D0358041

AQA

A2 Geography

Amanda Barker
David Redfern
Malcolm Skinner

Philip Allan Updates, an imprint of Hodder Education, an Hachette UK company, Market Place, Deddington, Oxfordshire OX15 0SE

Orders

Bookpoint Ltd, 130 Milton Park, Abingdon, Oxfordshire OX14 4SB
tel: 01235 827827
fax: 01235 400401
e-mail: education@bookpoint.co.uk

Lines are open 9.00 a.m.–5.00 p.m., Monday to Saturday, with a 24-hour message answering service. You can also order through the Philip Allan Updates website: www.philipallan.co.uk

© Philip Allan Updates 2008

ISBN 978-0-340-94612-1

Impression number   8 7 3 6 5
Year   2015 2014 2013 2012 2011

The front cover photographs are reproduced by permission of Corel, Amanda Barker.

All Office for National Statistics material is Crown copyright, reproduced under the terms of PSI Licence Number C200700185

Printed in Dubai

Hachette UK's policy is to use papers that are natural, renewable and recyclable products and made from wood grown in sustainable forests. The logging and manufacturing processes are expected to conform to the environmental regulations of the country of origin.

P01949

Contents

Unit 4

Introduction

This textbook covers the subject content for the AQA specification in A2 geography, unit by unit and option by option, as it is laid out in the specification. It forms a backbone for studies of AQA geography but should be supplemented by reference to topical sources of information including newspapers, television, periodicals aimed at post-16 geography students and the internet.

The following are key features of the content:

➤ concepts are clearly explained, and related issues are explored and analysed
➤ relevant, up-to-date and detailed case studies are provided
➤ a variety of stimulus material is provided, including full-colour maps, graphs, diagrams and photographs
➤ sample examination questions are included at the end of Unit 3 for each option, and in Chapters 7 and 8 (Unit 4)
➤ the skills required for the units that assess practical abilities are covered in depth

The sample questions included can be used for formal or informal assessment. Further advice and guidance can be found in the *AQA A2 Geography Unit 3 Student Unit Guide*, also published by Philip Allan Updates.

Additional exam guidance, sample A2 questions, mark schemes and commentary are provided to accompany this book at: www.hodderplus.co.uk/philipallan.

Scheme of assessment at A2

The scheme of assessment is modular. The A2 examination consists of two units that make up 60% and 40%, respectively, of the total award.

Unit 3

Unit 3 is based on **contemporary geographical issues**. The exam lasts $2\frac{1}{2}$ hours and consists of structured questions and essay questions carrying 90 marks in total. Candidates must answer three questions:

➤ **Section A** — one structured question (25 marks) from one of the **three physical** options (Plate tectonics and associated hazards, Weather and climate and associated hazards, Ecosystems: change and challenge).
➤ **Section B** — one structured question (25 marks) from one of the **three human** options (World cities, Development and globalisation, Contemporary conflicts and challenges).
➤ **Section C** — one essay question (40 marks) from an option not answered above.

Therefore all students must study **at least three** options: one physical, one human and one other (either physical or human).

Unit 4

For **Unit 4** there is a choice of assessment route. Either:
- **Unit 4A (Geography fieldwork investigation)**, or
- **Unit 4B (Geographical issue evaluation)**.

Both papers are $1\frac{1}{2}$ hours in length and carry 60 marks. In **Unit 4A,** there are two sections, Section A and Section B. **Section A** (40 marks) assesses a personal fieldwork investigation you have undertaken with the broad task of: 'the individual investigation of a geographical argument, assertion, hypothesis, issue or problem'. There are no restrictions on the type of topic studied other than it should be geographical and include primary, and where relevant secondary, data collection. It should be based on a small area of study and be linked to the content of the specification. This is a very wide brief. This investigation/fieldwork must be completed at a level above that at AS.

 Section B (20 marks) assesses fieldwork, investigative and research skills that are unfamiliar to you. Questions are set using data, skills and techniques used in presentation and analysis to enable you to interpret, analyse and evaluate geographical information and apply understanding in unfamiliar contexts. Most of these skills are described in the *AQA AS Geography* textbook published by Philip Allan Updates, and therefore only the additional A2 skills are explained here.

 Unit 4B is a geographical issue evaluation exercise based on pre-release material in an advance information booklet (AIB). Within the tasks there may be some questions relating to data gathering (including fieldwork), presentation and analysis. Candidates will be tested on their ability to apply understanding in unfamiliar contexts using fieldwork-based stimulus material. As with Unit 4A Section B, most of these skills are described in *AQA AS Geography* and only the additional A2 skills are explained here.

 The context for the issue evaluation exercise can arise from any area of the specification, either in isolation or combined with any other aspect as and when appropriate. The AIB will be made available from 1 November for the January examination and 1 April for the June examination.

Stretch and challenge

Assessments at A2 provide greater stretch and challenge for all candidates. This includes the use of more open-ended questions which require responses to be structured by the candidates. Specifically, this means:
- the use of a variety of demanding command words in questions — for example discuss, analyse, evaluate, justify
- greater connectivity between sections of questions
- a requirement for extended writing in all units
- the use of a wider range of question types to address different skills (for example open-ended questions) and a requirement for the detailed use of a range of case studies

For example, within Unit 3, the command words 'discuss' and 'evaluate' can be used in Sections A and B, and in Section C 'critically evaluate', 'analyse' and

'assess' may be used. The use of open-ended questions such as 'To what extent do you agree…' provides opportunities for thorough, well-developed and critical responses. In Unit 4A, similar command words are used, and in Unit 4B, the further high-level command 'justify' may be used in the issue evaluation context. The command 'comment on' is often used in data stimulus questions.

Analyse…

This requires you to break down the content of a topic into its constituent parts, and to give an in-depth account. It is important that you present a logical account that is both relevant and well-organised.

Discuss…

Candidates are expected to present arguments for and against an issue. You should make good use of evidence and appropriate examples, and express an opinion about the merits of each case. In other words, you should construct a verbal debate. In any discussion there are both positive and negative aspects — some people are likely to benefit and others are not. Candidates are invited to weigh up the evidence from both points of view, and may be asked to indicate where their sympathies lie.

Evaluate…, Assess…

These command words require more than the discussion described above. In both cases an indication of the candidate's viewpoint, having considered all the evidence, is required. 'Assess' asks for a statement of the overall quality or value of the feature or issue being considered, and 'evaluate' asks you to give an overall statement of value. Your own judgement is requested, together with a justification for that judgement.

The use of 'critically' often occurs in such questions, for example 'Critically evaluate…'. In this case you are being asked to look at an issue or problem from the point of view of a critic. There may be weaknesses in the argument and the evidence should not be taken at face value. You should question not only the evidence itself but also its source, and how it was collected. The answer should comment on the strengths of the evidence as well as its weaknesses.

Justify…

This is one of the most demanding command words. At its most simplistic, a response to this command must include a strong piece of writing in favour of the chosen option(s) in a decision-making exercise, and an explanation of why the other options were rejected. However, decision making is not straightforward. All the options in a decision-making scenario have positive and negative aspects. The options that are rejected will have some good elements and, equally, the chosen option will not be perfect in all respects. The key to good decision making is to balance the pros and cons of each option and to opt for the most appropriate based on the evidence available.

A good answer to the command 'justify' should therefore provide the following:
➤ For each of the options that are rejected, an outline of their positive and negative points, but with an overall statement of why the negatives outweigh the positives.

➤ For the chosen option, an outline of the negative and the positive points, but with an overall statement of why the positives outweigh the negatives.

Comment on…

You should refer to the data, but then make a statement arising from the data that is relevant, appropriate and geographical, but above all not directly evident. You are being invited to 'think like a geographer'.

Synoptic assessment

The definition of synoptic assessment in the context of geography is as follows:

> Synoptic assessment involves assessment of candidates' ability to draw on their understanding of the connections between different aspects of the subject represented in the specification and demonstrate their ability to 'think like a geographer'.

For this specification, synoptic assessment is included in each of the A2 units. Examples of synoptic assessment are:

➤ decision-making/problem solving/issue evaluation exercises requiring candidates to draw together relevant knowledge, understanding and skills, to tackle a decision, problem or issue that is new to them

➤ an essay question covering geographical issues or problems that require candidates to integrate and apply relevant knowledge, understanding and skills

➤ an essay question exploring key geographical concepts through linkages between physical, human and environmental geography

➤ an assessment of a particular region or area, on a scale that allows candidates to draw together and apply relevant knowledge, understanding and skills of processes or concepts of the specification

➤ reporting of a fieldwork enquiry which has encompassed a variety of themes and issues

Essay-writing skills

For many students essay writing is one of the most difficult parts of the exam. But it is also an opportunity to demonstrate your strengths. Before starting to write an essay you must have a plan of what you will write, either in your head or on paper. All such pieces of writing must have a beginning (introduction), a middle (argument) and an end (conclusion).

The introduction

This does not have to be long — a few sentences should do. It may define the terms in the question, set the scene for the argument to follow or provide a brief statement of the idea or viewpoint to be developed in the main body of the answer.

The argument

This is the main body of the answer. It should consist of a series of paragraphs, each developing one point only and following on logically from the previous one.

Try to avoid paragraphs that list information without any depth, and avoid writing all you know about a particular topic without any link to the question set. Make good use of examples, naming real places (which could be local to you). Make examples count by giving accurate detail specific to those locations.

At A2, the essay is important, particularly in Section C of Unit 3. There are many marks available, and the answer must be coherent and clear. Examiners are looking for students who demonstrate good (and sometimes critical) knowledge and understanding of concepts. Show confidence in the use of language.

The conclusion

In an essay answer the conclusion should not be too long. It should reiterate the main points stated in the introduction, but now supported by the evidence and facts given in the argument. It should address the command word in the question, such as 'evaluate' or 'assess'. There should be evidence of synthesis.

Should you produce plans in the examination?

If you produce an essay plan at all, it must be brief, taking only 2 or 3 minutes to write on a piece of scrap paper. The plan must reflect the above formula — make sure you stick to it. Be logical, and only give an outline — retain the examples in your head, and include them at the most appropriate point in your answer.

Other important points

Always keep an eye on the time. Make sure you write clearly and concisely. Do not give confused answers, endlessly long sentences or pages of prose with no paragraphs. Above all: *read the question and answer the question set*.

How are questions marked?

Examination questions for AQA are marked according to levels based on certain criteria. The following general criteria relate to knowledge, understanding and critical application, and the quality of written communication:

Level 1

A Level 1 answer is likely to:
- ➤ display a basic understanding of the topic
- ➤ make one or two points without the support of appropriate exemplification or application of principle
- ➤ give a basic list of characteristics, reasons and attitudes
- ➤ provide a basic account of a case study, or provide no case study evidence
- ➤ give a response to one command in a question where two or more commands are stated, e.g. 'describe and suggest reasons'
- ➤ demonstrate a simplistic style of writing, perhaps lacking close relation to the terms of the question and unlikely to communicate complexity of subject matter
- ➤ lack organisation, relevance and specialist vocabulary
- ➤ demonstrate deficiencies in legibility, spelling, grammar and punctuation, which detract from the clarity of meaning

Level 2

A Level 2 answer is likely to:
- display a clear understanding of the topic
- make one or two points with support of appropriate exemplification and/or application of principle
- give a number of characteristics, reasons, attitudes (i.e. more than one)
- provide clear use of case studies
- give responses to more than one command, e.g. 'describe and explain...'
- demonstrate a style of writing that matches the requirements of the question and acknowledges the potential complexity of the subject matter
- demonstrate relevance and coherence with appropriate use of specialist vocabulary
- demonstrate legibility of text, and qualities of spelling, grammar and punctuation that do not detract from the clarity of meaning

Level 3

A Level 3 answer is likely to:
- display a detailed understanding of the topic
- make several points with support of appropriate exemplification and/or application of principle
- give a wide range of characteristics, reasons, attitudes etc.
- provide highly detailed accounts of a range of case studies
- respond well to more than one command
- demonstrate evidence of discussion, evaluation, assessment and synthesis depending on the requirements of the assessment
- demonstrate a sophisticated style of writing incorporating measured and qualified explanation and comment as required by the question, and reflecting awareness of the complexity of subject matter and incompleteness/tentative-ness of explanation
- demonstrate a clear sense of purpose so that the responses relate closely to the requirements of the question with confident use of specialist vocabulary
- demonstrate legibility of text, and qualities of spelling, grammar and punctuation which contribute to complete clarity of meaning

Level 4

In addition to the Level 3 requirements, an answer at the highest level is likely to:
- provide strong evidence of thorough, detailed and accurate knowledge, critical understanding of concepts and principles and specialist vocabulary
- give explanations, arguments and assessments or evaluations that are direct, logical, perceptive, purposeful and show both balance and flair
- demonstrate a high level of insight, and an ability to identify, interpret and synthesise a wide range of material with creativity
- demonstrate evidence of maturity in understanding the role of values, attitudes and decision-making processes

For more details of the assessment process, see the online exam guidance at www.hodderplus.co.uk/philipallan.

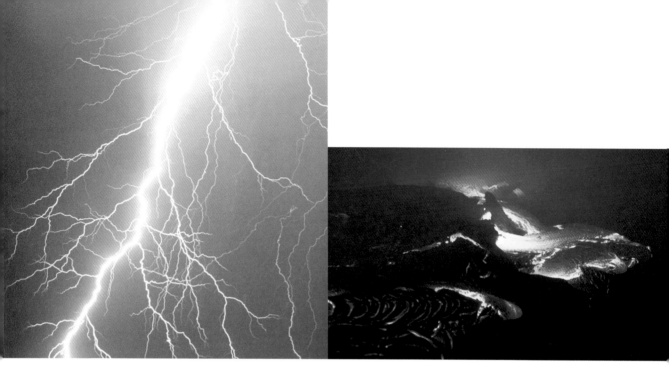

Unit 3

Contemporary geographical issues

Physical options

Plate tectonics and associated hazards

Plate movement

Plate tectonic theory revolutionised the study of earth science. As soon as maps of the Atlantic Ocean were produced, people noticed that the continents either side seemed to fit together remarkably well — the bulge of South America fitting into the indent below west Africa. Francis Bacon had noted this fit as early as the seventeenth century but it did not attract any serious attention as no one thought the continents could move.

The theory of plate tectonics

In 1912 a German, Alfred Wegener, published his theory that a single continent existed about 300 million years ago. He named this super-continent Pangaea, and maintained that it had later split into the two continents of Laurasia in the north and Gondwanaland in the south. Today's continents were formed from further splitting of these two masses. Wegener published this theory of continental drift and claimed that it was supported by several pieces of evidence that these areas were once joined.

> **Key terms**
>
> **Hot spot** A point on the surface of the Earth located above a plume of rising magma. The Hawaiian Islands lie above such a spot.
>
> **Plate** The lithosphere (the crust of the Earth and the upper part of the mantle) is divided into a number of segments known as plates. These rigid slabs float on the underlying semi-molten mantle (asthenosphere) and are moved by convection currents within it.
>
> **Plate tectonics** A theory that attempts to explain the formation and distribution of the Earth's major structural features in terms of a series of plates that make up its surface.
>
> **Seismic waves** Shock waves released by the rupture of rock strata at the focus of an earthquake. They travel through the rocks and are measured and recorded on a seismograph.
>
> **Tsunami** (Japanese for 'harbour wave') Sea waves, which can be very large, generated by shallow-focus underwater earthquakes (the most common cause), volcanic eruptions, underwater debris slides and large landslides into the sea.
>
> **Volcano** An opening or vent through which magma, molten rock, ash or volatiles erupt on to the surface of the Earth.

Geological evidence for the theory included:
➤ the above-mentioned fit of South America and Africa
➤ evidence of the glaciation of the late Carboniferous period (290 million years ago), deposits from which are found in South America, Antarctica and India. The formation of these deposits cannot be explained by their present position; they must have been formed together and then moved. There are also striations on rocks in Brazil and west Africa which point to a similar situation
➤ rock sequences in northern Scotland closely agree with those found in eastern Canada, indicating that they were laid down under the same conditions in one location

Biological evidence for the theory included the following:
➤ fossil brachiopods found in Indian limestones are comparable with similar fossils in Australia
➤ fossil remains of the reptile *Mesosaurus* are found in both South America and southern Africa. It is unlikely that the same reptile could have developed in both areas or that it could have migrated across the Atlantic
➤ the fossilised remains of a plant which existed when coal was being formed have been located only in India and Antarctica

Development of the theory

Wegener's theories were unable to explain how continental movement could have taken place and his ideas gained little ground. From the 1940s onwards, however, evidence began to accumulate to show that Wegener could have been correct.

The mid-Atlantic ridge was discovered and studied. A similar feature was later discovered in the Pacific Ocean.

Examination of the ocean crust either side of the mid-Atlantic ridge suggested that sea-floor spreading was occurring. The evidence for this is the alternating polarity of the rocks that form the ocean crust. Iron particles in lava erupted on the ocean floor are aligned with the Earth's magnetic field. As the lavas solidify, these particles provide a permanent record of the Earth's polarity at the time of eruption (palaeomagnetism). However, the Earth's polarity reverses at regular intervals (approximately every 400,000 years). The result is a series of magnetic 'stripes' with rocks aligned alternately towards the north and south poles (Figure 1.1). The striped pattern, which is mirrored exactly on either side of a mid-oceanic ridge, suggests that the ocean crust is slowly spreading away from this boundary. Moreover, the oceanic crust gets older with distance from the mid-oceanic ridge.

Sea-floor spreading implies that the Earth must be getting bigger. As this is not the case, then plates must be being destroyed somewhere to accommodate the increase in their size at mid-oceanic ridges. Evidence of this was found with the discovery of huge oceanic trenches where large areas of ocean floor were being pulled downwards.

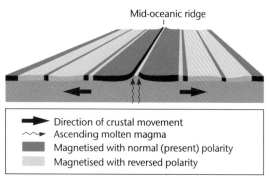

Mid-oceanic ridge

➤ Direction of crustal movement
〜➤ Ascending molten magma
■ Magnetised with normal (present) polarity
▨ Magnetised with reversed polarity

Figure 1.1 Magnetic 'stripes' on the Atlantic Ocean floor

The Earth's layers

Before the development of plate tectonic theory, earth scientists divided the interior of the Earth into three layers: the crust, the mantle and the core. The **core** is made up of dense rocks containing iron and nickel alloys and is divided into a solid inner core and a molten outer one, with a temperature of over 5,000°C. The **mantle** is made up of molten and semi-molten rocks containing lighter elements, such as silicon and oxygen. The **crust** is even lighter because of the elements that are present, the most abundant being silicon, oxygen, aluminium, potassium and sodium. The crust varies in thickness — beneath the oceans it is only 6–10 km thick but below continents this increases to 30–40 km. Under the highest mountain ranges the crust can be up to 70 km thick.

The theory of plate tectonics has retained this simple threefold division, but new research has suggested that the crust and the upper mantle should be divided into the lithosphere and the asthenosphere. The **lithosphere** consists of the crust and the rigid upper section of the mantle and is approximately 80–90 km thick. It is divided into seven very large plates and a number of smaller ones (Figure 1.2). Plates are divided into two categories, oceanic and continental, depending on the type of material from which they are made (see Table 1.1). Below the lithosphere is the semi-molten **asthenosphere**, on which the plates float and move.

Figure 1.2 Tectonic plates and their margins

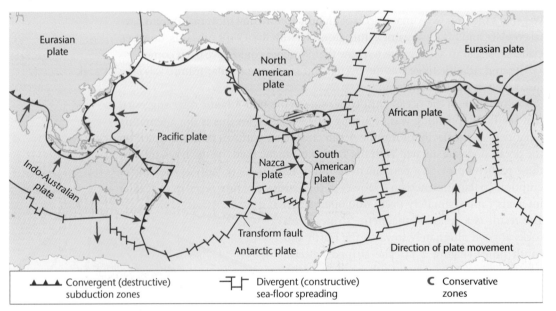

Table 1.1
Differences between continental and oceanic crust

	Continental crust	Oceanic crust
Thickness	30–70 km	6–10 km
Age	Over 1,500 million years	Less than 200 million years
Density	2.6 (lighter)	3.0 (heavier)
Composition	Mainly granite; silicon, aluminium, oxygen (SIAL)	Mainly basalt; silicon, magnesium, oxygen (SIMA)

Hot spots around the core of the Earth generate thermal convection currents within the asthenosphere, which cause magma to rise towards the crust and then spread before cooling and sinking (Figure 1.3). This circulation of magma is the vehicle upon which the crustal plates move. The crust can be thought of as 'floating' on the more dense material of the asthenosphere. This is a continuous process, with new crust being formed along the line of constructive boundaries between plates (where plates move away from each other) and older crust being destroyed at destructive boundaries (where plates are moving towards each other).

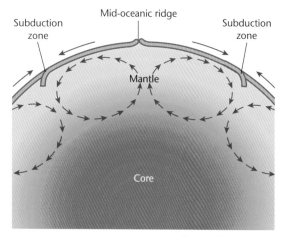

Figure 1.3
Convection currents and plate movement

Features of plate margins

Constructive (divergent) margins

Where plates move apart in oceanic areas they produce mid-oceanic ridges. Where they move apart in continental crust they produce rift valleys. The space between the diverging plates is filled with basaltic lava upwelling from below. Constructive margins are therefore some of the youngest parts of the Earth's surface, where new crust is being continuously created.

Figure 1.4
Cross-section of the mid-Atlantic ridge

Oceanic ridges

Oceanic ridges (Figure 1.4) are the longest continuous uplifted features on the surface of the planet, and have a total length of 60,000 km. In some parts they rise 3,000 m above the ocean floor. Their precise form appears to be influenced by the rate at which the plates separate:

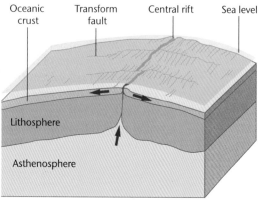

➤ a slow rate (10–15 mm per year), as seen in parts of the mid-Atlantic ridge, produces a wide ridge axis (30–50 km) and a deep (3,000 m) central rift valley with inward-facing fault scarps

➤ an intermediate rate (50–90 mm per year), such as that on the Galapagos ridge (Pacific), produces a less well-marked rift (50–200 m deep) with a smoother outline

➤ a rapid rate (>90 mm per year), such as on the east Pacific rise, produces a smooth crest and no rift

Volcanic activity also occurs along the ridge, forming submarine volcanoes, which sometimes rise above sea level, e.g. Surtsey to the south of Iceland (Iceland itself was formed in this way and is the largest feature produced above sea level on a divergent margin, Photograph 1.1). These are volcanoes with fairly gentle sides because of the low viscosity of basaltic lava. Eruptions are frequent but relatively gentle (effusive).

As new crust forms and spreads, transform faults occur at right angles to the plate boundary. The parts of the spreading plates on either side of these faults may move at differing rates, leading to friction and ultimately to earthquakes. These tend to be shallow-focus earthquakes, originating near the surface.

Photograph 1.1 Iceland, on a divergent margin, the mid-Atlantic ridge, has a lot of geothermal activity

Emily Hunter-Higgins

Rift valleys

At constructive margins in continental areas, such as east Africa, the brittle crust fractures as sections of it move apart. Areas of crust drop down between parallel faults to form **rift valleys** (Figure 1.5). The largest of these features is the African rift valley which extends 4,000 km from Mozambique to the Red Sea. From the Red Sea it extends north into Jordan, a total distance of 5,500 km (Figure 1.6). In some areas, the inward-facing scarps are 600 m above the valley floor and they are often marked by a series of parallel step faults.

Figure 1.5 Cross-section of a rift valley

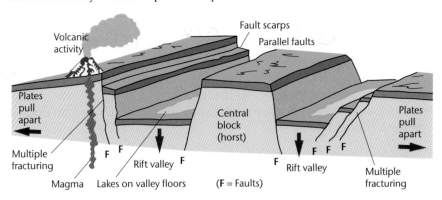

The area is also associated with volcanic activity (for example the highest mountain in Africa, Mt Kilimanjaro). The crust here is much thinner than in neighbouring areas, suggesting that tension in the lithosphere is causing the plate to thin as it starts to split. The line of the African rift is thought to be an emergent plate boundary, the beginning of the formation of a new ocean as eastern Africa splits away from the rest of the continent.

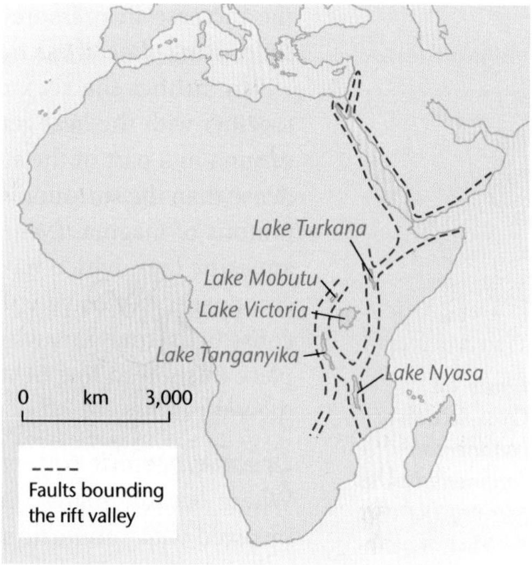

Destructive (convergent) margins

There are two types of plates, so there are three different convergent situations:

➤ oceanic plate moves towards continental plate
➤ oceanic plate moves towards oceanic plate
➤ continental plate moves towards continental plate

Figure 1.6 The African rift valley

Oceanic/continental convergence

Where oceanic and continental plates meet, the denser oceanic plate (see Table 1.1) is forced under the lighter continental one. This process is known as **subduction**. The downwarping of the oceanic plate forms a very deep part of the ocean known as a **trench** (Figure 1.7). A good example of an ocean trench is off the western coast of South America where the Nazca plate is subducting under the South American plate, forming the Peru–Chile trench.

Sediments that have accumulated on the continental shelf on the margin of the land mass are deformed by folding and faulting. Along with the edge of the continental plate, these are uplifted to form **fold mountains** (Figure 1.7), such as the Andes along the Pacific side of South America. As the oceanic plate descends,

Figure 1.7 Cross-section of oceanic/continental plate convergence at a destructive plate margin

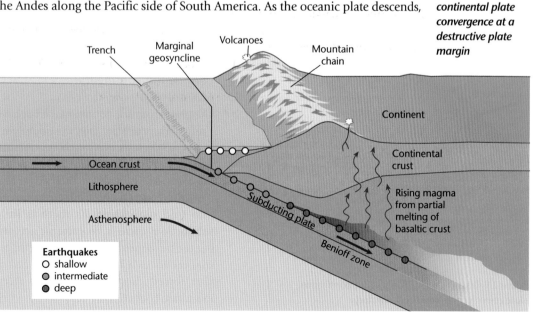

the increase in pressure can trigger major earthquakes along the line of the subducting plate; these may be shallow-, intermediate- or deep-focus.

The further the rock descends, the hotter the surroundings become. This, together with the heat generated from friction, begins to melt oceanic plate into magma in a part of the subduction zone known as the Benioff zone. As it is less dense than the surrounding asthenosphere, this molten material begins to rise as plutons of magma. Eventually, these reach the surface and form volcanoes. The andesitic lava, which has a viscous nature (flows less easily), creates complex, composite, explosive volcanoes (contrast this with the basaltic emissions on constructive margins which tend to be gentle eruptions). If the eruptions take place offshore, a line of volcanic islands known as an **island arc** can appear, e.g. the West Indies.

Figure 1.8 Cross-section of continental/ continental plate convergence at a destructive plate margin

Oceanic/oceanic convergence

Where oceanic plates meet, one is forced under the other and the processes involved with subduction begin. Ocean trenches and island arcs are the features associated with this interaction, as it takes place well offshore. A good example is on the western side of the Pacific Ocean where the Pacific plate is being subducted beneath the smaller Philippine plate. Here the ocean floor has been pulled down to form the very deep Marianas trench. A line of volcanic islands, including Guam and the Marianas, has been formed by upwelling magma from the Benioff zone (Figure 1.8).

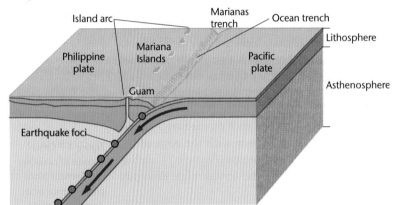

Continental/continental convergence

The plates forming continental crust have a much lower density than the underlying layers, so there is not much subduction where they meet. Instead, as the plates move towards each other, their edges and the sediments between them are forced up into fold mountains. As there is little subduction, there is no volcanic activity, but the movement of the plates can trigger shallow-focus earthquakes. Material is also forced downwards to form deep mountain roots (Figure 1.9).

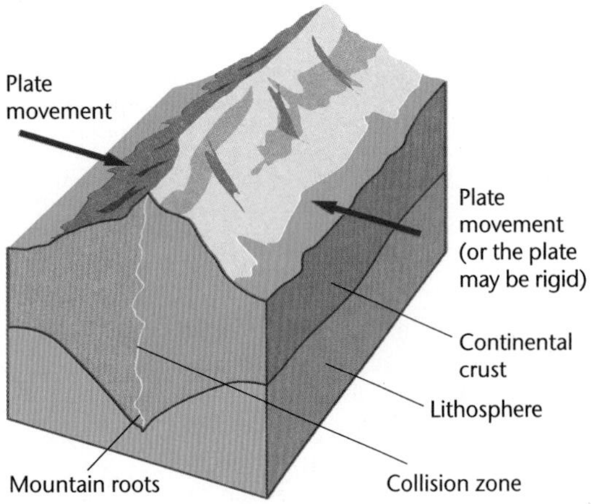

Figure 1.9 Cross-section of continental/continental plate convergence (collision boundary)

Corel

The best example of such a margin is where the Indo-Australian plate is being forced northwards into the Eurasian plate. The previous intervening ocean, known as the Sea of Tethys, has had its sediments forced upwards in large overfolds to form the Himalayas, an uplift that is continuing today. The Himalayan range of fold mountains, containing the highest mountain on the planet (Mt Everest 8,848 m), is up to 350 km wide and extends for 3,000 km (Photograph 1.2).

Photograph 1.2 The Annapurna range in the Himalayas has been formed at a convergent margin

Conservative margins

Where two crustal plates slide past each other and the movement of the plates is parallel to the plate margin, there is no creation or destruction of crust. At these conservative margins (sometimes called passive) there is no subduction and therefore no volcanic activity.

The movement of the plates, however, creates stresses between the plate edges and, as sections of the plates rub past each other, the release of friction triggers shallow-focus earthquakes, for example San Francisco 1906 and 1989, Los Angeles 1994. These earthquakes occurred at the best-known example of a conservative margin — the San Andreas fault in California, where the Pacific and North

Figure 1.10 The San Andreas fault system: a conservative plate margin

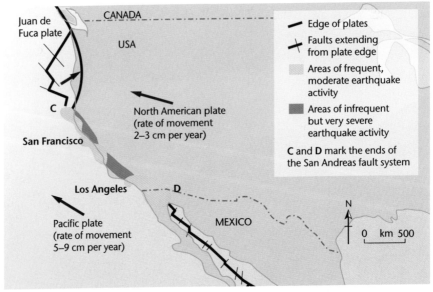

American plates move parallel to each other (Figure 1.10). Both plates are moving in the same direction but not at the same speed. Stresses set up by this movement cause transform faults to develop, running at right angles to the main San Andreas fault.

Hot spots

Vulcanicity is normally associated with plate margins but, in the centre of the Pacific Ocean, we find the volcanic Hawaiian islands that are not connected with any plate boundary. It is believed that this volcanic area is caused by a localised hot spot within the Pacific plate. A concentration of radioactive elements inside the mantle may cause such a hot spot to develop. From this, a plume of magma rises to eat into the plate above. Where lava breaks through to the surface, active volcanoes occur above the hot spot.

Figure 1.11 The Hawaiian hot spot

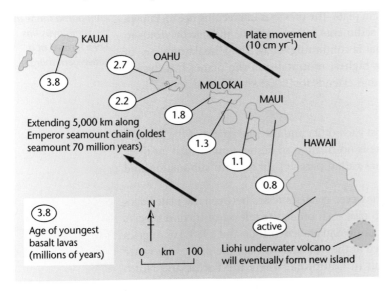

The hot spot is stationary, so as the Pacific plate moves over it, a line of volcanoes is created. The one above the hot spot is active and the rest form a chain of islands of extinct volcanoes. The oldest volcanoes have put so much pressure on the crust that subsidence has occurred.

Plate margin	Movement of plates	Tectonic features	Examples
Constructive	Divergent: two plates moving away from each other	New crust is formed from upwelling magma: mid-oceanic ridges, effusive ridge (shield) volcanoes, shallow-focus earthquakes, median rift valleys	Mid-Atlantic ridge
		Continental rift valleys	East African rift valley
Destructive (1) Subduction	Convergent: two plates moving towards each other	(1a) Oceanic to oceanic: trenches, island arcs, explosive volcanoes, earthquakes (shallow, intermediate and deep)	On the margins of Pacific plate, with subduction under other, separate sections of the plate — Tonga trench
		(1b) Oceanic to continental: trenches, fold mountains, explosive volcanoes, earthquakes (shallow, intermediate and deep)	Andean type: Nazca plate subducting under South American plate
(2) Collision		(2) Continental to continental: fold mountains, shallow-focus earthquakes	Himalayan type: Indian plate colliding with Eurasian plate
Conservative	Two plates shearing past each other	Shallow-focus earthquakes	San Andreas fault: Pacific plate and North American plate
Not at plate boundaries	Hot spots: may be near the centre of a plate	Plume volcanoes	Hawaiian islands: Emperor seamount chain

This, together with marine erosion, has reduced these old volcanoes to seamounts below the level of the ocean. Figure 1.11 shows the line of the Hawaiian islands and their ages. From this evidence it is clear that the Pacific plate is moving northwest. This is further proof that the Earth's crust is moving, as originally suggested by Alfred Wegener.

Table 1.2 Relationship of tectonic activity to plate margins

Table 1.2 summarises the relationship of tectonic activity to plate margins.

Vulcanicity

Distribution

Most volcanic activity is associated with plate tectonic processes and is mainly located along plate margins (Figure 1.12). Such activity is therefore found:
- along oceanic ridges where plates are moving apart. The best example is the mid-Atlantic ridge — Iceland represents a large area formed by volcanic activity
- associated with rift valleys. The African rift valley has a number of volcanoes along it including Mt Kenya and Mt Kilimanjaro
- on or near subduction zones. The line of volcanoes, or 'ring of fire', that surrounds the Pacific Ocean is associated with plate subduction. This tends to be the most violent of all activity
- over hot spots such as the one in the middle of the Pacific Ocean which has given rise to the Hawaiian islands

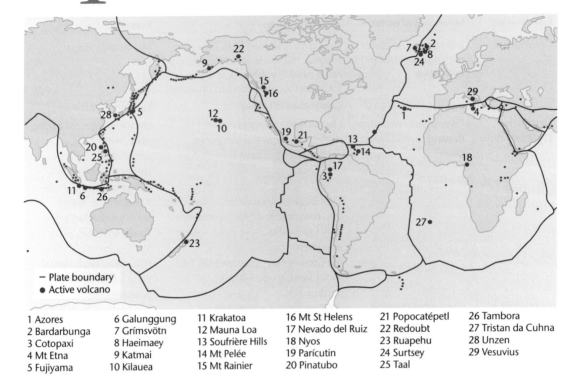

- – Plate boundary
- ● Active volcano

1 Azores	6 Galunggung	11 Krakatoa	16 Mt St Helens	21 Popocatépetl	26 Tambora
2 Bardarbunga	7 Grímsvötn	12 Mauna Loa	17 Nevado del Ruiz	22 Redoubt	27 Tristan da Cuhna
3 Cotopaxi	8 Haeimaey	13 Soufrière Hills	18 Nyos	23 Ruapehu	28 Unzen
4 Mt Etna	9 Katmai	14 Mt Pelée	19 Parícutin	24 Surtsey	29 Vesuvius
5 Fujiyama	10 Kilauea	15 Mt Rainier	20 Pinatubo	25 Taal	

Figure 1.12 Global distribution of active volcanoes

Volcanic eruptions

There are variations in the form, frequency and type of volcanic eruption. These are related to the different kinds of plate margin, emissions and lava. For example, constructive and destructive plate margins produce different types of lava, and this leads to different types and frequencies of eruption. How these different plate margins affect volcanic eruptions and landforms is summarised in Figure 1.13.

Corel

Photograph 1.3 Hambledown Tor on Dartmoor is an example of a batholith

Intrusive volcanic landforms

When magma is forced to the surface, only a small amount of the mass actually reaches that level (Figure 1.14). Most of the magma is **intruded** into the crust where it solidifies into a range of features. These are often exposed at the surface by later erosion.

Batholiths are formed deep below the surface when large masses of magma cool and solidify. As the magma cools slowly, large crystals are formed in the rock (e.g. granite). Batholiths are often dome-shaped and exposed by later erosion. This is the

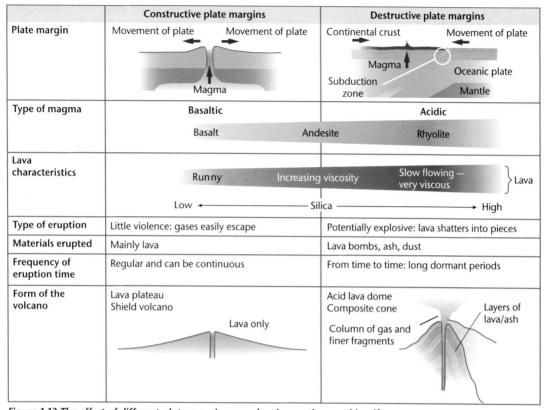

	Constructive plate margins	Destructive plate margins
Plate margin	Movement of plate Movement of plate Magma	Continental crust Movement of plate Magma Oceanic plate Subduction zone Mantle
Type of magma	Basaltic	Acidic
	Basalt Andesite Rhyolite	
Lava characteristics	Runny Increasing viscosity Slow flowing — very viscous } Lava Low ← Silica → High	
Type of eruption	Little violence: gases easily escape	Potentially explosive: lava shatters into pieces
Materials erupted	Mainly lava	Lava bombs, ash, dust
Frequency of eruption time	Regular and can be continuous	From time to time: long dormant periods
Form of the volcano	Lava plateau Shield volcano Lava only	Acid lava dome Composite cone Layers of lava/ash Column of gas and finer fragments

Figure 1.13 The effect of different plate margins on volcanic eruptions and landforms

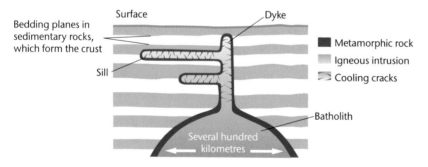

Figure 1.14 Intrusive vulcanicity

case on Dartmoor (Photograph 1.3) and the Isle of Arran (Scotland). Batholiths can be several hundreds of kilometres in diameter. The area surrounding the batholith is altered by the heat and pressure of the intrusion to form a **metamorphic aureole** (limestone, for example, can be transformed into marble). Batholiths are unaffected by the characteristics and structure of existing rock. Sometimes smaller injections of magma form a lens shape that is intruded between layers of rock. This then forces the overlying strata to arch upwards, forming a dome. This feature is known as a **laccolith**, and it may be exposed by later weathering and erosion to form a small range of hills, for example the Eildon Hills on the Scottish Borders.

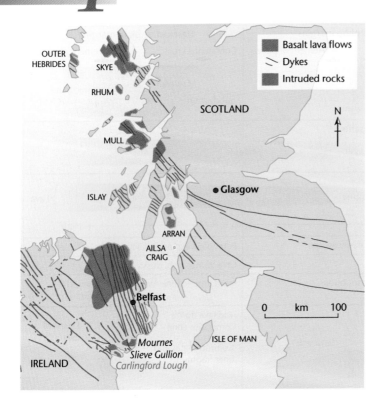

Figure 1.15 Dykes and lava flows in Scotland and Ireland

Dykes are vertical intrusions with horizontal cooling cracks. They cut across the bedding planes of the rocks into which they have been intruded. Dykes often occur in groups where they are known as dyke swarms. Many Scottish islands, such as Mull and Skye, have clusters of dykes, all associated with one intrusive event (Figure 1.15).

Sills are horizontal intrusions along the lines of bedding planes. Sills have vertical cooling cracks. Examples include the Great Whin Sill (which carries part of Hadrian's Wall) and Drumadoon on the Isle of Arran. Both sills and dykes are commonly made up of **dolerite**.

Extrusive volcanic landforms

Extrusive vulcanicity involves two forms of lava:

➤ **Basaltic lava** is formed from magma that is low in silica. This makes for a more fluid magma that allows gas bubbles to expand on the way up to the surface, so preventing sudden explosive activity.

➤ **Andesitic** and **rhyolitic** lavas are formed from silica-rich (acid) magma that is very viscous. This often solidifies before reaching the surface, leading to a build-up of pressure and, ultimately, to a violent explosion.

The main types of extrusive volcanic landforms are as follows:

➤ **Lava plateaux** are formed from fissure eruptions (Figure 1.16). The extensive lava flows are basaltic in nature, so they flow great distances. A good example is the Antrim lava plateau in Northern Ireland, the edge of which can be seen at Giant's Causeway. Lava plateaux are generally flat and featureless.

Basaltic lava flows a considerable distance over gentle slopes

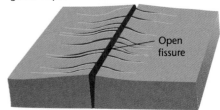

Figure 1.16 Fissure eruption

➤ **Basic/shield volcanoes** are also formed from free-flowing lava. The resulting volcanoes have gentle sides and cover a large area, for example Mauna Loa, Hawaii.

➤ **Acid/dome volcanoes** are steep-sided convex cones, consisting of viscous lava, which is probably rhyolite. The best examples can be seen in the Puy region of central France.

➤ **Ash and cinder cones** are formed from ash, cinders and volcanic bombs ejected from the crater. The sides are steep and symmetrical, for example Paricutín, Mexico.

➤ **Composite cones** are the classic pyramid-shaped volcanoes, consisting of layers of ash and lava that is usually andesitic (Figure 1.17). Examples include Mt Etna on Sicily and Mt Fuji in Japan.

➤ **Calderas** occur when the build-up of gases becomes extreme and a huge explosion removes the summit of the cone, leaving an opening several kilometres in diameter. The caldera may become flooded by the sea, or a lake may form within it. Examples include Krakatoa in Indonesia and Santorini in Greece.

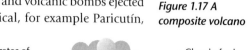

Figure 1.17 A composite volcano

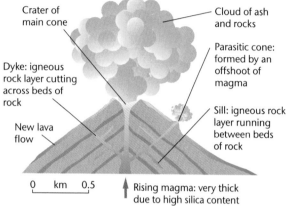

Crater of main cone

Cloud of ash and rocks

Parasitic cone: formed by an offshoot of magma

Dyke: igneous rock layer cutting across beds of rock

Sill: igneous rock layer running between beds of rock

New lava flow

0   km   0.5

Rising magma: very thick due to high silica content

The nature of volcanic eruptions

Vulcanologists have traditionally classified volcanoes according to the nature of the eruption (Figure 1.18). This classification is based on the degree of violence of the explosion, which is a consequence of the pressure and amount of gas in the magma.

Minor volcanic forms

Minor volcanic forms include:

➤ **solfatara** — small volcanic areas without cones, produced by gases (mainly sulphurous) escaping to the surface, for example around the Bay of Naples in Italy

➤ **geysers** — these occur when water, heated by volcanic activity, explodes onto the surface, for example Old Faithful, Yellowstone National Park, USA

➤ **hot springs/boiling mud** — sometimes the water, heated below, does not explode onto the surface. If this water mixes with surface deposits, boiling mud is formed. Such features are very common in Iceland. There are hot springs at Bath in the west of England

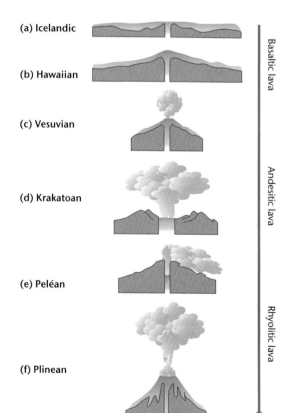

(a) Icelandic

(b) Hawaiian

(c) Vesuvian

(d) Krakatoan

(e) Peléan

(f) Plinean

Basaltic lava

Andesitic lava

Rhyolitic lava

Figure 1.18 Forms of volcanic eruption

Intrusive and extrusive volcanic activity in the UK

Apart from hot springs, the UK has no current volcanic activity. However, there is much geological evidence of such activity, which occurred during the mountain-building periods of the Caledonian, Hercynian and Alpine orogenies (Figure 1.19).

Figure 1.19 Examples of intrusive and extrusive volcanic activity in the British Isles

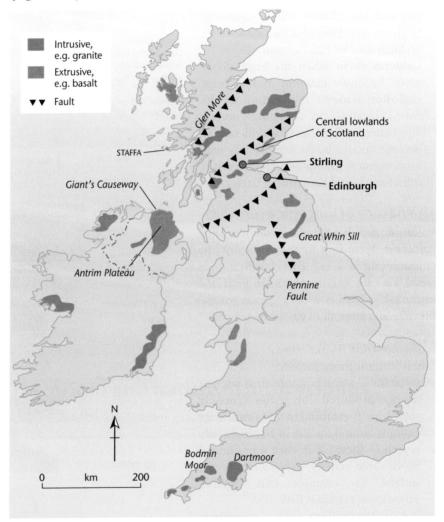

> **Granites** and other examples of **intruded rocks** occur across the Grampians in Scotland, in Ireland and particularly in the southwest of England where the top of an exposed batholith is seen in areas such as Dartmoor and Bodmin Moor. Here, weathering and erosion have combined to give a distinctive landscape of upland plateaux capped by rock outcrops, which are known as **tors** (see Photograph 1.3, page 12).

➤ **Dykes** and **sills** are also common. The dyke 'swarms' that radiate across the Isle of Arran in Scotland contain around 500 such features in a 20 km stretch of coastline. Dykes generally occur as small ridges in the landscape because they are more resistant than the surrounding rocks. The Great Whin Sill runs across large distances in the north of England, forming an upstanding cliff-like feature. Many rivers produce high waterfalls as they plunge over it, for example High Force and Cauldron Snout in the Tees valley in the Pennines. It is also the defensive base for man-made features such as Hadrian's Wall and Bamburgh Castle.

➤ **Basaltic flows** can be seen where the Antrim lava plateau formed in Northern Ireland. When the lava cooled, vertical cracks in the flow resulted in hexagonal columns. These are exposed at the coast — the Giant's Causeway. The same volcanic feature can be seen in Fingal's Cave on the Isle of Staffa in Scotland.

➤ A **volcanic plug** from a long-extinct volcano (active over 300 million years ago) forms the site of Edinburgh Castle. Stirling Castle is also built on a volcanic plug.

The impact of volcanic activity

A volcanic event can have a range of impacts, affecting the area immediately around the volcano or the entire planet. Effects can be categorised into primary and secondary. **Primary** effects consist of:

➤ **tephra** — solid material of varying grain size, from volcanic bombs to ash particles, ejected into the atmosphere

➤ **pyroclastic flows** — very hot (800°C), gas-charged, high-velocity flows made up of a mixture of gases and tephra

➤ **lava flows**

➤ **volcanic gases** — including carbon dioxide, carbon monoxide, hydrogen sulphide, sulphur dioxide and chlorine. Emissions of carbon dioxide from Lake Nyos in Cameroon in 1986 suffocated 1,700 people

Secondary effects include:

➤ **lahars** — volcanic mud flows such as those that devastated the Colombian town of Armero after the eruption of Nevado del Ruiz in November 1985

➤ **flooding** — melting of glaciers and ice caps such as the Grímsvötn glacial burst on Iceland in November 1996

➤ **tsunamis** — giant sea waves generated after violent caldera-forming events such as that which occurred on Krakatoa in 1883 — the tsunamis from this eruption are believed to have drowned 36,000 people

➤ **volcanic landslides**

➤ **climatic change** — the ejection of vast amounts of volcanic debris into the atmosphere can reduce global temperatures and is believed to have been an agent in past climatic change

Volcanic effects become a hazard when they impact upon the human and built environments, killing and injuring people, burying and collapsing buildings, destroying the infrastructure and bringing agricultural activities to a halt.

Volcanic events: case studies

Case study   **Eruption of Mt Nyiragongo, Congo, January 2002**

Mt Nyiragongo lies in the Virunga Mountains in the Democratic Republic of Congo (Figure 1.20) and it is associated with the African rift valley (see pages 6–7).

The main crater of the volcano is 250 m deep, 2 km wide and often contains a lava lake. Since records of the area began in the nineteenth century, the volcano has erupted more than 30 times. Together with its neighbouring volcano, Mt Nyamuragira, it is responsible for approximately 40% of Africa's recorded volcanic eruptions. Lava erupted by Mt Nyiragongo is very fluid and has been known to flow downhill at speeds greater than 90 km h^{-1}.

Although there had been some seismic activity in the area, the eruption in January 2002 was unex-

pected. Nonetheless, warnings of the lava flows enabled most people to flee from their effects. This was a large eruption, opening a fissure 13 km long on the southern flank of the volcano, spewing lava up to 2 m deep, which flowed in the direction of Goma and Lake Kivu.

The major effects of the eruption were:
- Lava flows destroyed at least one-third of Goma, a town with over 200,000 inhabitants.
- The commercial centre of the town was destroyed, along with water and power supplies and many of the medical facilities, including three health centres and one hospital.
- The lava covered the northern third of the runway at Goma airport.

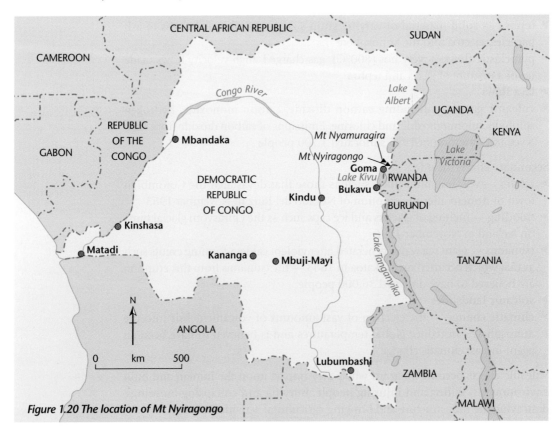

Figure 1.20 The location of Mt Nyiragongo

Getty

Photograph 1.4 The Hotel Jambo in Goma surrounded by lava

- The death toll reached 147.
- It was estimated that more than 350,000 people fled the area, many over the border to Rwanda, particularly to the town of Gisenyi. This caused an enormous problem in providing food and shelter in this small country.
- Sulphurous lava entered Lake Kivu, polluting the lake, which is a major source of drinking water in the area.
- There was a fear that the increase in temperature of Lake Kivu, caused by the lava, could allow toxic gases to be released from the lake bed.
- Several earthquakes accompanied the eruption, one measuring over 5 on the Richter scale. The tremors were strong enough to cause structural damage to some buildings in the area.
- Thousands of people required medical attention, at first from the effects of smoke and fumes from the lava, which caused eye irritation and respiratory problems, and then from diseases such as dysentery, linked to drinking contaminated water.
- There was much looting from abandoned homes and commercial properties. Many people were killed when a petrol store, which they were attempting to loot, exploded. It is believed that the looters were hoping to sell the petrol in order to buy food.

The authorities' initial response to the eruption was to issue a 'Red Alert' for Goma and the surrounding area. This enabled a full evacuation to take place. This prompt response was one factor in keeping the death rate relatively low.

Two days after the eruption, the UN began to bring in humanitarian aid. Emergency rations were initially of high-energy foods such as biscuits, which were followed by more substantial food aid (maize, beans and cooking oil) as communications began to improve. The UN also set up camps to house displaced people. The organisation has estimated the cost of providing food, blankets, household utensils, temporary shelter, clean water, sanitation and healthcare to the refugees at $15 million. However, a much higher cost will be incurred in rebuilding Goma's infrastructure, homes and livelihoods. The lava flows destroyed many businesses, resulting in a massive increase in unemployment in the area.

> **Case study** **Eruptions of Mt Etna, 1991–93**

Mt Etna (3,323 m), towering above Catania, the second largest city in Sicily (Figure 1.21), has one of the world's longest documented records of eruptions, dating back to 1500 BC (Photograph 1.5). The stratovolcano, truncated by several small calderas, was constructed over an older shield volcano. The most prominent feature is the Valle del Bove, a 5–10 km horseshoe-shaped caldera or depression open to the east. This was created when the volcano experienced a catastrophic collapse during an eruption, generating an enormous landslide.

Persistent explosive eruptions, sometimes with minor lava emissions, take place from one or more of the three prominent summit craters (central, northeast and southeast). There are a number of vents on the side of the volcano from which lava emerges and cinder cones are often constructed over the vents of lava flows on the lower flanks. Lava flows have reached the sea over a broad area on the southeast flank of Mt Etna.

Although it can be destructive, the volcano is not regarded as particularly dangerous. Thousands of people live on its slopes and in the surrounding areas, working the fertile volcanic soils.

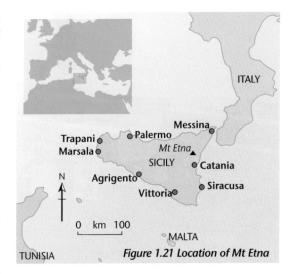

Figure 1.21 Location of Mt Etna

Towards the end of 1991, lava began to pour from vents high on the eastern flank of the volcano in the Valle del Bove, and to advance on the settlement of Zafferana. A series of protective measures was introduced to halt the lava flow, or at least slow its speed:

■ A **large earth barrier** was constructed across the end of the Val Calanna at the southern end of the Valle del Bove. This was several tens of metres

Photograph 1.5 Mt Etna erupting in 2002

high and more than 400 m long and it held back the lava for several months. The aim was to slow the lava advance temporarily while other protective measures were put in place or the eruption ended.

■ During the spring of 1992, the accumulated lava began to spill over this barrier and down into the valley leading to Zafferana. **Smaller barriers** erected across the valley were rapidly overwhelmed by the advancing lava which destroyed orchards and a few small buildings.

■ It was decided to cut off the flow by blocking the primary feeder channel. This was first attempted by **dropping concrete blocks** from helicopters through the roof of the upper lava tube.

■ Finally, in May 1992, engineers **blasted openings** in the lava tube. This was to encourage a new direction of flow, partly on top of the existing flow, rather than feeding it. The lava front stopped advancing on Zafferana, and the eruption ended 10 months later in early 1993.

Although this was probably the most successful attempt at changing the course of a volcanic eruption at that time, there remain doubts as to whether the flow would have reached Zafferana anyway. Figure 1.22 shows a number of lava flows from the volcano since the seventeenth century. The success of the above schemes was based upon the following favourable factors:

■ low effusion rates during the eruption

■ high elevation of the eruptive vents. These were between 2,200 and 2,350 m in altitude and therefore well away from inhabited areas. The lava had to flow more than 8 km before it became a serious threat

■ the possibility of diverting the lava flow into uninhabited areas (at least 7 km from the nearest village)

It is not always possible to stop lava flows on Mt Etna. In 2002, there was a more serious eruption and lava flows completely destroyed the ski station of Piano Provenzana (the village included two hotels, two restaurants, several ski hire firms, a dozen souvenir shops and a ski school). It also damaged part of another station at Rifugio Sapienza. Clouds of ash rained down on the area, affecting the city of Catania in particular.

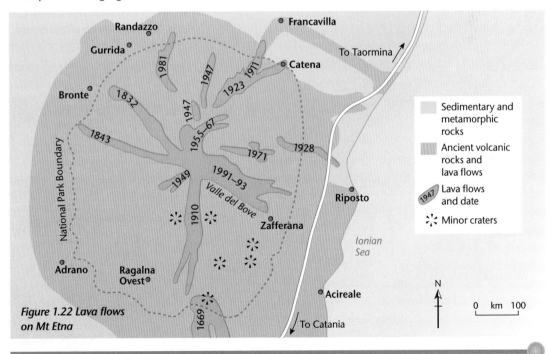

Figure 1.22 Lava flows on Mt Etna

Case study **The Soufrière Hills eruption, Montserrat, 1995–97**

In July 1995, after lying dormant for many centuries, the volcano located in the Soufrière Hills on the island of Montserrat in the Caribbean (Figure 1.23) began to erupt. Early activity included ash emissions, steam explosions and numerous earthquakes, the steam and ash reaching heights of more than 2,500 m. The volcano entered a quieter period for a while, but in March 1996 it again produced a huge ash cloud accompanied by dome growth and small pyroclastic flows.

In early 1997 there was continued dome growth with small explosions and ballistic projectiles. The climax occurred on 25 June when large explosions within the volcano resulted in extensive pyroclastic flows from an eruption estimated at 4–5 million m^3 of material. Most of this material flowed down the northern flank of the volcano, damaging houses and killing some inhabitants. Only 40 km^2 of the island's 100 km^2 was considered safe to live on. The island's capital, Plymouth, was eventually buried in over 10 m of ash and mud, the airport and docking facilities were destroyed, and the southern part of the

island was rendered uninhabitable (Photograph 1.6). Since 1997 the volcano has been relatively quiet with only minor activity.

During and after the eruption of the Soufrière Hills volcano, the British government had to provide, or assist in, the following, as Montserrat was still a dependent territory:

■ setting up of exclusion zones (see Figure 1.24)
■ evacuation of 7,000 of the island's 11,000 inhabitants to neighbouring islands such as Antigua, or resettlement in the UK, and financial help with all resettlement
■ resettlement of some of the population from the volcanic south to the 'safer' north of the island
■ setting up of temporary shelters in the north
■ re-establishment of air and sea links with the island
■ building of new permanent housing
■ moving the capital from Plymouth to Salem
■ providing farming areas for those resettled in the north

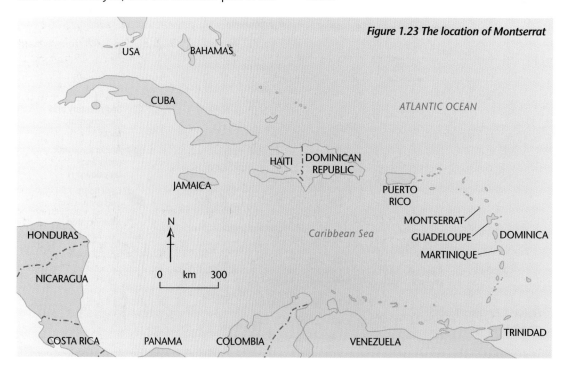

Figure 1.23 The location of Montserrat

TopFoto

- setting up the Montserrat Volcano Observatory (MVO) to monitor the Soufrière Hills activity. Today this is run under contract by the British Geological Society (BGS)

Photograph 1.6 The former capital of Montserrat, Plymouth, covered by dust and ashes from the Soufrière Hills volcano, August 1997

The UK government spent more than £100 million in assisting migration and restoring services, agriculture and employment on the island. By the early twenty-first century, a number of new homes had been built, although many inhabitants were still living in temporary accommodation. Other features of the island's redevelopment include:

- attempts to restore some of the tourist industry lost during the eruptions
- the return of some refugees from the UK and elsewhere
- the construction of a new airport known as Gerald's. This cost £11 million and was opened in 2005
- the development of port facilities at Little Bay
- the construction of a new football pitch, mainly funded by FIFA. Montserrat is now back in the world cup preliminaries but in February 2008 it occupied the last place in the FIFA rankings (along with five other nations)

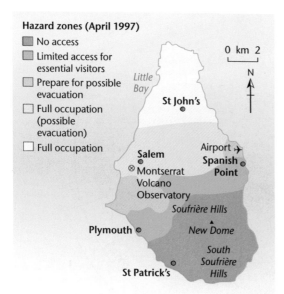

Hazard zones (April 1997)

- ■ No access
- ■ Limited access for essential visitors
- ■ Prepare for possible evacuation
- □ Full occupation (possible evacuation)
- □ Full occupation

Figure 1.24 Montserrat danger zones

Seismicity

Causes of earthquakes

Figure 1.25 The focus and epicentre of an earthquake

As the crust of the Earth is mobile, there tends to be a slow build up of stress within the rocks. When this pressure is suddenly released, parts of the surface experience an intense shaking motion that lasts for just a few seconds. This is an earthquake. The point at which this pressure release occurs within the crust is known as the **focus**, and the point immediately above that on the Earth's surface is called the **epicentre** (Figure 1.25). The depth of the focus is significant and three broad categories of earthquake are recognised:

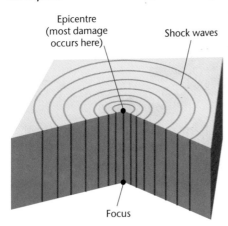

➤ shallow-focus (0–70 km deep): these tend to cause the greatest damage and account for 75% of all the earthquake energy released
➤ intermediate-focus (70–300 km deep)
➤ deep-focus (300–700 km deep)

Seismic waves radiate from the focus rather like the ripples in water when a rock is thrown into a pond. There are three main types of seismic wave, each travelling at different speeds (Figure 1.26):

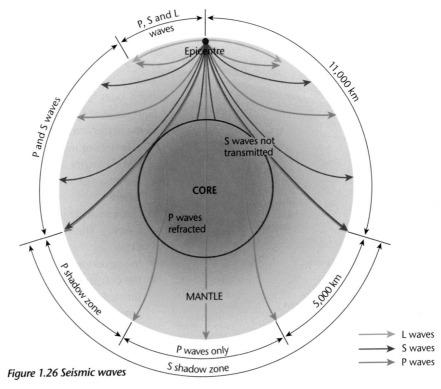

Figure 1.26 Seismic waves

- **primary (P) waves** travel fastest and are compressional, vibrating in the direction in which they are travelling
- **secondary (S) waves** travel at half the speed of P waves and shear rock by vibrating at right angles to the direction of travel
- **surface (L) waves** travel slowest and near to the ground surface. Some surface waves shake the ground at right angles to the direction of wave movement and some have a rolling motion that produces vertical ground movement

P and S waves travel through the interior of the Earth and are recorded on a seismograph. Studying earthquakes and the seismic waves they generate has made it possible to build up a picture of the interior of the Earth.

Distribution

The vast majority of earthquakes occur along plate boundaries (Figure 1.27), the most powerful being associated with destructive margins. At conservative margins, the boundary is marked by a fault, movement along which produces the earthquake. Perhaps the most famous of these is the San Andreas fault in California which represents the boundary between the North American and Pacific plates. In reality, the San Andreas system consists of a broad complex zone in which there are a number of fractures of the crust (Figure 1.28).

Some earthquakes occur away from plate boundaries and are associated with the reactivation of old fault lines. An example is the event that occurred on 23 September 2002 in the UK midlands. This earthquake measured 4.8 on the Richter scale, and the epicentre was located in Dudley, west of Birmingham. It is believed that the cause was movement along an old fault line known as the Malvern lineament.

It has been suggested that human activity could be the cause of some minor earthquakes. Examples are the building of large reservoirs in which the water puts pressure on the surface rocks, or subsidence of deep mine workings.

Figure 1.27 Global distribution of earthquakes

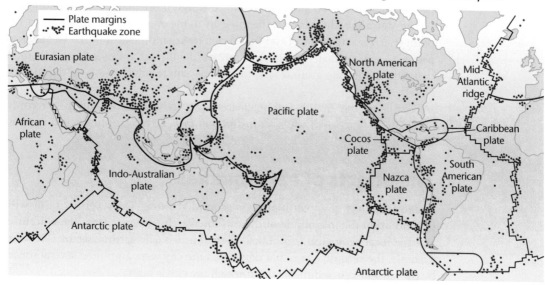

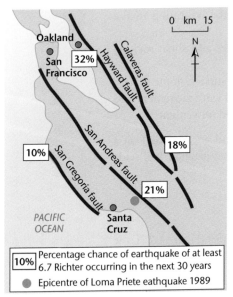

*Figure 1.28
Earthquake
probability in the
San Francisco area*

Percentage chance of earthquake of at least 6.7 Richter occurring in the next 30 years

● Epicentre of Loma Priete eathquake 1989

Table 1.3 The Richter scale

Number (logarithmic)	Effects
1–3	Normally only detected by seismographs, not felt
4	Faint tremor causing little damage
5	Widely felt, some structural damage near epicentre
6	Distinct shaking, less well-constructed buildings collapse
7	Major earthquake causing serious damage (e.g. Kobe 1995, Turkey 1999)
8	Great earthquake causing massive destruction and loss of life (e.g. Mexico City 1985, San Francisco 1906)
9–10	Very rare great earthquake causing major damage over a large region. Ground seen to shake

Magnitude and frequency

The magnitude of earthquakes is measured on two scales. The **Richter scale** (Table 1.3) is a logarithmic scale — an event measured at 7 on the scale has an amplitude of seismic waves ten times greater than one measured at 6 on the scale. The energy release is proportional to the magnitude, so that for each unit increase in the scale, the energy released increases by approximately 30 times.

The largest event ever recorded was measured at 8.9 on the scale. The earthquake in Dudley described above, at 4.8 on the scale, was large for the UK but small compared with major earthquakes such as the 1999 Turkish earthquake that measured 7.4 on the Richter scale. This earthquake killed more than 14,000 people, injured 25,000 and completely destroyed more than 20,000 buildings.

The **Mercalli scale** measures the intensity of the event and its impact. It is a 12-point scale that runs from Level I (detected by seismometers but felt by very few people — approximately equivalent to 2 on the Richter scale) to Level XII (total destruction with the ground seen to shake — approximately 8.5 on the Richter scale).

Seismic records enable earthquake frequency to be observed, but these records only date back to 1848 when an instrument capable of recording seismic waves was first developed.

The effects of earthquakes

The initial effect of an earthquake is **ground shaking**. The severity of this will depend upon the magnitude of the earthquake, the distance from the epicentre and the local geological conditions. In the Mexico City earthquake of 1985, for example, the seismic waves that devastated the city were amplified several times by the ancient lake sediments upon which the city is built.

Secondary effects are as follows:

➤ **soil liquefaction** — when violently shaken, soils with a high water content lose their mechanical strength and start to behave like a fluid
➤ **landslides/avalanches** — slope failure as a result of ground shaking
➤ **effects on people and the built environment** — collapsing buildings, destruction of road systems and other forms of communications, destruction of service provision such as gas, water and electricity, fires resulting from ruptured gas pipes and collapsed electricity transmission systems, flooding, disease, food shortages, disruption to the local economy. Some of the effects on the human environment are short term; others occur over a longer period and will depend to a large extent on the ability of the area to recover
➤ **tsunamis** — giant sea waves (tsunami means 'harbour wave' in Japanese) generated by shallow-focus underwater earthquakes (the most common cause), volcanic eruptions, underwater debris slides and large landslides into the sea

Tsunamis

In the open ocean tsunamis have a very long wavelength (sometimes more than 100 km) and a low wave height (under 1 m), and they travel quickly at speeds greater than 700 km h^{-1} (some tsunamis take less than a day to cross the Pacific Ocean). On reaching shallow water bordering land they increase rapidly in height.

Often, the first warning for coastal populations is the wave trough in front of the tsunami, which causes a reduction in sea level, known as a drawdown. Behind this comes the tsunami itself, which can reach heights in excess of 25 m. The event usually consists of a number of waves, the largest not necessarily being the first. When a tsunami reaches land, its effects will depend upon:

➤ the height of the waves and the distance they have travelled
➤ the length of the event that caused the tsunami
➤ the extent to which warnings can be given
➤ coastal physical geography, both offshore and in the coastal area
➤ coastal land use and population density

The wave will wash boats and wooden coastal structures inland, and the backwash may carry them out to sea. Both the water itself and the debris that it carries cause drowning and injuries. The effects of most tsunamis are felt at least 500–600 m inland, depending upon the coastal geography. Buildings, roads, bridges, harbour structures, trees and even soil are washed away. Tsunamis generated by the explosion of the volcano Krakatoa in 1883 are estimated to have drowned more than 35,000 people and produced waves that travelled around the world, the highest being over 40 m.

Around 90% of all tsunamis are generated within the Pacific basin and are associated with the tectonic activity taking place around its edges. Most are generated at convergent plate boundaries where subduction is taking place, particularly off the Japan–Taiwan island arc (25% of all events). Since the devastating tsunami of December 2004 (see case study below), the area has been affected by at least two major tsunamis:

➤ July 2006, south Java coast — generated by an earthquake of magnitude 7.7 on the Richter scale 180 km offshore, a tsunami devastated the area around Pangandaram, resulting in more than 600 deaths
➤ April 2007, Solomon Islands — the tsunami swept across the islands, killing at least 15 people

The geological record indicates that huge tsunamis have affected areas such as the Mediterranean basin (e.g. the Santorini eruption around 1450 BC) and the North Sea area. Around 7250 BP the Storegga slide, caused by huge submarine debris slides off Norway, produced tsunamis more than 6 m high in Scotland and other areas bordering the North Sea. It is believed that these tsunamis continued across the Atlantic to affect the coastlines of Spitsbergen, Iceland and Greenland.

Case study — Indian Ocean tsunami, 26 December 2004

Pressure had been building up for some time where the Indo-Australian plate subducts beneath the Eurasian plate south of Myanmar, and on Boxing Day 2004 there was a slippage along the plate edge some 25 km beneath the Indian Ocean. A section of sea bed on the Eurasian side of the fault rose several metres, generating a powerful earthquake which measured about 9.0 on the modified Richter scale. This makes it one of the biggest earthquakes ever recorded.

The epicentre of this earthquake was just off the northwestern tip of the island of Sumatra (see Figure 1.29). The earthquake triggered a tsunami that raced across the Indian Ocean, devastating islands (the Maldives, and the Andaman and Nicobar Islands) and the coastlines of the countries bordering the ocean, particularly Indonesia (Sumatra), Malaysia, Thailand, Myanmar, India and Sri Lanka. In some places the wall of water that came ashore was more than 25 m in height. Tsunami warning systems are in place in the Pacific basin but no such system had been set up in the Indian Ocean. The populations of these countries had no idea of what was about to arrive.

The main effects of the tsunami were:
■ an estimated 300,000 people were killed by the waves
■ tens of thousands of people were injured by the force of the waves and the debris that they carried
■ many of these coastal areas, particularly in Thailand, Sri Lanka and the Maldives, are popular

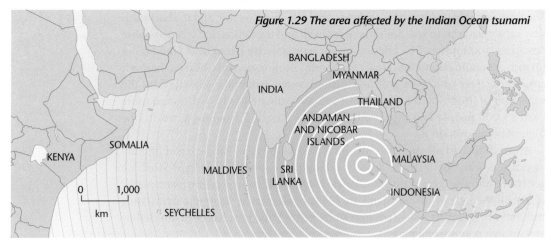

Figure 1.29 The area affected by the Indian Ocean tsunami

BANGLADESH
MYANMAR
INDIA
THAILAND
ANDAMAN AND NICOBAR ISLANDS
SOMALIA
KENYA
MALDIVES
SRI LANKA
MALAYSIA
INDONESIA
0   1,000
km
SEYCHELLES

tourist destinations, particularly over the Christmas holiday, so many hundreds of the dead and missing were from Europe
- whole towns and villages were swept away, particularly in northern Sumatra, the nearest land to the epicentre — it has been estimated that more than 1,500 villages were destroyed in this area alone (Photograph 1.7)
- destruction of property resulted in millions of people being made homeless
- there was massive damage to the tourist infra-structure, particularly hotels, bars, restaurants and shops
- there was widespread damage to coastal commu-nications, particularly bridges and railway lines — in one instance in Sri Lanka, a train was swept off the tracks resulting in more than 1,000 deaths
- damage to the economies of these coastal areas, particularly agriculture and fishing, left hundreds of thousands of people unable to feed themselves — the damage was so severe in places that coastal economies will be seriously affected for many years

- many hospitals and clinics were washed away or damaged, so a great deal of medical aid had to be brought in from outside the affected areas
- despite the enormous human cost, the insurance industry estimated that the disaster could cost less than $5 billion

On the western side of the Indian Ocean, countries did receive a warning of what was to come and were able to take action. Kenya, for example, reacted quickly, moving thousands of tourists off beaches to safety.

One positive result of this tsunami is that a warning system has now been set up among the countries that border the Indian Ocean. This would have been of little use in northern Sumatra as it was so close to the epicentre of the earthquake, but other countries would have benefited from some warning.

Photograph 1.7 Devastation caused by the tsunami: a lone mosque left standing in a flattened village in Aceh, Sumatra

TopFoto

Earthquake events: case studies

Case study Gujarat earthquake, India, 26 January 2001

One of the most powerful earthquakes to strike the Indian subcontinent in the last 100 years was centred near the small town of Bhuj in Gujarat (Figure 1.30). This earthquake, with a focus 17 km below the Earth's surface, was measured at 7.9 on the Richter scale. The shock waves from the event were felt over the border in Pakistan, where several people were killed. They were also felt on the other side of the subcontinent in Bangladesh and Nepal.

The death toll was high, as many buildings were not able to withstand the tremors, even in an area that was known to be seismically active. One resident complained that 'ours was not a well-designed building, it was built 12 years ago but it just fell to pieces as all the beams and pillars buckled instantly'. A month after the event, the Indian government issued the following information about the effects of the earthquake:

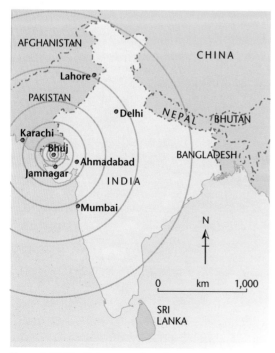

Figure 1.30 The Gujarat earthquake, 2001

- the death toll was put at just under 20,000, although some experts have estimated that at least 30,000 died in the earthquake. No accurate count of the dead and injured was available many days after the earthquake as the authorities were unable to cope with the magnitude of the disaster, the collapse of the district administration and a complete breakdown of communications with the outside world
- more than 160,000 people were seriously injured
- over 1 million people were made homeless
- approximately 345,000 dwellings were destroyed, ranging from blocks of flats to simple mud-built houses
- more than 800,000 buildings suffered some form of damage
- small towns such as Bhuj, Bhachau and Anjar had at least 90% of their dwellings destroyed and many smaller villages were totally devastated (Photograph 1.8)
- in Bhuj all four hospitals were destroyed. This made it difficult to deal with the many injured survivors. Emergency services had to be brought into the area from other parts of India and from overseas
- much of the cultural heritage of the area was destroyed including forts, palaces, temples and monuments, many of them centuries old
- communications were severely disrupted and power lines brought down

In the aftermath, one of the most disturbing aspects of the event was widespread looting of damaged property, which the authorities struggled to bring under control. In the days following the earthquake there were several hundred aftershocks, most of them small but one over 5 on the Richter scale. These aftershocks caused considerable damage to buildings weakened by the main earthquake.

Rescue teams were sent from many parts of the world to save people trapped beneath fallen buildings. Britain sent a 69-strong team sponsored by the Department for International Development. In addition to rescue operations, disinfectant was sprayed on the collapsed buildings to prevent the spread of disease from so many rotting bodies. Water purification tablets were also issued.

The Indian government sent 5,000 troops into the area along with 40 military aircraft (including helicopters) and three naval vessels, two of which were to act as floating hospitals, each capable of treating more than 200 patients. Military personnel trans-

Photograph 1.8 Devastation in Bhuj following the Gujarat earthquake

ported medical aid, food, tents and communication equipment by air to the worst affected areas.

The authorities feared widespread epidemics of typhoid and cholera following the event. However, prompt action meant that these did not occur, although there was evidence of widespread diarrhoea and gastroenteritis. In an area still heavily dependent on agriculture, the loss of 20,000 cattle had an enormous impact. The overall cost of the earthquake has been estimated at $4–5 billion and it has been suggested that more than 1 million people have been in receipt of some form of aid as a result of the event.

TopFoto

Case study: Northridge earthquake, Los Angeles, USA, 17 January 1994

Since 1933 there have been five earthquakes in the Los Angeles area that measured at least 5.8 on the Richter scale (Figure 1.31). They were:

- 1933 Long Beach, 6.4 Richter, 120 people died
- 1971 San Fernando, 6.6 Richter, 65 people died
- 1987 Whittier Narrows, 5.9 Richter, 8 people died
- 1991 Sierra Madre, 5.8 Richter, 2 people died
- 1997 Northridge, 6.7 Richter, 57 people died

The Northridge earthquake occurred at 4.30 a.m. on Monday 17 January 1994 and was the result of movement along a previously unknown thrust fault. The focus of the earthquake was at a depth of 18.4 km. The ground acceleration (the measurement of ground shaking) was the highest ever instrumentally recorded in a North American earthquake. The early morning occurrence is one of the factors

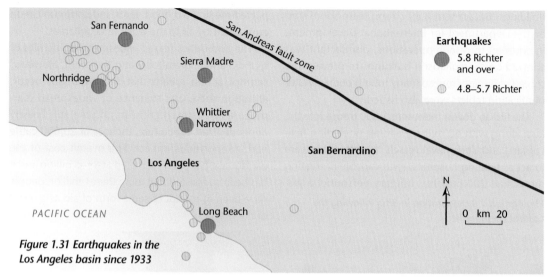

Figure 1.31 Earthquakes in the Los Angeles basin since 1933

suggested for the low death toll. If the earthquake had occurred later, more people would have been away from their homes, many on the roads of the area. It was also a federal holiday (Martin Luther King Day).

The main effects of the earthquake were:

- 57 people killed and more than 1,500 seriously injured (it has been estimated that over 10,000 people received some form of injury)
- 12,500 buildings suffered moderate to serious damage
- 11 major roads were seriously damaged and had to close for the rebuilding of some sections
- roads were damaged up to 32 km from the epicentre
- more than 11,000 landslides were triggered, some of them blocking roads and damaging water lines
- the landslides also damaged homes, particularly in the Pacific Palisades area
- more than 20,000 people were immediately made homeless
- 11 hospitals suffered some structural damage and were unable to serve their local neighbourhoods
- 600 aftershocks were recorded in the days following, resulting in damage to already weakened buildings (for example, a magnitude 5.6 earthquake occurred 11 hours after the main event)
- 80 km to the south, the scoreboard at the

Anaheim Stadium collapsed onto seating (the stadium was empty at the time)
- several days after the event, 9,000 premises did not have electricity, 20,000 had no gas supply, 48,500 had little or no water supply
- the estimated cost of the damage exceeded $30 billion and more than 700,000 applications were made to federal and state assistance programmes for financial help

The damage caused by the earthquake demonstrated that some types of building structure did not perform well. These included multistorey wood-frame buildings and those with a weak first floor (such as those with parking areas on the ground floor).

As California is an area of known seismic activity, area building codes were in place to ensure that new buildings could withstand earthquakes. School buildings and hospitals, which were required to be reinforced, survived fairly well. The Olive View hospital in Sylmar, for example, which was destroyed in the 1971 San Fernando earthquake, withstood the Northridge event as it had been rebuilt to a more exacting standard. As a result of the Northridge event, the state legislature decreed that all hospitals in California should, by 2005, have earthquake-proof acute care units and emergency rooms.

Case study — Market Rasen earthquake, Lincolnshire, UK, 27 February 2008

The Market Rasen earthquake was the strongest to hit Britain for nearly 25 years and occurred at 12.56 a.m. As with all recorded British earthquakes, no buildings collapsed, no bridges fell down and nobody was killed. The earthquake measured 5.2 on the Richter scale and occurred at a depth of 18.6 km. The epicentre was 4 km north of Market Rasen (Lincolnshire) and the resulting tremors were felt for hundreds of kilometres. There were several after-shocks, the strongest being only 2.2 on the Richter scale (Figure 1.32).

As the British Isles are not on or near a plate boundary, major earthquakes are unknown. As the plates move, however, tensions set up within them

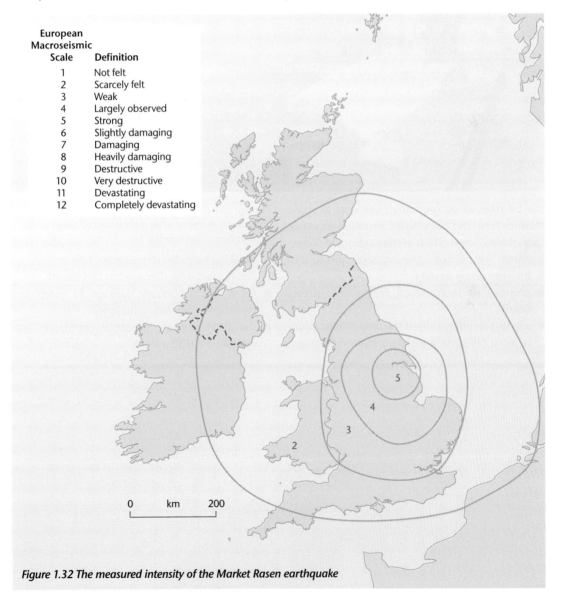

European Macroseismic Scale	Definition
1	Not felt
2	Scarcely felt
3	Weak
4	Largely observed
5	Strong
6	Slightly damaging
7	Damaging
8	Heavily damaging
9	Destructive
10	Very destructive
11	Devastating
12	Completely devastating

Figure 1.32 The measured intensity of the Market Rasen earthquake

Photograph 1.9 The damage to David Bates' room in Wombwell, Barnsley after a chimney collapsed in the Market Rasen earthquake

can be relieved by ground movements at some distance from the boundaries, resulting in minor earthquakes. Some effects of the earthquake were:

- homes were shaken, causing panic and calls to the emergency services
- chimney stacks collapsed, falling onto streets below
- a falling chimney caused the only serious injury when it fell onto a sleeping man in Barnsley, breaking his pelvis (Photograph 1.9)
- house roofs were damaged as tiles fell off
- there was secondary damage to roads and pavements from falling masonry
- the total cost to insurance companies was estimated at £30 million

Weather and climate and associated hazards

Major climate controls

The structure of the atmosphere

The atmosphere is a mixture of transparent gases held to the Earth by gravitational force. It consists of mainly nitrogen (78.09% by volume) and oxygen (20.95%). Other gases include argon, carbon dioxide, water vapour containing hydrogen, neon, helium, krypton, xenon, ozone, methane and radon. By international convention the top of the upper atmosphere is assumed to be at 1,000 km, but gravity and compression mean that most of the atmosphere is concentrated near to the Earth's surface. Approximately 50% lies within 5.6 km of the surface and 99% within 40 km.

In the study of weather and climate the most important part of the atmosphere is the **troposphere** (Photograph 2.1). Most of our climate and weather processes operate within 16–17 km of the Earth's surface in this lower atmospheric zone. In the troposphere

Corel

Photograph 2.1 Most weather occurs in the troposphere

> **Key terms**
>
> **Atmosphere** The mixture of gases surrounding the Earth.
>
> **Mesosphere** The layer of atmosphere above the stratosphere to an altitude of about 80 km above the surface of the Earth.
>
> **Stratosphere** The layer of atmosphere above the troposphere in which the temperature does not decrease with increasing altitude.
>
> **Thermosphere** The outermost layer of the Earth's atmosphere (to approximately 100 km from the Earth's surface), where the temperature falls with increasing altitude.
>
> **Tropopause** The boundary or interface between the troposphere and the stratosphere.
>
> **Troposphere** The layer of atmosphere extending approximately 8–17 km upwards from the Earth's surface, in which temperature decreases with increasing height.

temperatures generally decrease with height (averaging 6.5°C per kilometre). The top of this layer is marked by a boundary called the **tropopause** where temperatures remain fairly constant. This is found at a height of approximately 8 km at the poles and 17 km in the tropics and it can vary with seasonal changes in climate. The tropopause acts as a temperature inversion, forming an effective ceiling to convection in the troposphere and so provides an upper limit to the Earth's weather systems. Within the troposphere vertical convection currents disturb the atmosphere and air masses flow horizontally from one latitude to another.

Above the troposphere, the **stratosphere** extends to approximately 50 km above the Earth's surface. Within this layer temperatures increase with height. This layer is free of cloud and dust, and here ozone absorbs and filters out ultraviolet radiation. Warming is greater over the polar regions than in the tropical latitudes and these temperature differences cause strong horizontal air movements at great heights.

Global warming has been linked to recent changes in the stratosphere, brought about by human activity. The upper limit of the stratosphere is marked by the **stratopause**.

Figure 2.1 The vertical structure of the atmosphere

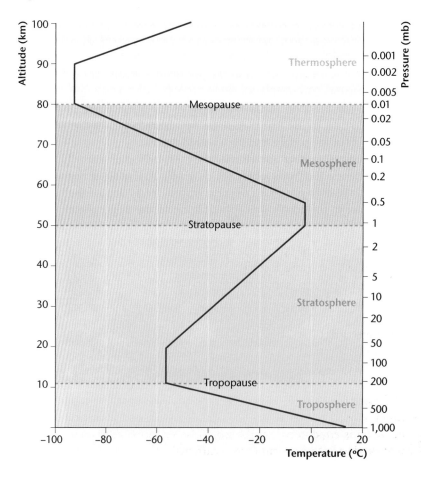

AQA A2 Geography

The uppermost layers of atmosphere are the **mesosphere** and the **thermosphere** (Figure 2.1). Within the mesosphere temperatures again decrease with altitude. However, in the most distant layer, the thermosphere, temperatures rise again at a constant rate to as much as 1,500°C.

The atmospheric heat budget

The Earth and its atmosphere receive heat energy from the sun. The atmospheric heat budget of the Earth depends on the balance between incoming **solar radiation (insolation)** and outgoing radiation from the planet (Figure 2.2). Geological records show that, on average, the energy budget has remained constant over the last few thousand years. This means that the incoming and outgoing energies must be equal. However, there is evidence to suggest that global warming has occurred over recent decades.

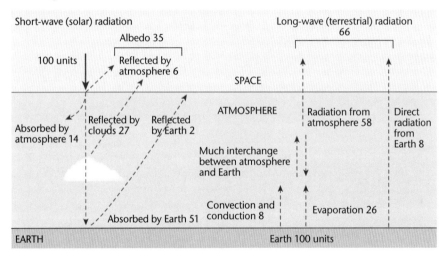

Figure 2.2 Solar energy budget

The Earth receives energy from the sun as incoming radiation. Some of this is lost as it passes through the atmosphere but overall the surface has a net *gain* of energy. The only places where there is a deficit are the polar regions. Only about 24% of the incoming solar radiation reaches the surface of the Earth, because of absorption, reflection and scattering.

The atmosphere, in contrast, has a net *deficit* of energy. Because of this difference, heat is transferred from the surface of the Earth to the atmosphere by radiation, conduction and by the release of latent heat.

There are variations in energy and heat between different latitudes. Low latitudes have a net surplus of energy, mainly because of their relative proximity to the sun. The high latitudes (polewards 40°N and 40°S) have a net deficit. Theoretically, this differential heating should result in the equatorial regions being much hotter and the poles much colder than they are. Since the poles are not becoming colder, and the equatorial regions are not becoming hotter, heat must be being transferred between the two. This occurs by means of air movement (winds), and water movement (ocean currents).

Planetary surface winds

Wind is the horizontal movement of air on the Earth's surface. Winds result from differences in air pressure and they always blow from high to low pressure. Pressure differences occur spatially because of global and local variations in temperature. When the air temperature of a place increases, the air in that area expands and rises, thus reducing air pressure. Conversely, when the temperature falls, the air becomes denser, it sinks and air pressure increases. The gradual change in air pressure over an area, seen in the pattern of isobars on a weather map, is called the **pressure gradient**. This gives rise to the movement of air from an area of relatively high pressure to an area of relatively low pressure.

The three cell model (see page 40) helps to explain the global pattern of surface winds (Figures 2.3 and 2.4). This pattern is generalised; in reality the pattern of

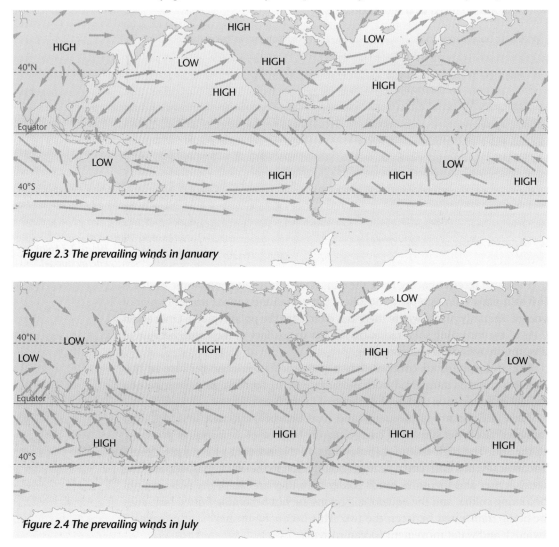

Figure 2.3 The prevailing winds in January

Figure 2.4 The prevailing winds in July

surface winds changes seasonally, and land and sea influence wind direction at the small scale. Winds also affect temperatures. The temperature of the wind is influenced by its area of origin and by the surface over which it has travelled. Winds blowing on to the land from the sea are relatively warm in winter and help to raise air temperatures. In the summer they depress air temperatures because the sea over which they have travelled is cooler than the land surface.

Atmospheric pressure and winds

Atmospheric pressure is the pressure exerted by the weight of air in the atmosphere at the surface of the Earth. The unit of atmospheric pressure is the millibar (mb) and it is measured using a barometer. The average atmospheric pressure at sea level is 1,013 mb. Points of equal atmospheric pressure are joined on a weather map by lines called **isobars** (see Figure 2.13, page 50).

The layers of the atmosphere closest to the ground surface have the greatest weight acting upon them, so pressure is greatest here. Air pressure decreases with altitude. At the top of the highest mountains it is very low. Air passengers are protected from low air pressure in the upper atmosphere by pressurised cabins.

Atmospheric pressure also varies horizontally, because it is a direct function of temperature. When the temperature rises, air expands and rises by convection, and pressure decreases. Conversely, when the temperature falls, air contracts and becomes denser, causing an increase in pressure.

High pressure occurs where air is descending and is associated with dry weather. This is because air warms as it descends, leading to the evaporation of most water vapour.

Low pressure occurs where air is rising. It is generally linked to precipitation and windy conditions. As it ascends air cools, and cannot hold as much water vapour. The water condenses into droplets, which become clouds at condensation level.

The general atmospheric circulation system

The differential heating of the Earth's surface by the sun is sufficient to create a pattern of pressure cells. The movement of air within each cell is generally circular and is responsible for the transfer of surplus energy from equatorial regions to other parts of the Earth.

In 1686 Hadley proposed that warm tropical air rises and spreads towards the poles at high altitude, with a return flow towards the equator at low level. He modified this in 1735 to include the effects of the Earth's rotation, deflecting winds towards the right in the northern hemisphere and to the left in the southern hemisphere. This single-cell model failed to explain the westerly winds in the temperate latitudes.

Key terms

Altitude Height of the land above sea level (metres).

General atmospheric circulation The pattern of wind and pressure belts within the atmosphere. The circulation is complex but certain movements occur regularly enough for us to recognise patterns of air pressure, distribution and winds.

Jet stream A narrow belt of fast-moving air near the top of the troposphere.

Latitude The angular distance a place lies, either north or south, from the equator.

Lapse rate The rate at which temperature changes with altitude.

Rossby waves A series of large waves that occur in the westerlies in the mid-latitudes in both the northern and southern hemispheres.

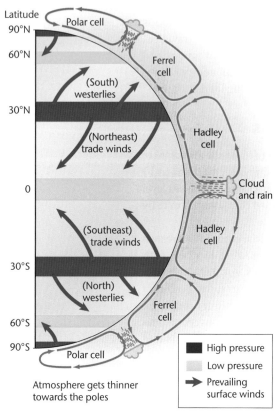

Figure 2.5 The three-cell model of atmospheric circulation

Further improvements were made in 1856 by Ferrel. He proposed that three cells form in each hemisphere, resulting in major areas of high and low pressure at the surface. High pressure forms where the air is falling and low pressure where it is rising. The three-cell model forms the basis of our understanding of global circulation.

The three cells in each hemisphere are known as the Hadley cell, the Ferrel cell and the Polar cell (Figure 2.5).

The Hadley cells

The two Hadley cells, one in each hemisphere, form the basis of tropical air circulation as shown in Figure 2.6, and are responsible for the seasonal changes in climate of those regions that experience a wet and dry climate.

Each Hadley cell can be divided into four components:

➤ Between the two cells there is an area of low pressure in equatorial latitudes which is known as the **inter-tropical convergence zone** or ITCZ. As the sun is always high in the sky, the ground heats rapidly by day and there is much surface evaporation. As the hot air rises in convection currents, an area of low pressure develops. This rising air cools and the water vapour eventually condenses, giving heavy rainfall.

➤ At high altitudes the air moves polewards. This air usually circulates as upper westerly winds around the planet as a result of the deflection effect of the rotation of the Earth, known as the **Coriolis effect**. The net effect, though, is for the air still to move polewards.

Figure 2.6 The circulation of the Hadley cells

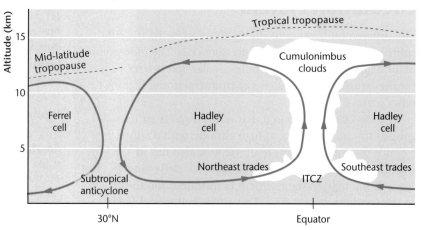

> Around 30°N and 30°S the colder air at higher altitudes begins to sink, or subside, back to the Earth's surface. As this air descends, it warms and any residual moisture evaporates. At the surface, high pressure is created, with cloudless skies. These areas are known as the **subtropical anticyclones**.

> On reaching the ground, some of the air returns towards equatorial areas as consistent winds known as the **trade winds**. These air movements are also subject to the Coriolis effect and blow from a northeasterly direction in the northern hemisphere and from the southeast in the southern hemisphere. The two trade wind systems move air towards the equator where it forms the ITCZ.

The Ferrel and Polar cells

The Ferrel cell occurs at higher latitudes (between 30° and 60°N and 30° and 60°S). This is responsible for the climate types occurring in the mid-latitudes. As Figure 2.5 shows, air on the surface is pulled toward the poles, forming the warm southwesterly winds in the northern hemisphere and the northwesterlies in the southern hemisphere. These winds pick up moisture as they travel over the oceans. At around 60°N and 60°S, they meet cold air, which has drifted from the poles. The warmer air from the tropics is lighter than the dense, cold polar air and so it rises as the two air masses meet. This uplift of air causes low pressure at the surface and the unstable conditions that follow result in the mid-latitude depressions, characteristically experienced in the cool temperate western maritime (CTWM) climate.

On reaching the troposphere, some of this rising air eventually returns to the tropics as part of the Ferrel cell circulation; some is diverted polewards, as part of the Polar cell.

On the surface at the north and south poles, descending air from the Polar cell results in high pressure. In both the northern and southern hemispheres winds are pulled from the high-pressure poles towards the mid-latitude low-pressure belt, which occurs at around 60°N and 60°S. The Earth spinning on its axis causes the prevailing surface winds to be deflected to the left in the southern hemisphere and to the right in the northern hemisphere. Thus cold air is transported away from high latitudes and warm air is brought in by the Polar cell. This helps to address the energy deficit.

The three-cell model does not allow for the influence of depressions/anticyclones or high-level jet streams in the redistribution of energy. It was refined by Rossby in 1941 to take these into account. More recent approaches, known as wave theory models, have been developed to explain the behaviour of the upper-air westerly air streams (Rossby waves) and jet streams (Figure 2.7).

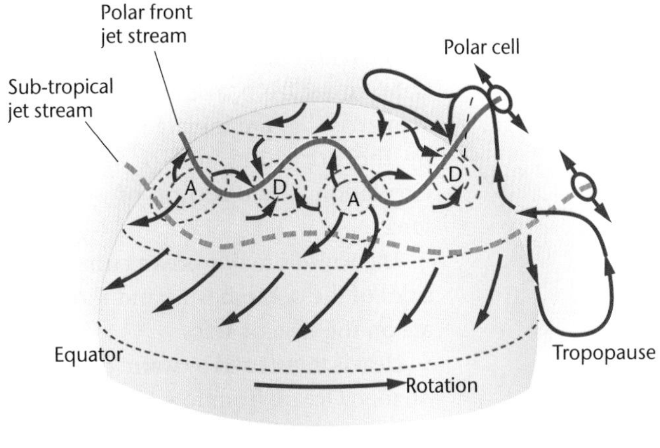

Figure 2.7
A generalised model of global circulation

Polar front jet stream
Polar cell
Sub-tropical jet stream
Equator
Tropopause
Rotation

In the upper atmosphere winds blow around the Earth in a westerly direction. Pilots first noticed this when they were blown off course when flying north to south, and they also found that they could travel more quickly than expected when flying from west to east.

Rossby waves follow a wavy undulating pattern as they travel around the Earth's upper atmosphere. The waves occur between four and six times in each hemisphere and they can stretch from the polar latitudes to the tropical latitudes. It is not known why they exist but some people believe that they are caused by the upper air flow being forced to divert around the great north–south mountain ranges of the Rockies and Andes. Once a wave motion has begun, it is perpetuated around the planet. The waves have considerable variation in amplitude during the year.

Within the upper westerly winds are bands of extremely fast-moving air (up to 250 km h^{-1}) called **jet streams**. A jet stream can be hundreds of kilometres in width but with a vertical thickness of just 1,000–2,000 m. On average they are found at altitudes of 10,000 m. They are the product of a large temperature gradient between two air masses. There are two main locations of jet streams:

➤ The **polar front jet stream** (PFJS) — a westerly band of wind, associated with the meeting place of cold polar and warm tropical air high above the Atlantic Ocean, between latitudes 40 and 60°N and 40 and 60°S. The precise location of the jet stream varies, but pilots seek to ride in it when going from west to east and to avoid it when flying from east to west. It marks the division between the Polar and Ferrel cells, and helps to explain the formation of mid-latitude low-pressure weather systems, or depressions.

➤ The **subtropical jet stream** (STJS) — also generally westerly and associated with the poleward ends of the Hadley cells at approximately 25°N and 35°S. However, in summer above west Africa and southern India this jet may become easterly. This is due to higher temperatures over land than over the more southerly sea areas.

Oceanic circulation

The large-scale movement of water within the oceans is part of the horizontal transfer of heat from the tropics to the polar regions and is responsible for around 20% of the total transfer of heat within the energy budget. Each ocean has its own circular pattern of currents (called a **gyre**) that are produced as masses of water move from one climatic zone to another. However, the patterns are all similar as they are initiated by the same factors. Ocean currents are set in motion by the prevailing surface winds associated with the general atmospheric circulation. The direction of water movement is also deflected by the Coriolis force.

The world's major ocean currents are particularly dominant along the western sides of the ocean basins and those that are less well-defined and relatively weak are on the eastern sides.

Heat is transferred by warm ocean currents, such as the North Atlantic Drift in the Atlantic Ocean, from low to high latitudes. This warming influence is particularly

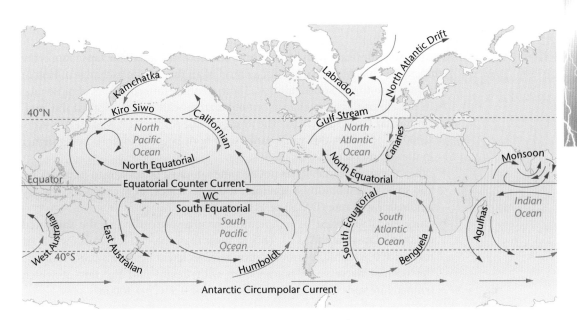

Figure 2.8 Oceanic circulation

dominant in winter between latitudes 40° and 65° where winds blow onshore on the western sides of continents. Cold ocean currents have less effect upon temperatures because they usually occur under offshore winds. One exception is the Labrador current off the east coast of North America (Figure 2.8).

Latitude

Insolation varies with latitude because of variations in day-length and the angle of incidence of the sun's rays. The Earth spins on its axis once every 24 hours and, at the same time, it moves in a large circular path around the sun, once per year. Its axis is tilted in relation to this path.

➤ **Length of daylight hours** — in the tropics there is little seasonal difference in the length of day and night; both last about 12 hours. In summer at the north and south poles it never properly becomes dark and in the winter there are up to 24 hours of darkness. Between the equator and the poles the length of night and day varies gradually with latitude. Heat energy from the sun can only be received during the hours of daylight. Therefore, the polar regions are cold during the dark winter months, but warmer in summer because of the long daylight hours.

➤ **Angle of incidence** — the midday sun remains high in the sky in the tropics all year round. The sun's rays are concentrated and strong. Outside the tropics the angle of the sun is lower and the sun's rays travel a greater distance through the Earth's atmosphere, losing energy. On reaching the surface each ray heats up a larger area than in the tropics so the sun's energy is less concentrated.

Photograph 2.2 At the poles the angle of the sun's incidence is low

Ingram

Altitude

Temperatures decrease with height above sea level. The **adiabatic lapse rate** is the temperature change with height for a parcel of air that has no exchange of heat or moisture with the air surrounding it. There are three different types of lapse rate:

➤ In the atmosphere the change of temperature with height is called the **environmental lapse rate** (ELR). The average value for the ELR is 6.5°C for every 1,000 m. However, this value varies with both height and time, being higher in the summer season.

➤ When the air is dry, i.e. it has not become saturated by cooling to its dewpoint and so relative humidity is less than 100%, its temperature changes at the **dry adiabatic lapse rate** (DALR) of 1°C per 100 m.

➤ Once air is saturated its temperature changes according to the **saturated adiabatic lapse rate** (SALR). This is lower than the DALR because when air reaches 100% humidity condensation releases latent heat. This process offsets the normal decrease of temperature with height and the rate at which temperature varies with altitude is taken to be 0.5°C per 100 m.

The climate of the British Isles

Basic climatic characteristics

The main influences on the **climate** of the British Isles are its latitude and its maritime position. It lies within the **cool temperate western maritime (CTWM)** climate belt. It does not experience extremes of temperature and it receives precipitation throughout the year. One of the most striking features of the **weather** in the British Isles is its unpredictability. This is due in part to the dominance of low-pressure weather systems. Climate graphs (Figures 2.9 and 2.10) present a view of the average conditions taken over at least 30 years.

Temperature

Mean summer temperatures in the UK are lower than average for the latitude. Although daily maximum temperature can reach 30°C, average monthly values seldom exceed 18°C. This is due to the cooling influence of the Atlantic Ocean. In winter the average temperatures are above freezing (between 2°C and 7°C). In some coastal locations, such as Cornwall and Pembrokeshire, relatively high average winter values (above 6°C) result from the warming influence of the sea and ensure a year-round growing season. The annual range of temperature within the CTWM is relatively small but increases with distance from the west coast.

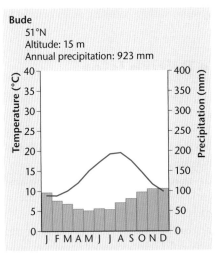

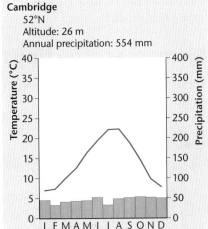

Figure 2.9 Climate graph for Bude, Cornwall   *Figure 2.10 Climate graph for Cambridge*

Cambridge in East Anglia has an annual temperature range of 14°C (Figure 2.11) compared with 10°C for Plymouth in Devon.

Precipitation

Precipitation is experienced throughout the year but varies with relief. In upland areas, in particular those close to western coasts, rainfall totals can exceed 2,500 mm. A short distance further east, on lowland in the shadow of the mountains, annual totals can be as little as 500 mm. Most of the rainfall is brought by frontal systems moving from west to east, releasing moisture as they cross the land. In general, summer is the driest season, followed by winter. This is because high-pressure weather systems (anticyclones) are more likely to become established in these seasons and block the approaching fronts, deflecting them to the north or south.

Wind

The prevailing wind direction is southwest and this is governed by the general atmospheric circulation system. However, although Britain receives most air streams from the west, easterly winds do occur. They generally bring spells of dry weather.

Winds from the west can be strong and gales are common, particularly during the autumn. These winds are influenced by low-pressure weather systems, where rising air in the centre of the low

Key terms

Anticyclone A high-pressure weather system with diverging air near the ground. Winds in the northern hemisphere flow clockwise in the system and the weather is dry.

Climate The average weather over an area, usually taken from records of the last 30 years. Climate describes the seasonal pattern of temperature and precipitation.

Cool temperate western maritime climate (CTWM) The seasonal pattern of weather experienced in the mid-latitudes (between 45° and 60°) on the western side of continental land masses.

Depression A low-intensity cyclone or low-pressure weather system, frequently experienced in the CTWM climate. This weather system is associated with rising air, wind and precipitation. In the northern hemisphere winds blow in an anticlockwise direction towards the centre of the low pressure.

Weather Day-to-day state of the atmosphere.

results in a steep pressure gradient on the ground surface, causing air to rush in to replace that which has risen.

Air masses affecting the British Isles

Several air masses may approach western Europe. Each brings with it a range of weather conditions (Figure 2.11):

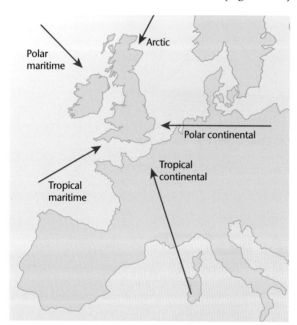

Figure 2.11 Air masses affecting the British Isles

➤ **Arctic** — from the north, brings extremely cold temperatures and snow in winter and early spring.

➤ **Polar maritime** — from the northwest Atlantic, is accompanied by cold, moist weather.

➤ **Polar continental** — from the east, brings bitterly cold temperatures in winter, and possibly snow to eastern England.

➤ **Tropical maritime** — from the southwest, causes the weather to be mild and wet in winter but cool and moist in summer.

➤ **Tropical continental** (in summer only) — from the southeast, brings hot, dry, heatwave conditions.

The weather associated with an air mass is related to the source region. A frontal system develops when two contrasting air masses meet.

The origin and nature of depressions

Depressions are low-pressure weather systems. They have the following characteristics:

➤ they are areas of low atmospheric pressure, often below 1,000 mb

➤ they are represented on a weather map by a system of closed isobars with pressures decreasing towards the centre

➤ they usually move rapidly from west to east across the British Isles

➤ isobars are usually close together, producing a steep pressure gradient from the outer edges to the centre

➤ winds are often strong and blow inwards towards the centre of the low in an anticlockwise direction

➤ a place in the southern part of the British Isles will often experience a change of wind direction from south to southwest to west to northwest as the depression moves across from west to east. In such circumstances the wind is said to **veer**

➤ in the northern parts of the British Isles the wind changes direction from southeast to east to northeast to east and is said to **back**

University of Dundee

Formation of a depression

A depression affecting the British Isles originates in the North Atlantic where two different **air masses** meet along the polar front (see Figure 2.12 and Photograph 2.3). The two air masses involved are:

➤ polar maritime air, which is dense, moist and cold
➤ tropical maritime air, which is light, moist and warm

Photograph 2.3 Satellite photograph showing a depression to the west of the British Isles

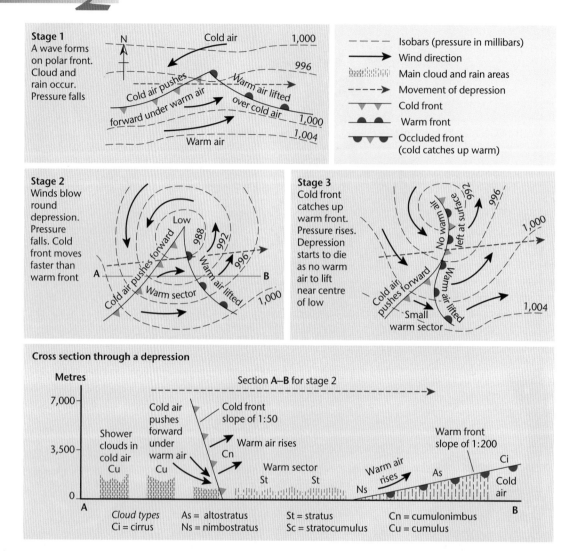

Figure 2.12
The stages of a depression

As these two bodies of air move towards each other the warmer, less dense air from the south rises above the colder, dense air from the north. The rising air is removed by strong upper atmosphere winds (the **jet stream**), but as it rises the Earth's rotational spin causes it to twist. This twisting vortex produces a wave at ground level in the polar front, which increases in size to become a depression.

Two separate parts of the original front have now developed (stage 2 in Figure 2.12):

➤ the **warm front** at the leading edge of the depression where warm, less dense air rises over the colder air ahead
➤ the **cold front** at the rear of the depression where colder dense air pushes against the warmer air ahead

In between these two fronts lies the **warm sector** — an area of warm and moist air. As the depression moves eastwards, the cold front gradually overtakes the warm front to form an **occlusion** in which the colder air undercuts the warmer air so that it no longer touches the ground.

Weather conditions

The weather conditions associated with a depression depend on whether the area in question has polar maritime air or tropical maritime air over it. Polar maritime air brings average temperatures for the season in winter (5–8 °C in January) but noticeably cooler temperatures for the season in summer (16–18 °C in July). Rain showers are common in both seasons, with the possibility of sleet in winter.

Tropical maritime air brings humid and mild weather in winter, with temperatures well above the seasonal norm at 12–14 °C in January. Low stratus cloud and fog are also common. In summer it may cause advection fog in western coastal areas, but elsewhere temperatures will be warm — 25 °C in July. There will be the threat of showers and possibly thunderstorms due to the combination of high humidity levels and low pressure.

Table 2.1 summarises the main weather changes associated with the passage of a depression over an area in the British Isles. It should be used in conjunction with the cross-section through a depression shown in Figure 2.12.

Table 2.1 Weather changes associated with the passing of a depression

Weather element	Cold front			Warm front		
	In the rear	At passage	Ahead	In the rear	At passage	Ahead
Pressure	Continuous steady rise	Sudden rise	Steady or slight fall	Steady or slight fall	Fall stops	Continuous fall
Wind	Veering to northwest, decreasing speed	Sudden veer, southwest to west. Increase in speed, with squalls	Southwest, but increasing in speed	Steady southwest, constant	Sudden veer from south to southwest	Slight backing ahead of front. Increase in speed
Temperature	Little change	Significant drop	Slight fall, especially if raining	Little change	Marked rise	Steady, little change
Humidity	Variable in showers, but usually low	Decreases sharply	Steady	Little change	Rapid rise, often to near saturation	Gradual increase
Visibility	Very good	Poor in rain, but quickly improves	Often poor	Little change	Poor, often fog/mist	Good at first but rapidly deteriorating
Clouds	Shower clouds, clear skies and cumulus clouds	Heavy cumulo-nimbus	Low stratus and stratocumulus	Overcast, stratus and stratocumulus	Low nimbostratus	Becoming increasingly overcast, cirrus to altostratus to nimbostratus
Precipitation	Bright intervals and scattered showers	Heavy rain, hail and thunder-storms	Light rain, drizzle	Light rain, drizzle	Rain stops or reverts to drizzle	Light rain, becoming more continuous and heavy

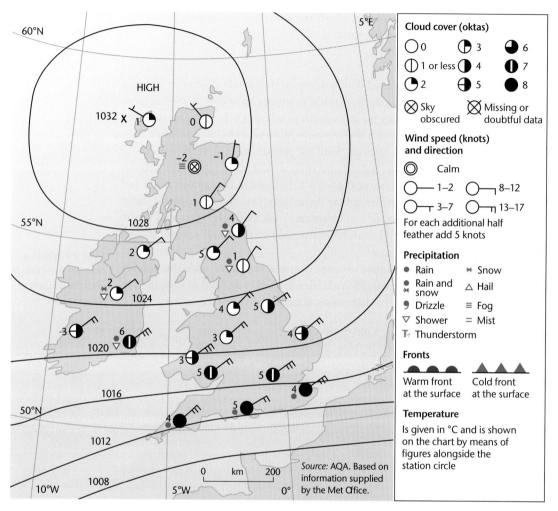

Figure 2.13 An anticyclone over Scotland in winter

The origin and nature of anticyclones

Anticyclones have the following characteristics (Figure 2.13):

➤ they are areas of relatively high atmospheric pressure

➤ they are represented on a weather map by a system of closed isobars with pressures increasing towards the centre

➤ anticyclones move slowly and may remain stationary over an area for several days or even weeks

➤ the air in an anticyclone subsides (falls from above), warming as it falls. This produces a decrease in its relative humidity which leads to a lack of cloud development, and dry conditions

➤ isobars are usually far apart, and therefore there is little pressure difference between the centre and edges of the anticyclone

➤ winds are weak, and flow gently outwards in a clockwise direction in the northern hemisphere, anticlockwise in the southern hemisphere

*Photograph 2.4
A winter anticyclone
traps pollution in
the air over Burnley.
The polluted air can
be seen as a brown
haze over the town*

Associated weather conditions in winter and summer

In winter anticyclones result in:

➤ cold daytime temperatures — from below freezing to a maximum of 5°C
➤ very cold night-time temperatures — below freezing with frosts
➤ generally clear skies by day and by night. Low-level cloud may linger and **radiation fogs** (caused by rapid heat loss at night) may remain in low-lying areas
➤ high levels of atmospheric pollution in urban areas, caused by a combination of subsiding air and lack of wind. Pollutants are trapped by a **temperature inversion** (when air at altitude is marginally warmer than air at lower levels, see Photograph 2.4)

In summer, anticyclones mean:

➤ hot daytime temperatures — above 25°C
➤ warm night-time temperatures — may not fall below 15°C
➤ generally clear skies by day and night
➤ hazy sunshine in some areas
➤ early morning mists, which disperse rapidly
➤ heavy dew on the ground in the morning
➤ the east coast of Britain may have sea **frets** or **haars** caused by onshore winds
➤ thunderstorms may occur when the air has high relative humidity

Anticyclones that establish themselves over Britain and northwest Europe and remain stationary for many days are described as **blocking anticyclones**. Depressions that would normally travel across the British Isles on a westerly airstream are steered around the upper edge of the high, away from the area. Extreme weather conditions are then produced — dry and freezing weather in winter, and heatwaves in summer.

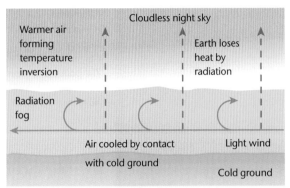

Figure 2.14 How radiation fog forms

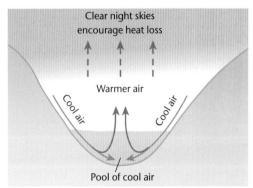

Figure 2.15 Fog formation under a temperature inversion in a valley

Fogs

Fogs are common features of anticyclonic conditions. Fog is cloud at ground level that restricts visibility to less than 1 km. It consists of tiny water droplets suspended in the atmosphere. There are two main types of fog — radiation fog and advection fog.

Radiation fog

Radiation fog forms under clear night skies when a moist atmosphere cools through the radiation of heat from the ground surface. The cooling extends some distance above the ground surface and is encouraged by light winds that allow slight mixing of the air. The air is cooled to its **dew point**, at which condensation occurs (Figure 2.14).

This type of fog is common in winter, when long hours of darkness allow maximum cooling. In such cases, the fog may persist all day. It disperses either through an increase in wind speed or through warming of the air (and evaporation).

Radiation fog is common under temperature inversions, which often occur in valleys (Figure 2.15). In the evening, with clear skies and high humidity, the air on the upper slopes chills more quickly than that in the valley bottom. Cooling increases the density of the air, and it begins to move downslope. The cooler air accumulates in the valley bottom, pushing the warmer air upwards. The cold air now in the valley bottom will cool to its dew point, and create a dense fog that can last all day, and cause a severe frost.

Advection fog

Advection fog forms when a mass of relatively warm air moves horizontally across a cooler surface. The air is cooled to its dew point and condensation occurs. This type of fog is most common around coasts and over the

**Figure 2.16
Advection fog**

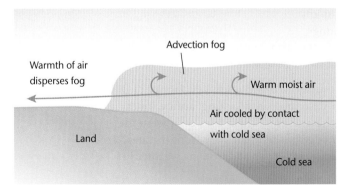

sea in summer. In such areas it is sometimes called a **fret** or **haar**. As the fog moves inland, it is warmed and evaporates (Figure 2.16).

Storm events

Atmospheric processes

Gales are a common feature of the CTWM climate. They are generally at their worst during the autumn, when the sea temperature is still warm enough to fuel powerful low-pressure cells. Sometimes, during this season, the relics of tropical storms from the Caribbean find their way across the Atlantic. However, by the time they reach the European coast much of their energy has been lost because of lower temperatures.

The magnitude of gales is greatest in the exposed western coastal areas of the UK. They are associated with low-pressure weather systems and occur where there is a steep pressure gradient. Surface winds always blow from high to low pressure. Strong winds and a steep gradient in pressure can be recognised on a weather chart by closely spaced isobars.

The atmospheric processes that cause winds are outlined earlier in this chapter; in the case of strong winds, these processes occur more rapidly than normal.

Severe gales occur when the air pressure drops to a very low level. This occurred in the 'the storm of the century' that hit southern England in 1987 (see case study). The air pressure at the centre of the low measured 974 mb (the average value for air pressure at sea level is 1,013 mb).

Storms of this nature are rare in the mid-latitudes, but when they do occur the scale of the damage is significant. However, the magnitude of the event can never equal that of a major hurricane. This is because in the mid-latitudes the air pressure at the centre of an intense depression does not fall to such an extremely low level as it does in the tropics. Therefore, the wind speed caused by the steep pressure gradient in a tropical revolving storm is never quite matched.

Impact

The Beaufort scale can be used to categorise wind strength. A 'moderate' gale has wind speeds of between 50 and 60 km h^{-1}, and this sets whole trees in motion. A 'fresh' gale breaks twigs from trees and has wind speeds between 61 and 73 km h^{-1}. A 'strong' gale has winds of between 74 and 86 km h^{-1} and can cause slight damage to buildings, particularly roofs. A 'whole' gale is classed as having wind speeds between 87 and 100 km h^{-1}. It uproots trees and causes structural damage to buildings. Winds in excess of 100 km h^{-1} are classed as storms and are capable of causing widespread damage to buildings and infrastructure. Storms of this magnitude are rare in the British Isles, but when they do occur they cause widespread disruption for a short period of time. Wind speeds above 120 km h^{-1} are unlikely to be experienced in the British Isles. Storms of such magnitude are classified as hurricanes.

Every year gales are expected to result in short-term disruption to transport and power supplies, but such damage is usually minor.

Case study   **The great storm, southern Britain, 1987**

In October 1987, the 'storm of the century' occurred in England. Meteorologists incorrectly predicted that this low-pressure weather system would sweep over France and Spain. However, it veered northwards instead and hit southern England (Figure 2.17). By midnight on 15 October, gusts exceeding 150 km h^{-1} (normally classed as hurricane strength) were recorded over exposed coastal areas. The emergency services were stretched to their limits throughout the night, dealing with fallen trees, accidents and power cuts.

If the storm had occurred 8 hours later, during the rush hour, the impacts would have been much worse. The immediate effects were 19 people dead, colossal damage to property and power cuts to 13 million homes. Train and ferry services were cancelled, caravan parks wrecked and boats broke from their moorings and were washed ashore. Insurance claims were estimated to be over £1.5 billion. The clear-up took many months, particularly where structural damage to buildings had occurred. One of the most significant long-term impacts of this storm was the destruction of some 15 million trees, uprooted by the hurricane-strength winds (Photograph 2.5).

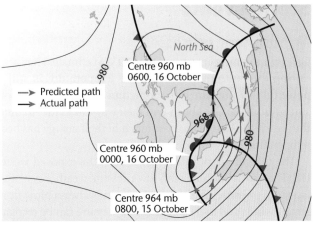

Figure 2.17 Predicted and actual paths of the great storm in southeast England, 1987

Photograph 2.5 Uprooted trees in Kew Gardens following the great storm of 1987

Tropical climates

We have seen that the climate of the British Isles is influenced by its location in the mid-latitudes and close to the Atlantic Ocean. Within the tropics, as in the temperate latitudes, there are variations in climate types. These are influenced by latitude, pressure systems and their winds, continentality or distance from the sea, ocean currents and mountain ranges. You are required to study one from the following three tropical climate types:

Key terms

Climatic hazard A natural event brought about by weather or climate that threatens life and property.

Convection When the lower air in the atmosphere is heated by the ground it expands and rises. This leads to instability within the atmosphere and formation of cumulonimbus clouds.

Monsoon The seasonal reversal of pressure and wind direction, commonly associated with heavy precipitation, experienced when winds blow in from the ocean in southeast Asia during the months of May to October.

Tropical revolving storm A term that covers hurricanes, tropical cyclones, typhoons and willy-willies. These intense low-pressure weather systems are associated with catastrophic wind speeds and torrential rainfall.

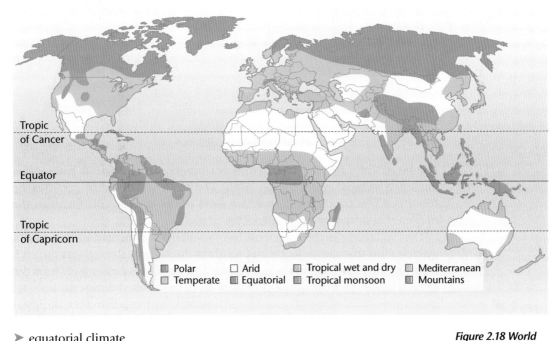

Figure 2.18 World climatic regions

➤ equatorial climate
➤ tropical wet and dry climate
➤ tropical monsoon climate

Figure 2.18 shows the global distribution of these three climate types.

The inter-tropical convergence zone

A major influence on all tropical climates is the position of the inter-tropical convergence zone (ITCZ) and the role of associated subtropical anticyclones. The ITCZ occurs along a line where the northeast trade winds blowing away from the subtropical high-pressure cell in the northern hemisphere meet the southeast trade winds blowing in a similar fashion from the subtropical high in the southern hemisphere. Convergence occurs at the point where the trade winds meet.

*Figure 2.19
Movements of the
ITCZ*

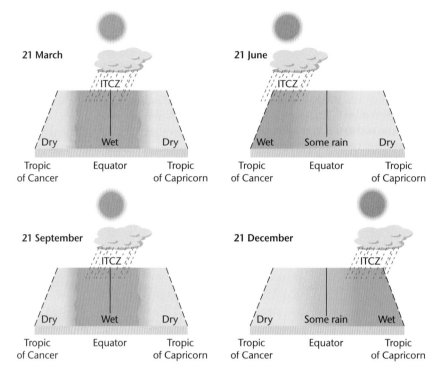

Combined with intense heating in the low latitudes, this causes air to rise and this in turn is helped by divergence aloft. The tendency of air to be lifted by convergence is greater on the western sides of the oceans. This increases the frequency of storms in those parts of the tropics.

The ITCZ marks an area of intense low pressure. It is associated with an area of precipitation that moves north and south of the equator throughout the year, following the movement of the sun (Figure 2.19). It moves further away from the equator in the northern hemisphere than might be expected during the summer months, in particular over the great continental landmass of Asia. During these months the land is heated intensely.

*Figure 2.20
Equatorial climate,
Uaupés, Amazon
lowlands*

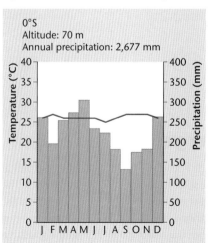

Equatorial climate

The equatorial climate occurs in lowland areas within 5–10° latitude of the equator and is sometimes referred to as the tropical rainy climate (Figure 2.20).

There is little variation in the length of daylight hours throughout the year because the sun is never far from its zenith. This means that day and night are both around 12 hours and the annual temperature range is small, normally as low as 3°C. Mean monthly temperatures are 26–28°C. The diurnal temperature range is greater than the annual range. Night-time temperatures rarely fall below 18°C and daytime temperatures may rise to 35°C. With high humidity and constant temperatures this climate can be oppressive.

The constant uplift of warm, unstable air is caused by the convergence of tropical air masses in these latitudes and results in low pressure throughout the year. Close to the equator pressure gradients are small and therefore winds are gentle.

Rainfall is high, over 2,000 mm per year, and the daily pattern is repetitive and predictable. The morning is hazy and, as this clears, convection currents develop and produce cumulus clouds. These build up and intensify during the afternoon heat to form cumulonimbus clouds. Heavy rain develops in the late afternoon or early evening. Convection uplift is related to the position of the ITCZ and rainfall totals double the normal maximum can occur when the sun is directly overhead at the spring and autumn equinox. However, rainfall patterns can vary from this, particularly in locations far from the ocean such as the eastern Amazon basin, where some parts of the year are drier than average.

On the forest floor there is little breeze. On the equator there is a lack of wind because this is where the trade winds converge.

Tropical wet and dry climate

The tropical wet and dry climate is also known as the tropical continental climate. It is found polewards of the equatorial climate, generally between latitudes 5° and 15° north and south of the equator, within the central parts of large continents (Figure 2.21). As latitude increases so does the length of the dry season. Therefore, in reality there is a gradual transition from the equatorial climate to the tropical wet and dry climate.

There is a hot wet season, with temperatures above 26°C and heavy convectional rain. This occurs when the

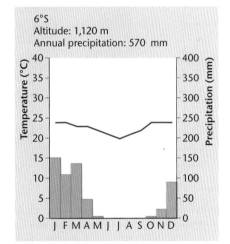

Figure 2.21 Tropical wet and dry climate, Dodoma, Tanzania

ITCZ moves polewards with the overhead sun, causing low pressure to develop and producing strong convection and heavy rainfall. Rainfall totals are greater nearer to the equator (around 1,200 mm) but can be as little as 500 mm on the borders of this climate regime.

For the rest of the year there is a hot dry season when high pressure dominates. There is a double peak in temperatures coinciding with the sun being directly

overhead. This corresponds to a period when offshore trade winds blow across the area from a dry interior source. The trade winds are steady and strong and are created as air is pulled towards the low pressure around the ITCZ. During the dry season the sun shines in cloudless skies and temperatures can reach 40°C or more. The diurnal range of temperature is greater than the annual. At night heat escapes rapidly in the clear skies and temperatures can drop below 10°C.

Tropical monsoon climate

Large parts of southeast Asia experience what is known as a monsoon climate that is marked by distinct wet and dry seasons (Figure 2.22). The word monsoon is derived from the Arabic for season, but in meteorology it is associated with the seasonal reversal in wind direction seen particularly in the Indian subcontinent and other parts of southeast Asia. The Himalayas are a major influence on this climate type, as the high mountains interfere with the general circulation of the atmosphere.

Figure 2.22 Tropical monsoon climate, Chittagong, Bangladesh

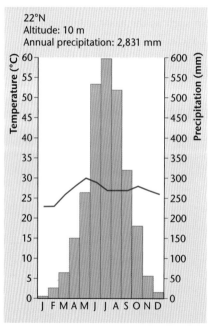

Seasonal contrasts in temperature occur between the land masses and the oceans because of the differential heating capacity of solids and liquids. As water both heats up and cools down relatively slowly, the seasonal shifts of heat and pressure zones are relatively small over the oceans. In contrast, over the large continental land mass that forms Asia, temperature variations are much greater. During the summer months the land is heated intensely and, because solids have a greater capacity for heat transfer, temperatures are much higher than over the oceans.

In June the ITCZ moves polewards, towards the Tropic of Cancer, but extends further north than might be expected (as far as 30°N) over northern India (Figure 2.23). This is due to the intense heating that takes place there. Winds blow from a southwesterly direction, deflected by the Coriolis force as the Earth spins. This low pressure draws in warm moist unstable air from the Indian Ocean, bringing heavy rain. Rainfall totals are further increased by the uplift of the air over the foothills of the Himalayan mountain range, and by intense convection.

In January the ITCZ and the subtropical jet stream move south over the equator and towards the Tropic of Capricorn (Figure 2.23). At the same time the continental landmass at the centre of Asia experiences intense cooling and a large area of high pressure develops. Winds blow from the northeast, away from this

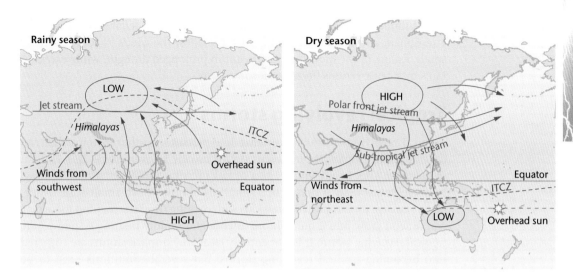

Rainy season

LOW
Jet stream
Himalayas
ITCZ
Overhead sun
Winds from southwest
Equator
HIGH

Dry season

HIGH
Polar front jet stream
Himalayas
Sub-tropical jet stream
Equator
Winds from northeast
ITCZ
LOW
Overhead sun

Figure 2.23 Seasonal wind reversal of the monsoon over southeast Asia

high-pressure cell, bringing dry conditions to most of the Indian subcontinent. From November to February mean monthly temperatures range between 19°C and 23°C. The eastern coast of India and Sri Lanka may receive some rain from this monsoon as the winds pass over the Bay of Bengal.

The mean monthly temperature rises to its annual maximum (up to 30°C) just before the monsoon 'bursts' in May (slightly later in some parts of southeast Asia). At this time of year clear skies, associated with continued high pressure and sinking air, allow more intense heating than in the wet season when low pressure generates clouds that absorb and reflect some of the incoming radiation. Tropical revolving storms (called cyclones in this region) can occur during the rainy season, when up to 2,500 mm of rain falls. These intense low-pressure weather systems bring violent winds, torrential rainfall and thunderstorms.

Corel

Photograph 2.6 Indonesia experiences a monsoon climate

The timing of the arrival of the monsoon is not always reliable because upper atmospheric conditions have to be correct to allow the winds to come from the south. Failure of the monsoon may result in prolonged drought, while excessive rains may cause serious flooding in some years.

Tropical revolving storms

Tropical revolving storms are intense low-pressure weather systems that can develop in the tropics. These violent storms usually measure some 200–700 km in diameter. They begin with an area of low pressure, caused by surface heating, into which warm air is drawn in a spiralling manner. Such small-scale disturbances enlarge into tropical depressions with rotating wind systems and these may continue to grow into a much more intense and rapidly rotating system — the tropical revolving storm. It is not entirely clear why tropical storms are triggered into becoming tropical revolving storms, but several conditions need to be present:

➤ an oceanic location with sea temperatures above 27°C — this provides a continuous source of heat to maintain rising air currents

➤ an ocean depth of at least 70 m — this moisture provides latent heat, rising air causes the moisture to be released by condensation and the continuation of this process drives the system

➤ a location at least 5° north or south of the equator in order that the Coriolis force can bring about the maximum rotation of air (the Coriolis force is weak at the equator and will stop a circular air flow from developing)

➤ low-level convergence of air in the lower atmospheric circulation system — winds have to come together near the centre of the low-pressure zone

➤ rapid outflow of air in the upper atmospheric circulation — this pushes away the warm air, which has risen close to the centre of the storm

Figure 2.24 The structure of a tropical revolving storm

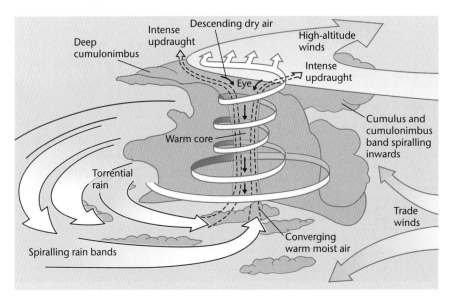

The tropical revolving storm exists while there is a supply of latent heat and moisture to provide energy and low frictional drag on the ocean surface. Once the system reaches maturity, a central eye develops. This is an area 10–50 km in diameter in which there are calm conditions, clear skies, higher temperatures and descending air. Wind speeds of more than 300 km h^{-1} have been observed around the eye. Figure 2.24 shows the structure of a typical mature tropical revolving storm. Once the system reaches land or colder waters polewards, it will decline as the source of heat and moisture is removed.

Distribution

Tropical revolving storms occur between latitudes 5° and 20° north and south of the equator (Figure 2.25). Once generated they tend to move westwards and are at their most destructive:

➤ in the Caribbean Sea/Gulf of Mexico area where they are known as **hurricanes** (11% of all tropical revolving storms)
➤ on the western side of central America (east Pacific) (17%)
➤ in the Arabian Sea/Bay of Bengal area where they are known as **cyclones** (8%)
➤ off southeast Asia where they are known as **typhoons** (main area with one-third of all tropical revolving storms)
➤ off Madagascar (southeast Africa) (11%)
➤ in northwestern Australia, where they are known as **willy-willies**, and the southwestern Pacific (20%)

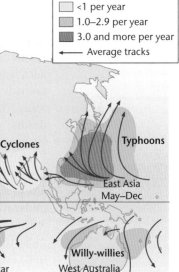

Average per year
- <1 per year
- 1.0–2.9 per year
- 3.0 and more per year
- ← Average tracks

East Pacific
June–Oct

Hurricanes

Caribbean
Aug–Oct

Cyclones

Typhoons

South Asia
Oct–Nov

East Asia
May–Dec

Equator

Southwest Pacific
Jan–Mar

Madagascar
Dec–Mar

Willy-willies
West Australia
Jan–Mar

Magnitude and frequency

Tropical revolving storms are measured on the Saffir-Simpson scale, which has five levels based upon central pressure, wind speed, storm surge and damage potential. Scale 5, for example, has:

Figure 2.25 Global distribution and seasons of tropical revolving storms

- central pressure at 920 mb or below
- wind speed at 69 m s^{-1} (250 km h^{-1}) or greater
- storm surge at 5.5 m or greater
- damage potential that refers to 'complete roof failure of many buildings with major damage to lower floors of all structures lower than 3 m above sea level. Evacuation of all residential buildings on low ground within 16–24 km of coast is likely'

The average lifespan of a tropical storm is 7–14 days. Every year about 70–75 tropical storms develop around the world, of which approximately 50 will intensify to become tropical revolving storms.

Impacts

The vulnerability of people to this hazard depends upon a range of factors, both physical and human. The main physical factors include:
- intensity of the storm (Saffir-Simpson scale 1–5)
- speed of movement, i.e. length of time over area
- distance from the sea
- physical geography of the coastal area — width of coastal plain/size of delta, location of any mountain ranges relative to the coast

Human responses include the preparations a community has made to resist the effects of the event, and these are considered in the next section. There are several ways in which tropical cyclones pose a hazard to people and the built environment:
- **Winds** often exceed 150 km h^{-1} and have been known to reach over 300 km h^{-1}. Such winds can bring about the collapse of buildings, cause structural damage to roads and bridges, bring down transmission lines and devastate agricultural areas. They can also hurl large pieces of debris around and this may cause deaths.
- **Heavy rainfall**, often more than 100 mm per day, causes severe flooding, landslides and mudslides. High relief can exaggerate already high rainfall figures and totals in excess of 500–700 mm per day have been recorded.
- **Storm surges** result when wind-driven waves pile up and the ocean heaves up under reduced pressure. These can flood low-lying coastal areas and, in flat areas such as the Ganges delta, flooding may extend far inland. Storm surges cause the majority of deaths from tropical revolving storms and agriculture often takes a long time to recover because the soil becomes contaminated with salt. The storm surge that accompanied Hurricane Katrina in 2005 broke through the levées on the banks of the Mississippi that protected the city of New Orleans, causing billions of dollars of damage.

Prediction

Predicting tropical revolving storms depends on the monitoring and warning systems available. Weather bureaus such as the National Hurricane Center in Florida (USA) collect data from geostationary satellites and from land- and sea-based recording centres. The USA also maintains round-the-clock surveillance by weather aircraft of tropical storms that have the potential to become hurricanes and affect the Caribbean/Gulf of Mexico area. Such information is compared with computer models to predict a path for the storm and to warn people to evacuate the area.

There is a high economic cost associated with evacuation and false alarms can cause people to become complacent and refuse future advice. It has been estimated that the cost of evacuating coastal areas in the USA is roughly $1 million per kilometre of coastline. This figure is made up of losses in business and tourism and the provision of protection. As tropical revolving storms have a tendency to follow an erratic path, it is not always possible to give more than 12–18 hours warning.

Developing countries, whose communications are not so advanced as those in developed countries, may not be as well prepared and this can lead to a higher death toll. However, progress is being made and some coastal areas of developing countries, including the Bay of Bengal and some central American coasts, do have adequate warning systems. In 1997 a tropical cyclone warning in the Cox's Bazaar area of Bangladesh allowed the evacuation of 300,000 people, resulting in fewer than 100 deaths.

Case study Hurricane Katrina, USA, 2005

In 2005 Hurricane Katrina was the eleventh named tropical storm, fourth hurricane and first category 5 hurricane in what was to become one of the most active hurricane seasons ever recorded in the Atlantic area. The storm first developed on 23 August over the southeastern Bahamas and was upgraded and named Katrina the next day.

On 28 August Katrina was upgraded to category 4 and it became clear that it was heading for the coasts of Mississippi and Louisiana (Figure 2.26). It continued to intensify on that day, rapidly becoming a category 5 hurricane, with sustained wind speeds of 280 km h^{-1}, gusts of up to 345 km h^{-1} and a central pressure of 902 mb, making it the fifth most intense Atlantic basin hurricane on record.

Advance warnings were in force by 26 August and the possibility of 'unprecedented cataclysm' was already being considered. President Bush declared a state of emergency on 27 August in Louisiana, Alabama and Mississippi, 2 days before the hurricane was expected to make landfall. Risk assessments conducted in preparation for such an

event had been published; for example the *National Geographic* magazine had run an article less than 12 months before the storm occurred. However, when it happened, the authorities found it difficult to respond to the sheer scale of the disaster. At a news conference on 28 August, shortly after Katrina had been upgraded to a category 5 storm, the mayor of New Orleans ordered that the city be evacuated.

Most of the population managed to leave in private cars and on school buses, but some 150,000 people remained, mostly by choice. As a last resort, refugees who had been 'left behind' were encouraged to seek protection in the massive Louisiana Superdrome. Basic supplies of food and water were delivered to support 150,000 people for 3 days.

When Katrina hit Louisiana on the morning of 29 August, it was accompanied by a massive storm surge, up to 10 m high in places. Although it had weakened to a category 3 storm as it reached the border of Louisiana and Mississippi, the storm was so intense that its powerful winds and storm surge smashed the entire Mississippi Gulf Coast as it passed through (Photograph 2.7).

The main effects of the storm were:

- Power and water supplies were disrupted. Almost 233,000 km^2 were declared a disaster zone, an area almost as large as the UK. This left an estimated 5 million people without power, and it took almost 2 months for the entire area to be reconnected.
- More than 1 million people became refugees, displaced from their homes. One month after the storm, refugees from Katrina were registered in all 50 states. Although 75% of evacuees had stayed within 400 km of their origin, tens of thousands had located more than 1,000 km away.
- In New Orleans, a city mostly below sea level, the complex system of flood defences, including levées, was breached and 80% of the city was deluged by floodwater.
- Reports at the time claimed that those most affected by the hurricane were the black American urban dwellers — the poorer and most disadvantaged members of society. It was alleged that the authorities would have responded differently if those suffering were white. Many criticised

President Bush for being slow to visit the disaster area.

- Looters ran riot through the abandoned homes and shops in New Orleans. This resulted in the deployment of the Mississippi National Guard, which was given orders to treat looters ruthlessly.
- The financial cost of the storm broke all records in the USA, with damage estimated to be in the region of $200 billion.
- Many oil rigs and refineries in the Gulf area were damaged. An immediate effect of this was that the price of oil shot up (to over $60 per barrel), affecting people worldwide. For the first time, the price of petrol in the UK reached £1 per litre.
- The famous New Orleans' French Quarter was severely damaged, affecting tourism revenue.
- Hundreds of thousands of people were temporarily displaced from their homes. Of the 180,000 houses in the city of New Orleans, 110,000 were flooded and 55,000 of these were too badly damaged to be repaired.
- The number of fatalities — some 1,242 people — was far below initial estimates. Of these, 1,035 were in Louisiana and 228 in Mississippi. Few people died in the aftermath of the storm because

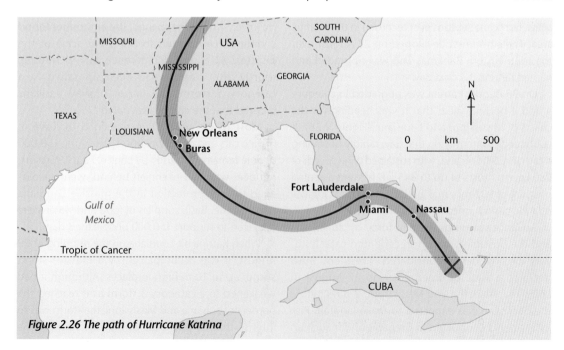

Figure 2.26 The path of Hurricane Katrina

Photograph 2.7 Devastation in Biloxi, Mississippi, following Hurricane Katrina

the USA had the infrastructure to ensure that people had access to clean water, medical care and food supplies.

■ Many businesses were affected by storm damage. Most were adequately insured, but some major insurance companies were forced to declare profit warnings to their shareholders following the storm.

■ Government aid was rapidly assigned to help recovery. The US Senate authorised a bill assigning $10.5 billion in aid in the first week of September.

On 7 September another $51.8 billion was allocated from Federal funds. Other countries also responded to the disaster — even Afghanistan.

■ The public donated $1.8 billion to the American Red Cross alone — more than the amounts raised for 9/11 and the 2004 Asian tsunami appeal.

Case study — Cyclone Nargis, Burma (Myanmar), 2008

Cyclone Nargis began on 27 April as an intense tropical depression in the Bay of Bengal. Meteorologists expected the storm to track over Bangladesh and farmers there were advised to speed up the harvest of their rice crop. However, the storm changed direction and headed towards Burma, where it made landfall over the Irrawaddy delta in the south of the country on 2 May (Figure 2.27). By this time it had intensified into a borderline category 3–4

storm, with winds gusting to 215 km h^{-1} as it passed close to the city of Yangon (formerly Rangoon). In some places 600 mm of rain fell as the cyclone passed and a storm surge was blown inland, further inundating the low-lying rice paddies of the Irrawaddy delta.

■ Five coastal regions — Yangon, Ayeyarwady, Bago, Mon and Kayin — were declared disaster zones by the government.

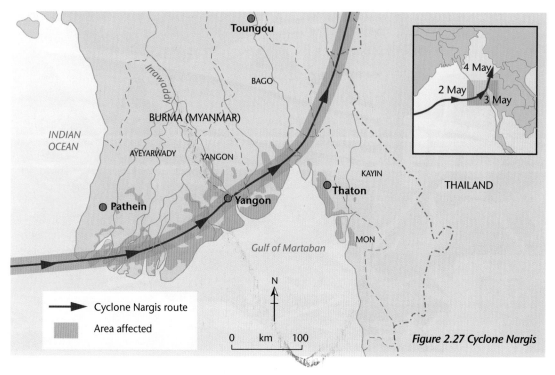

Figure 2.27 Cyclone Nargis

- The cyclone was the deadliest in this region since 1991, with the official death toll registering over 84,000. Another 54,000 people were declared missing.
- 5 million people were made homeless, and tens of thousands were injured.
- The cost of damage was estimated at $10 billion.

The Burmese military government was reluctant to allow Western aid agencies to enter the country. The UN and Red Cross declared that some 2.5 million people were in urgent need of assistance, food, water and shelter. Aid workers who did manage to get in reported that the area resembled a war zone.

Following international pressure the government eventually allowed entry to some foreign aid agencies towards the end of May 2008 and, belatedly, the relief operation started. Although official government aid from individual countries was also accepted, the Burmese government remained reluctant to allow foreign ships to dock or foreign troops to assist as it was afraid of invasion.

Climate on a local scale: urban climates

Cities create their own climate and weather. Some geographers refer to this as the 'climatic dome' within which the weather is different from that of surrounding rural areas in terms of temperature, relative humidity, precipitation, visibility, air

Table 2.2 The effects of urban areas on local climate

Element of climate	Effect of urban area (compared to nearby rural areas)
Temperature	
Annual mean	0.5–0.8°C increase
Winter minimum	1.0–1.5°C increase
Precipitation	
Quantity	5–10% increase
Days with less than 5 mm	10% increase
Relative humidity	
Annual mean	6% decrease
Winter	2% decrease
Summer	8% decrease
Visibility	
Fog in winter	100% increase
Fog in summer	30% increase
Wind speed	
Annual mean	20–30% decrease
Calms	5–20% increase
Extreme gusts	10–20% decrease
Radiation	
Ultraviolet in winter	30% lower
Ultraviolet in summer	5% lower
Total on horizontal surface	15–20% lower
Pollution	
Dust particles	1,000% increase

quality and wind speed (Table 2.2). For a large city, the dome may extend upwards to 250–300 m and its influence may continue for tens of kilometres downwind (Figure 2.28).

There are two levels within the urban dome. Below roof level there is an urban canopy where processes act in the space between buildings (sometimes referred to as 'canyons'). Above this is the urban boundary layer. The dome extends downwind and at height as a plume into the surrounding rural areas.

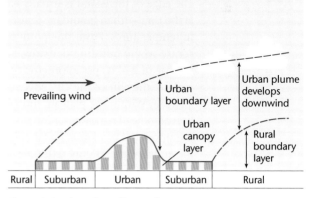

Figure 2.28 The urban climate dome

Temperatures: the urban heat island effect

The **urban heat island** is a warm spot in the 'sea' of surrounding cooler rural air. Cities tend to be warmer than rural areas for the following reasons:

➤ Building materials such as concrete, bricks and tarmac act like bare rock surfaces, absorbing large quantities of heat during the day. Much of this heat is stored and slowly released at night. Some urban surfaces, particularly buildings with large windows, have a high reflective capacity, and multistorey buildings tend to concentrate the heating effect in the surrounding streets by reflecting energy downwards.

➤ Heat comes from industries, buildings and vehicles, which all burn fuel. Although they regulate the temperature indoors, air conditioning units release hot air into the atmosphere. Even people generate heat and cities contain large populations in a small space.

➤ Air pollution from industries and vehicles increases cloud cover and creates a 'pollution dome', which allows in short-wave radiation but absorbs a large amount of the outgoing radiation as well as reflecting it back to the surface.

➤ In urban areas, water falling on to the surface is disposed of as quickly as possible. This changes the urban moisture and heat budget — reduced evapotranspiration means that more energy is available to heat the atmosphere.

Changes over time

The heat island effect is greatest under calm, high-pressure conditions, particularly with a temperature inversion in the boundary layer above the city. Heat islands are also better developed in winter when there is a bigger impact from city heating systems. Urban–rural contrasts are much more distinct at night when the effect of insolation is absent and surfaces that absorbed heat by day slowly release it back into the atmosphere. Heat islands are not constant — they vary both seasonally and diurnally.

Changes over space

The edge of the island is usually well defined and temperatures change abruptly at the rural–urban boundary. Some climatologists have likened the effect to a 'cliff' in temperatures. From this point temperature rises steadily to a peak in the city centre where building densities are highest. The rise tends to be gentle, at an average of 2–4°C per kilometre.

After the cliff of the city edge, this steady rise has often been referred to as a 'plateau'. Within the plateau, though, there are variations that reflect the distribution of industries, power stations, water areas and open spaces. This is due to **albedo**, the amount of insolation (solar radiation) that is reflected by the Earth's surface and the atmosphere. Highly reflective surfaces absorb very little insolation. They can reflect it back into the atmosphere and keep cool, or reflect it so that it focuses into a small area, which heats up. Darker surfaces tend to absorb insolation much better and then re-radiate it as long-wave energy that heats up the urban area.

Surfaces in the city tend to be much less reflective than those in rural areas — lots of tarmac but not a great deal of grass. In winter, rural areas keep snow for a much longer period and therefore have a greater albedo. Rural surface albedos include snow (0.86–0.95), sand (0.37), deciduous forest (0.17) and coniferous forest (0.14).

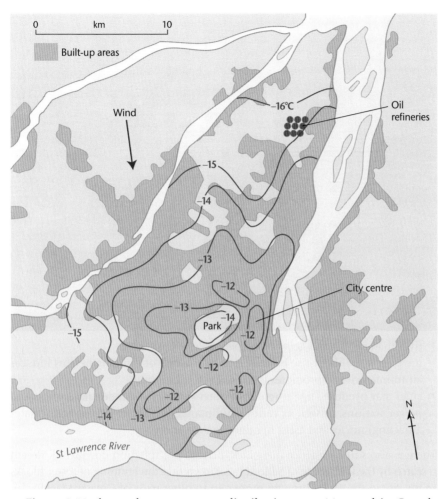

Figure 2.29 Temperature distribution over Montreal, 7 March, 7 a.m., with winds from the north at 0.5 m s⁻¹

Figure 2.29 shows the temperature distribution over Montreal in Canada (Photograph 2.8). The following can be clearly seen:

➤ lower temperatures on the side of the prevailing wind
➤ the plateau-like temperature zone running from the city edge towards the city centre, which has the highest temperatures
➤ the correlation between the highest density of building (city centre) and the highest temperatures
➤ the fall in temperature over the park area, which is an open vegetated space

Precipitation

There is some evidence that rainfall can be higher over urban than rural areas. This is partly because higher urban temperatures encourage the development of lower pressure over cities in relation to the surrounding area. Convection rainfall tends to be heavier and more frequent, as does the incidence of thunder and lightning. There are several possible reasons for this:

Photograph 2.8
Cities like Montreal
create an urban
heat island

> the urban heat island generates convection
> the presence of high-rise buildings and a mixture of building heights induces air turbulence and promotes increased vertical motion
> cities may produce large amounts of water vapour from industrial sources and power stations, as well as various pollutants that act as hygroscopic (water attracting) nuclei and assist in raindrop formation

There is also some evidence that cities increase precipitation downwind. Recent research by the University of Salford has shown that the building of tower blocks in the city in the 1970s brought more rain to other parts of Greater Manchester. The prevailing wind tends to be westerly here, and rainfall in areas downwind of Salford, such as Stockport, has increased by as much as 7% over the past few decades.

Snow is less common in cities, and that which falls melts faster.

Fog

In cities the occurrence of fog increased along with industrialisation. Records of London weather show that in the early 1700s there would have been about 20 days of fog every year but by the end of the 1800s this had risen to over 50 days. It was discovered in the 1950s that the average number of particles in city air in the more developed world was much greater than in rural areas. The particles acted as condensation nuclei and encouraged fog formation at night, usually under high-pressure weather conditions.

In the UK the Clean Air Acts of the 1950s resulted in a dramatic reduction in smoke production and particulate emissions, and a decrease in the number of

foggy days. As cities in less developed countries industrialise they are experiencing more fog. Cities such as New Delhi and Beijing suffer regular winter fogs. These can cripple transportation networks and become hazardous to human health when they trap pollutants.

Thunderstorms

Thunderstorms develop in hot humid air and are characterised by violent and heavy precipitation associated with thunder and lightning. In urban areas the chance of thunderstorms is increased, particularly during the late afternoon and early evening in the summer months.

Thunderstorms are produced by convectional uplift under conditions of extreme instability. Cumulonimbus clouds may develop up to the height of the tropopause, where the inversion produces stability. The updraught of air through the central area of the towering cloud causes rapid cooling and condensation. This leads to the formation of water droplets, hail, ice and super-cooled water, which coalesce during collisions in the air. During condensation, latent heat is released that further fuels the convectional uplift. As raindrops are split in the updraught, positive electrical charge builds up in the cloud. When the charge is high enough to overcome resistance in the cloud, or in the atmosphere, a discharge occurs to areas of negative charge in the cloud or to Earth. This produces lightning. The extreme temperatures generated cause a rapid expansion of the air which develops a shock wave. This is heard as thunder.

Air quality

Particulate pollution and photochemical smog

Air quality in urban areas is often poorer than in rural areas. The main pollutants of urban areas, and some of their effects, are:

➤ **Suspended particulate matter** — the solid matter in the urban atmosphere, which derives mainly from power stations and vehicle exhausts (particularly from burning diesel fuel). Such particles are usually less than 25 µm in diameter and are responsible for fog/smog, respiratory problems, soiling of buildings and may contain carcinogens. Other particulates in the atmosphere include cement dust, tobacco smoke, ash, coal dust and pollen. Coastal cities also have vast numbers of sea salt particulates. Particulates are sometimes referred to as **PM10s**, as the bulk of particles have a diameter of less than 10 µm.

➤ **Sulphur dioxide** produces haze, acid rain, respiratory problems (including asthma), damage to lichens and plants and corrosion of buildings.

➤ **Oxides of nitrogen** cause accelerated weathering of buildings, photochemical reactions, respiratory problems, acid rain and haze.

➤ **Carbon monoxide** is associated with heart problems, headaches and fatigue.

➤ **Photochemical oxidants** (ozone and peroxyacetyl nitrate [PAN]) are associated with smog, damage to plants and a range of discomforts to people including headaches, eye irritation, coughs and chest pains.

Air pollution varies with the time of year and with air pressure. Concentration of pollutants may increase five or six fold in winter because temperature inversions trap them over the city (Figure 2.30).

*Figure 2.30
An urban
temperature
inversion*

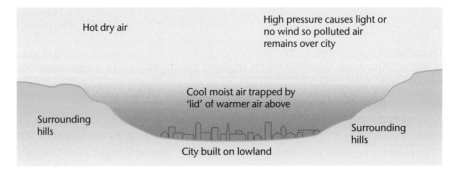

The mixture of fog and smoke particulates produces **smog**. This was common in European cities through the nineteenth and first half of the twentieth centuries because of the high incidence of coal burning, particularly on domestic fires. Britain suffered particularly badly, many of the smogs being so thick they were known as 'pea-soupers'. In December 1952, smog in London was responsible for more than 4,000 deaths. This persuaded the British government that legislation needed to be introduced to control coal burning.

More recently there has been an increase in **photochemical smog**. The action of sunlight on nitrogen oxides (NO_x) and hydrocarbons in vehicle exhaust gases causes a chemical reaction, which results in the production of ozone. (Do not confuse this low-level ozone with the high-level ozone in the atmosphere, which protects the Earth from damaging ultraviolet radiation.) Los Angeles has had a serious problem with photochemical smog because of its high density of vehicles, frequent sunshine and topography that traps photooxidant gases at low levels.

Photochemical smog is a particular hazard during anticyclonic conditions because once the air has descended it is relatively static owing to the absence of wind. Such weather systems tend to be stable and can persist for weeks during the summer months. Many cities are located in river basins so the relief ensures a sheltered location, perfect for the establishment of photochemical smog. Athens is often quoted as the worst affected city in Europe, but conditions can be equally bad in inland British cities such as Oxford and Bath. In London, high levels of nitrogen dioxide have been shown to occur at certain times of the day. These come from vehicle exhaust emissions during the rush hour.

Pollution reduction policies

There are a number of ways in which governments and other organisations have tried to reduce atmospheric pollution in cities.

Clean Air Acts

After the London pea-souper of 1952, the government decided legislation was needed to prevent so much smoke entering the atmosphere. The act of 1956 introduced smoke-free zones into urban areas and this policy slowly began to clean up the air. The 1956 act was reinforced by later legislation. In the 1990s, for example, tough regulations were imposed on levels of airborne pollution, particularly on PM10s. Local councils in the UK are now required to monitor pollution in their areas and to establish **Air Quality Management Areas** where levels are likely to be exceeded. Some have planted more vegetation to capture particulates on leaves.

Vehicle control in inner urban areas

A number of cities have looked at controlling pollution by reducing the number of vehicles that come into central urban areas. In Athens, for example, the city declared an area of about 2.5 km² in the centre **traffic-free**. Many British towns and cities have pedestrianised their CBDs and have promoted **'park and ride'** schemes. In London, attempts to control vehicle numbers have included the introduction of a **congestion charge** (in effect, a road toll), which means that vehicle owners have to pay if they wish to drive into the centre. In Mexico City, the city council passed **driving restriction** legislation known as the *Hoy no Circula* (don't drive today). This bans all vehicles from the city on one weekday per week, the vehicle's registration number determining the day. If conditions worsen, the legislation allows for a ban of two weekdays and one weekend day.

Photograph 2.9 Vehicles that run on hydrogen fuel cells are one way of reducing air pollution in cities

More public transport

Attempts have been made to persuade people to use public transport instead of cars. Such schemes have included Manchester's development of a **tram system** (Metrolink), the introduction of **bus-only lanes** into city centres and the encouragement of **car-sharing schemes**.

Zoning of industry

Industry has been located downwind in cities if at all possible and planning legislation has forced companies to build higher factory chimneys to emit pollutants above the inversion layer.

Vehicle emissions legislation

Motor vehicle manufacturers have been made to develop more efficient fuel-burning engines and to introduce **catalytic converters**, which remove some of the polluting gases from exhaust fumes. However, catalytic converters actually increase emissions of carbon dioxide, and they only work once the car has warmed up, on longer journeys. The switch to **lead-free petrol** has also reduced pollution in the UK.

Winds

Urban structures and layout have an effect on wind speed, direction and frequency. There are three main types of effects:

➤ The surface area of cities is uneven because of the varying height of the buildings. Buildings exert a powerful frictional drag on air moving over and around them. This creates turbulence, giving rapid and abrupt changes in both wind direction and speed. Average wind speeds are lower in cities than in the surrounding areas and they are also lower in city centres than in suburbs.

➤ High-rise buildings may slow air movement but they also channel air into the 'canyons' between them. Winds in such places can be so powerful that they make buildings sway and knock pedestrians off their feet.

➤ On calm and clear nights when the urban heat island effect is at its greatest, there is a surface inflow from the cooler areas outside the city to the warmer areas in the city centre.

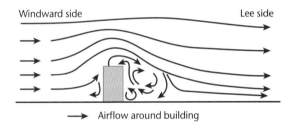

Windward side   Lee side

➤ Airflow around building

Figure 2.31 The effects of large urban buildings on winds

Winds are therefore affected by the size and shape of buildings. Figure 2.31 shows how a single building can modify an airflow passing over it. Air is displaced upwards and around the sides of the building and is also pushed downwards in the lee of the structure.

Figure 2.32 shows the windward side of a building in more detail. The air pushes against the wall here with relatively high pressures. As the air flows around

Figure 2.32 Airflow modified by a single building

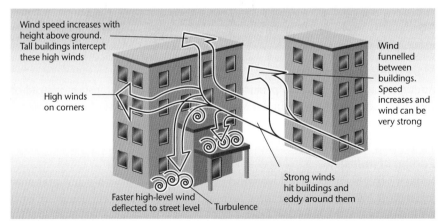

Wind speed increases with height above ground. Tall buildings intercept these high winds

High winds on corners

Wind funnelled between buildings. Speed increases and wind can be very strong

Faster high-level wind deflected to street level

Turbulence

Strong winds hit buildings and eddy around them

the sides of the building it becomes separated from the walls and roof and sets up suction in these areas. On the windward side the overpressure, which increases with height, causes a descending flow. This forms a vortex when it reaches the ground and sweeps around the windward corners. This vortex is considerably increased if there is a small building to windward.

In the lee of the building there is a zone of lower pressure, causing vortices behind it. If two separate buildings allow airflow between them, then the movement may be subject to the **Venturi effect** in which the pressure within the gap causes the wind to pick up speed and reach high velocities. Some buildings have gaps in them, or are built on stilts, to avoid this problem, but a reasonable flow of air at street level is essential to remove pollution.

Usually buildings are part of a group and the disturbance to the airflow depends upon the height of the buildings and the spacing between them. If they are widely spaced, each building will act as an isolated block, but if they are closer, the wake of each building interferes with the airflow around the next structure and this produces a complex pattern of airflow (Figure 2.33).

When buildings are designed it is important that pollution emitters (chimneys) are high enough to ensure that pollutants are released into the undisturbed flow above the building and not into the lee eddy or the downward-flowing air near the walls.

(a) Widely-spaced buildings act like single buildings

(b) Narrower-spaced buildings – flows interfere

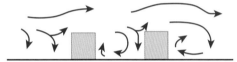

Figure 2.33 Airflow in urban areas modified by more than one building

Global climate change

Evidence for climate change

The climate of the British Isles has changed significantly since the Pleistocene ice age, which ended around 10,000 or 11,000 years ago. At the end of the Pleistocene, in the period known as the pre-Boreal, the climate began to warm up and that trend has continued ever since. There have, however, been some fluctuations during which the climate has cooled, the best-known being the 'little ice age' from the mid-sixteenth century to around 1800. During this period of global cooling the Thames regularly froze over and fairs were held on the ice. Table 2.3 shows the main climatic periods in the British Isles since the Pleistocene.

Key terms

Climatic change Evidence shows that change has always been a feature of the Earth's climate. Apart from the Pleistocene ice age, recent research has revealed a series of climatic trends on a variety of timescales.

Global warming The recent gradual warming of the Earth's atmosphere largely as a result of human activity.

Climatic period	Time before present (years)	Climatic conditions
Sub-Atlantic to present day		Temperatures fluctuate; cooler than the present day
		A cool coastal climate with cooler summers and increased rainfall
		A marked cool period between AD 1300 and AD 1800 — the little ice age
	2,500	A period of warming in the last 200 years
Sub-Boreal		Temperatures falling but rainfall relatively low at the beginning of this period, increasing later
		Period known as the neoglacial in Europe, with evidence of ice advance in alpine areas
	5,000	Warm summers and colder winters
Atlantic		Temperatures reach the optimum for many trees and shrubs — 'the climatic optimum'
	7,500	A warm 'west coast' type of climate, with higher rainfall
Boreal		Climate becoming warmer and drier
	9,000	A continental-type climate
Pre-Boreal		Mainly cold and wet, but becoming warmer and drier
	10,300	Changing from tundra/sub-arctic to more continental

Table 2.3 Climatic periods since the Pleistocene ice age

Evidence for climatic change is taken from a variety of sources, which can be used to reconstruct past climates. Most of the evidence is indirect — climatic changes are inferred from changes in indicators that reflect climate, such as vegetation.

Pollen analysis

Species have climatic requirements that influence their geographical distributions. Each plant species has a distinctively shaped pollen grain and if these fall into oxygen-free environments, such as peat bogs, they resist decay. Changes in the pollen found in different levels of the bog indicate changes in climate over time.

One limitation of this method is the fact pollen can be transported considerable distances by wind or sometimes wildlife.

Dendrochronology

This is the analysis of tree rings from core samples. Each year, the growth of a tree is shown in its trunk by a single ring made up of two bands: a band reflecting rapid spring growth when the cells are larger and a narrower band of growth during the cooler autumn. The width of the ring depends on the conditions of each year. A wide band indicates a warm and wet year, a narrower one cooler and drier conditions.

Recent investigations, however, have shown that trees respond more to levels of moisture than to temperature. Dendrochronology has a limitation in that few trees are older than about 4,000 years. It has been possible to extend surveys further back using remains of vegetation preserved in non-oxygen conditions.

Ice-core analysis

Glacial ice can be studied by drilling cores from areas such as Antarctica and Greenland. The carbon dioxide trapped within the ice is a climatic indicator — levels tend to be lower during cooler periods and higher when it is warmer. Another method is to look at oxygen isotope levels (see below).

Sea-floor analysis

Core samples from the ocean floor reveal shifts in animal and plant populations, which indicate climatic change. The ratio of the isotopes oxygen-18 to oxygen-16 in calcareous ooze can also be measured. This is linked to the ice-core analysis described above. During colder phases, when water evaporated from the oceans and precipitated onto the land eventually forms glacial ice, water containing lighter oxygen-16 is more easily evaporated than that containing heavier oxygen-18. As a result, the oceans have a higher concentration of oxygen-18, while the ice-sheets and glaciers contain more of the lighter oxygen-16. During warmer periods, the oxygen-16 held in the ice is released and returns to the oceans, balancing out the ratio. Studies of isotope curves showing the ratio of oxygen-16 to oxygen-18 therefore give a picture of climate change.

Recent investigations have suggested that isotope variations are an indication of changes in the volume of ice rather than water temperature, but as ice volume itself reflects climatic conditions, such studies have tended to confirm earlier findings.

Radiocarbon dating

Carbon-14 is a radioactive isotope of carbon (normally carbon-12). Plants take in carbon during photosynthesis. As carbon-14 decays at a known rate and carbon-12 does not decay, comparison of the levels of the two isotopes present in plant remains indicate the age at which the plant died. The type of vegetation present at any particular time is an indicator of the climate of that period. This method can accurately date organic matter up to 50,000 years old.

Coleoptera

Remains of Coleoptera beetles are common in freshwater and land sediments. Different species of this beetle tend to be found under different climatic conditions. Knowledge of the present climatic range of the different species, and the age of sediments in which remains are found, allows past climatic conditions to be determined.

Changing sea levels

The presence of rias and fjords indicates rising (eustatic) sea levels flooding glacial and river valleys. Changes in sea levels are indicators of climate change — the volume of sea water changes as it warms/cools.

Glacial deposits

These show records of ice advance during colder periods and retreat during warmer times.

Historical records

Historical records include cave paintings, depth of grave digging in Greenland, diaries, documentary evidence of events (such as 'frost fairs' on the Thames) and evidence of areas of former vine cultivation. Since 1873 daily weather reports have been documented, and the Royal Society has encouraged the collection of data since the seventeenth century. Parish records are a good source of climate data.

Recent evidence for global warming

Figure 2.34 shows how average world temperature has risen since records were first kept in 1860. Although the overall rise seems small, the 10 hottest years have all occurred since 1980, and the 1990s was the hottest decade. The first years of the twenty-first century continued that trend and global warming has probably become the major environmental issue of our time. Although scientists have been slow to commit themselves about cause and effect, there is no doubt that the planet is heating up.

Figure 2.34 Average variation in Earth-surface temperature from the mean since 1860

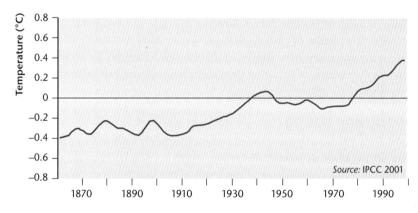

Photograph 2.10 Heavy industry has contributed to increased carbon dioxide in the atmosphere

Climatic changes have happened in the past, but present evidence seems to suggest that the recent increase in temperature has been brought about by pollution of the atmosphere, in particular the release of huge amounts of carbon dioxide from fires, power stations, motor vehicles and factories (Photograph 2.10).

Possible causes of climate change

Several theories have been put forward to explain climate change. Suggestions have included the following:
- ➤ variations in solar activity (sunspot activity)
- ➤ changes in the Earth's orbit and axial tilt (which affect the amount of solar radiation reaching the surface)
- ➤ meteorite impact
- ➤ volcanic activity (increasing dust in the atmosphere)
- ➤ plate movement (redistribution of land masses)
- ➤ changes in oceanic circulation
- ➤ changes in atmospheric composition, particularly the build-up of carbon dioxide and other greenhouse gases (the enhanced greenhouse effect)

The enhanced greenhouse effect

Carbon dioxide in the troposphere allows incoming short-wave radiation from the sun to pass through and warm the Earth. Some of this radiation is reflected back from the Earth's surface into space at a longer wavelength (Figure 2.35). Greenhouse gases in the troposphere, such as carbon dioxide, absorb some of this long-wave radiation and radiate it back to the Earth's surface. This trapping of heat is known as the greenhouse effect and is part of the natural process of heat balance in the atmosphere. In fact, it is essential for life on Earth — without the greenhouse effect the planet would be about 30°C colder. The greenhouse

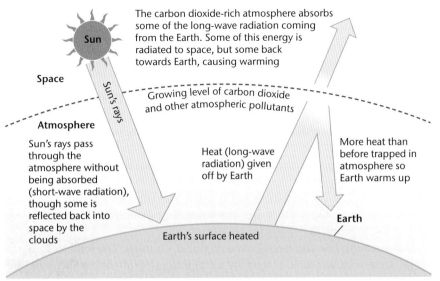

The carbon dioxide-rich atmosphere absorbs some of the long-wave radiation coming from the Earth. Some of this energy is radiated to space, but some back towards Earth, causing warming

Sun

Space

Sun's rays

Growing level of carbon dioxide and other atmospheric pollutants

Atmosphere

Sun's rays pass through the atmosphere without being absorbed (short-wave radiation), though some is reflected back into space by the clouds

Heat (long-wave radiation) given off by Earth

More heat than before trapped in atmosphere so Earth warms up

Earth

Earth's surface heated

Figure 2.35 The greenhouse effect

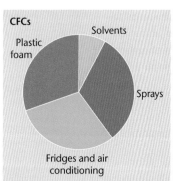

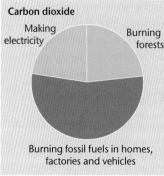

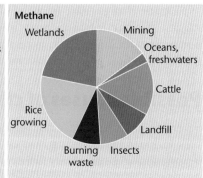

Figure 2.36 Where greenhouse gases come from

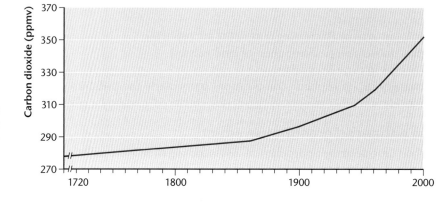

Figure 2.37 Changes in the concentration of carbon dioxide in the atmosphere, 1720–2000

gases responsible for trapping heat include carbon dioxide, chlorofluorocarbons (CFCs), methane, nitrous oxide and ozone.

Provided the amount of carbon dioxide and water vapour in the atmosphere stay the same and the amount of solar radiation is unchanged, then the temperature of the Earth remains in balance. This natural balance, however, has been influenced by human activity (Figure 2.36). The atmospheric concentration of carbon dioxide has increased by about 15% in the last 100 years and the current rate of increase is estimated to be 0.4% per year (Figure 2.37). This, together with increases in levels of other greenhouse gases such as methane and nitrous oxide, has upset the natural balance and led to global warming.

It is generally agreed that these continuing atmospheric changes will lead to a further rise in temperature, but it is difficult to predict the extent or speed of change. If carbon dioxide levels double, then temperatures could rise by a further 2–3 °C, with greater rises at higher latitudes, perhaps of the order of 7–8 °C.

One of the main reasons for the increase in carbon dioxide has been the burning of fossil fuels such as coal, oil and natural gas, which contain hydrocarbons, in the industrialised nations of the world. Now that countries such as China are industrialising heavily they are consuming huge quantities of fossil fuels, and adding to the problem.

Deforestation has also been linked to global warming. The rainforests of the world act as a 'carbon sink' as trees are a major store of non-atmospheric carbon.

The more vegetation there is, the more carbon dioxide is taken up by trees and plants. Tropical rainforests are rapidly diminishing because of the demand for space and resources in countries such as Brazil. Continued deforestation will contribute to the build-up of carbon dioxide in the atmosphere.

Large-scale cattle-rearing for beef in areas of cleared forest contributes in another way, as the cattle emit methane. Ironically, where rainforests have been flooded to create reservoirs for the production of hydroelectric power, decaying vegetation within reservoirs releases carbon dioxide too.

Effects of global warming

Global warming has serious implications for sea levels, climate patterns and economic activity. Some of the likely effects are described below.

Rising sea levels

The sea-level rise in the twentieth century has been estimated as 1.5 cm, but in the twenty-first century levels could rise between 5 and 10 cm per decade (Table 2.4). This will be sufficient to cause serious flooding in coastal areas and increased erosion in others. For low-lying countries such as the Netherlands and Bangladesh, and for many Pacific and Indian Ocean islands, rising sea levels will have catastrophic consequences. There will also be the huge cost of providing substantial flood defences. Many British estuaries may need defences similar to the Thames Barrier.

Table 2.4 Predicted sea-level rises resulting from global warming

Year	Sea-level rise (cm)	
	Best estimate	Worst estimate
2020	5	8
2040	12	20
2060	25	40
2080	35	60
2100	48	85

Climatic change

Many places will experience warmer summers. One estimate for the UK suggests that, by 2030, average temperatures could rise by more than 2°C. Continental areas could see reduced rainfall, producing desert-like conditions in places previously good for agriculture, such as Spain.

Some climatologists believe that if global warming leads to changes in the pattern of ocean currents, the UK could experience a much colder climate (see pages 84–85).

Such climatic changes would have widespread effects on vegetation, wildlife and agriculture. The ability of some regions to provide food for the population would diminish, leading to mass migrations as people searched for new areas in which to grow crops. Some areas, though, could benefit. There could be more land suitable for agriculture in countries such as Russia and Canada.

Extreme events

Heatwaves, floods, droughts and storms will all last longer and show an increasing intensity. With higher temperature there will be increased evaporation over the oceans, leading to greater global precipitation.

Effects on tropical climate

Case study The Amazon basin (equatorial)

The Amazon basin in South America, vegetated by tropical rainforest, lies within the equatorial climate zone and covers an area of some 8,235,430 km², mainly in Brazil. The Amazon River flows through the basin from its source high in the Andes towards its mouth in the Atlantic Ocean, and is the largest single source of freshwater runoff on Earth, representing 15–20% of global river discharge. At present the Amazon rainforest acts as a carbon sink. It absorbs around 35% of the world's annual carbon dioxide emissions and produces more than 20% of the world's oxygen. It contains the greatest biodiversity on Earth, providing a habitat for more than half the world's estimated 10 million species of plants, animals and insects. Predicted impacts of climate change on this region include:

■ An increase in temperature of 2–3°C by 2050, which is likely to result in increased rates of evapo-transpiration and a more vigorous hydrological cycle. Sea temperatures are also expected to warm, particularly in the Pacific Ocean. This will have a knock-on effect on the El Niño Southern Oscillation (ENSO), which is likely to occur more frequently.

■ A decrease in precipitation during the dry season (which can last up to 4 months of the year) is expected. Reduced rainfall and prolonged drought are features of an El Niño year and these will be experienced more frequently. It is possible that more intense rainfall will be experienced during the wet season.

■ Sea levels are currently rising by some 5 mm per year along the delta of the Amazon. Increased erosion and flooding is likely to have an impact on low-lying areas and will destroy the coastal mangrove forests.

■ Up to 40% of plant species may no longer be viable in the Amazon rainforest by 2080 if predicted climate changes occur. Large areas of the evergreen tropical rainforest may be succeeded by mixed forest and savanna grassland vegetation.

■ As the dry season lengthens trees will have more time to dry out so there is likely to be an increased incidence of spontaneous forest fires. These will add to carbon dioxide emissions.

■ Forest die-back as a result of vegetation succession and fire is predicted to result in the Amazon region becoming a net source of carbon dioxide rather than a carbon sink by the year 2050, exacerbating the rate of global warming.

■ Glaciers in the Andes provide the source for as much as 50% of the discharge of the Upper Amazon. Over the last 30 years Peruvian glaciers have shrunk by 20% and it is predicted that Peru will lose all its glaciers below a height of 6,000 m by 2050. This will have a further impact on the Amazon's hydrological cycle.

Case study The African savanna (tropical wet/dry)

The tropical wet/dry savanna climate is experienced over a huge area of western Africa surrounding the rainforests to the north and south of the equator. This is essentially a zone of transition. Close to the equator the dry season is very short but increases in duration with increases in latitude. Opinions are divided about the likely impacts of climate change within this region. However, many scientists believe that:

■ Overall the savanna lands are likely to experience an increase in temperature of some 1.5°C by 2050. Surrounding sea temperatures are not expected to rise to the same extent (0.6–0.8°C), resulting in a greater temperature differential between land and sea.

- Precipitation is expected to increase by 15% within the savanna lands closer to the equator but might decrease by 10% in areas towards the northern and southern fringes of the climate zone, for example in the Horn of Africa. This is likely to be due partly to the Sahara heating up more than the Atlantic Ocean, causing more moisture to be drawn in from the ocean during the wet season.

- An increase in the variability of rainfall will lead to more frequent droughts and flooding in some areas. During the wet season 25–50% more rainfall is expected to fall. More frequent drought will contribute to desertification, particularly along the extreme fringes of the savanna biome.

However, in areas where annual rainfall remains below 650 mm the savanna ecosystem is likely to be more stable than in those regions where they rise above this.

- A rise in sea level of 25 cm is predicted by 2050, so low-lying areas along the coast will experience an increase in coastal erosion and flooding. Coral reefs along the east coast of Africa may be lost.

- Higher rainfall totals in savanna lands closer to the equator are likely to result in an increased growth of trees and scrub in what was previously grass-land. Changes to the tree–grass balance will have an impact on plant and animal life and on the water and carbon cycles. Increased rates of evap-otranspiration may result in lower annual discharge in rivers such as the Nile and the Zambezi.

Case study — Bangladesh (monsoon)

Bangladesh lies within the global climatic zone experiencing the tropical wet monsoon climate. Its population was estimated by the United Nations to be over 150 million in 2008. It is one of the most densely populated countries in the world with some 1,102 people per km². As one of the poorest nations in the world it is also one of the most ill-prepared to face the challenges presented by climate change but is likely to be seriously affected by global warming. Predicted effects include:

- An increase in average temperatures of 1.5–2.0°C by 2050.

- An increase of 10–15% in annual precipitation by 2050 and an increase in the frequency and severity of cyclones during the wet season as a result of warmer sea temperatures in the Bay of Bengal.

- A 20% increase in river discharge, partly from the predicted increase in precipitation but also because of glacier melt in the Himalayas, where the rivers Brahmaputra, Meghna and Ganges have their source.

- A significant rise in sea level along the coastline and inland along the countless tidal inlets. In

2001 the World Bank reported rising sea levels of 3 mm per year (compared with the world average of 2 mm). It predicted that by 2050 a 1 m rise in sea level was possible if no preventative action was taken. This would result in 15% of the total land area of Bangladesh being inundated by salt water.

- An estimated 13–30 million people could be displaced from their homes by permanent flooding and the total annual rice crop is likely to fall by at least 30% because of the loss of land. Loss of land on such a large scale is likely to result in mass migration into northeast India and there is likely to be increased international tension between the two countries, in addition to internal political instability.

- Coral reefs will become irreparably damaged by severe storms, and this will have a knock-on effect on rare marine species, such as dolphins and turtles.

- The Sundarbans is a cluster of islands totalling 10,000 km² in area, stretching along the coast from Bangladesh into India. It is home to the

Photograph 2.11 Flooding in Bangladesh is likely to increase due to sea-level rise and increased river flow

world's largest natural mangrove forest and was declared a UNESCO World Heritage site in 1997. The Sundarbans is Asia's largest natural 'carbon sink' and supports many species including the endangered Royal Bengal Tiger, the Indian python and the estuarine crocodile. Climate change may lead to the loss of this unique area: complete flooding of low-lying islands, retreat of shorelines, salinisation of the soil and a rise in the water table.

Effects on the British Isles

As a result of global warming, the UK could experience warmer summers, longer hot spells, droughts and increased storm activity. However, if warm Gulf Stream current was diverted away from the UK (see Figure 2.38) the climate could become as cold as northern Canada.

Coastal regions

Increases in mean sea levels and in the frequency and magnitude of storms, storm surges and waves would lead to more coastal flooding. Sea levels around Britain are predicted to rise by between 12 and 37 cm by 2050, which would make a number of low-lying areas vulnerable, particularly the coasts of East Anglia and Lancashire, the Humber estuary, the Essex mudflats, the Thames estuary, parts of the north Wales coast, the Clyde/Forth estuaries and Belfast Lough. Flooding

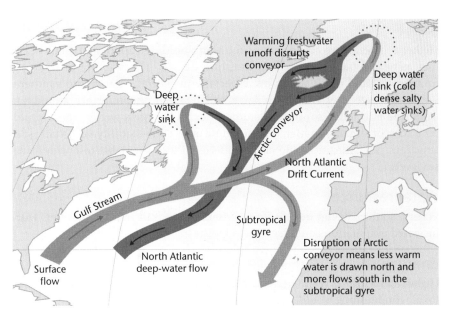

Figure 2.38 Effect of melting Arctic ice on ocean currents

would lead to disruption in transport, manufacturing and the housing sector. In addition, there would be longer-term damage to agricultural land and coastal power stations, and water supplies could be contaminated by salt infiltration.

Agriculture

Climate changes are likely to have a substantial effect on plant growth. Higher temperatures could result in:

➤ a decrease in yields of cereal crops
➤ an increase in yields of sugar beet and potatoes
➤ an increase in the length of the growing season for grasses and trees, bringing higher productivity
➤ the introduction of new crops and species — the UK could even become a major wine-producing region
➤ an increase in some pests, such as the Colorado beetle which causes serious damage to potatoes

Flora, fauna and landscape

A sustained rise in temperatures could have the following effects:

➤ a significant movement of species northwards and to higher elevations
➤ the extinction of some native species that are unable to adapt to the increasing temperatures
➤ the loss of species that occur in isolated damp, cool or coastal habitats
➤ the invasion and spread of alien weeds, pests and diseases
➤ an increased number of foreign species of invertebrates, birds and mammals, which may out-compete native species
➤ the disappearance of snow from the tops of the highest mountains

Soils

Higher temperatures could reduce the water-holding capacity of some soils, increasing the likelihood of soil moisture deficits. The stability of building foundations and other structures, especially in central, eastern and southern England where clay soils with large shrink–swell potential are abundant, would be affected if summers became drier and winters wetter. There could be a loss of organic matter, which would affect the stability of certain soil structures. Soil structure could also be affected if the water table rose with rising sea levels.

Water resources

Water resources would benefit from wetter winters, but warmer summers with increased evaporation could have the opposite effect.

Energy use

Higher temperatures could decrease the need for heating, but a growing demand for air conditioning would increase electricity consumption.

Responses to global warming

International responses

Carbon dioxide has an effective lifetime in the atmosphere of about 100 years, so its concentration responds slowly to changes in emissions. At the 1992 Earth Summit in Rio de Janeiro the developed countries agreed to stabilise carbon dioxide emissions. This would slow down the rate of climate change, but to prevent carbon dioxide concentrations from rising we need to *reduce* current global emissions by about 60%.

In 1997, at a follow up meeting in Kyoto, Japan, more than 100 governments signed a Climate Change Protocol. This set more specific targets for pollution mitigation and proposed schemes to enable governments to reach these targets. Most governments agreed that by 2010 they should have reduced their atmospheric pollution levels to those of 1990. The Kyoto Protocol came into force in February 2005 and by 2006 it had been ratified by 162 countries. This agreement will expire in 2012. There are three things to note:

➤ Some countries are already polluting at levels significantly above those of 1990. The USA, for example, releases 15% more carbon dioxide at the start of the twenty-first century than it did 10 years ago. Despite this, President Bush refused to ratify the Kyoto proposals, claiming that 'the agreement was fatally flawed' and that the emissions targets were unattainable and potentially damaging to the US economy.
➤ Some countries are disproportionately responsible for releasing greenhouse gases. In 1996, the USA released 21% of global carbon dioxide even though it had only 4% of the world's population. China, now one of the foremost

industrial nations of the world and responsible for a considerable amount of pollution, is not required to reduce its emissions as it was not considered an industrial giant in 1997.

➤ Some countries, particularly the least developed countries which have little industry and few vehicles, release low levels of greenhouse gases.

Carbon credits

Following the Kyoto meeting, a system of global carbon credits was introduced, under which each country is set an annual carbon dioxide pollution limit. Major polluters can buy 'carbon credits' from less polluting countries, which are not using up their own quotas. If polluting countries still go over the limit, a number of options might be forced on them:

➤ a fine

➤ investment in ways to reduce domestic carbon dioxide emissions (e.g. wind or solar power, Photograph 2.12)

➤ paying for improved technologies in other countries or for other countries to plant trees (in February 2000 the Japanese paid the government of New South Wales in Australia £50 million to plant over 40,000 ha of trees in 20 years)

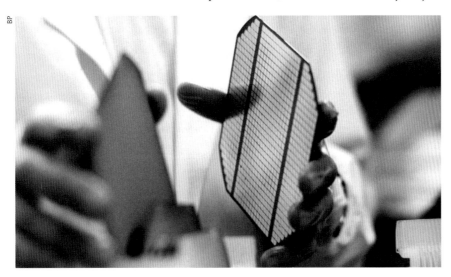

*Photograph 2.12
A solar panel factory. Solar power is a way of reducing carbon emissions*

Critics argue that this system is flawed because it serves the interests of the developed countries, which are the major polluters, and allows them to go on polluting. Such people believe that the mass industrialisation and consumerism which underpin the economies of the developed world are unsustainable. It is unlikely, though, that the citizens of the developed world will be willing to give up their current lifestyles. The monitoring systems have also been criticised — countries are expected to monitor themselves, leaving much room for cheating and 'massaging' of the figures.

One result of the carbon credit system in the UK has been the introduction of a climate change levy — a tax on energy used by industry, commerce and the public sector. This came into effect in April 2001. It is designed to help meet the

target agreed in the Kyoto Protocol, which commits the UK to a 12.5% reduction in emissions of six greenhouse gases by 2010. Many people now believe that the carbon credit system is the best way to reduce, if not entirely eradicate, atmospheric pollution in the twenty-first century.

Post Kyoto

In July 2005 the G8 world leaders and delegates from China, India, Brazil, South Africa and Mexico attended a conference in Gleneagles, Scotland where they agreed that urgent action needed to be taken to make significant reductions in greenhouse gases. The G8 countries are home to some 13.5% of the total world population but contribute around 39% of current greenhouse gas emissions.

They devised the Gleneagles Action Plan, which included plans for increased energy efficiency in buildings and appliances, cleaner fuels, renewable energy and the promotion of research and development into cleaner technologies.

By 2006 it became clear that a global agreement was needed to take the place of the Kyoto Protocol after 2010. A UN climate change convention in Bali in December 2007 was attended by more than 180 countries. The main outcome of this was the 'Bali roadmap', which started a 2-year process of negotiations on new emissions targets to be finalised at the UN Copenhagen Conference in 2009. When the G8 world leaders met in 2008 in Japan, they made a commitment to halve their greenhouse gas emissions by 2050.

National responses: the UK

In the government's 2006 **Climate Change Programme,** policies and priorities for action were set out to address the issue of climate change both in the UK and internationally. These included strategies to reduce greenhouse gas emissions, manage the impacts of climate change and improve energy efficiency:

➤ On the domestic front, building regulations were tightened to ensure that new housing was properly insulated and had energy-saving boilers.
➤ In transport, vehicle excise duty and company car tax were amended to ensure financial incentives for those driving vehicles with the lowest carbon dioxide emissions.
➤ The Carbon Trust was granted £65 million from the government over 5 years to help provide loans to small and medium-sized businesses investing in improved energy efficiency.
➤ In Scotland woodland creation schemes were sponsored and a package of measures designed to reduce nitrous oxide emissions from fertilisers was introduced.
➤ The **Climate Change and Sustainable Energy Act** of 2006 placed an obligation on the Department for Environment, Farming and Rural Affairs (DEFRA) to report annually on levels of emissions of greenhouse gases and the success of measures set out in its Climate Change Programme.

More recently, the **Climate Change Bill** (2008) aimed to manage and respond to climate change in the UK in a range of different ways including:

➤ setting ambitious targets for reduction in emissions. For example, using 1990 as a baseline, there should be a reduction in carbon dioxide emissions of 26% by 2020 and 60% by 2050

➤ an annual review of the initial targets by the independent Committee on Climate Change, whose job will be to consider whether these targets should be raised

➤ the creation of 5-year carbon budgets, which set binding limits on carbon dioxide emissions

➤ encouraging the purchase of carbon credits from overseas

➤ expansion of the Renewable Transport Fuels Operation which will increase the proportion of biofuels used in transport

➤ assisting local authorities to improve their household waste reduction and recycling schemes

Local responses

Sustainable development has become a key concept in the twenty-first century. In order to maintain current standards of living and to slow the predicted impacts of global warming, societies need to use their resources more wisely. At the regional scale, many local governments have developed initiatives to respond to environmental problems such as global warming. Some cities, such as Manchester, are planning to follow London's lead, using a congestion charge to limit the traffic entering their inner cities. Most of the initiatives introduced in cities to help reduce problems of urban pollution, such as tram services and park and ride schemes, will also curb the rise in carbon emissions. At an individual level households can contribute by:

➤ **Insulating** their homes properly with cavity wall insulation, loft lagging and double glazing. New housing is governed by regulations on insulation and grants are often available to insulate older housing.

➤ **Recycling**. Local councils have targets for recycling and provide separate containers for collection of paper and cardboard, glass and aluminium cans, plastic and compostable waste.

➤ **Using energy wisely**. Individuals can cut their energy bills by turning off lights, turning down the central heating, not leaving the television and computer on stand-by and using energy-efficient light bulbs.

➤ **Using public transport** and joining car-sharing schemes, walking or cycling. Many primary schools have promoted 'walk to school' schemes.

Photograph 2.13 Some communities in Britain, like Wolvercote in Oxfordshire, have declared themselves low carbon and introduced schemes to reduce their carbon footprint

Ian Curtis

Ecosystems: change and challenge

Nature of ecosystems

The structure of ecosystems

Key terms

Biomass The total mass of plant and animal life in an ecosystem.

Biome Ecosystem at a continental scale covering a large area, with vegetation characteristics that are predominantly influenced by the climate. A biome can also be judged by the speed at which the vegetation grows.

Ecosystem A dynamic, stable system characterised by the interaction of plants and animals with each other and with the non-living components of the environment. An ecosystem can be considered at any scale from a small area, such as a pond or hedge, up to an area as large as the Earth itself.

Environment All the conditions in which an organism lives.

Food chain A hierarchy of organisms in a community. Each member feeds upon another in the chain and is eaten in turn.

Food web When organisms within a community eat more than one type of food and food chains become interlinked, a food web is created.

Trophic level A feeding level within a food chain. The first level is made up of vegetation or primary producers.

The components of an ecosystem are categorised as either biotic or abiotic. **Biotic** means the living environment, so components include:

➤ vegetation (living and decomposing)
➤ mammals, insects, birds and microorganisms

The mass of material in the bodies of animals and plants is called the **biomass**. It is mainly plant tissue.

Photograph 3.1 An ecosystem can be considered at any scale

Corel

Abiotic means the non-living, chemical and physical components of the ecosystem and includes:

➤ climate — in particular the seasonal pattern of temperature and precipitation
➤ soil characteristics
➤ underlying parent rock
➤ relief of the land
➤ drainage characteristics

As with any system there are inputs, outputs, stores and flows. Ecosystems are open systems because energy and living matter can both enter and leave the system.

➤ **Inputs** — the most important input is energy from the sun, which drives photosynthesis and so enables plants to grow. Other inputs include animals that arrive from elsewhere, and water, transported into the ecosystem by precipitation or rivers.
➤ **Outputs** — nutrients are transferred out of the system in a number of ways. Animals can physically move; water can move out of the ecosystem in rivers and by evapotranspiration, throughflow and groundwater flow.
➤ **Flows** — within an ecosystem nutrients can be transferred from one store to another, for example from the soil to the vegetation through capillary uptake by plant roots.
➤ **Stores** — the three main stores of nutrients are in the vegetation, plant litter and soils.

Energy flows and nutrient cycling

Plants are able to capture light energy from the sun and use it to make carbohydrates from carbon dioxide and water. This process of photosynthesis is the way in which plants grow and increase their biomass.

Figure 3.1 A model of the mineral nutrient cycle

Within all ecosystems, nutrients are required for plant growth and are recycled from one store to another. For example, leaves fall from trees and as they decompose nutrients are returned to the soil. The commonly accepted way of demonstrating the cycling of nutrients within the main stores of a biome is by a **Gersmehl diagram** (Figure 3.1). Circles of proportionate size are drawn to represent the stores of nutrients within the biomass, litter and soil. Nutrient transfers, inputs and outputs are represented by arrows of varying thickness, depending on the relative rates of transfer between the stores.

➤ Inputs include nutrients such as carbon and nitrogen dissolved in precipitation and minerals from weathered parent rock.

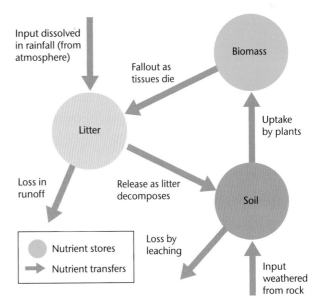

➤ **Outputs** include loss of nutrients from the soil by leaching and by surface runoff.
➤ **Flows** or **transfers** include leaf fall from the biomass to the litter, decomposition of litter transferring nutrients to the soil, and uptake of nutrients from the soil by trees and other plants.

Trophic levels, food chains and webs

Energy transfer within an ecosystem can be illustrated by a pyramid diagram showing the four main trophic levels (Figure 3.2). At each trophic level, some of the energy contained is available as food for the next level in the hierarchy. Each layer in the pyramid from the bottom up decreases in size because around 90% of the energy contained within each level is lost through life processes, particularly respiration, movement and excretion. Only 10% is available for the next level as food, so the number of living organisms within an ecosystem decreases as the trophic level increases.

Figure 3.2
An energy pyramid

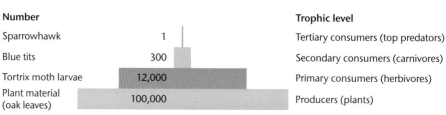

Number		Trophic level
Sparrowhawk	1	Tertiary consumers (top predators)
Blue tits	300	Secondary consumers (carnivores)
Tortrix moth larvae	12,000	Primary consumers (herbivores)
Plant material (oak leaves)	100,000	Producers (plants)

➤ **Producers** or **autotrophs** are the first and lowest layer in the pyramid. They are green plants and produce their own food through photosynthesis using energy from sunlight.
➤ **Primary consumers** or **herbivores** occupy the second trophic level. These insects, fish, birds and mammals eat the producers.
➤ **Secondary consumers** or **carnivores** are meat-eaters and survive primarily by consuming the herbivores.
➤ **Tertiary consumers** are at the top of the trophic pyramid. They are the top predators and eat the secondary consumers. They may be **omnivores**.
➤ **Detritivores** and **decomposers** operate at each trophic level. A detritivore is an animal that feeds on dead material or waste products; a decomposer is an organism that breaks down dead plants, animals and waste matter. Fungi and bacteria are decomposers.

Trophic pyramids can be illustrated by examining simple food chains that exist within a particular ecosystem. A food chain also shows the flow of energy through an ecosystem. There are usually four links in a food chain, as there are four levels in a trophic pyramid. Each link in the chain feeds on and obtains energy from the preceding link and, in turn, is consumed by and provides energy for the following link. Examples of simple food chains include:

rose leaf → aphid → blue tit → sparrowhawk
phytoplankton → zooplankton → cod → human
corn → field mouse → weasel → fox

In reality, a large number of individual food chains operate within a single ecosystem. The overall picture can be shown as a food web (Figure 3.3). Many animals have a varied diet and any one species of animal or plant is likely to be the food for a number of different consumers. As a result, there are complex feeding interactions within an ecosystem. Humans, as omnivores, operate at several trophic levels.

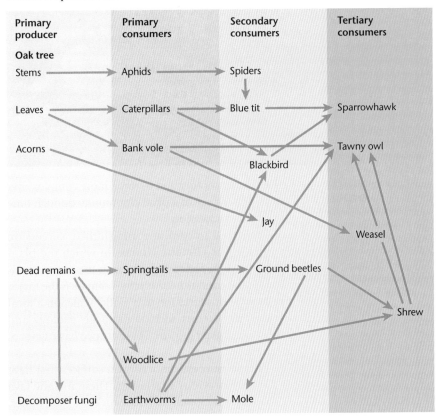

Figure 3.3
A food web

Ecosystems in the British Isles

Succession and climatic climax

The composition of vegetation depends on the interaction between all the components that make up the environment — the plants' habitat. These include natural factors such as climate, relief and soils, and human influence through clearance, fires and livestock grazing. Plants will survive under suitable conditions, depending on environmental factors and competition. Plant populations vary from

Photograph 3.2 Plants colonising bare lava on Mt Rangitoto, New Zealand: a primary succession

Jane Buckett

one area to another and become more complex over time. The change in a plant community through time is called a **succession**.

If allowed to continue undisturbed, succession will reach its **climatic climax**, in which the plant species live in perfect balance with the current environmental conditions. Although climate is the major influence on vegetation at a global scale, on a local scale other factors such as drainage, geology and relief affect plant growth. There are two basic types of succession:

➤ **Primary succession** occurs on surfaces that have had no previous vegetation. These include lava flows (Photograph 3.2), bare rock and sand dunes. There are two main types of primary succession. **Xeroseres** are formed on dry land. This group can be subdivided into lithoseres on bare rock and psammoseres on sand dunes. **Hydroseres** are formed in water — haloseres in salt water and hydroseres in fresh water.

➤ **Secondary succession** follows the destruction or modification of an existing plant community. This can occur naturally, perhaps after a landslide or a fire caused by lightning. It can also occur through human activity, such as deforestation to provide farmland.

Development of a succession

As a succession develops it passes through a series of stages called **seres**. Here the processes of invasion, colonisation, competition, domination and decline operate to influence the composition of the vegetation.

When plants first invade bare ground (through the processes of dispersal and migration), groups of a particular species, or colonies of two or more species, become established. These **pioneer species** are extremely hardy plants, adapted to survive in harsh conditions. Long-rooted salt-tolerant marram grass growing on a sand dune is an example of a pioneer plant. Pioneers compete for available space, light, water and nutrients and, as they die, they help to modify the habitat, adding organic matter to the developing soil. They can affect the microclimate of the area (wind speed at ground level, shelter, temperature and humidity) and soil conditions (organic content, nutrient recycling, acidity and water retention). The roots of the pioneer plants help to break up and weather the surface and so aid soil formation.

As the ground is improved by the creation of an immature soil, other plants are able to colonise and change the existing balance of species. Each stage of the colonisation provides better conditions for plant growth than the previous one, so an increasing number of species is found. The addition of organic matter (from decaying vegetation) to the developing soil improves its structure and water-retention qualities. This allows the growth of taller and more aggressive plants that are more demanding of water, nutrients and anchorage. Taller plants also provide shelter from the sun and wind, which in turn allows other plants to become established. In each stage of a plant succession, there are dominant plants. These are the tallest plants and cover the most ground.

Over time, sometimes even thousands of years, a period of relative stability is reached in which the vegetation has reached its climax, with dominants excluding rivals less suited to the current environmental conditions. Once the major dominants are in place the number of species begins to decline. Climax is usually dominated by the tallest species that can grow in the given conditions. At this stage the community becomes 'closed' — saturation point has been reached with all potential niches occupied. This is known as the **climatic climax community**, the natural vegetation having reached a stable balance with the climate and soils of the area.

Some biogeographers believe that within one climate, local factors such as drainage, geology, relief and even microclimates can create variations in the climatic climax community. This idea is known as **polyclimax theory**.

Figure 3.4 The development of a lithosere on a raised beach

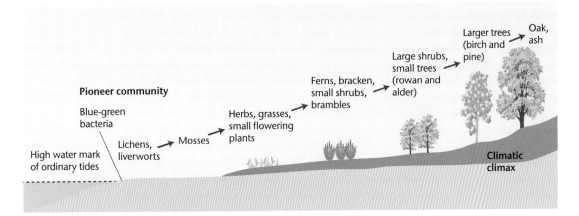

A lithosere

A lithosere is a succession that begins life on a newly exposed rock surface. This might have been created by the eruption of a volcano, leaving a new, bare lava surface, as happened when Surtsey erupted in Iceland in 1963.

Another example of a lithosere is a raised beach, created either by falling sea levels or by the isostatic uplift of land from the sea (Figure 3.4). Raised beaches can be seen on the west coast of Scotland. In the UK, a lithosere on a raised beach develops as follows:

➤ The bare rock surface is initially colonised by bacteria and algae, which can survive where there are few nutrients. Bare rock tends to be very dry and there is rapid surface runoff.

➤ The pioneers begin to colonise, starting with lichens which can withstand the acute water shortage. They begin to break down the rock and assist water retention.

➤ As water retention improves, mosses begin to grow. These also improve water retention and weathering to produce the beginnings of a soil in which more advanced plants can grow.

➤ Ferns, herbs and flowering plants appear. As these die back, bacteria convert their remains into humus, which helps to recycle nutrients and further improve soil fertility.

➤ Shrubs start to grow, shading out the grasses and herbs.

➤ Pioneer trees become established. These are mainly fast-growing species such as willow, birch and rowan.

➤ Slower-growing tree species begin to develop, such as ash and oak. Initially they are in the shade of shrubs, so they only appear in the later stages of the succession. They are the dominants of the climatic climax community — temperate deciduous woodland.

A hydrosere

A hydrosere develops as follows:

➤ In a freshwater environment, such as a pond, submerged aquatics are the first plants to develop. These help to trap sediment which enables other species, such as aquatics with floating leaves, to move in.

➤ The next seral stage is the growth of reed beds and swamp conditions. As plant debris accumulates along with silt and sediment it rises above the water level to produce a carr or fen.

➤ Colonisation by alder and fern begins. These plants further modify the environmental conditions, improving drainage and mineral content of the immature soil and so allowing the entry of willow and ash.

➤ Eventually the climatic climax vegetation of deciduous oak or beech woodland is reached. Throughout the succession there are progressive changes to soil condition, ground-level microclimate and animal activity.

Examples of a psammosere (sand dune) and halosere (salt marsh) plant successions are covered in *AQA AS Geography* on pages 92–95.

The climatic climax: temperate deciduous woodland

A biome is a global-scale ecosystem and is a naturally occurring organic community of plants and animals in the climatic climax stage of succession. Comparing maps of the world's climate (Figure 3.5) and vegetation (Figure 3.6) zones (biomes) reveals marked similarities. A third map showing zonal

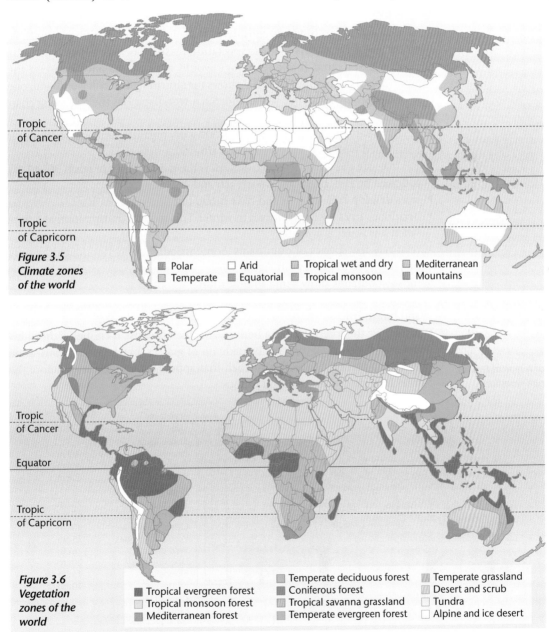

Figure 3.5 Climate zones of the world

▪ Polar	□ Arid	▪ Tropical wet and dry	▪ Mediterranean
▪ Temperate	▪ Equatorial	▪ Tropical monsoon	▪ Mountains

Figure 3.6 Vegetation zones of the world

	▪ Temperate deciduous forest	▪ Temperate grassland
▪ Tropical evergreen forest	▪ Coniferous forest	▪ Desert and scrub
▪ Tropical monsoon forest	▪ Tropical savanna grassland	□ Tundra
▪ Mediterranean forest	▪ Temperate evergreen forest	□ Alpine and ice desert

soil distribution at the same scale would also bear comparison. Within any ecosystem, the three main components — climate, vegetation and soils — are closely linked in equilibrium.

Tropical rainforests and temperate deciduous woodlands are both examples of high-energy biomes. Each has its own distinctive vegetation. Each biome type, no matter on which continent it occurs, shows similarities in climate, soils, plants and animal life. Low-energy biomes are the tundra in the high latitudes and the hot deserts in the low latitudes. Here, the vegetation is scant and net primary productivity is low.

In a natural state a biome is considered to be in dynamic equilibrium with its environment. This means that the vegetation exists in perfect balance with the climate and soils and that any change would alter the balance between the components of the biome. Figure 3.7 shows the structure of an oak woodland, one type of temperate deciduous woodland. Such woodland has the following characteristics:

➤ a net primary productivity (NPP) of 1,200 g dry organic matter per m^2 per year (compared with 2,200 g m^{-2} $year^{-1}$ for tropical rainforest)
➤ tall trees are the dominant species. Oak is the tallest (and can reach 30–40 m) followed by elm, beech, sycamore, ash and chestnut
➤ trees develop large crowns and have broad but thin leaves
➤ deciduous trees shed their leaves in winter. This reduces transpiration at a time when less water is available
➤ relatively few species of dominants. Some woodlands are dominated by only one tree species (such as in Figure 3.7)
➤ most woodlands show some stratification
➤ below the canopy is a shrub layer with smaller trees such as holly, hazel, rowan and hawthorn
➤ just above the forest floor is a herb layer, which is dense if enough light filters through the shrub layer. This is made up of grasses, bracken, ferns and some flowering plants such as the bluebell that appear early in the year, before the trees have developed their full canopy

Figure 3.7 Structure of a typical English oak woodland

	Average height
Tree layer	
Oak	20 m
Shrub layer	
Bramble	1.5 m
Rose	1.5 m
Rowan	2.8 m
Herb layer	
Nardus grass	25 cm
Fern bracken	60 cm
Other grass	30 cm
Wood anemones	15 cm
Wild garlic	6 cm
Dog's mercury	20 cm
Bluebells	15 cm
Primroses	10 cm
Ground layer	
Mosses	2 cm

Jane Buekett

*Photograph 3.3
Deciduous
woodland is the
UK's climatic climax
community*

- ➤ epiphytes, e.g. lichens and mosses, grow on the trunks and branches of trees
- ➤ mosses grow on the forest floor and a thick layer of leaf litter is readily broken down by soil microbes and animals

Photograph 3.3 shows beech woodland in the UK.

Arresting factors

Plant successions can be stopped from reaching the climatic climax, or deflected towards a different climax, by human interference. The resulting vegetation is known as a **plagioclimax**. Examples of human activity that create plagioclimaxes are:
- ➤ deforestation or afforestation
- ➤ animal grazing or trampling
- ➤ fire clearance

A **secondary succession** is one that develops on land that has previously been vegetated. For example, an area might have been cleared for farming but later abandoned. This abandoned land becomes colonised in a secondary succession. The stages of secondary succession may be more rapid than those of primary succession because organic matter is already present in the soil. The pioneer stage may be short or absent altogether. Climatic climax might be reached in a much shorter time than if the succession had started on a new surface.

Secondary succession can also follow natural events such as a change in climate, a disease, a mudflow, a volcanic eruption or a spontaneous fire, which can be the result of lightning.

A plagioclimax: heather moorland

A good example of a plagioclimax in the UK is heather moorland. Many of the uplands in Britain were once covered by a climax vegetation of deciduous

woodland, particularly oak forest. Heather (*Calluna vulgaris*) would have featured, but only in small amounts. Gradually the forests were removed, for a variety of purposes. As the soils deteriorated without the deciduous vegetation, hardy plants such as heather came to dominate the uplands. Sheep grazing became the major form of agriculture and the sheep prevented the regeneration of climax woodland by destroying young saplings.

Figure 3.8 The heather nutrient cycle

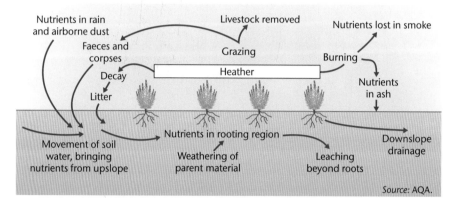

Figure 3.9 The heather cycle

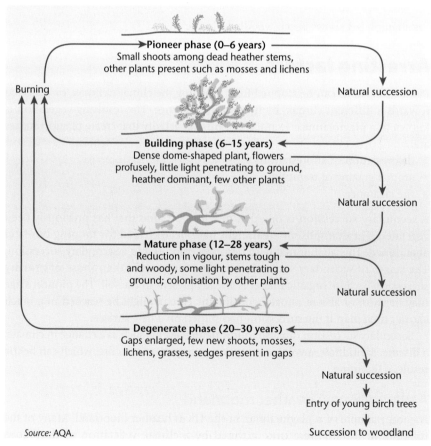

Source: AQA.

Many of these uplands have been controlled by managed burning to encourage new heather shoots. Burning has eliminated the less fire-resistant species, leading to the dominance of heather. One of the aims of burning heather is to ensure that as much as possible of the available nutrient fund is conserved in the ecosystem. In many areas, heather is burnt on average every 15 years. If a longer time elapses there is too much woody tissue, the fires burn too hot, and nutrients are lost in the smoke.

Figures 3.8 and 3.9 show the cycle associated with the heather system. If the burning was not continued, the heather moorland would degenerate, eventually allowing the growth of trees and a succession to woodland. Much of the present vegetation of the UK is a plagioclimax, largely as a result of clearance from the Roman and Anglo-Saxon periods through to the eleventh century. By this time only about 10% of the original woodland remained in England and Wales.

Tropical biomes

In the tropical rainforest biome, because of the constant high temperature and rainfall, the vegetation grows more quickly than anywhere else on Earth. This produces the greatest amount of organic matter, referred to as **net primary productivity** (NPP).

Tropical rainforest and monsoon forest are high-energy biomes but savanna grasslands have a lower NPP (Table 3.1). Each has its own distinctive vegetation, adapted to the climate.

Table 3.1 Net primary productivity per biome

Biome	Mean NPP (g m^{-2} year^{-1})
Tropical rainforest	2,200
Monsoon forest	1,600
Savanna grassland	900

Key terms

Biodiversity The variety of species within an ecosystem.

Leaching/eluviation Soluble bases are removed from a soil by downward-percolating water in environments where precipitation exceeds evaporation.

Net primary productivity (NPP) The amount of energy fixed in photosynthesis minus the energy lost by respiration in plants, measured in grammes per square metre per year (g m^{-2} year^{-1}).

Soil The outermost layer of the Earth's crust, providing the foundation for all plant life. Soil is made up of organic, mineral and animal constituents differentiated into layers (horizons) of variable depth. It is created by the interaction of physical, chemical and biological processes.

The greatest biodiversity exists within tropical rainforests which are believed to contain half the world's gene pool. Tropical rainforests have been stable ecosystems for up to 100 million years. In their undisturbed state they have continued to gain new species.

The tropical equatorial rainforest biome

The tropical rainforest biome circles the Earth, mainly between latitudes 10°N and 10°S of the equator. It occurs in the Amazon basin in South America, in the

Democratic Republic of Congo and the Guinea coast of Africa, parts of southeast Asia, Indonesia and northern Australia.

Climate

The equatorial climate has little seasonal variation. Temperatures remain high throughout the year: mean monthly values seldom fall below 25°C and maximum values are unlikely to rise above 28°C (see Figure 2.20, page 56).

In locations further from the equator a dual peak of temperature can occur annually. In such locations the sun is directly overhead twice a year as it appears to move from the Tropic of Cancer to the Tropic of Capricorn between the summer and winter solstices. The daily (diurnal) range of temperature tends to be higher than the annual range of monthly averages. During sunny spells, often in the morning or late afternoon when the skies have cleared after a thunderstorm, temperatures can rise above 30°C. At night, if the sky is cloud free, temperatures can drop quite rapidly, sometimes to below 20°C. This is because there are no insulating clouds to keep the heat in. Annual precipitation is high, often in excess of 2,000 mm. Rain falls all year round at the equator because the inter-tropical convergence zone (ITCZ, a low-pressure belt) dominates atmospheric conditions here.

A little further away from the equator, a short dry season occurs. This is because of the annual movement of the ITCZ as it travels between the Tropics of Cancer and Capricorn and affects atmospheric pressure. In the months of May, June and July there is a dry season in the southern hemisphere because the ITCZ is directly over the Tropic of Cancer, pulling with it wet low-pressure weather into the northern hemisphere. The opposite occurs at the end of the year in late November, December and early January.

As with temperature, the pattern of rainfall in the rainforest varies during the day. In the morning, skies are generally clear. Evapotranspiration is rapid as the sun beats down on the humid forest and the low-pressure conditions allow this air to be rapidly uplifted. As the air rises it cools and water vapour condenses into clouds. These clouds continue to build until the early afternoon. By this time they are of the towering cumulonimbus variety and a dense grey in colour. In the middle of the afternoon, heavy rain, often with thunder and lightning, returns the previously uplifted moisture back to ground level. The cycle begins again and the day ends as it started with clear skies.

Humidity is high throughout the year — the rainforest has been likened to a natural greenhouse. Continuous evapotranspiration adds water vapour to the air.

Day and night are the same length at the equator. Dawn arrives at around 6 a.m. and night falls quickly at 6 p.m. There is little twilight. Twelve hours of sunlight every day allow photosynthesis to take place all year.

On the forest floor there is little breeze. On the equator there is a distinct lack of wind because this is where the trade winds converge.

Soils

In any undisturbed biome the underlying soil will have developed naturally over a long period of time and be in balance with its environment. Such a soil is known as a **zonal soil**. This is a mature soil and its characteristics strongly reflect the climate and vegetation. The zonal soil type associated with the tropical rainforest is a **latosol** (Figure 3.10).

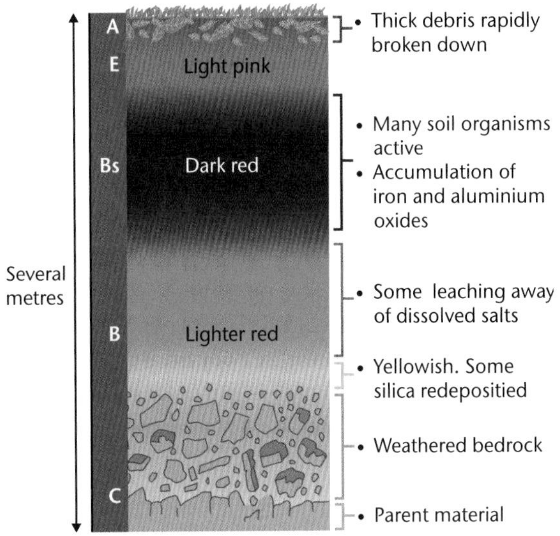

Characteristic features

A latosol can be more than 40 m deep. The constant hot wet climate of the rainforest provides perfect conditions for chemical weathering of the bedrock and there is a constant supply of minerals from the parent rock to the soil. **Ferrallitisation** is the name for the process by which the bedrock is broken down by chemical weathering into clay minerals and sesquioxides (hydrated oxides of iron and aluminium).

Figure 3.10 Profile of a latosol

The red colour of the soil is partly the result of the presence of iron and aluminium minerals. As there is a moisture surplus in the equatorial climate (because rainfall exceeds evapotranspiration), there is downward movement of water through the soil. Silica minerals are washed out of the A horizon and transported downwards by this water in a process known as **leaching** or **eluviation**. Iron and aluminium compounds are less soluble and are left behind. The iron compounds give the soil its rich red colour.

The latosol is nutrient poor. Plant uptake of nutrients is roughly equal to the input from decomposed litter. Although there is a constant supply of organic matter from falling leaves and decaying vegetation, the year-round growing season ensures that, as soon as litter is broken down into humus, it is absorbed by the growing vegetation.

Figure 3.11 shows the soil moisture budget for Yaoundé in the Cameroon, 4°N of the equator. Precipitation is greater than potential evapotranspiration for at least 8 months of the year, when monthly rainfall exceeds 100 mm. During these months there is a soil moisture surplus. The soil is saturated, which leads to surface runoff. Rivers regularly flood during the wettest months.

The short dry season from December to early January occurs when the sun is directly over the Tropic of Capricorn. July also has slightly lower than average rainfall. During December and January the movement of the ITCZ into the

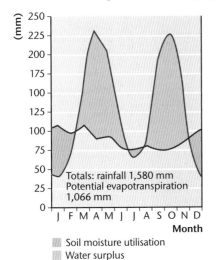

Totals: rainfall 1,580 mm
Potential evapotranspiration 1,066 mm

Soil moisture utilisation
Water surplus
— Potential evapotranspiration
— Rainfall

Figure 3.11 Soil moisture budget for Yaoundé, Cameroon

southern hemisphere results in the arrival of higher pressure in Cameroon, and lower rainfall totals. Soil moisture utilisation occurs throughout this period, as evaporation and transpiration exceed precipitation. However, because the dry season is so short there is no period of soil moisture deficit within the soil.

Vegetation

The rainforest is the most diverse and productive biome in the world but it is also the most fragile. Those remote parts of the forest untouched by modern society have developed over thousands of years and are said to be in a state of dynamic equilibrium. The vegetation is in harmony with its environment and is a climatic climax community where the dominant species are the hardwood trees. This balance can be easily disturbed by human activity.

➤ The net primary productivity of the rainforest is 2,200 g m^{-2} yr^{-1}. This means that energy from sunlight is used by plants to produce 2,200 g of living matter for every square metre of land each year. This figure is high because the growing season lasts all year and the litter is rapidly decomposed, replacing nutrients taken up by the vegetation.

➤ The forest has an evergreen appearance because, although most of the trees are deciduous, individual species lose their leaves at different times of the year. There are always some trees in full leaf.

➤ There can be up to 300 species of tree in every square kilometre. They include mahogany, teak, rosewood, rubber, balsa and brazil nut.

Figure 3.12 The layered structure of tropical rainforest

➤ The forest has a layered appearance, with the tallest trees (emergents), standing up to 45 m tall, above the canopy (Figure 3.12). The canopy absorbs most of the sunlight and intercepts most of the precipitation.

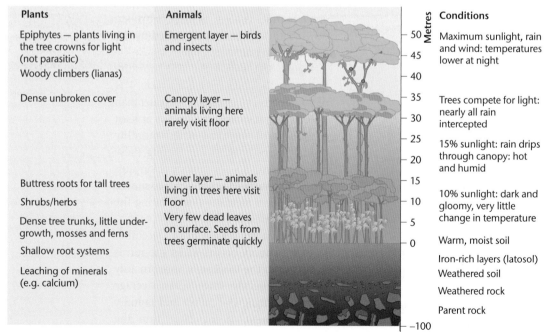

➤ When a tree dies naturally it brings down others as it falls, creating a small clearing in the forest. New trees grow quickly, taking advantage of the light. The fallen trees decompose rapidly, assisted by detritivores and by the hot, humid conditions.

➤ Fungi grow on trees and other plants and inhabit the forest floor. They have an important role in decomposing litter.

The vegetation has developed and adapted to the physical conditions of the rainforest in a number of ways:

Amazon-Images/Alamy

Photograph 3.4 Buttress roots on a tree in the Amazon rainforest

➤ The trees grow rapidly upwards towards the light and their trunks are slender with few branches. The leaves are at the tops of the trees, where they absorb sunlight and photosynthesise. The bark is thin because the trees do not need protection from harsh winter temperatures. The tallest trees have flexible trunks that allow movement. At 50 m above ground level the winds can be strong, so this allows trees to sway without breaking.

➤ Since the minerals needed by the trees are found only in the top layer of the soil and there is an abundant supply of water, the tree roots do not go deep into the soil but spread out on the forest floor. Buttress roots, emerging up to 3 m above the ground, help to stabilise the tallest trees (Photograph 3.4).

➤ The leaves have adapted to the regular heavy rainfall by developing drip-tips. These allow excess water to be easily shed. In addition, some leaves are thick and leathery to withstand the strong sunlight and reduce loss of water from the plant.

➤ Away from the riverbanks the forest floor is dark so some plants, called epiphytes, grow on the trees. The tree is not damaged by this, as it would be by a parasite. Lianas are examples of epiphytes.

Rainforests form the habitat for a huge number of species of birds, insects and other animals.

Impact of human activity: deforestation

Destruction of the world's tropical rainforests is a major environmental issue. Deforestation is the deliberate clearance of woodland by cutting, burning or the application of a defoliant, such as that used during the 1960s by American troops to clear the jungle in Vietnam. In some developing countries and newly industrialising countries (NICs) tropical rainforests, such as those in the Amazon basin

in South America, and in Indonesia and Malaysia in the far east, are being destroyed at an alarming rate. There are claims that half of the world's original rainforests have already been cleared, with an area the size of the UK being removed each year. By 2010, if the present rate of destruction continues, Brazil and the Democratic Republic of Congo will be the only countries with a significant area of rainforest remaining.

Climatic climax vegetation has been destroyed and this has resulted in both secondary succession and plagioclimax. The vegetation that eventually grows to replace the original rainforest tends to be smaller in height and less diverse, with a reduction in the overall biomass.

Causes of deforestation

The demand for hardwood, such as teak, for building and furniture is increasing and many developing countries rely on export earnings from timber to help pay their debts and finance major development projects. Deforestation also occurs to provide land for rubber plantations, cattle ranches for beef farming, soya plantations, roads and railways. In the Brazilian rainforest, rivers have been dammed and large areas flooded to provide water for hydroelectric power stations. An example of such a reservoir lies behind the Tucuruí dam on the Tocantins River in Amazonia. Forest is also being cleared in Brazil for mining. There are vast resources of aluminium and iron ores in the ground beneath the rainforest and the Carajás mining project in Amazonia has resulted in the destruction of large areas of climax vegetation.

Most countries with large areas of rainforest are still developing economically. During the 1960s and 1970s, the population of southeast Asia and South America increased rapidly because birth rates exceeded death rates. Population pressure led to increasing clearance of rainforest. In Indonesia, the transmigration policy encouraged people to move from the overcrowded island of Java to less populated islands such as Sumatra, where rainforest was cleared to make way for settlements and agriculture.

Impacts of deforestation

Impacts can be physical, economic, social and cultural. They mainly occur on a local scale, but some impacts can be global.

As habitats shrink, plant species become endangered and the food chain within the forest is disrupted. Some animal species, for example tigers and orang-utans, are threatened by extinction.

The vegetation protects the latosol soils from the regular heavy tropical downpours. Once the trees are removed the topsoil is open to erosion and to leaching of nutrients and minerals. Runoff causes sediment to block river channels and increases flooding.

The microclimate of the forest is disturbed by deforestation — the daily water cycle of rapid evapotranspiration followed by afternoon precipitation cannot occur and there is less cloud cover, so a greater temperature range. Burning associated with forest clearance leads to local air pollution and contributes to climate change.

Deforestation can have economic benefits in terms of income from mining, farming and exports of hardwood. However, the culture of indigenous people is destroyed and they may be forced to move from their land.

The savanna grassland biome

Although this global ecosystem is characteristically found within the tropics on all the continental landmasses, it is most often associated with the savanna grasslands of Africa.

Climate

The tropical wet and dry climate of Africa (Figure 3.13) shows seasonal variations in wind direction, precipitation and temperature. It is transitional between the equatorial rainforests, where rain can be expected all year, and the hot deserts, which have minimal precipitation. Variations occur with increasing latitude from the equator. The climate, however, is generally characterised by a dry season in the cooler period and a wet season in the hotter period, during which up to 90% of the annual precipitation falls (Figure 3.14).

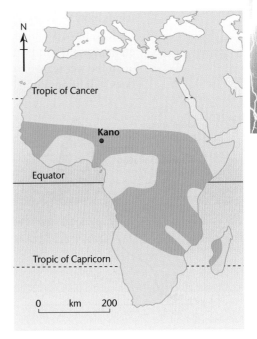

Figure 3.13 The tropical wet and dry regions of Africa

Precipitation varies as follows:

➤ on the equatorial rainforest margins more than 1,000 mm falls per year, the rainy season lasting 10–11 months

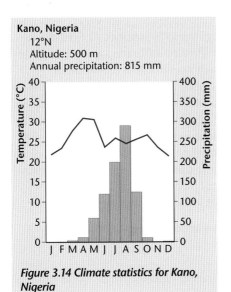

Figure 3.14 Climate statistics for Kano, Nigeria

➤ on the desert/semi-arid margins there is less than 500 mm per year with only 1 or 2 months rainy season away from the equator, so the reliability of the rainfall decreases

Temperature varies as follows:
➤ on the equatorial rainforest margin, temperatures range from 22°C in the wet season to 28°C in the dry season
➤ on the desert margins the temperatures range from 18°C in the wet season to 34°C in the dry season

During the dry season, the subtropical anticyclone moves over the desert margins. The subsiding air of the encroaching high pressure suppresses convection, giving rise to clear skies and high daytime temperatures. The trade winds blow from the high pressure towards the ITCZ and in doing so move air from the land towards the coasts. Such air is very dry, and in north Africa often produces an unpleasant wind with a low moisture content known as the harmattan.

In the wet season, the ITCZ migrates polewards (see Figure 2.19, p. 56). As it does so it brings rainfall because uplift and convection are fed by moist, unstable, tropical maritime air. Areas at the poleward limit are only briefly affected, and therefore only have a short wet season with low annual rainfall totals. Towards the equator, the wet season lasts during the time the ITCZ has moved polewards, giving a much longer rainy season with higher total rainfall amounts. There are two periods of maximum precipitation in some areas, when the ITCZ moves polewards and when it returns.

Ecological responses

Soil moisture budgets

Figure 3.15 shows the soil moisture budget for an area in northern Ghana. Precipitation is greater than potential evapotranspiration between July and September, whereas the reverse is true between October and June. There are four distinct periods that can be seen in the soil moisture budget for this area:

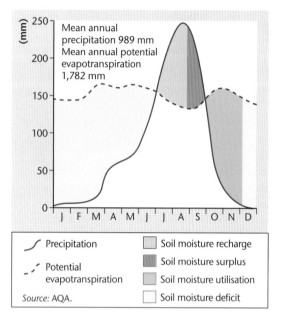

Precipitation

Potential evapotranspiration

Source: AQA.

Soil moisture recharge

Soil moisture surplus

Soil moisture utilisation

Soil moisture deficit

Figure 3.15 Soil moisture budget for Navrongo, northern Ghana (11°N)

➤ **Soil moisture recharge** occurs through July and early August and this is when precipitation first becomes greater than evapotranspiration. Rainwater begins to fill the empty pores in the soil. When they are full the soil is said to have reached its field capacity.

➤ **Soil moisture surplus** occurs in late August and September. At field capacity, the soil is saturated and rainwater has difficulty infiltrating the ground. This causes surface runoff and explains the high river levels of late summer.

➤ **Soil moisture utilisation** occurs from October, as evapotranspiration begins to exceed precipitation. There is more water evaporating from the ground surface and being transpired by plants than is falling as rain. Water is also drawn up the soil by capillary action and this leads to further evaporation.

➤ **Soil moisture deficit** occurs by December when the soil moisture is used up and there is a water deficit. Plants can only survive by being drought resistant or through irrigation. This period lasts until precipitation again becomes greater than evapotranspiration in early July and soil moisture recharge can begin.

This area in northern Ghana therefore shows the following characteristics:

➤ a lengthy period of moisture deficit
➤ a short period of moisture surplus
➤ total annual potential evapotranspiration greater than total annual precipitation

Number of wet months	10–12	9–10	7–9	4–6	1–3	0
Mean annual rainfall (mm)	Mainly >2,000	Mainly >1,500	Mainly >1,000	750–1,000	> 400 | < 400	<250

Figure 3.16 Section south to north through west Africa showing variations in vegetation

metres 50 —						
Main vegetation	Moist tropical forest	Tree (parkland) savanna		Grassland savanna	Shrub savanna | Semi-desert	Desert

Adaptations by vegetation

The vegetation of the wetter areas consists of tall coarse grasses (elephant grass) with many deciduous trees. It is known as the tree savanna. In drier areas towards the desert margins, shorter tussock grass becomes dominant, with bare soil between the tufts of grass. This is often accompanied by drought-resistant trees such as acacia and baobab. These areas are known as the grassland and shrub savannas (Figure 3.16).

Trees in these areas tend to be deciduous, losing their leaves in the dry season, although some evergreens are also present. These have hard leathery leaves to reduce transpiration losses. Other plants are microphyllous (small-leaved), for the same reason.

In the **tree savanna**, a parkland exists. Here isolated trees have low umbrella-shaped crowns that shade root areas and reduce soil moisture evaporation. The trees show xerophytic characteristics (adaptations to dry surroundings), with dense cell fluids, hard waxy leaves, thorns and protected stomata, which all reduce water loss. The two main trees of the savanna are:

Photograph 3.5 Baobab and shrubs, Tanzania

> acacia, which has a crown structure often flattened by the trade winds. It loses its leaves in the dry season
> baobab ('upside-down tree'), which has a thick spongy trunk, long tap roots and bears leaves for only a few weeks. Like the acacia, the baobab is pyrophytic — it can withstand fire, mainly because of its insulating bark (Photograph 3.5)

TopFoto

In the **grassland savanna** the grasses between the trees are shorter and more sparse. They are perennial, dying back during the dry season and regrowing from root nodules when it rains. The grasses are tussocky, enabling them to retain some moisture. The naturally created straw dies down and protects roots.

In the **shrub** or **scrub savanna** there are many acacia trees, thorn bushes and short tufted grasses. Many species generate short stems from a single stock, with deep, branched roots and dormant seeds that compete for water. In some plants, even the stems may be capable of photosynthesis, so plants can have fewer leaves and retain more water. Some grasses are feathery and wiry, and turn their blades away from the strong sun to reduce water loss.

Impact of human activity

Human activity has two main effects on the vegetation:

➤ Grass is burnt off to ensure better growth of young grass next season for grazing. This regular burning makes it difficult for young trees and bushes to become established. Their place is taken by herbaceous plants and by the few indigenous woody plants that can survive fire, like acacia and baobab, which are therefore common in the savanna.
➤ Woody plants are killed by cattle eating their foliage. Thorny, animal-repellent trees and shrubs, such as acacia, therefore become numerous.

There is a belief among some biogeographers that humans have had a much greater influence than climate on the development of savanna vegetation. Some even suggest that grassland may therefore not be the climatic climax community.

The tropical monsoon forest biome

What remains of the tropical monsoon forest biome is mainly found in parts of southeast Asia experiencing a tropical monsoon climate. Before 1900 monsoon forest was the main vegetation type in large parts of the region, but by the start of the twenty-first century most of this had been removed by human activity. In India only 7% of the original forest cover remains.

Tropical monsoon forest is still well developed in Burma (Myanmar), inland from the coast, and in Thailand, Laos, north Vietnam and Cambodia. Within this geographical region vegetation varies with altitude, so tropical monsoon forest gives way to other types of vegetation on high land. In addition, along the coastlines around river deltas and creeks there are mangrove forests.

There are small areas of vegetation with similar characteristics to the tropical monsoon forest in northern Australia and Madagascar. However, in Africa and South America annual precipitation totals are lower in areas fringing the tropical rainforests, so savanna-type vegetation is more likely to exist. The natural vegetation of most of Bangladesh was originally tropical rainforest, even though it lies within the area of tropical monsoon climate, as the presence of rivers meant that there was no seasonal shortage of water for vegetation.

Climate

The tropical monsoon climate experiences high temperatures throughout the year, with a fairly small annual range (19–30°C) because of its location within the tropics. Although annual precipitation totals are high, sometimes in excess of those experienced in the equatorial zone, there is a marked dry season. During the summer months, from late May to October, winds blow in from the oceans (southwest) bringing with them exceptionally moist air and heavy rainfall. For the rest of the year the air is much drier as the winds blowing in the opposite direction (northeast) have their source over land. This climate is explained in detail in Chapter 2 (see Figures 2.22 and 2.23, pages 58–59).

Ecological responses

Soil moisture budgets

Precipitation is much higher than potential evapotranspiration during the wet season, usually between May and early November, whereas the reverse is true for the rest of the year. However, high rainfall totals during the wet season result in saturation of the soil, and some of this moisture can be utilised by vegetation in the first few months of the dry season, even though evapotranspiration then exceeds precipitation. A soil moisture deficit occurs by January, and deciduous trees lose their leaves in response to drought conditions. This period lasts until the arrival of the monsoon rains in late spring. The period of moisture deficit is shorter than that experienced in the tropical savanna biome.

Soils within this biome are typically lateritic, with similar qualities to those found in tropical rainforests (see Figure 3.10, page 103). The months of water surplus during the wet monsoon season result in the leaching of bases and silica, and very little humus is allowed to develop in the top layers.

Adaptations by vegetation and animals

Tree growth is more open than in the tropical rainforest and the canopy is not continuous. The tallest trees are smaller, from 12 m to 35 m, and provide an incomplete cover. This means there is less competition for light, allowing greater development of vegetation (often evergreen species) at lower levels. In some parts of the forest dense undergrowth of bamboos, known as 'jungle', exists. There are fewer species of trees, typically around 40 per hectare compared with 200 per hectare in the tropical rainforest. Common species are sal, pyinkado and teak, all of which are economically valuable. Trees do not possess buttress roots and they develop large round crowns with more branching lower down their trunk than in the rainforest. The bark is often thick and rough to protect them from the harsh climate of the dry season; leaves are thin and generally smaller than in the tropical rainforest.

Different species of plants and trees flower more or less at the same time (at the start of the dry season) and fruit during the wet season. Deciduous trees forming the upper layer of forest shed their leaves in response to a lack of moisture to reduce transpiration during the dry season. This allows light to reach the forest floor and leads to the development of dense undergrowth. Although epiphytes,

typically orchids, and lianas are present, they are fewer in number than in the rainforest.

Mangrove forests have developed along coastal areas protected from wave action, such as deltas and tidal creeks, particularly in Bangladesh, northeast India and Burma (Myanmar). These saline environments where fine sediments with high organic content are deposited give rise to a dense network of trees with massive interlocking root systems, adapted to survive in anaerobic conditions. The mangrove forests fringing the Bay of Bengal help to protect the land from savage cyclones and storm surges during the wet monsoon season and provide a habitat for marine crustaceans.

The monsoon and mangrove forests were once home to abundant wildlife. Some of the most well-known animal inhabitants of these ecosystems in southeast Asia include the Royal Bengal tiger, the Indian elephant, leopard, rhinoceros, crocodile and wild bear. Bird species include peacock, jungle fowl and black partridge and aquatic creatures include dolphin and turtle. Many of these species are now endangered by ever-shrinking habitats and, in some cases, by hunting.

Impact of human activity

Tropical monsoon and mangrove forests are fragile ecosystems, easily lost once removed. Following deforestation it is almost impossible for existing food webs to continue and all trophic levels are affected. Human activity has resulted in a massive decrease in natural vegetation in southeast Asia's mangrove forests over the last 25 years, faster than the loss of tropical rainforests during the same period. The United Nations Food and Agriculture Organisation estimates that 20% of the mangrove forests that existed in 1980 have been destroyed through coastal development of shrimp fishing and tourism, and the use of wood for timber and charcoal.

Removal of the monsoon forests occurred most rapidly in the first half of the twentieth century, mainly as a result of increasing population pressure. Lowland forest was cleared to make way for agricultural land and to provide fuelwood for the rapidly increasing populations in this region. More recently, timber such as teak has been exploited for export to developed countries. It is estimated that only 7% of the original monsoon forest still exists on the Indian subcontinent, and that which does is in small fragmented parcels, making it difficult for animals to maintain their traditional migratory patterns. Many indigenous species are endangered. It is estimated that just 300 Royal Bengal tigers still exist in the wild. Although some remaining areas of monsoon and mangrove forest are designated as National Parks and have additionally been given 'Protected Area' status by the United Nations, it is possible that the damage already done is irreversible.

Development issues in the three biomes

Table 3.2 highlights species diversity and the percentage of species currently under threat from extinction in countries in the three tropical climate types you need to know about. It also shows the percentage of natural landscape protected by

	Brazil (tropical equatorial rainforest)	Tanzania (savanna grassland)	Bangladesh (tropical monsoon forest)
Total land area protected (%)	18	39.6	0.5
Higher plants (number of species)	56,215	10,008	5,000
Threatened (%)	0.7	2.4	0.2
Mammals (number of species)	578	375	131
Threatened (%)	13	9	17
Breeding birds (number of species)	1,712	1,056	604
Threatened (%)	7	3.5	4
Reptiles (number of species)	651	335	113
Threatened (%)	3	1.5	18
Amphibians (number of species)	695	132	231
Threatened (%)	3.5	30	0
Fish (number of species)	471	331	81
Threatened (%)	9	8.5	10

Table 3.2 Species diversity and percentage threatened: three biomes

legislation. It is interesting to note that, although Brazil has the greatest species diversity, a smaller proportion of its land is protected than in Tanzania. It also appears that a higher proportion of species are threatened in Brazil than in Tanzania, where nearly 40% of the total area is designated National Parkland. On the other hand, Bangladesh, one of the most densely populated countries on Earth, has very little protected land, the lowest species diversity and the highest percentage of mammals, reptiles and fish under threat.

Species diversity is of crucial importance because:
➤ plants photosynthesise and produce the oxygen we breathe
➤ trees act as a carbon sink, absorbing emissions created from the burning of fossil fuels
➤ some species help to keep the human race alive by purifying water, fixing nitrogen, recycling nutrients and waste
➤ insects pollinate crops

In all three biomes the natural environment is threatened by population growth and economic development. The tropical monsoon lands have experienced the greatest pressure, and very little natural vegetation remains here in comparison with the savanna grasslands and the tropical rainforests. It remains to be seen whether future sustainable development allows these unique ecosystems to coexist with economic development and the predicted outcomes of climate change.

Ecosystem issues on a local scale

Changes in ecosystems resulting from urbanisation

Urban areas contain a wide variety of habitats including:
➤ industrial sites
➤ derelict land
➤ residential gardens and allotments
➤ parks and other open green areas
➤ transport routes (both used and disused) such as canals, roadside verges and railway embankments
➤ waste disposal areas
➤ urban forests
➤ water bodies

This variety means that it is difficult to make generalisations about urban ecology — all these habitats contain different mixes of flora and fauna. Human impact also makes urban habitats somewhat unstable.

Urban niches

Many urban habitats are specialised. Within one site, a number of different niches or microhabitats might be available for plants and animals to colonise. Photograph 3.4 shows an abandoned and neglected urban site. On this small part of the site, the following niches available for plants would include:

Photograph 3.6 Urban niches on a derelict site

Phil Banks

➤ horizontal bare tarmac
➤ vertical stone walls
➤ vertical brick walls
➤ tops of walls
➤ rubble-strewn ground (different types of rubble create their own microhabitats)

Colonisation of wasteland

Plant succession, the change in a community of species over time, is brought about by changes in the microenvironment which occur because of the supply of new species, the competition between species and changes in habitat. A number of different successions occur within urban areas, depending upon the type of habitat initially colonised, but one of the most studied is that which takes place on an abandoned or neglected area (such as that in Photograph 3.6). On such an area a lithosere-type succession (bare rock succession) develops. The types of plants that can initially colonise such a site are influenced by the following:

➤ **slope** — on horizontal surfaces and gentle slopes debris accumulates that eventually develops into soil
➤ **moisture availability** — on horizontal surfaces and gentle slopes rainwater accumulates or drains away slowly; on steep slopes faster runoff creates dry areas
➤ **aspect** — south-facing slopes are warmer and drier
➤ **porosity** (the ability to hold water) — surfaces that can hold water are colonised more quickly
➤ **surface roughness** — allowing plants to get a hold: glass and metal are too smooth for most plants
➤ **pollution levels** — these depend on the previous use of the site. Substances that are toxic to plants, such as lead, may contaminate the ground

The succession on an abandoned industrial site, for example, would occur as follows:

➤ **Stage 1 The pioneers** — mosses and lichens are the first plants to develop on bare surfaces. They are able to exist in areas where there is little water, obtaining nutrients by photosynthesis and from the bare concrete beneath them. The concrete is slowly weathered by the production of acids. When the plants die, they provide a thin mat of organic matter which, mixed with the weathered mineral matter, produces a protosoil that other plant species can root into.
➤ **Stage 2 Oxford ragwort** — cracks in the surface provide sheltered places for seeds to germinate and also retain moisture and dust, which help plants to root. The most common invaders are plants with windblown seeds such as Oxford ragwort. This has a long flowering season (180–190 days May–November) which enables it to produce millions of seeds. Other common plants at this stage include American willowherb, annual meadow-grass, buddleia, groundsel, knotgrass, dandelion, mugwort, wormwood, white clover and perennial rye-grass. Many of these plants are known as ruderal species, because

they are able to tolerate waste ground, rubbish and debris. At this stage, plant succession is usually rapid.

➤ **Stage 3 Tall herbs** — as these higher plants die off, they produce a thicker and more nutrient-rich soil. Taller plants that are more demanding of good growth conditions can then become established. One of the most common is rosebay willowherb, which spreads initially by seeds and then by rhizomes which can extend up to 1 m a year (rhizomes are elongated horizontal underground plant stems producing shoots above and below ground). Other common plants at this stage include Michaelmas daisy, goldenrod, fennel, goat's-rue, garden lupin, tansy, Jacob's ladder and columbine. These plants gradually shade out the smaller plants, stopping them photosynthesising.

➤ **Stage 4 Grassland** — as soil enrichment continues, the amount of grass in the vegetation increases. The smaller meadow grasses and bents of earlier stages are replaced by taller species. At this stage the area takes on the appearance of grassland containing scattered clumps of tall herbs. One of the invaders is Japanese knotweed. Thickets of this plant can grow up to 3 m in height and their dense canopies shade out most species beneath them.

➤ **Stage 5 Scrub woodland** — as the processes of soil enrichment and competition continue, the taller herbaceous plants are replaced by shrubs and, eventually, trees. The early woody plant colonists (e.g. grey willow, birch) all possess light, windborne seeds, but when the herbaceous vegetation thickens it becomes difficult for these small-seeded plants to establish unless there has been some disturbance to the succession, such as fire. The later trees have larger seeds that can enter closed vegetation. These include sycamore, laburnum, rowan and hawthorn. Dense thickets of bramble and other scrubby plants develop. These are able to compete because they can grow roots into deeper crevices in the rock or concrete.

As the plant succession develops, there are changes in the fauna. Soil fauna, such as earthworms, increase in number as soil improves. There is an increase in the number and diversity of the insect population. These in turn provide food for small mammals which then allow the presence of predators such as kestrels and the urban fox. The arrival of trees may bring squirrels, feeding on the available nuts and seeds.

On any site such as this, there will be variations caused by differences in the nature of the surface being colonised. These are known as **sub-stratum** variations and can lead to several parallel successions developing. Surfaces can be acid or alkaline, and can include wetland, concrete, tarmac and rubble. On one site in Sheffield it was discovered that, even on rubble-strewn areas, there were different successions on different types of rubble. Investigation revealed that there were three sub-strata present:

➤ crushed brick and mortar rubble
➤ several metres of whole and half-bricks on a slight slope
➤ a granular layer of ash and slag

Each of these had distinct successions taking place at different rates, with different species involved.

Ecologies along routeways

Routeways are distinctive habitats because exotic species of plants and insects may be brought in by traffic. They also represent wildlife corridors comparable with rural hedgerows.

Railway lines enable animals to move around the city. During the days of steam, there were frequent fires on the lines which burnt off tall species and allowed light through, encouraging light-demanding species to establish (e.g. primrose and foxglove). Windborne seeds can be sucked along by trains, allowing the establishment of plants such as Oxford ragwort. Because the track is fenced off, a lack of human interference encourages wildlife such as badgers and urban foxes, and bramble-filled areas provide nesting sites for a variety of birds.

Roads act in a similar way, providing homes on verges and embankments for kestrels and scavenging birds. The nitrogen-rich exhaust fumes boost the growth of some wild flowers and these, in turn, increase the presence of insects and animals further up the food chain. The number of wild flowers, however, can be reduced by mowing, depending on when it is carried out. Some roadsides are managed: trees, shrubs and flowers are planted. In London streets, the London plane tree is commonly planted as it is well-adapted to the urban environment.

Canals act like long ponds, providing a habitat for a variety of aquatic plants (e.g. yellow flag iris), waterfowl (e.g. moorhens, ducks, kingfishers) and water-loving insects (e.g. dragonflies, damselflies).

Introduction of new species

Many of the plant and animal species found in urban areas are recently introduced, and there are relatively few indigenous (native) species. Cities are centres for the establishment and spread of foreign species. Figure 3.17, for

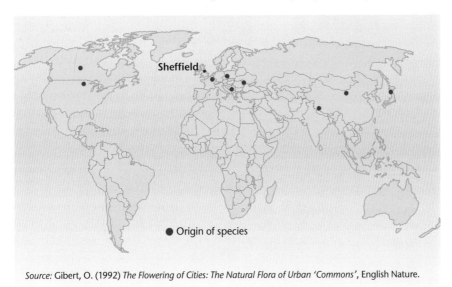

Figure 3.17 Origins of introduced species on a small urban common in Sheffield

Source: Gibert, O. (1992) *The Flowering of Cities: The Natural Flora of Urban 'Commons'*, English Nature.

example, shows the results of a survey of a small urban common in Sheffield. Species that were recorded included:

➤ from **North America**: Canadian goldenrod, Michaelmas daisy
➤ from **Europe**: sycamore, laburnum, wormwood, goat's-rue
➤ from **China and Japan**: buddleia, Japanese knotweed

Such species could have been introduced to the area by escapes from gardens, plants brought in by collectors or amateur gardeners, wind-blown seed or seed carried by animals and forms of transport.

Urban areas are attractive for immigrant species because of the variety of habitats, the constant creation of new habitats and the reduced level of competition.

Gardens and parks

Gardens (private and public), allotments, parks, cemeteries, playing fields and school property are all areas where the vegetation is managed (Photograph 3.7). Species are introduced, many from overseas, and others are removed or controlled by mowing, weeding or the use of pesticides and herbicides. Sports fields, for example, reduce the diversity of plant species by maintaining grass pitches where once there were meadows with a variety of plants. Other reasons for management of such areas include the following:

➤ **altruistic motives** — giving a dull urban landscape more colour, developing green areas to provide amenity space and improving aesthetic value
➤ **improving the visual outlook** — hiding eyesores (screening of factories, for example) to encourage businesses or residents to move in

Photograph 3.7 Allotments are examples of urban areas where vegetation is managed by weeding and planting

- schools may produce a diverse environment for **study purposes**
- local businesses (shops and factories) may want a pleasant site to **attract customers**
- local authorities may provide the public with an **arboretum**
- groups such as birdwatchers may wish for a diverse environment to **attract new species**
- to act as **noise and pollution inhibitors**
- to **provide shade** in hot urban environments
- to **reduce soil erosion** on embankments

Changes in the rural–urban fringe

The rural–urban fringe is the countryside immediately surrounding towns and cities. It was defined in 1942 by George Wehrwein as 'the area of transition between well recognised urban land uses and the area devoted to agriculture'. The rural–urban fringe is home to a wide range of activities and residents, and is seen as an attractive location for developments including business parks, airports, theme parks and high-cost housing. Other pressures for development include the need for improved transport networks, landfill sites and sewage works. In southeast England alone 500,000 new homes are needed over the next 25 years. Although the fringe is under pressure from development, many such areas in the UK are designated green belt, with regulations that strictly control new development.

Open countryside in the rural–urban fringe is frequently degraded. Farmers face problems from fly-tipping, illegal encampments, trespass and vandalism. Secondary succession may begin on untended fields, with the growth of weeds, thorns and brambles. Despite lack of investment, land values are often high because of speculation regarding potential for future development. There is a belief that derelict, unkempt land has an advantage in gaining planning permission.

However, recent government policy is in favour of **sustainable development** of the rural–urban fringe and the recycling of derelict or degraded land, e.g. through the planting of woodland, to improve the local landscape. In addition to woodland, many urban areas have seen the creation of 'country parks' in land on their fringe. Country parks are relatively unmanaged and harbour more natural plant communities, providing potential breeding sites for bird species such as lapwing and skylark, both of which nest on the ground.

Ecological conservation areas

Conservation areas are developed for a variety of reasons, some of which are listed in the section above on gardens and parks. Other reasons include:
- encouraging wildlife back into cities
- making cheap use of an otherwise derelict area that would be more expensive to set up as a park

> ➤ reducing maintenance costs in an area
> ➤ maintaining a diverse species base and reintroducing locally extinct species

Work done in such areas includes planting of trees, planting of native species, dredging of ponds and other water bodies, and soil improvements. Groups and organisations behind such conservation include local authorities, national government, Natural England, Joint Nature Conservation Committee, conservation volunteers, Groundwork, the National Urban Forestry Unit, the National Trust, English Heritage, potential users of the site and local inhabitants.

There is a range of **attitudes** to conservation of vegetated areas in urban environments. Different groups have different priorities, and these affect their view of conservation. For example, local authorities have planning needs, and have to balance the desire to make use of derelict land against the potential cost to local taxpayers. Conservation groups want to create environments where traditional species can re-establish. Local people often want a safe environment for leisure pursuits and may, through Fields in Trust (formerly the National Playing Fields Association), wish to establish sports fields. Urban wildlife groups prefer areas that provide cover for wildlife. Issues of conservation include the eventual management plan for an area, the resolution of ownership, cost and the satisfaction of the needs of various user groups.

Case study Dulwich Upper Wood conservation area

Dulwich Upper Wood is in southeast London, close to the site of the old Crystal Palace. It is a 2-ha remnant of a much larger wooded area that once stretched some distance across south London. The park is open at all times and has a network of trails, some of which are suitable for wheelchairs.

Species in the wood

The wood developed from the abandoned gardens of old Victorian houses (now demolished) and a small core of ancient woodland. Trees include sycamore, oak, ash, yew and chestnut, and there is also a magnificent line of lime trees. As most of the ground in the wood is deeply shaded, few of the garden plants remain apart from shrubs such as rhododendron and laurel. Plants from the ancient woodland have survived, including wood anemone, lords and ladies, bluebell and yellow pimpernel.

There are over 250 different types of fungi (mushrooms and toadstools), which are best seen in autumn. These live on dead wood or leaf litter, helping to break down these materials and return nutrients to the soil.

Many mammals, such as foxes, bats, mice and hedgehogs, live in the wood and more than 40 species of birds nest here, including woodpeckers and owls. There are also butterflies, moths and a great variety of other insects.

What makes the site interesting?

Figure 3.18 and the description above give some suggestions as to why the area is so interesting to ecologists and conservationists. Reasons include:
■ conservation of both abandoned Victorian gardens and ancient woodland
■ a number of both preserved and re-created habitats including coppiced areas, wet areas and a pond, herb garden and foxglove area
■ the site is both managed and allowed to grow wild in different areas
■ there is a range of different habitats

■ there is plenty of wildlife on the site including mammals, more than 40 species of birds and a wide variety of insects

■ 'original' habitats have been preserved, enabling native species of plants and animals to survive

■ it is a good example of how habitats can be preserved and created and yet still allow the public access through a network of trails

■ the site has an educational value with a posted nature trail

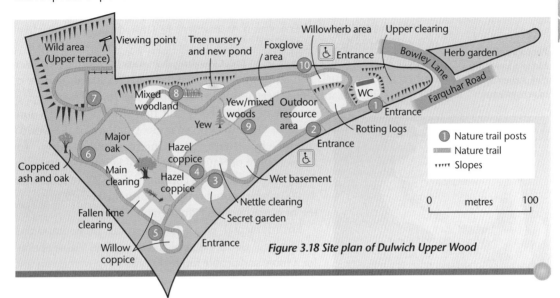

Figure 3.18 Site plan of Dulwich Upper Wood

Ecosystem issues on a global scale

Human activity, biodiversity and sustainability

As the world's population continues to grow, increasing stress is being put on resources and environmental systems such as water, air and land. Population growth and economic development, particularly over the last 200 years, have resulted in a spiralling demand for natural resources and a reduction in natural ecosystems and biodiversity.

In 1972 a group of scientists (Meadows et al.) from the Massachusetts Institute of Technology published a report on the world's population and resources, called *The Limits to Growth*. This predicted that at some time during the twenty-first century the world's carrying capacity would be reached, and that population growth and economic activity would result in disastrous consequences for the Earth. In a follow-up report published in 1992 called *Beyond the Limits* they came to the conclusion that:

society has gone into overshoot...a state of being beyond the limits without knowing it. These limits are more like speed limits than barriers at the end of the road: the rate at which nature can reduce our pollution. We are overshooting such crucial resources as food and water whilst overwhelming nature with pollutants such as those causing global warming. A sustainable future will require profound social and psychological readjustments in the developed and developing worlds.

In 2005 the Millennium Ecosystem Assessment (a United Nations initiative) stated that humans have changed ecosystems more rapidly and extensively over the past 50 years than ever before, to meet growing demands for food, fresh water, timber, fibre and fuel. The result of this change has been a substantial loss of diversity of life on Earth. It has been estimated that up to one-third of plant species are threatened globally and that climate change could result in the extinction of up to 1 million of the world's species by 2050. The International Union for Conservation of Nature and Natural Resources's 2007 *Red List of Threatened Species* concluded that 39% of more than 41,000 species tested could be threatened by extinction in the next few decades (Photograph 3.8).

*Photograph 3.8
Many species are threatened by loss of ecosystems*

Environmental issues have become more important politically, at global, national and local levels. Viable options for a more sustainable future do exist and governments and international organisations such as the United Nations and the World Wide Fund for Nature are working to educate people, to protect ecosystems and to support sustainable development. Global warming, a serious consequence of economic development, presents one of the biggest challenges to natural communities worldwide. The 1997 Kyoto conference on the environment resulted in most industrialised countries agreeing to cut their carbon dioxide emissions by 30% by 2010. This was the first step towards a global agreement to protect the environment. An agreement known as the 'Convention on Biological Diversity' was also signed at Kyoto, with objectives to conserve and sustainably use biological diversity while equitably sharing the benefits of the use of genetic resources.

In 2002, at the World Summit on Sustainable Development held in Johannesburg, key issues were sustainable management of the global resource base, poverty eradication and better healthcare. The last two were seen as ways in which global population growth could be reduced, but the first resolved to strengthen efforts to halt biodiversity loss by 2010.

The UK government was one of the first to commit to protection of the environment, producing the UK Biodiversity Action Plan (BAP) in 1994. This set out aims and activities to cover a 20-year period including:

➤ protecting the best sites for wildlife — around 10% of the UK has been designated as a Site of Special Scientific Interest (SSSI) or Area of Special Scientific Interest (ASSI)
➤ targeting action on priority species and habitats — in 2007 the UK Biodiversity Partnership published a list of 1,149 priority species and 65 habitats with a focus on their conservation over the next decade

➤ embedding consideration of biodiversity and ecosystem services in all sections of policy and decision making

➤ encouraging people to change their behaviour in relation to environmental issues

➤ ensuring that the UK plays a proactive role in the development of multilateral environmental agreements, and implementing them in the UK

Management of fragile environments

A fragile environment or ecosystem is one that lacks resilience to a change in conditions. Many ecosystems are vulnerable to change, the cause of which can include human activity, the introduction of foreign species and natural events such as flooding or drought. According to the United Nations, fragile environments include arid and semi-arid areas, mountainous areas, polar locations, freshwater and intertidal wetlands, rainforests and coral reefs. Many are regional in scale, crossing national boundaries, others are at a small scale in isolated and fragmented pockets. This section considers the success of management strategies in contrasting locations in the three tropical biomes you need to know about, all of which are considered to be fragile ecosystems.

Case study **The Central Amazon Conservation Complex (tropical rainforest)**

Over the last century the degradation and destruction of Brazil's tropical rainforests has had a severe impact on natural habitats and biodiversity. Despite this, some parts of the forest have remained intact and undisturbed and are now protected from development by law. The Central Amazon Conservation Complex is one such area, located to the north and northwest of Manaus within the watershed of the Rio Negro (a major tributary of the Amazon) (Figure 3.19). More than 6 million hectares in size, it is a corridor of land linking together three separate reserves (the combined area of which is larger than Switzerland):

■ Jaú National Park (2,272,000 ha)
■ Mamirauá Sustainable Development Reserve Focal Zone (260,000 ha)
■ Amanã Sustainable Development Reserve (2,230,000 ha)

This conservation complex is a UNESCO World Heritage site and has also been designated a World Wide Fund for Nature (WWF) priority region for conservation. It encompasses the second largest area of protected rainforest in the world. The region

Figure 3.19 Map showing location of Jaú National Park

is sparsely populated, its small population living close to the rivers in small settlements. There are no roads or railways and the only means of transport is by boat, an 18-hour journey from Manaus.

The indigenous Amerindians follow a traditional way of life, cultivating small plots of land and supplementing their crops with meat, fish and fruit collected from the forest. A small number of settlers of Portuguese descent were originally rubber tappers and today they continue to trade in forest products. There have been some incidences of hunting and poaching by outsiders for commercial gain, activities banned by the authorities. Partly because of its isolated location the Conservation Complex has few outside pressures from development. No major projects, such as hydroelectric dams, gas pipelines or mining affect the watershed of the Rio Negro. There is little tourism — perhaps a couple of thousand visitors per year. The Carabinani Falls in the Jaú National Park provide the main focus for tourists.

The Amazon Conservation Complex contains one of the most diverse wildlife communities in the world. With an average 180 tree species to every hectare, the range of fauna includes:

- nearly 200 species of mammals (including 20 species of rodents and marsupials and more than 100 species of bat alone)
- more than 500 species of birds (including parrots and macaws)
- reptiles and amphibians including coral snakes, iguanas and boa constrictors
- more than 300 species of fish and countless insects, such as ants and termites

Some of these are endangered, including varieties of anteater, armadillo, spider monkey, puma, manatee, tortoise, turtle, alligator and dolphin. Commercial hunting is banned, although the indigenous inhabitants are permitted to hunt for their own consumption.

Management

Management of the Conservation Complex has three main functions:

- to protect the land and to minimise the impact of human activity

- to research, catalogue and protect biodiversity
- to manage specific activities, such as tourism

The main aim of those working to protect the environment is to manage the natural resources sustainably, protecting fauna and flora. A zoning plan has been drawn up that defines four main types of area within the complex, with different management strategies:

- **primitive zone** — land of great natural value where there has been minimum human intervention. This has the greatest level of protection
- **extensive use zone** — where there has been a small amount of activity
- **intensive use zone** — where the environment has already been significantly altered by human activity. This is still protected but some economic activity is allowed
- **special use zone** — land on which the core services required to monitor and protect the natural rainforest are located

In the Marimauá Sustainable Development Focal Zone a significant amount of land has experienced 'intensive use'. This area has a population of more than 5,000 in some 23 settlements, mainly close to the river. A management strategy was developed by local communities together with representatives from mining and tourism industries, local government officials, members of the IBAMA (Brazilian Institute of Environment and Natural Renewable Resources) and officials from other international research organisations. The plan resulted in the following actions and outcomes:

- hunting and logging for commercial gain is prohibited
- inhabitants of the rainforest receive environmental education and improved healthcare
- increased economic production from the available natural resources is promoted to ensure a sustainable future for those living in the rainforest
- zoning and protection have been established and have resulted in an increase in the productivity of forest and aquatic resources

Case study

Serengeti National Park and Ngorongoro Conservation Area, Tanzania (savanna grasslands)

Photograph 3.9 Serengeti is home to endangered species

The Serengeti National Park and the Ngorongoro Conservation Area together form a UNESCO Biosphere Reserve and are also designated World Heritage sites. Located in the north of the country, close to the border with Kenya, the parkland occupies an area of 2,305,100 ha and consists of immense open plains and volcanic uplands (Figure 3.20). The Serengeti and Ngorongoro are known for their herds of wildebeest (estimated 1.3 million), Thomson's gazelle (400,000) and plains zebra (200,000), all of which follow a seasonal migration pattern, pursued by their natural predators such as lions, cheetah and leopard. The area is home to other endangered species such as the African elephant (perhaps only 2,000 remaining, Photograph 3.9), rhinoceros, hippopotamus and giraffe. More than 500 bird species, including 34 raptors, 6 vultures, ostrich, stork and flamingo, inhabit the plains and waterways.

The Serengeti ecosystem is one of the oldest on Earth. It is populated by the Masai Mara, nomadic herdsmen who have lived in harmony with their natural environment for thousands of years. This sustainable, extensive system of land management

Figure 3.20 Serengeti National Park and Ngorongoro Conservation Area, Tanzania

requires large areas for the grazing of cattle, goats and sheep. However, the Masai Mara's cultural code forbids the eating of wild animals and so biodiversity is protected.

History

In the early twentieth century Tanzania was under British rule. During this colonial period wild game was hunted for fur and ivory. The Serengeti plains were not settled extensively by Europeans because the tsetse fly and a relatively low and seasonal rainfall deterred commercial cattle ranching and the cultivation of crops. The first game reserve was established in 1921 to preserve lions, which until then had been viewed as vermin by the Europeans. The Serengeti National Park was created some 30 years later. Controversial legislation was passed which resulted in the Masai Mara losing their right to live and graze their cattle in the Serengeti. To compensate for this loss, the Ngorongoro Conservation Area was set up in 1959. Its aim was to promote the interests of both the Masai Mara and the wildlife. Today some 52,000 Masai Mara live in the Conservation Area under strict regulations. They are forbidden to cultivate the land or to build permanent settlements, but must live in traditional seasonally built homes called *bomas*. The only people allowed to live in the Serengeti National Park are those employed as rangers or other park workers or by the tourist industry.

Since independence the Serengeti National Park and the Ngorongoro Conservation Area have been managed by the Tanzanian government. In the late 1960s and early 1970s the Serengeti National Park began to decline as economic recession meant there was a lack of finance for conservation projects. Wardens and park rangers were often not paid and were ill-equipped to protect wildlife. The elephant and rhinoceros populations were depleted by poachers during this period and the outlook was bleak. During the 1980s the economic situation improved and tourism began to boom, leading to a rise in the park's income. This allowed the park authorities to rebuild the infrastructure and to re-establish anti-poaching units. Tourism is an impor-

tant source of revenue in the park and in recent years there have been around 90,000 visitors a year. Although tourism is managed sustainably, it is estimated that some 200,000 animals are still illegally killed by poachers every year, resulting in declining numbers of warthog, giraffe, eland, topi, impala and buffalo.

Management

Recently, the approach to management of local communities has changed from one of 'exclusion' to one of 'inclusion'. Buffer zones, called Community Wildlife Management Areas, have been put in place around the Serengeti National Park. Local people are encouraged, and have legal rights, to make decisions regarding the management of wildlife in these areas. It is hoped that this will help to curb illegal poaching.

Nomadic pastoralists still inhabit land on the fringes of the protected areas but their traditional way of life is threatened as grazing land becomes increasingly scarce. Population pressure in a country with a birth rate of 36 per 1,000, a 2% annual population growth and where 36% of the population live below the poverty line has resulted in ever-increasing pressure on existing resources. The development of irrigation systems has enabled commercial agriculture to encroach into marginal areas and, in recent years, transnational corporations have offered incentives to village communities to grow crops for biofuels. Sedentary farming threatens traditional migration routes of both wildlife and nomadic pastoralists. A new threat to the natural grasslands is the invasion of the non-native Mexican prickly poppy, which rapidly takes over on overgrazed land, crowding out native species that are needed to sustain existing patterns of wildlife.

In spite of the pressure, Tanzania has committed itself to protecting more than 42,000 km² of land. This is approximately one-third of its territory. In the UK only about a tenth of the land is protected. The main aim is to preserve the country's rich natural heritage and to provide secure breeding grounds for its flora and fauna, safe from the conflicting interests of a growing human population.

Case study: The Sundarbans Reserved Forest, Bangladesh (tropical monsoon forest)

The Sundarbans mangrove forests and swamps lie within the delta of the Ganges, Brahmaputra and Meghna rivers in the Bay of Bengal, (40% in India and 60% in Bangladesh) (Figure 3.21). At the beginning of the twenty-first century the area under mangrove forest and swamp was approximately 10,000 km², roughly half the size it was 200 years ago. Population pressure in Bangladesh is intense. Today 1,000 people inhabit every square kilometre, compared with 200 people in 1901. Large areas of forest have been cleared to provide more space for agriculture and settlement.

Threats

A number of risks threaten the Sundarbans:

■ **Climate change**. Sea levels are rising at 3 mm year⁻¹. This will cause flooding of low-lying delta land, the retreat of shorelines, salinisation of soils and changes to the water table.

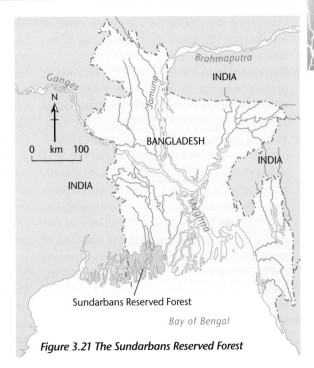

Figure 3.21 The Sundarbans Reserved Forest

Photograph 3.10 Deer in mangrove forest in the Sundarbans

Images & Stories/Alamy

- **Abstraction of water** from rivers upstream for irrigation during the dry season. The Farraka Barrage was constructed on the Ganges River in India in 1974. Its effect was a 40% reduction in flow during the dry season at the river's delta in Bangladesh. This led to increased salinity of the land and water.
- **Deforestation** in the Himalayas has resulted in greater volumes of silt being carried and deposited by the rivers as they reach the delta, altering the balance of the ecosystem.
- Some **3 million people** live in small villages around the edges of the Sundarbans. The land and waterways within the area provide a livelihood for up to 500,000 fishermen, woodcutters and gatherers of honey, golpatta leaves and grass.
- **Fishing camps** are a major disturbance in the area, with some illegal hunting and trapping of species such as turtles. The nutrient-rich waters of the Sundarbans provide a rich harvest of shellfish, such as shrimp and prawn. Crustaceans form the largest proportion of the biomass.
- **Water pollution**. Industries in and around the ports of Khulna and Mongla have particularly affected aquatic wildlife in recent years.
- **Natural disasters**. In November 2007 a cyclone killed 3,000 people. Cyclone Sidr caused damage to 40% of the reserved forest. Foliage was stripped from branches and most of the larger trees were uprooted. The Forest Department's entire operational capacity was lost when all field stations, boats and equipment were destroyed. Experts estimated that, without outside help, it might take 15 years for this part of the Sundarbans to recover.

Flora and fauna

The Sundarbans consists of a vast network of rivers, mudflats and islands, called chars, vegetated by mangroves. Mangroves are salt-tolerant trees and are restricted to the intertidal zone along the coast, extending inland along tidal stretches of river. They act as natural buffers against storm surges and protect the land from tropical cyclones which occur during the summer monsoon season.

Endangered predators in this eco-region include the Royal Bengal tiger (estimated numbers around 350), the estuarine crocodile and the Indian python. Spotted deer and wild boar are the main prey of the tiger, which also has a reputation in the region as a 'man eater'. This wetland is home to hundreds of species of birds — one of its greatest attractions. These include nine species of kingfisher, eagles, herons, egrets, storks and numerous other waders. Mudskippers (fish that can climb out of the water) occur in large numbers, and turtles and the Gangetic freshwater dolphin are also found here. In recent decades species such as the Javan rhinoceros, water buffalo, swamp deer and gaur have become locally extinct and many other animals, including the Bengal tiger and varieties of turtle, are at alarmingly low numbers.

Management

The Sundarbans was declared a UNESCO World Heritage site in 1997 and a Biosphere Reserve in 2001. Its protection is considered to be of international importance. There are seven conservation areas, including three wildlife sanctuaries. In the Bangladesh-controlled area of the Sundarbans, they are managed locally by the Forest Department and make up some 15% of the eco-region. Under the wildlife act of 1974 it is illegal to cultivate the land within the conservation areas or to introduce domestic animals, hunt, damage or set fire to the vegetation.

In reality there are not enough staff or structures in place to enforce the law. The threats to the area require more cross-border cooperation with India, as well as financial support from official sources of aid and non-governmental organisations. Management plans drawn up by outside agencies stress the need for a participative approach. Plans must include a high degree of local community involvement to allow sustainable use of the forest. Schemes to generate income, such as aquaculture, the development of alternative energy sources, local crafts and animal husbandry are required.

Unit 3

Contemporary
geographical
issues

Human
options

World cities

The global pattern of urbanisation

At a global scale, rapid urbanisation has occurred over the last 50 years. Almost 50% of the world's population lives in towns and cities (Figure 4.1), and 19% lives in cities of more than 1 million people. The most urbanised continents are Europe, North America, South America and Oceania; the least urbanised are Asia and

*Photograph 4.1
Hong Kong: 40% of
Asia's population
lives in cities*

Key terms

Counter-urbanisation The movement of people from large urban areas into smaller urban areas or into rural areas, thereby leapfrogging the rural–urban fringe. It can mean daily commuting, but could also require lifestyle changes and the increased use of ICT (homeworking or teleworking).

Re-urbanisation The movement of people and economic activities back into city centres. One characteristic of re-urbanisation is the refurbishment, by more affluent people, of old housing stock in former run-down inner-city areas. This process is known as **gentrification**.

Size of urban area This varies according to the boundaries chosen. Each boundary is likely to give a different estimate of population. An urban area might comprise:
- the administrative boundary
- the contiguous built-up area (including both the inner and outer suburbs)
- the contiguous built-up area and the physically separate suburbs

- the contiguous built-up area and the commuter hinterland

Suburbanisation The movement of people from living in the inner parts of a city to living on the outer edges. It has been facilitated by the development of transport networks and the increase in ownership of private cars. These have allowed people to commute to work.

Urban growth An increase in the number of urban dwellers. Classifications of urban dwellers depend on the census definitions of urban areas, which vary from country to country. They usually include one or more of the following criteria: population size, population density, average distance between buildings within a settlement, legal and/or administrative boundaries.

Urbanisation An increase in the proportion of a country's population that lives in towns and cities. The two main causes of urbanisation are natural population growth and migration into urban areas from rural areas.

Africa. However, in terms of urban growth, the number of urban dwellers is by far the largest in Asia, with 1.4 billion people living in towns and cities, which is 40% of the population.

Urbanisation is increasing most rapidly in Africa and Asia. This trend is expected to continue, so that by 2025 almost half the population of these continents will live in urban areas and 80% of urban dwellers will live in developing countries.

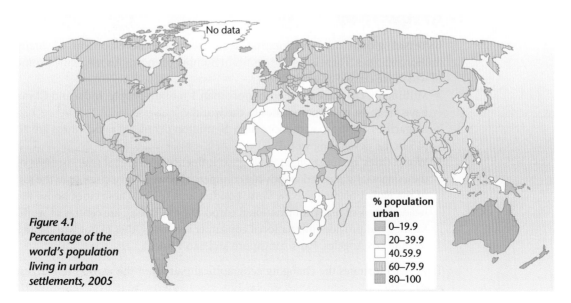

Figure 4.1
Percentage of the world's population living in urban settlements, 2005

% population urban
- 0–19.9
- 20–39.9
- 40.59.9
- 60–79.9
- 80–100

No data

- Africa
- Asia
- South America
- North America
- Europe
- Oceania

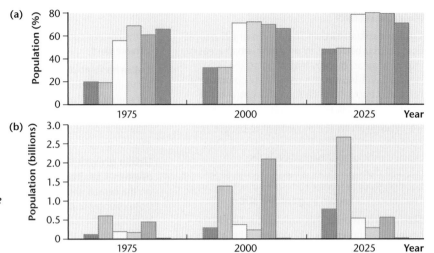

Figure 4.2
Predicted pattern
of urbanisation,
1975–2025, by
(a) per cent and
(b) number of people

However, a consequence of the rapid economic development taking place in parts of China, India and southeast Asia is that the level of urbanisation will increase very rapidly here. Rates of economic development and rates of urbanisation are rising simultaneously in these countries.

In Europe, Oceania and North America, the more economically developed areas of the world, urbanisation levels peaked in the 1970s and have fallen steadily since then.

The graphs in Figure 4.2 illustrate the complexity of this topic. The predicted pattern of urbanisation based on percentages appears to vary little between 2000 and 2025. However, the pattern based on actual numbers of people is very different.

The growth of millionaire cities and megacities

Increased global urbanisation has resulted in the development of many millionaire cities. There is also a significant number of enormous megacities, some of which are classed as world cities.

➤ **Millionaire cities** are those with more than 1 million people. India and China have the most millionaire cities in the world.

➤ **Megacities** are those with more than 10 million people, of which there are 20 (15 in the developing world).

➤ **World cities** are those which have great influence on a global scale, because of their financial status and worldwide commercial power. Three cities sit at the top of the global hierarchy: New York, London and Tokyo. These cities house the headquarters of many transnational corporations (TNCs), are centres of world finance and provide international consumer services. Other major world cities include Los Angeles, Paris, Singapore and São Paulo.

Table 4.1 illustrates the changing geographical pattern of the world's ten largest cities.

Rank	1960	Population (millions)	2008	Population (millions)
1	New York	14.2	Tokyo–Yokohama	34.4
2	London	10.7	New York	20.3
3	Tokyo	10.7	Seoul–Incheon	20.1
4	Shanghai	10.7	Jakarta	19.9
5	Beijing	7.3	Mumbai	19.4
6	Paris	7.2	São Paulo	19.1
7	Buenos Aires	6.9	Mexico City	18.4
8	Los Angeles	6.6	Delhi	17.6
9	Moscow	6.0	Osaka–Kobe–Kyoto	17.2
10	Chicago	6.0	Manila	17.0

Table 4.1 The world's ten largest cities, 1960 and 2008

Contemporary urbanisation processes

Urbanisation

The causes of urban growth

Natural population growth

Urban areas tend to have relatively low age profiles. Young adults (15–40 years), have traditionally migrated from rural areas. They are in their fertile years — the years during which people have children — and so the rates of natural increase are higher in cities than in the surrounding rural areas.

Rural–urban migration

The reasons for rural–urban migration are often divided into 'push' and 'pull' factors. **Push factors** cause people to move away from rural areas, whereas **pull factors** attract them to urban areas. In countries with lower levels of economic development push factors tend to be more important than pull factors.

Push factors are largely due to poverty caused by:
➤ population growth, which means the same area of land has to support increasing numbers of people, causing over-farming, soil erosion and low yields
➤ agricultural problems, including desertification because of low rainfall, systems of inheritance that cause land to be subdivided into small plots, systems of tenure and debt on loans taken out to support agricultural change
➤ high levels of local diseases and inadequate medical provision

> changes introduced to try to pay off the interest on national debts. Land previously used to grow food for local people is now used to produce cash crops for sale to more developed countries
> natural disasters such as floods (Mozambique), tropical storms (Bangladesh) and earthquakes (Gujarat, India) — people flee rural areas and do not return
> wars and civil strife cause people to flee their land

Pull factors include the prospect of:
> employment in factories and service industries (e.g. hotels), which is better paid than work in rural areas
> earning money from the informal sector, e.g. selling goods on the street, providing transport (taxi/rickshaw driver), prostitution
> better quality social provisions, from basic needs such as education and healthcare to entertainment and tourism
> a perceived better quality of life in the city, fed by images in the media

 Case study | **Urbanisation in São Paulo, Brazil**

São Paulo is the largest city in the southern hemisphere. In 2008, the population of the metropolitan area was 19 million. Its population density is 21,000 persons km^{-2}, which is twice that of Paris and three times that of Los Angeles. The city continues to grow in size — between 1991 and 2001 the population increased by 16% — but the rate of increase is slowing. There is reduced rural–urban migration and the rate of natural increase has slowed. In addition the population of the central areas is decreasing and that of the peripheral areas is increasing. Such decentralisation mirrors that of cities in the wealthier parts of the world.

São Paulo initially grew as a centre of agriculture, exporting coffee and cotton. It is now a major industrial centre with manufacturing and service industries. An attractive feature of the city is its temperate climate due to its elevated position compared with the tropical coastal lowlands (Figure 4.3).

The environment

It has been estimated that 25% of all vehicles in Brazil circulate in São Paulo. In recent years, much has been done to improve air quality and reduce the levels of sulphur dioxide and lead. However, levels of other pollutants such as ozone, carbon monoxide and suspended particulates are still of concern.

The city authorities spend $1 million a day on rubbish collection. Disposing of this waste is a problem. In 2001, the city had only two landfill sites. Two huge waste incinerators, each burning 7,500 tonnes a day, came into operation during that year.

Figure 4.3 Map showing the location of São Paulo

Variations in the quality of life

Although São Paulo is prosperous compared with the country as a whole, the city has the highest unemployment rate in the country and there is a huge divide between rich and poor (Photograph 4.2). In 2002, the city authorities conducted a survey of living standards. The richest district, Moema, had a human development index (HDI) equivalent to the Portuguese national average; the poorest district, Marsilac, had an HDI lower than that of Sierra Leone (the world's poorest country according to the UN).

This has a big social impact. In 1999, São Paulo recorded 11,500 homicides, compared with 670 in New York. The affluent elite use helicopters to hop from rooftop to rooftop and escape the squalor and danger of the streets. São Paulo has 240 helipads compared with ten in New York.

Three different housing types dominate:

- **condominiums** — luxury housing blocks for wealthy people both within the city and on the periphery, protected by high walls and security gates
- **corticos** — inner-city dilapidated rental accommodation in subdivided nineteenth-century tenement buildings. Many consist of blocks of one-room dwellings in which up to four people live
- **favelas** — or informal settlements made up of small, poorly built dwellings

Photograph 4.2 Sao Paulo: favelas in the foreground and modern apartments behind

It is estimated that substandard housing occupies 70% of the area of São Paulo and that up to 60% of the population growth of recent years has been absorbed by the favelas. They occupy the poorest, most peripheral and hazardous areas — floodplains and steep hill slopes. Heliopolis is São Paulo's largest area of favelas. Here, 100,000 people live in a mix of absolute and semi-poverty.

Basic favelas are densely packed informal settlements made of wood, corrugated iron and other makeshift materials. More established favelas are made from concrete blocks, with tiles replacing the corrugated roofing material. Services are poor, with little running water, mains drainage or rubbish collection. The streets are frequently open sewers that flood when it rains. Electrical power is limited, and there is a lack of schools, teachers, hospitals and healthcare professionals. Drinking water is often polluted, causing disease (typhoid, cholera and dysentery). Many people who live in the favelas are unemployed or underemployed, finding work in the informal sector of the economy.

Housing improvement schemes

Some large-scale improvement in favelas has occurred as a result of:

■ residents expecting to remain where they are
■ changes in public policies during the past 20 years, from slum removal to slum upgrading

A number of attempts have been made by the government to tackle the housing problem by building new housing, upgrading slums or funding self-help projects. During the early 1990s, the city supplied funding directly to community groups, which allowed families to either build their own or to renovate existing housing. The authorities also provided serviced plots for building with mains water, electricity, sewerage and roads — such **site and service schemes** were a low-cost solution to the housing problem. However, despite a great deal of publicity, the annual house building total only increased to 8,000 during this period.

Since 2000 greater investment in such projects has been made. In the Santo André area of the city an Integrated Programme of Social Inclusion to alleviate poverty has included provision of micro-credit facilities for small-scale entrepreneurs, community health-care workers and literacy programmes.

Cooperation between the authorities and the local community is essential to provide the best services.

Elsewhere in the world

Most newcomers to a city in the less developed world would like to rent a proper house. However, even if they could afford to rent, there are usually not enough houses available. Instead:

➤ Many new arrivals move in with friends or relatives.
➤ Some people sleep on the streets. In some cities, thousands of people live rough. Most railway stations in India have a well-established resident population. People know who 'owns' each patch of pavement and the street people protect each other from outsiders. Street dwellers can include families in which three generations live together. There are also gangs of orphaned or abandoned children.
➤ Many people squat. They build a makeshift house on unused land, in an area of similar houses. This creates a squatter settlement or shanty town.

People squat on three main types of land:

➤ land that is not suitable for building because it is too steep, too marshy or too polluted
➤ land close to the city centre that has not been built on because no-one knows who owns it, or the owner has left it empty, hoping it will increase in value
➤ land on the edge of the city that was once farmland but was abandoned as the city spread

It is not uncommon for local authorities to help people in such settlements by providing them with water and electricity, while leaving them to do most of the building work. Around the world, squatter settlements (shanty towns) have a variety of local names:

➤ in Spanish-speaking Latin American cities — barrios
➤ in Portuguese-speaking Brazil — favelas
➤ in Mumbai, India — zopadpattis
➤ in Calcutta, India — bustees

Slums of despair	Slums of hope
High unemployment and underemployment	Some formal employment and much informal employment
Weak family and friendship structures	Strong family and friendship structures
Poorly built housing and little on-going improvement	Housing improvement through individual and group action
Poor water supply and sewerage	Water supply being improved with help from authorities; sewage usually stored in septic tanks and removed by tanker
Easy spread of infections and disease	Infections and disease under control
Illegal hook-ups to the electricity mains, or no supply at all	Illegal hook-ups to the electricity mains, which are gradually being replaced by legal connections
Widespread crime, prostitution, drug-dealing and other social problems due to poverty and lack of police control	Crime, prostitution and drug dealing not widespread because of strong social structures and cooperation between the community and the police
Settlement appears untidy and poorly organised; much litter, rubbish and piles of junk around houses	Settlement appears tidy and fairly well organised; piles of junk around houses are the raw materials of earning a living (recycling activities); much evidence of informal economy
City authorities opposed to settlement; threats to bulldoze houses make squatters insecure and cause the settlement to deteriorate	Cooperation between the settlement and the authorities, which do their best to provide an infrastructure of roads, bus services, education, healthcare, electricity and water

Slums of hope or slums of despair?

Squatter settlements are often seen as places of deprivation — slums of despair. It is true that in many cases the physical, economic and social conditions are very poor. However, it is all a matter of perception. Other people see them as 'slums of hope' (Table 4.2). In reality, most settlements have some features of both hope and despair.

Table 4.2 Slums of hope or slums of despair?

Urban regeneration in the developing world

City authorities in these areas are aware of the problems of large squatter settlements, but rarely have enough resources to tackle them.

➤ In some cities, such as Lagos in Nigeria and Caracas in Venezuela, the authorities have built **high-rise apartment blocks** to re-house people. However, in most places there is not enough money available to do this.

➤ In some countries, the authorities have helped migrants to the city by allowing them to build houses in **site and service schemes**. An area of land that is not too far from workplaces in the city is divided into individual plots by the authorities. Roads, water and sanitation may be provided. Newcomers can rent a plot of land and build their own house, following certain guidelines. When they have more money, they can improve their house.

➤ Once people have built a house, no matter how basic it is, they are likely to improve it — providing they are confident they will not be evicted from the land. If people are to improve their homes they must be given legal ownership of the land. **Self-help schemes** are important in almost all big cities. People improve

Photograph 4.3
A woman walking
to her shack
through polluted
water in a Manila
slum that has no
sewage system,
Philippines

their houses slowly, for example by replacing mud walls with bricks or breeze blocks, fitting proper windows and doors, and adding rooms and upper floors. City authorities usually provide water from standpipes in the street and, later, help with sanitation and waste collection. Commercial bus operators will start services to the settlement and the local community may build health centres. In this way, people work together to improve the area. Over time it changes from a poor, illegal settlement to a legal, medium-quality housing area.

The brown agenda

Cities in the less developed world are affected by the **brown agenda**, a mix of social and environmental problems brought about by rapid growth and industrialisation associated with economic development. It has two components:

➤ traditional issues associated with the limited availability of good-quality land, shelter and services such as clean water
➤ problems resulting from rapid industrialisation, such as toxic or hazardous waste, water, air and noise pollution, and industrial accidents owing to poor standards of health and safety

In all cases it is the low-income groups in the cities that suffer most.

In many of these cities, water is contaminated by sewage and untreated industrial waste (Photograph 4.3). City managers have to tackle such pollution issues with insufficient resources. However, environmental problems are not always solved by technology and capital. The empowerment of low-income communities to bring about their own improvements is equally important.

International bodies (such as the UN) have proposed city-specific solutions to the brown agenda. A suggested management framework to enable these solutions to be carried out is as follows:

➤ A basic urban environmental profile should be undertaken. There should be public consultation over what the main issues are, and a political commitment to improve.

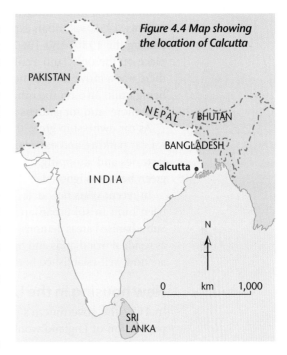

> The risks, impacts and purposes of improvement strategies should be assessed. A cost–benefit analysis of all the available options should be undertaken.
> Action plans should be put into place. Specific task forces aimed at specific districts and/or citywide problems should be created.
> Local support groups should be established, with training for community leaders. Further consultation and involvement at a local level are priorities.

You could assess the extent to which the above principles are being followed in the case study of Calcutta.

Case study Calcutta, India

Calcutta lies in the Ganges delta, at the centre of an area that has a dense, overcrowded rural population (Figure 4.4). The soils of the delta are fertile, but the area suffers many natural disasters. It is often flooded by monsoon rains or by cyclones. In the late twentieth century, the area suffered from wars and civil conflicts. Each new war or flood brings refugees flocking to Calcutta.

Issues

The land is low-lying, so many of the squatter settlements (bustees) flood easily. The floods not only destroy homes, they also bring disease in the polluted floodwater. Until recently, Calcutta had a reputation for some of the worst slums in the world. It was here that Mother Teresa cared for thousands of street people.

Solutions

The Calcutta Metropolitan Development Authority (CMDA) has tried to improve the infrastructure by:
■ reinforcing the banks of the River Hooghly and attempting to stop people from squatting on the lowest-lying land near the river
■ improving sewage disposal — in the 1960s there were about 1,000 sewage-related deaths a year from cholera, but in recent years there have been very few
■ improving the water supply — there is now at least one tap for every 25 bustee houses

Figure 4.4 Map showing the location of Calcutta

PAKISTAN

NEPAL BHUTAN

BANGLADESH

Calcutta

INDIA

N

0   km   1,000

SRI LANKA

■ replacing mud tracks between the shacks with concrete roads
■ installing street lighting in many bustees, to improve safety and to give some light to people with no electricity in their homes
■ widening roads and improving public transport from the bustees into the city centre

The CMDA does not work on the bustee houses. The occupiers must improve their homes themselves

Suburbanisation

Characteristics, causes and effects

Suburbanisation has resulted in the outward growth of urban development that has engulfed surrounding villages and rural areas. During the mid to late twentieth century, this was facilitated by the growth of public transport systems and the increased use of the private car. The presence of railway lines and arterial roads enabled wealthier commuters to live some distance away from their places of work.

The towns and cities of the UK demonstrate the effects of past suburbanisation. In the 1930s there were few planning controls and urban growth took place alongside main roads — this was known as ribbon development. By the 1940s this growth, and growth between the 'ribbons', became a cause for concern. This led to the creation of **green belts** — areas of open space and low-density land use around towns where further development was strictly controlled.

Since 1950, suburban expansion has increased and has been better planned. During the 1950s and 1960s large-scale construction of council housing took place on the only land available, which was the suburban fringe. In the 1970s, there was a move towards home ownership, which led to private housing estates being built, also on the urban fringe. Building in these areas allowed people to have more land for gardens and more public open space.

As car ownership grew, the edge of town, where there is more land available for car parking and expansion, became the favoured location for new offices, factories and shopping outlets. In a number of cases, the 'strict control' of the green belts was ignored.

In recent years new detached and semi-detached houses and bungalows have been built in suburban areas, along with local shopping centres and schools. Suburbanised areas demonstrate other key elements of the rural–urban fringe, such as residual woodlands and parks, cemeteries, golf courses and playing fields. Many are now well-established housing areas, highly sought after in the property market.

New housing in the UK

In 1997 the government's population projections suggested that by 2021 the population of England would rise by 7% but the number of households would rise by 18%. There are two main reasons why there is likely to be a faster growth in households than in population:

➤ the increase in the adult population, which accounts for 77% of the growth in demand for households. This is due to the change in the age structure of the population with a fall in the proportion of younger age groups and a rise in the proportion of those in older age groups

➤ changes in the way in which people choose to live, in particular, more divorces and later marriages. 71% of new households will be single people

The following solutions have been suggested:

➤ **Increasing the number of people living in homes that already exist** — using empty or abandoned private and council houses, and providing tax incentives to encourage people to take in lodgers or to share their homes.

➤ **Building new houses on brownfield sites (in towns and cities)** — this includes developers buying up large houses and their gardens in established suburban areas, demolishing them and building several new houses on the same land.

➤ **Allowing building in rural areas and small towns on land that has not been 'previously developed'** — greenfield sites are cheaper to develop than brownfield sites and there is still plenty of rural land available.

Most new houses will be built in rural areas and small towns in the south and southeast of England, where demand is greatest. The main proposed areas of development are the Thames Gateway, Ashford in Kent, Milton Keynes, the Solent Gateway and the Cambridge to Stansted M11 corridor.

The main features of brownfield and greenfield sites are summarised in Table 4.3.

Table 4.3 Brownfield and greenfield sites compared

Brownfield sites	Greenfield sites
Derelict sites in urban areas	New sites, usually on agricultural land in green belts around urban areas
The land is available, but can be costly to reclaim if it has been polluted by industrial use; this information may not be readily available	Land is not available unless planning permission has been obtained; there is usually a public enquiry and a delay of several years, adding to the costs
Housing is likely to be built at a high density to reflect the cost of the land; there is less demand for such housing as it is in less fashionable areas	Housing will be relatively low density; there is great demand for such housing as it is in fashionable areas
Infrastructure is normally present, though existing facilities can become overloaded	Infrastructure costs are high as new sewerage, water, gas and electricity supplies have to be considered; new schools and health facilities may be needed too
Sites tend to be small patches of land	Sites tend to be larger
The environment is generally improved	The environment is changed from rural to urban use

Counter-urbanisation

Characteristics, causes and effects

Counter-urbanisation is the migration of people from major urban areas to smaller urban settlements and rural areas. Counter-urbanisation does not lead to suburban growth, but to growth in rural areas beyond the main city. The difference between rural and urban areas is reduced as a consequence of this movement.

A number of factors have caused the growth of counter-urbanisation. One is that people want to escape from the air pollution, dirt and crime of the urban environment. They aspire to what they see as the pleasant, quiet and clean environment of the countryside, where land and house prices are cheaper. Car ownership and greater affluence allow people to commute to work from such areas. Indeed, many employers have also moved out of cities. Between 1981 and 1996, rural areas gained more than 1 million jobs. Improvements in technology such as the internet have allowed more freedom of location. Someone working from a home computer can access the same global system as a person in an office block in the centre of a city.

At the same time there has been a rising demand for second homes and earlier retirement. The former is a direct consequence of rising levels of affluence. Alongside this is the need for rural areas to attract income. Agriculture is facing economic difficulties and one straightforward way for farmers to raise money is to sell unwanted land and buildings.

Counter-urbanisation affects the layout of rural settlements. Modern housing estates are built on the edges of small settlements, and small industrial units on the main roads leading into the settlement. Former open areas are built on, old properties and some agricultural buildings are converted and modernised. As with gentrified areas in inner cities (discussed later in this chapter), there is tension between the newcomers and the locals.

One of the main areas of conflict is that, despite the influx of new people, local services often close down. Bus services to many rural communities have disappeared, schools and post offices have closed, and churches have closed as parishes are amalgamated into larger units. The main reason for these changes is that the newcomers have the wealth and the mobility to continue to use the urban services some distance away.

The evidence for counter-urbanisation in an area includes:
➤ an increase in the use of a commuter railway station in the area, including car parking for commuters
➤ increased value of houses in the area

Photograph 4.4
New housing in
Cordrona village,
near Peebles, UK

> the construction of more executive housing in the area, often on newly designated building land, following the demolition of old properties
> conversions of former farm buildings to exclusive residences

Counter-urbanisation is one of a number of processes contributing to social and demographic change in rural settlements, sometimes referred to as the **rural turnaround**. The main changes include:
> the out-migration of young village-born adults seeking education and employment opportunities elsewhere
> the decline of the elderly village-born population, through deaths
> the in-migration of young to middle-aged married couples or families with young children
> the in-migration of younger, more affluent people, which results in increased house prices

These changes do not take place uniformly within all rural settlements. There are considerable variations between and within parishes. The ones with the most change are **key settlements** that have a range of basic services and good access to commuter routes. Such settlements are called **suburbanised villages**.

Land-use patterns of suburbanised villages

Like suburban areas in towns and cities, suburbanised villages have experienced much change in recent years. The influx of new population has been reflected in changes to the land-use structure of the area. These changes include new detached and semi-detached houses and bungalows, both on individual plots and on estates of varying sizes, and the conversion of farm buildings (Photograph 4.4). The model in Figure 4.5 summarises the types of change that have occurred in suburbanised villages. Compare it with the main features of a similar village you have studied.

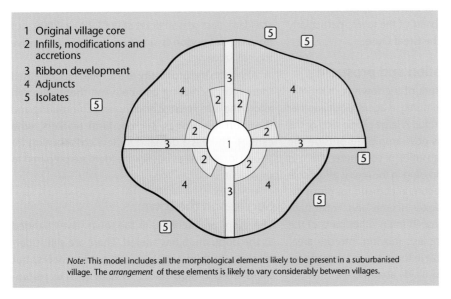

Figure 4.5 A model of a suburbanised village

1 Original village core
2 Infills, modifications and accretions
3 Ribbon development
4 Adjuncts
5 Isolates

Note: This model includes all the morphological elements likely to be present in a suburbanised village. The *arrangement* of these elements is likely to vary considerably between villages.

The small town of St Ives, in Cambridgeshire, is about 100 km north of London. It lies on the A1123, 8 km east of Huntingdon and 25 km northwest of Cambridge, just off the A14 trunk road (Figure 4.6). The town is close to both the A1 trunk road and the main east coast railway line. Regular trains to London make the area accessible.

St Ives is a picturesque town on the Great Ouse. It has a narrow six-arched bridge with a central chapel that was built in the fifteenth century. The town has connections with Oliver Cromwell and his statue stands in the market place. There are fine Georgian and Victorian houses in the Broadway and in Bridge Street. There are also other splendid buildings, including the Corn Exchange and All Saints Church. The building styles contribute to the character of the place and add to the attraction of living there.

The surrounding rural area is mainly farmland. However, in recent years there have been many housing developments on the periphery of the town. A substantial number of exclusive apartments have also been built in the heart of the town, particularly on the south bank of the Great Ouse.

Changing population and prosperity

The population structure of the town is changing. One section of the community is ageing, but another is becoming more youthful. A large proportion of the working population is now employed outside the town. There has been an influx of commuters from in and around London. Housing in the area is affordable and there has been a boom in demand for property. People in St Ives have higher incomes and higher standards of living than those in many other parts of the UK. Retired people are also moving into the area. Their impact is noticeable in the increased demand for bungalows and small riverside apartments.

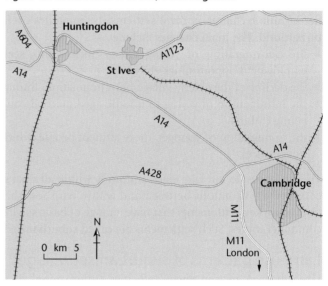

Figure 4.6 The location of St Ives, Cambridgeshire

Commuting to London increased during the 1990s. The main line was electrified and journey times were much reduced. The station at Huntingdon is about 50 minutes from Kings Cross in central London. It is estimated that 25% of St Ives' working population now commutes to London each day. These people prefer living in a rural/small town environment and travelling daily to London. An annual standard-class season ticket cost £3,920 in 2008, but housing in London is significantly more expensive than in St Ives.

Although the prosperity of the town has increased there is an increasing gap between those who can afford the rising cost of housing and commuting and those on low wages, such as farm workers, who cannot. There is a demand for low-cost housing for young local families but few builders are prepared to provide it.

Services in the town

The shops and services in the town have changed as the population has altered. There are still supermarkets, butchers, bakers and greengrocers, but there are also high-status services such as restaurants, antique dealers, designer clothes shops and knick-knack shops. A number of estate agents have offices in the town, as do branches of banks and building societies. The secondary school roll is increasing.

As in other rural areas, the bus service to St Ives is infrequent, although it is better than many others because the town lies on a route between Cambridge and Huntingdon. Bus services are available at priority times — the start and end of the school day and on market days.

Pressure to increase the housing stock has become greater, fuelled by demand from commuters. There is resistance to building more homes from the local residents, but many of these are new to the area themselves and do not want their newly chosen environment changed. If more house building takes place developers will be encouraged to make it blend in with the current urban landscape. There will need to be an acceptable density of buildings, use of appropriate construction materials, provision of open space, preservation of vistas and tasteful provision of street furniture (road signs, seating, lamp posts). Any development must make a positive contribution to the character of the area.

Case study: Eco-towns in the UK

In 2008 the government announced plans to build up to ten eco-towns by 2020. These will be small new towns of between 5,000 and 20,000 homes. The developments are intended to produce zero carbon emissions, and to provide sustainable living using the best new design criteria and architecture. A number of sites have been short-listed (Figure 4.7).

The essential requirements of these new towns are:

■ they must be new settlements, separate from existing towns but well linked to them
■ they should provide a good range of facilities — a secondary school, a medium-scale retail centre, good-quality business space and leisure facilities

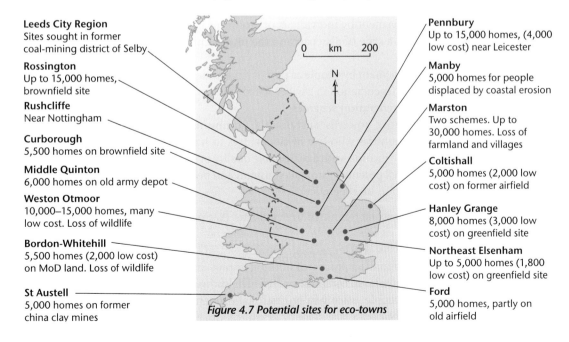

Leeds City Region
Sites sought in former coal-mining district of Selby

Rossington
Up to 15,000 homes, brownfield site

Rushcliffe
Near Nottingham

Curborough
5,500 homes on brownfield site

Middle Quinton
6,000 homes on old army depot

Weston Otmoor
10,000–15,000 homes, many low cost. Loss of wildlife

Bordon-Whitehill
5,500 homes (2,000 low cost) on MoD land. Loss of wildlife

St Austell
5,000 homes on former china clay mines

Pennbury
Up to 15,000 homes, (4,000 low cost) near Leicester

Manby
5,000 homes for people displaced by coastal erosion

Marston
Two schemes. Up to 30,000 homes. Loss of farmland and villages

Coltishall
5,000 homes (2,000 low cost) on former airfield

Hanley Grange
8,000 homes (3,000 low cost) on greenfield site

Northeast Elsenham
Up to 5,000 homes (1,800 low cost) on greenfield site

Ford
5,000 homes, partly on old airfield

Figure 4.7 Potential sites for eco-towns

- affordable housing should make up between 30% and 50% of the total through a wide range and distribution of tenures in mixed communities, with a particular emphasis on large family homes
- a management body must help develop the town and provide support and services for people and businesses moving there

Some of the proposed sites have met with opposition from local residents and councils. One of these is Weston Otmoor, southwest of Bicester in Oxfordshire. It lies west of the M40 and straddles the A34. The local council has expressed concern at the loss of green belt land, and the effects that the new town will have on rural roads and nature conservation sites (Otmoor is an important wetland). It is also concerned at the impact it will have on the regeneration of existing towns in the area such as Bicester.

A local action group — the Weston Front Action Group — has argued against the site on the grounds of loss of green belt and loss of a Site of Special Scientific Interest (SSSI), but this could be a case of 'nimby-ism' (not in my back yard). The chairman of the Oxfordshire Campaign to Protect Rural England (CPRE) argues that the minister's view that the development would be on brownfield land is flawed. He says that only a small proportion of the proposed site could be classed as brownfield — that which would come from a Ministry of Defence airfield.

The developers want to build a new settlement of the future, with a shopping centre over the A34. They also want to revitalise the public transport system, including building a new east–west rail link to Milton Keynes, and free tram and bus services around the town and into Oxford.

Re-urbanisation

Characteristics, causes and effects

Re-urbanisation is the movement of people into the city centre or inner city as part of urban regeneration.

There are three main processes:

➤ in-movement by individuals or groups of individuals into older housing that was in a state of disrepair and the improvement of that housing — **gentrification**

➤ in-movement by people as part of large-scale investment programmes aimed at urban regeneration in a wider social, economic and physical sense — **property-led regeneration schemes**

➤ the move towards **sustainable communities**, allowing individuals and communities who live in city centres to have access to a home, a job and a reliable income, with a reasonable quality of life and opportunities to maximise personal potential through education and health provision, and through participation in local democracies

The last two are examined in detail later (see pages 154 and 158).

Gentrification

Gentrification is a process of housing improvement. It is associated with a change in neighbourhood composition in which low-income groups are displaced by more affluent people, usually in professional or managerial occupations. Regeneration of inner cities can take place by gentrification, but it is different from the schemes

described on pages 154–157 in that it is carried out by individuals or groups of individuals, and not by supported bodies. Gentrification involves the rehabilitation of old houses and streets on an individual basis, but is openly encouraged by groups such as estate agents, building societies and local authorities.

One of the positive outcomes of gentrification is that the social mix of the area is changed and becomes more affluent. The purchasing power of the residents is greater, which leads to a rise in the general level of prosperity. There is an increase in the number of bars, restaurants and other higher-status services. The refurbishment that takes place in each house leads to the creation of employment in areas such as design, building work, furnishings and decoration.

There are, however, clear disadvantages of gentrification. Local people on low incomes find it increasingly difficult to purchase houses, as the price of refurbished property rises. Indeed, the size of the privately rented sector diminishes as more properties are sold off. Friction may arise between the 'newcomers' and the original residents.

Gentrification is taking place in the central parts of many towns and cities in the UK. Well-documented examples include Notting Hill and Islington in London.

Case study Gentrification in Notting Hill, London

Brief history

Notting Hill is now a bustling urban area but in the mid-eighteenth century it was a country hamlet, known for its gravel pits and roadside inns frequented by travellers. The 'tollgate', which gave the main road its name (Notting Hill Gate), appeared at this time. Later, industrialisation brought workers from the countryside, with landlords building tiny

Photograph 4.5 Portobello Road market

TopFoto

---

terraced houses to rent to them. In Victorian times, Notting Hill was a rough, working-class area and by the 1950s it was an area of slums and inner-city deprivation. In 1958, it was the scene of race riots following continuous harassment of the newly arrived Afro-Caribbean community by the 'Teddy Boys' of the British Union of Fascists. A second riot during the Notting Hill Carnival of 1976 inspired the punk anthem, *White Riot* by the Clash.

Today…

In the past 30 years gentrification of previously working-class neighbourhoods has sent property prices rocketing. Houses can cost more here than in upmarket Mayfair. Notting Hill's secluded communal gardens, sandwiched between the rows of houses and scarcely visible from the street, make it London's most desirable area for families. Movie stars, rock singers, media types and fashion designers (such as Stella McCartney) have moved into the area, which has acquired the sort of atmosphere associated with the King's Road, Chelsea in the 1960s. The area received a great deal of publicity from the movie *Notting Hill*, though gentrification was taking place long before the film was released.

The area possesses a number of fashionable places to eat and be seen, including:
- Veronica's (Hereford Road) — devotes itself to reviving Britain's culinary heritage, serving historical dishes from 2,000-year-old menus
- the Westbourne Pub — with trendy crowds and a great selection of beers
- Lazy Daisy Café (Portobello Road) — famous for its delicious puddings and cakes
- the Sausage and Mash Pub (also Portobello Road)
- the Golbourne Road area — well known for its Portuguese and Moroccan restaurants

The Portobello Road, hosting a famous street market, is also in Notting Hill (Photograph 4.5). Since 1837, people have been able to buy almost anything here. The market (known locally as 'The Lane') has antiques and bric-a-brac to the south, fruit and vegetables in the middle, and second-hand clothing and bedding to the north.

On August bank holiday, Notting Hill hosts the famous carnival. It is the largest outside Rio de Janeiro, attended by over 1 million people, and lasts for 3 days. The large Afro-Caribbean population, and others, have an all-day street party with loud music, dancing and colourful costumes.

Urban decline and regeneration

Characteristics and causes of urban decline

Urban deprivation

Inequalities occur in all urban areas — enormous contrasts in wealth can be found over relatively small distances. When you do fieldwork in an area, you can sense if a neighbourhood is improving or deteriorating. The wealthy and the poor seem to concentrate spatially — a form of social segregation. There are a number of reasons for this:

➤ **Housing** — developers, builders and planners tend to build housing on blocks of land with a particular market in mind. Wealthier groups can choose where they live, paying premium prices for houses well away from poor areas, with pleasing environments and services such as quality schools and parks. The poorer groups have no choice and have to live where they are placed in welfare housing, or where they can find a cheap place to rent.

➤ **Changing environments** — housing neighbourhoods change over time. Houses that were built for large families in Georgian and Victorian times are now too big for the average UK family. Many have been converted into multi-let apartments for private renting to people on low incomes. Conversely, former poor areas are being gentrified. The 'right to buy' legislation of the 1980s transformed many council estates, as houses were bought by their occupants and improved.

➤ **The ethnic dimension** — ethnic groups originally come to the country as new immigrants. When they first arrive they often suffer discrimination in the job market and may be either unemployed or employed in low-paid jobs. They are only able to afford to buy cheap housing (inner-city terraces) or they have to rent privately. Therefore, newly arrived migrants concentrate in poor areas in the city, often clustered into multicultural areas (see chapter 6). Such ethnic groupings tend to persist into later generations.

Measuring inequalities

It is possible to measure the quality of life in an area using primary data, such as the quality, density and condition of housing and the nature of the physical and social environment (Figure 4.8). It is also possible to use secondary data from a

Figure 4.8 Measures of quality of life

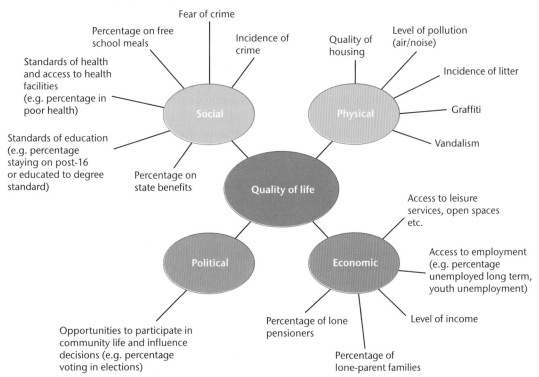

census to assess deprivation levels. This may include poverty, in terms of low income, or shown by poor health or the lack of possessions, such as cars. It is common for the poorest parts of an urban area to suffer from **multiple deprivation** (a combination of social, environmental and economic deprivation).

Urban social exclusion refers to the problems faced by residents in areas of multiple deprivation. These people are excluded from full participation in society by their social and physical circumstances. They cannot access a decent job because of poor education, or obtain decent housing because of poverty. They often suffer from poor health and from high levels of crime in an unattractive physical environment. In a city, inequality can cause lack of social cohesion and in extreme cases lead to civil unrest. Governments have to address social injustices for a variety of social, economic and political reasons.

The inner city

The characteristic features of inner-city areas are:
- high population out-migration figures
- many boarded-up shops
- many empty and derelict properties
- the closing of schools, particularly primary schools, and low levels of education
- high levels of unemployment
- high incidence of crime, vandalism and graffiti
- low levels of participation in local democracy

The causes of inner-city decline

More than 4 million people live in the inner cities of the UK. These areas are typified by economic decline, personal poverty, social problems and environ-mental decay (Figure 4.9).

Economic decline

Since the 1950s, there has been a widespread movement of employment away from the large conurbations to smaller urban areas and to rural areas. This fall in employment has been largely in traditional manufacturing industries, formerly based on coal, steam power and railways. These industries were located in today's inner-city areas. Between 1960 and 1981, more than 1.6 million manufacturing jobs were lost in the major urban areas. This accounted for 75% of job losses nationally.

This decline in manufacturing was accompanied by the growth of service industries. However, this growth did not compensate for the massive job losses in manufacturing. In addition, service industries did not require the same skills as manufacturing industries. In the late 1980s and early 1990s jobs in services in inner-city areas also fell, by 7% compared with a national increase in such jobs of 11%.

Deindustrialisation in the inner cities was accompanied by the expansion of employment in rural areas and small towns. This shift can be partly explained by:
- The changing levels of technology and space requirements of manufacturing industry, which resulted in a shortage of suitable land and premises in inner cities. Investment moved from urban to rural locations.

Figure 4.9 The web of inner-city decline, despair and deprivation

Decline

Population loss

Declining industries

Lack of capital investment

Lack of social investment

Poor infrastructure for industrial expansion

Ageing population

Despair

Housing stress

Lack of skills

Illness

Loss of jobs

Social unrest

Overcrowding

Riots

Unemployment

Rising crime rates

Slums

Run-down terraced housing

Inner city

Low public participation

Deprivation

Poorly built towerblocks

Poverty

Vandalism

Political extremism

Population loss

Lack of adequate open space

High number of single parents

High concentration of ethnic groups

Pollution

Traffic congestion

Dereliction

Inadequate public services

Difficult schools

Poor recreational and entertainment facilities

High proportion of low social classes

➤ Globalisation of production, which led to declining profits and increased competition. To remain competitive, companies were forced to acquire other companies, introduce new technology, and move to new locations in the UK and overseas.

Inner cities contained many of the types of workplace most likely to be closed — old plants with the oldest production techniques, lowest productivity and most unionised workforces.

Unemployment thus became a major problem for the inner-city areas of the former industrial regions of Liverpool, Sheffield, Glasgow, Newcastle-upon-Tyne and Birmingham. Unemployment was particularly high among school leavers, the poorly qualified, the poorly skilled and ethnic minorities. In 1994, the inner cities of Britain had an unemployment rate 50% higher than that in the rest of the country.

Population loss and social decline

Between 1951 and 1981, the UK's largest conurbations lost 35% of their population and migration was the key cause. For example, in the 1970s, out-migration from the inner areas of Liverpool and Manchester led to a population

decline of over 25%. Many of these people were looking for better employment opportunities.

In the 1960s and 1970s the out-movement of people led to a growth in small towns around the large conurbations. In the 1980s, a significant proportion of the out-migration from cities involved people moving to rural areas, a process known as counter-urbanisation (see page 141).

The key causes of population decline, therefore, are changing residential preferences, job growth and improvements in accessibility of suburban and rural areas, as well as the poor image of the inner city.

The people who have left the inner-city areas have tended to be the younger, the more affluent and the more skilled. This has meant that those left behind are the old, the less skilled and the poor. Therefore, economic decline of these areas has led to social decline.

The poor physical environment

The physical environment of the inner cities is usually poor, with low-quality housing, empty and derelict properties, vacant factories and unsightly, overgrown wasteland. There are high levels of vandalism, graffiti and flyposting and few amenities such as parks, open spaces and play areas. Urban motorways, with flyovers, underpasses and networks of pedestrian walkways, contribute further to the bleak concrete-dominated landscape.

Photograph 4.6 High-rise flats are often vandalised

Areas of nineteenth-century terraced housing are now often of poor quality and slum clearance schemes of the 1960s and 1970s created unsightly estates.

Inner-city high-rise developments

High-rise flats were a common feature of both inner-city renewal and peripheral council estates in the 1960s and 1970s. Some were well built, but many were not. People hated living in them because:

➤ they lacked community feel
➤ they were poorly ventilated and suffered from damp
➤ they were expensive to heat
➤ the open spaces designed to develop a sense of community spirit belonged to no-one, so no-one cared for them and they were vandalised
➤ poor design led to 'hidden' places where hooliganism and criminal activity took place (Photograph 4.6)

Cities were, therefore, saddled with a nightmare combination of run-down old housing and unpopular new housing. Many councils have either already demolished these flats or are considering doing so.

Political problems

There has been concern that the problems of inner-city residents have been marginalised politically. Inner cities have the lowest election turnouts in the UK, reflecting the degree to which the people feel rejected. In looking for solutions local people have elected members of far-right parties such as the British National Party to local councils. Urban regeneration policies have done little to relieve poverty.

During 2007 it emerged that local councils in the north of England and the midlands were being encouraged to demolish up to 4,000 houses a year, often Victorian terraced houses in inner-city areas, to meet government targets for new-builds. If they did not do so, they faced having their funds cut. Such moves are part of the Pathfinder regeneration scheme aimed to create up to 3 million homes by 2020. Under this scheme, it is suggested that 400,000 old houses will need to be demolished in the next 15 years, with clear financial incentives being given to facilitate clearance rather than repair.

Urban decline elsewhere: peripheral council estates

During the 1950s, 1960s and 1970s many local authorities built estates on the edges of urban areas to house overspill population and people who needed rehousing because of inner-city slum clearance. The estates consisted of uniform council houses — semi-detached, red brick with or without rendering, metal-framed windows, with gardens, limited garaging and colour-sequenced front doors. There were also tower blocks and maisonettes made of prefabricated materials.

These types of housing were a cheap way for local authorities to meet housing demand. Planning controls were limited, and construction was done in great haste. It seemed a good idea at the time to build these estates, using greenfield sites to provide decent homes, with open space and public amenities, for the poorer elements of society. However, the result was that communities the size of small towns were created on the outskirts of cities with no proper facilities or affordable transport links to the city centre or to places of work.

During the 1980s and 1990s the physical fabric and environmental quality of these estates deteriorated. Maintenance costs escalated to the point where, for many estates, demolition was the best option. The houses and flats have not proved popular under the right-to-buy legislation, and so many are still rented. This means that such estates contain above average proportions of the more vulnerable groups in society — low-income households, the unemployed, and the elderly living in poverty. They have a range of social and economic problems.

Urban regeneration

A number of governments since the Second World War have tried to regenerate declining urban areas. The main schemes that have taken place since 1980 are described below (see also gentrification, page 146).

Property-led regeneration

Urban Development Corporations (UDCs) were set up in the 1980s and 1990s to take responsibility for the physical, economic and social regeneration of selected inner-city areas with large amounts of derelict and vacant land. They are an example of what is known as property-led regeneration. They were given planning approval powers over and above those of the local authority, and were encouraged to spend public money on the purchase of land, the building of infrastructure and on marketing to attract private investment. The intention was that private investment would be four to five times greater than the public money initially invested.

Figure 4.10 Urban Development Corporations

The boards of UDCs, mostly made up of people from the local business community, had the power to acquire, reclaim and service land prior to private-sector involvement and to provide financial incentives to attract private investors. In 1981, two UDCs were established — the London Docklands Development Corporation (LDDC) and a Merseyside UDC. Eleven others followed, in areas such as the Lower Don Valley in Sheffield, Birmingham Heartlands, Trafford Park in Manchester and Cardiff Bay (Figure 4.10).

By 1993, UDCs accounted for nearly 40% of all urban regeneration policy expenditure. Over £12 billion of private-sector investment had been attracted, along with £4 billion from the public sector. They had built or refurbished 35,000 housing units, and created 190,000 jobs (Table 4.4).

Criticisms of UDCs

Some people argued that this amount of new employment was inadequate. There were two more significant criticisms. First, the UDCs were too dependent on property speculation and they lost huge sums of money through the compulsory purchase of land that later fell in value. Second, because they had greater powers than local authorities, democratic accountability was removed. Local people complained that they had no involvement in the developments taking place. Indeed, there were some examples, particularly in the London Docklands, where local people felt physically and socially excluded by prestigious new housing and high-technology office developments.

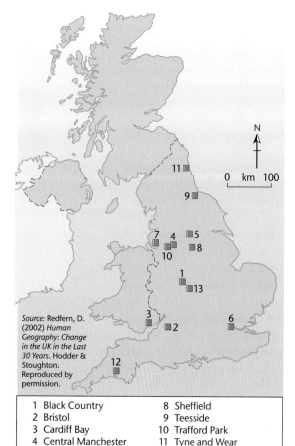

Source: Redfern, D. (2002) *Human Geography: Change in the UK in the Last 30 Years.* Hodder & Stoughton. Reproduced by permission.

1 Black Country	8 Sheffield
2 Bristol	9 Teesside
3 Cardiff Bay	10 Trafford Park
4 Central Manchester	11 Tyne and Wear
5 Leeds	12 Plymouth
6 London Docklands	13 Birmingham
7 Merseyside	Heartlands

Table 4.4 *Expenditure and targets of UDCs*

Location	Date started	Expenditure (£million)		Lifetime targets		
		1992/93	1995/96	Land reclaimed	Housing (units)	Jobs
London Docklands	1981	293.9	88	846.5	24,036	75,458
Merseyside	1981	42.1	34	384.0	3,544	23,357
Trafford Park	1987	61.3	29.7	400.6	3,774	21,440
Black Country	1987	68.0	36.6	525.3	1,403	10,212
Teesside	1987	34.5	47.5	210.8	311	25,618
Tyne and Wear	1987	50.2	43.5	517.7	4,842	34,043
Central Manchester	1988	20.5	13.7	60.0	661	4,590
Cardiff Bay	1988	—	—	250.0	950	2,200
Leeds	1988	9.6	—	35.3	2,581	5,074
Sheffield	1988	15.9	11.6	68.0	561	8,369
Bristol	1989	20.4	8.7	259.6	0	17,616
Birmingham Heartlands	1992	5.0	11.7	129.1	878	5,983
Plymouth	1993	n/a	10.6	12.7	93	491

Case study Central Manchester Development Corporation (CMDC)

CMDC is an example of a Development Corporation established after the LDDC, in 1988.

A partnership between the local authority and private developers was created. Its aim was to regenerate 200 ha of land and buildings in the southern sector of Manchester city centre. The area contained decaying warehouses, offices, former mills and contaminated land, unsightly railway viaducts and neglected waterways. It had been declared a conservation area in 1979.

Some of the buildings were refurbished into a range of uses including housing. For example, in the Whitworth Street district, warehouses were converted and redeveloped to create a village-like community of more than 1,000 household units, pubs, bars, restaurants and shops. The canals in the area were cleaned, and their banks were improved by the addition of lighting, seats and plants to upgrade the aesthetics of the area. This has now become a popular entertainment-based area for young people.

The CMDC engaged in widespread consultation and formulated a development strategy that complemented the plans of Manchester City Council. For example, Castlefield, which was once an area of disused canals, wharves and warehouses, became a mixture of housing (including some luxury apartments), office developments and leisure facilities.

The area also developed its tourist potential and now attracts over 2 million visitors a year. Attractions included the world famous tour of Granada Studios (now closed), the Manchester Museum of Science and Technology, the GMEX Centre (now known as Manchester Central) and the Bridgewater Concert Hall complex. The CMDC was disbanded in 1996, and planning powers have now reverted to Manchester City Council.

Partnerships between local and national governments and the private sector

City Challenge Partnerships represented a major switch of funding mechanisms towards competitive bidding. To gain funding a local authority had to come up with an imaginative project and form a partnership in its local inner-city area with the private sector and the local communities. The partnership then submitted a 5-year plan to central government in competition with other inner-city areas. The most successful schemes combined social aims with economic and environmental outcomes. By 1993, over 30 City Challenge Partnerships had been established and another 20 or more bids had been unsuccessful. By the end of that year partnerships accounted for over 20% of expenditure on inner-city regeneration.

How City Challenge worked

The City Challenge initiative was designed to address some of the weaknesses of the earlier regeneration schemes. The participating organisations — the partners — were better coordinated and more involved. This particularly applied to the residents of the area and the local authority. Separate schemes and initiatives operating in the same area, as had happened before, were not allowed — the various strands of the projects had to work together. Many earlier initiatives had concentrated on improving buildings, whereas City Challenge gave equal importance to buildings, people and values. Cooperation between local authorities and private and public groups, some of which were voluntary, was prioritised.

All the City Challenge areas suffered from high long-term and youth unemployment, a low skills base, poor levels of educational attainment, environmental deterioration, increasing areas of derelict land and growing commercial property vacancy. Public-sector housing was deteriorating in almost all the City Challenge areas due to a combination of poor initial design and inadequate maintenance. The population of these areas usually had a higher than national average incidence of healthcare problems, high levels of personal crime and fear of crime, a high proportion of single-parent families and households dependent on social security.

The priorities of the different City Challenge areas varied. In Liverpool, priority was given to environmental improvement, while in Wolverhampton a science park formed the centrepiece of the project. In Hulme, Manchester, housing improvement was the main focus (see case study).

Was the initiative successful?

Overall, the competition between areas for funding was believed to be successful — improving the quality of proposals and encouraging new and more imaginative ideas. The private sector, in particular, found the competitive principle attractive and argued that competition had encouraged local authorities to suggest solutions as well as identifying problems. However, the competitive nature of the scheme was criticised by others on the grounds that large sums of money should have been allocated according to need, not competitive advantage.

In some cases neighbouring authorities competed against each other when they could have worked together. It is rare for the limits of disadvantaged areas to coincide with an administrative boundary. The policy that all successful bidders should receive

exactly the same sum of money, irrespective of need, was also criticised. Finally, competing authorities were not given clear information about the criteria on which their application was to be judged — for some it was a stab in the dark.

By 1997 the Conservative government was able to publish statistics pointing to the success of City Challenge. Over 40,000 houses had been improved, 53,000 jobs had been created, nearly 2,000 ha of derelict land had been reclaimed and more than 3,000 new businesses had been established.

Case study — Hulme City Challenge Partnership

The Hulme area of Manchester was redeveloped as part of a slum clearance programme in the 1960s and a number of high-rise flats were built. Of the 5,500 dwellings, 98% were council owned. Over half of the dwellings were part of a deck access system, with many of the poor design features of prefabricated construction. The area had a low level of families with children, and a disproportionate number of single-person households. There was also a high number of single parents, and other people with social difficulties. There was some evidence that the local authority had used the area to 'dump' some of its more unfortunate residents.

Redevelopment

In 1992, under the Hulme City Challenge Partnership, plans were drawn up to build 3,000 new homes, with new shopping areas, roads and community facilities. A more traditional pattern of housing development was designed, with streets, squares, two-storey houses and low-rise flats. By 1995, 50 ha of land had been reclaimed, the majority of the former deck access flats had been demolished, 600 new homes for rent had been built, and more than 400 homes had been improved and refurbished. The main shopping area was totally refurbished, including the addition of an ASDA supermarket. A new community centre, including crèche facilities and other social provision, the Zion Centre, was also constructed. Crime in the area has been greatly reduced, and there is more of a social mix of people living in the area. The appearance of Hulme has altered radically.

Changing the reputation of Hulme gained in the 1970s and 1980s has been a long process, but appears to have been achieved. A green area, the Birley Fields, has been partly developed for a series of office blocks, and partly retained as urban parkland. The office development houses companies such as Michelin, Laing O'Rourke and the University of Manchester data centre. One significant part of 1970s Hulme that still exists is the Moss Side Sports and Leisure Complex. Upgraded for the 2002 Commonwealth Games, the centre has a gym and other sporting facilities. Hulme's proximity to the city centre has made it a popular place to live for a new generation of city dwellers; students of the University of Manchester also live in many of the student-focused residential developments in the area.

A symbol of the regeneration is the Hulme Arch. It supports Stretford Road as it passes over Princess Road. The construction of the bridge formed part of the regeneration of the area, both by re-establishing the former route of Stretford Road and by providing a local landmark.

The partners

A number of agencies and organisations were responsible for this transformation, including the Guinness Trust and Bellway Homes. These worked in close collaboration with each other and with Manchester City Council. The company responsible for Manchester airport also invested capital in the project. Hulme is a good example of how the public and private sectors can work together to improve a previously declining and socially challenging area.

Schemes and strategies of the twenty-first century

In the early years of the twenty-first century, the Labour government moved in two main directions in its attempts to regenerate and redevelop urban environments in the UK.

➤ It created **prestige project developments** (also known as **flagship projects**), such as the waterfront developments in Cardiff Bay, the Convention Centre area of Birmingham and the St Stephen's Development in Kingston-upon-Hull (see case study, page 168).

➤ It began to develop **sustainable communities** in a variety of UK towns and cities (see case study below). In theory, urban economic sustainability should allow people who live in cities to have access to a home, a job and a reliable income. Urban social sustainability should provide a reasonable quality of life and opportunities to maximise personal potential through education and health provision, and through participation in local democracies.

Case study   Sustainable communities in London

The Labour government stated that the sustainable communities initiative had the following general aims:

We will work closely with our key regional partners to identify practical steps to ensure that we have communities that:

■ are prosperous

■ have decent homes for sale or rent at a price people can afford

■ safeguard green and open space

■ enjoy a well-designed, accessible and pleasant living and working environment

■ are effectively and fairly governed with a strong sense of community

There is an urgent need for more affordable homes all over London to accommodate its growing population and to reduce homelessness. It is also essential that workers who are key to the delivery of the capital's public services are able to afford to live and work within its communities. The Government Office for London (GOL) is working with the Greater London Authority (GLA), local authorities and relevant agencies (the Housing Corporation, English Partnerships, the Commission for Architecture and the Built Environment [CABE] and English Heritage) to achieve these aims.

Examples

The **Holly Street estate redevelopment in Hackney** has transformed a whole community. In addition to the newly created neighbourhood of small streets, small blocks of flats and brick-built houses with pitched roofs and gardens, a sports and community centre, an elderly persons' day centre and a health centre have been provided. Alongside the aim of redeveloping the housing on the estate, the project sought to remove fear of crime, improve security and improve the mental and physical health of residents, thus reducing the pressure on health services.

Coin Street Community Builders (CSCB) is a social enterprise that has built social housing and commercial developments, including Oxo Tower Wharf, on London's South Bank. CSCB does not distribute profits from its commercial activities but uses them to cross-subsidise activities which otherwise would not be viable, including an arts and leisure programme. Its four housing developments are run by 'fully mutual' cooperatives and provide 220 affordable homes for people in housing need.

Greenwich Millennium Village is being developed on a brownfield site and is part of the larger Greenwich Peninsula development (Photograph 4.7). Over a period of 5 years, 1,377 homes are being built, including homes for social rent or shared ownership. Sustainability, energy efficiency, waste management and quality in design and construction are key features of this project. The Millennium Primary School and Health Centre in the village is providing education, training, healthcare, crèche and other community facilities on one site.

However, not everyone believes that these sustainable communities meet the aims given above. Here is an extract from a 'blog' of a local resident:

This is the Greenwich Millennium Village, usually referred to here as the Yuppie Village. It's built on the same gasworks site as the Millennium Dome (now the O2 Arena), and needed decontamination before construction began in 2000. The first residents moved in about 2 years ago. It's backed by the government, with the aim of 'increasing social inclusion and participation'.

This is nonsense — most places sell for hugely inflated prices. One-bed flats now go for nearly £200,000. All concerned like to dress it up as the future of urban living, a vital addition to a decaying area. But it's so distant from the rest of Greenwich, most locals have never even set foot in it. It may as well be another fenced-off estate.

Yuppie Village residents rarely go much further in the area than the tube station or the bus stop. Even though they are only 7 or 8 minutes' walk from the tube station, even on the finest morning you can see a queue of Yuppie Village residents gathering at its bus stop, only for their faces to drop when the already packed bus steams past. Walk? Oh no, that'd involve getting to know the area...

There is one nod to the area's heritage — the gasworks' war memorial was moved into one of the village's parks. Gas was one of Greenwich's biggest industries until North Sea gas came on stream in the 1970s. I wonder how many of the families of those who worked at the gasworks could afford to take advantage of the land their fathers and grandfathers worked on. Not many. And I should know — I come from one of those families.

Photograph 4.7 The O2 Arena on Greenwich Peninsula

English Partnerships

Retailing and other services

Changing patterns in the UK

The traditional pattern of retailing is based on two key factors:
➤ easy, local access to goods such as bread, milk and newspapers which are purchased on a regular basis, often daily and particularly so if perishable
➤ willingness to travel to a shopping centre for goods with a higher value which are purchased less often, such as household and electrical goods, clothes and shoes

For many years, these factors led to a two-tier structure of retailing. Local needs were met by corner shops in areas of terraced housing, and by suburban shopping parades. Higher-value goods were purchased in the town centre (the central business district — CBD) and required a trip by bus or car. In the last 30 years

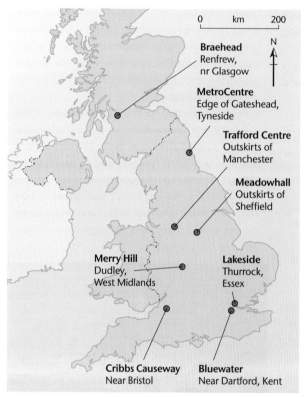

Figure 4.11 Location of out-of-town shopping centres in the UK

technology (in the form of the motor vehicle) has had a major influence on the patterns of retailing.

In the 1970s supermarkets and superstores began to be built in residential areas and town centres. These stores sold a full range of food and non-food items at the same check-out. This idea expanded into larger hypermarkets that also sold electrical goods and clothing and often had smaller specialist retail outlets under the same roof. An important factor in the development of these establishments was the use of the private car to load up once or twice a week with the 'family shop'.

In the 1980s non-food retail parks expanded. These housed DIY, carpet and furniture stores such as Focus, B&Q, MFI and Carpetright. Many such parks were built on the outskirts of towns or cities, with easy access to main roads, again to attract the car user. The warehouse-type buildings were often uniform in design, each distinguished by the display on the outside and by the internal design.

In the 1990s huge out-of-town shopping centres were built on the periphery of large urban areas and close to major motorways. They often had their own motorway junctions. Some of the best-known shopping areas in the country are in this category: MetroCentre (near Gateshead), Meadowhall (near Sheffield), the Trafford Centre (near Manchester), and Bluewater and Lakeside on either side of the Thames east of London (Table 4.5 and Figure 4.11).

Table 4.5 Out-of-town shopping centres

Shopping centre	Location	Approx. number of shops
Braehead	Near Glasgow	100
MetroCentre	Near Gateshead	320
Trafford Centre	Near Manchester	320
Meadowhall	Near Sheffield	270
Merry Hill	Near Birmingham	230
Cribbs Causeway	Near Bristol	150
Bluewater	Dartford (south of Thames)	330
Lakeside	Thurrock (north of Thames)	350

In the twenty-first century e-commerce and e-tailers are growing — electronic home shopping using the internet and digital and cable television systems. Supermarket chains such as Tesco, ASDA and Sainsbury's offer online shopping services, with delivery to the customer's door. The impact of this form of retailing on other types of shop has yet to be seen, but it seems unlikely to affect existing shopping locations seriously. People still want to examine items before purchase, and e-tailers depend upon mail delivery

services, both road and rail based, none of which can guarantee next-day delivery. At the same time, more traditional farmers' markets, selling local fresh produce, are growing in numbers for those customers who are willing to pay more than supermarket prices for healthier food with fewer food miles.

Factors affecting retail change

A number of factors have combined to produce the changes in retailing described above.

Increased mobility

Nearly all the changes described arise from increased ownership and use of the private car. Car parking in city centres is expensive and restricted. Out-of-town retail areas have large areas of free car parking. Locations next to motorway junctions offer speedy access compared to the congestion of city centres. Even at a local level, it is often easier to pull into a petrol-station forecourt to make a low-level purchase than to find a parking space outside a suburban shop. Petrol stations are no longer just places people go for fuel. They also supply newspapers, bread, milk, vegetables, fast food, lottery tickets and often have cash machines. The local petrol station has become the corner shop of the twenty-first century (Photograph 4.8).

Photograph 4.8 A petrol station in Essex: the corner shop of the twenty-first century?

The changing nature of shopping habits

People now purchase many items as part of a weekly, fortnightly or even monthly shop. The use of freezers in most homes means items that once had to be purchased regularly for freshness can now be bought in bulk and stored. This technology has dovetailed with the changing nature of employment. In many families all the adults work and do not have time to shop daily. Retailers have responded to this by developing more 'ready-made meal' products that can be stored in a domestic freezer.

Changing expectations of shopping habits

An increasing number of people see shopping as a family social activity. Consequently, many of the larger shopping areas combine retailers with cinemas, restaurants, fast-food outlets, crèches and entertainment areas. For example, the White Rose Centre near Leeds has an area set aside for men who accompany their partners but do not wish to 'shop until they drop'! It is claimed that at the Bluewater shopping centre near Dartford you are never more than 100 m away from a coffee bar (Photograph 4.9). Such marketing messages are used to make the customer feel more at ease.

Photograph 4.9 Bluewater shopping centre

The changing nature of retailing

There are only a few supermarket/hypermarket companies, each of which strives to be more competitive than the others. They seek to build on cheaper out-of-town locations and to increase their economies of scale. In this way they can afford to reduce prices and provide large car-parking areas.

Out-of-town retailing areas

Large areas have been devoted to major retail parks and this has involved the following:

Human options

- redevelopment and/or clearance of cheap farmland or a brownfield site
- the creation of extensive car parks
- the construction of a link to a motorway interchange or outer ring road
- the development of other transport interchange facilities — bus station, supertram, railway station
- the construction of linked entertainment facilities, e.g. Warner Village cinemas, fast-food outlets

Attitudes to the development of out-of-town retailing

The construction of such outlets has caused a lot of controversy. Those in favour of out-of-town retailing believe it provides greater opportunities to shop without the need to travel into city centres. It also creates jobs for local people, especially for students at weekends or young mothers who want to work part time.

Those opposed to out-of-town retailing believe it causes an increase in traffic in the area, which creates problems of safety, pollution, noise and parking in local residential streets. Twenty-four hour shopping means continual movement of both cars and delivery lorries, which may cause unacceptable noise levels at night.

Case study — The Trafford Centre, Manchester

When the Trafford Centre was opened in 1998 many people were concerned about the effect it would have on Manchester's CBD. Nearly 5.5 million people (almost 10% of the UK population) live within 45 minutes' drive of the centre. In 2005, 29.4 million people visited the centre. It was designed to be more than just a shopping centre, with a 1,600-seat food court, an 18-lane ten-pin bowling alley, a Laser Quest arena and a 20-screen cinema. Since its opening various additions have been made. A further expansion, called Barton Square, concentrating on furniture, kitchens and furnishings, was completed in 2006.

Advantages

The Trafford Centre offers the following:
- good motorway links — it is close to Junctions 9 and 10 of the M60, with easy links to the M6, M61, M62 and the M602 to Manchester city centre
- 11,000 free car parking spaces in discrete segments, each of which has its own automatic capacity-monitoring system that can relay messages to approach roads from the motorway network
- a bus station with the capacity to deal with 120 buses per hour

- facilities for the disabled, regularly spaced within the complex. These include a shop mobility unit, offering scooters and wheelchairs
- a weatherproof, air-conditioned and safe environment
- its own security system, with a tannoy and a meeting point for lost children
- a full range of services, such as a post office, banks and travel agents

Disadvantages

It has the following disadvantages, typical of out-of-town retail areas:
- heavy build-ups of traffic on the access road network, e.g. the M60, at certain times of the year, such as bank holidays and the run up to Christmas
- the atmosphere within the complex is artificial, although there are five themed sections named Peel Avenue, Regent Crescent, the Dome, Barton Square and the Orient
- all the outlets are those of chain stores — it is too expensive for local or independent businesses to rent space in the centre

- public transport services to the centre are restricted, though improving, which makes access difficult for elderly shoppers in particular. In 2004, 87% of visitors came by car. However, there are plans to provide a Metrolink connection and a rail link to the centre
- it is difficult for poorer people to gain access to the centre — for example, the homeless are kept out by security staff

Table 4.6 Visitor profile

Gender	
Male	35%
Female	65%

Age	
16–24	22%
25–34	26%
35–44	21%
45–54	16%
55+	15%

Method of travel	
Car	87%
Bus	8%
Walk	2%
Other	3%

Frequency of visits	
Once a week, or more often	24%
1–2 times a month	36%
2–6 times a year	27%
Less often	13%

Photograph 4.10 The Trafford Centre, Manchester

The Trafford Centre

Redevelopment of urban centres

The central business district (CBD) of a city contains the principal commercial areas and major public buildings and is the centre for business and commercial activities. The CBD is accessible from all parts of the urban area and has the highest land values in a city. These occur at the **peak land value intersection** (PLVI). The CBD is not static. It can grow outwards in some directions (**zones of assimilation**) and retreat in others (**zones of discard**).

In some CBDs, retailing is declining because of competition from out-of-town developments. This means there is a greater emphasis on offices and services. In a sizeable urban centre, there is often segregation of different types of businesses

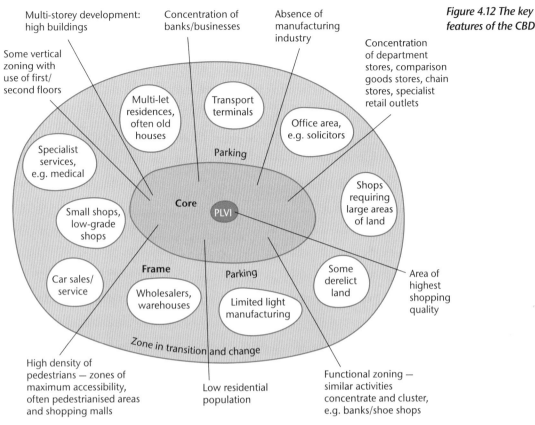

Figure 4.12 The key features of the CBD

Multi-storey development: high buildings

Concentration of banks/businesses

Absence of manufacturing industry

Concentration of department stores, comparison goods stores, chain stores, specialist retail outlets

Some vertical zoning with use of first/second floors

Multi-let residences, often old houses

Transport terminals

Parking

Office area, e.g. solicitors

Specialist services, e.g. medical

Core

PLVI

Shops requiring large areas of land

Small shops, low-grade shops

Frame

Parking

Some derelict land

Area of highest shopping quality

Car sales/service

Wholesalers, warehouses

Limited light manufacturing

Zone in transition and change

High density of pedestrians — zones of maximum accessibility, often pedestrianised areas and shopping malls

Low residential population

Functional zoning — similar activities concentrate and cluster, e.g. banks/shoe shops

PLVI = Peak land value intersection: the highest rated, busiest, most accessible part of a CBD

within the CBD, forming distinct quarters. Retailing tends to be separate from commercial and professional offices and forms a distinct inner core. The outer core is made up of offices and entertainment centres with some smaller shops. Beyond this, the outer part of the CBD (known as the frame) contains service industries, wholesalers and car parks, among other features (Figure 4.12).

The CBD has been affected by changes in retailing over the past 30 years in the UK.

CBDs in decline

Through each of the phases of retail change described above, the traditional town centre has continued to exist. However, on several occasions this area of retailing has been said to be dying, and in some small towns there has been a general decline. There are three main reasons for this:

➤ the loss of the retailing function (particularly food retailing, electrical goods and DIY) to out-of-town shopping centres. Evidence for this often quoted in the 1990s was the closure of branches of Marks and Spencer in some small towns

➤ the loss of offices to suburban or peripheral locations in prestige science parks

➤ the increasing costs of upkeep and development of the CBDs themselves. The

CBD is becoming increasingly expensive, congested and inaccessible, especially as the bulk of a city's population lives in suburban areas

Many decision makers are still worried that CBDs are in decline. A major concern is that run-down city centres can become dangerous places, particularly at night. Most people visiting a city arrive in the centre and a run-down CBD can discourage investment. Dereliction, vacant buildings, increased numbers of low-grade shops (e.g. charity shops and discount stores) and lack of investment all fuel decline (Figure 4.13). This situation is sometimes referred to as the 'dead heart' of a city (in the USA as an 'urban donut').

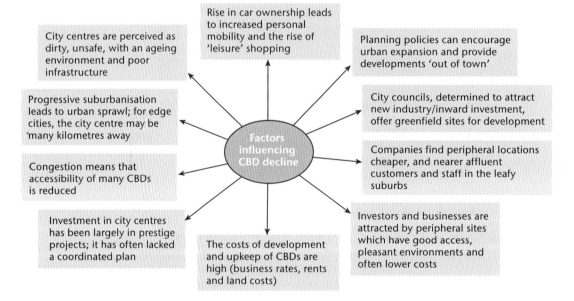

Figure 4.13 Factors influencing CBD decline

Planners see the CBD as an important social and cultural meeting point. However, the general public seems unconvinced about the worth of CBDs as they flock in thousands to shop in retail parks. Many companies have moved out to suburban offices in science parks.

However, despite the negative predictions, town centres still flourish alongside the new out-of-town locations. In some cases, the CBD has moved slightly in one or more directions. In other cases, it has reinvented itself with new indoor shopping areas or malls. The Eldon Centre in Newcastle and the Arndale Centres in many towns are examples. Another feature has been the gentrification of shopping areas, as in Brindleyplace in Birmingham.

Reversing the decline

A number of strategies are being devised to help reverse the decline of city centres, including:

➤ the establishment of business and marketing management teams to coordinate overall management of CBDs and run special events

➤ the provision of a more attractive shopping environment with pedestrianisation (which increases pedestrian safety), new street furniture, floral displays, paving and landscaping

➤ the construction of all-weather shopping malls that are air-conditioned in the summer and heated in the winter and which often have integral low-cost parking

➤ the encouragement of specialist areas, such as attractive open street markets, cultural quarters and arcades

➤ the improvement of public transport links to the heart of the CBD, including rapid transit systems, park-and-ride schemes and shopper buses (see pages 173–178)

➤ the extensive use of CCTV and emergency alarm systems to reduce crime and calm the fears of the public, particularly women (see below)

➤ the organisation of special shopping events such as Christmas fairs, late-night shopping and Sunday shopping — sometimes referred to as 'the 24-hour city'

➤ conservation schemes, such as the refurbishment of historic buildings in heritage cities like Chester, York, Bath and Cambridge, to attract shoppers and tourists

Making CBDs safer for women

Whether or not you feel safe in an area will influence whether or not you go there. CBDs have increasingly been perceived as threatening environments. Individuals or groups in society, for example some women, whose movements and activities are constrained by fear can be classed as disadvantaged. They suffer from reduced accessibility and a poorer quality of life. What can be done to alleviate these feelings and make women feel safer in CBDs?

One answer is segregated transport for women, for example:

➤ separate compartments on trains or night-buses

➤ priority taxis after 10 p.m. — in Manchester, this is known as the 'Lady Cab' service

➤ the formal licensing of mini-cabs in cities so that all private hire vehicles are registered and regulated

Improvements can be made to the street environment, including:

➤ CCTV, which is now widespread

➤ better maintenance of street lighting

➤ help points at key locations, for example subways, with emergency alarms connected to local police

➤ smoother pavements, few obstacles and better enforcement of on-kerb parking regulations to help women with prams (this is linked to required improvements for disability access)

➤ more seating in public places

➤ transparent bus shelters, to prevent people hiding behind them

➤ cutting hedges at the top and bottom, to increase light and safety

Multi-storey car parks are often seen as threatening environments. Here, suggested improvements include better lighting and the provision of ground-floor women-only sections.

Functions other than retailing

Many cities are encouraging the development of functions other than retailing to increase the attractions of a CBD, including:

➤ Encouraging a wider range of leisure facilities, including café bars, restaurants, music venues (such as the 'Arenas' in many city centres), cinemas and theatres. For example, the St Peter's Square area of Nottingham was made more attractive by planting shrubs, giving permission for open-air cafés and employing staff to clean the area in the early morning.

➤ Promoting street entertainment, such as at Covent Garden in London.

➤ Developing nightlife, such as clubbing, for example in Manchester and Leeds. (There are negative issues associated with this, including the high level of policing that is necessary.)

➤ Establishing theme areas, such as the gay area in Manchester and the cultural quarters in Sheffield and Stoke.

➤ Developing flagship attractions, for example the photographic museum in Bradford.

➤ Constructing new offices, apartments, hotels and conference centres to raise the status of the CBD for business and to encourages tourists to remain near the city centre.

➤ Encouraging residential activities to return to city centres, by providing flats to rent above shops, redeveloping old buildings (a form of gentrification) or building new up-market apartments (re-urbanisation) (see pages 146–148).

Most CBD managers are trying a range of these strategies and shoppers are being attracted back to city centres. However, this can only happen in conjunction with planning controls to limit the number of suburban or out-of-town shopping centres.

Some supermarket chains are turning their attention back to their existing and new CBD outlets. For example, Sainsbury's has developed Sainsbury's Local stores in CBDs and Tesco has opened Tesco Express stores. These CBD outlets do not sell the full range of goods found in the larger stores, but stock items targeted at local needs.

 Case study   ## The St Stephen's Development, Kingston-upon-Hull

The site of this development lies west of Ferensway and comprises 17 ha. It includes major work on the existing Grade II listed railway station.

Site

The brownfield site originally comprised a mixture of ownerships, buildings and vacant lots. The general ambience of the area was one of neglect and decay. Various piecemeal redevelopment schemes over the years came to nothing. The development sponsors, Kingston-upon-Hull City Council and Yorkshire Forward, now own or have acquired the whole site.

Scheme

The scheme provides:

Photograph 4.11 St Stephen's Development

St Stephens Hull

the Hull Truck Theatre Company, the Albemarle Music Centre (aimed at providing a range of music services to the youth of the city), 1,550 car parking spaces and over 200 new residential units
- a new integrated transport interchange

Both of these opened in September 2007. The basic design concept is built around a diagonal pedestrian route across the site which curves gently at either end to form an 'S'. At the east end of this route there is a mix of retail, leisure, hotel and cultural uses, with associated parking and servicing. The route is roofed over where it passes through the retail and leisure accommodation and this forms a covered street in the tradition of nineteenth-century arcade developments. At the west end of the pedestrian route there is an area of open space. New-build residential accommodation is proposed to the north and south of the open space.

Transport interchange

The new £10 million transport interchange scheme has transformed the old Paragon Rail Station and added a new bus station to provide a new gateway to the city.

The interchange is promoted by a partnership between Kingston-upon-Hull City Council, Citybuild, Yorkshire Forward, Network Rail, First Transpennine Trains, East Yorkshire Motor Services and Stagecoach Ltd.

- a flagship development that is intended to complement and reinforce city-centre activities by having a mixture of retail outlets, a 10,000 m² food store, a leisure complex, a hotel, a new home for

Sustainability issues in urban areas

Waste management

The average person in the UK produces 517 kg of household waste every year. Not only is the amount of waste increasing, but so is its toxicity and the length of time it is toxic for. Waste disposal in the UK is efficient, so people are not generally aware of the problems that waste is creating. The UK has lagged behind many other countries, particularly some in the EU, in recycling, reusing and managing household waste. We need to change our attitude to household waste — to see it as a resource to be managed rather than as a nuisance to be disposed of.

Recycling and alternatives

Table 4.7 Key UK waste targets (based on EU legislation)

There are a number of choices in how to manage waste. The least sustainable option is landfill. In 2005, 73% of UK household waste was treated in this way. Before landfill is used, other options should be explored (Table 4.7).

Waste Strategy 2000 recycling targets	25% of household waste to be recycled or composted by 2005
	30% of household waste to be recycled or composted by 2010
	33% of household waste to be recycled or composted by 2015
Waste Strategy 2000 recovery targets	40% of municipal waste to be recovered by 2005
	45% of municipal waste to be recovered by 2010
	67% of municipal waste to be recovered by 2015
European Union Landfill Directive targets	Biodegradeable municipal waste down to 75% of 1995 figures by 2010
	Biodegradeable municipal waste down to 50% of 1995 figures by 2013
	Biodegradeable municipal waste down to 35% of 1995 figures by 2020

Photograph 4.12 Paper and cardboard being taken for recycling in Cambridgeshire

TopFoto

Reduction

The best way of managing waste is to prevent it. Businesses are being encouraged to reduce the amount of packaging used. The government-funded group Envirowise gives advice to commercial enterprises on how they can reduce waste, and costs. Consumers can play a part by refusing to accept plastic bags, or by opting for products that do not use excessive packaging. Governments too can act — in Ireland there has been a €0.15 levy on plastic bags since 2002.

Re-use

Some re-use of milk containers, soft drinks bottles and jam jars has been attempted. However, the most successful example of re-use is the sale of 'bags for life'. In some parts of the world shops charge cash deposits on glass bottles to encourage their return.

Recycling

Waste products such as paper, glass, metal cans, plastics and clothes can be recycled if they can be collected economically (Photograph 4.12). However, the start-up costs of recycling schemes can be high and the market value of the material produced may be low. Householders may also be unwilling to sort recyclables from their other household waste.

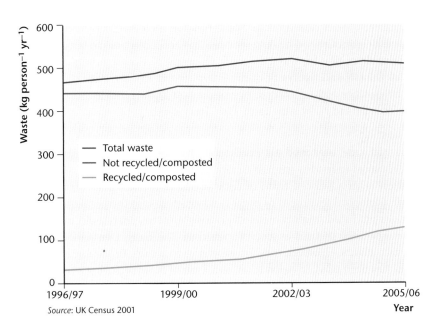

Source: UK Census 2001

*Figure 4.14
Household waste
and recycling in the
UK, 1996–2006*

Region	2000/01	2001/02	2002/03	2003/04	2004/05	2005/06
Northeast	4.1	5.2	6.6	12.2	15.4	21.1
Northwest	7.5	9.2	11.3	14.2	19.2	23.8
Yorkshire and the Humber	7.3	8.9	11.2	14.5	18.6	21.8
East Midlands	13.1	13.7	15.1	19.3	26.3	31.8
West Midlands	9.1	10.2	13.0	15.7	19.9	25.1
East	15.2	17.4	19.4	23.4	29.8	34.1
London	9.0	9.3	10.9	13.3	17.6	20.7
Southeast	16.4	17.7	19.6	22.8	26.1	29.2
Southwest	14.9	16.6	18.6	21.4	26.6	31.4
England	11.2	12.5	14.5	17.8	22.5	26.7

Although the proportion of household recycling in the UK is increasing (Table 4.8 and Figure 4.14), only 26% was recycled in 2005 — 135 kg per person. This still falls short of the EU's 30% target by 2010. Large quantities of steel and aluminium cans and paper are recycled in the UK, but recycling of plastic bottles is difficult to achieve on a profitable basis. Recycling also has hidden costs — transport from collection points to processing plants and the hot water and other materials needed for cleaning and processing.

Table 4.8 Regional household recycling rates (%)

Energy recovery

Waste material can be converted into energy. The main method is incineration. In the past, many councils burnt their waste, but this adds to carbon dioxide emissions and releases pollutants into the atmosphere as well as concentrating harmful substances such as dioxins in the ash. Many old, polluting incinerators

have therefore been closed down. Some modern incinerators generate electricity or power neighbourhood heating schemes and are considered by supporters to be a sustainable option for waste disposal. There are 17 licensed municipal incinerators in the UK and figures from the Environment Agency show that emissions have fallen since 1990. However, one of the best known incinerators, serving the Byker Wall flats in Newcastle-upon-Tyne, has closed.

Composting

On a small scale, organic waste (kitchen scraps and garden waste) can be used to make compost to fertilise gardens or farmland. On a much bigger scale, anaerobic digestion is an advanced form of composting that takes place in an enclosed reactor. Biological treatment of organic waste speeds up the breakdown process. The gases produced (mainly methane) can be burnt to generate electricity and the solid residue can be used as a soil conditioner. Germany, Denmark and Italy all have such plants. However, they are expensive to set up. In the UK dried sewage residue has been used, in pellet form, as a form of biomass fuel at a cement works in Derbyshire.

Landfill

Waste is dumped in old quarries or hollows, and this is convenient and cheap. However, it is unsightly and is a serious threat to groundwater and river quality because toxic chemicals can leach out and contaminate the water. Decaying matter at landfill sites also produces methane gas. This is not only explosive, it is also a strong greenhouse gas.

A major problem on landfill sites is the disposable nappy. Once paper, glass and plastic have been removed, nappies account for 15% of household waste. It costs £40 million a year to dispose of an estimated 1 million tonnes of nappy waste, of which 75% is urine and faeces. Most nappy waste is taken to landfill sites where it adds to the build-up of methane gas. Nappies take an estimated 500 years to break down.

In addition we are running out of space for landfill. In 2006 it was reported that the UK had capacity for only 9 more years of landfill before shortages of available sites began to occur. Furthermore, current EU legislation binds the UK to reducing the amount of waste sent to landfill to 75% of 1995 levels by 2010. The same legislation has also placed more stringent guidelines on the siting and structure of landfill.

All of this means that landfill is becoming an increasingly expensive option. Councils have a growing interest in 'pay-as-you-throw' schemes, under which households are charged according to the volume of waste they produce. However, evidence from Ireland, where such charging has been in operation since 2003, suggests that this creates more fly-tipping and household incineration.

Japanese cities operate a staggered system of waste collection (depending on waste type) using colour-coded translucent refuse sacks. Waste collectors are able to check on the content of the sacks. There are heavy fines for non-compliance, but overall the system works in an efficient and orderly manner.

Elsewhere in the world, refuse is seen as an opportunity to make money, as the following case study illustrates.

Case study: Waste disposal in Nairobi, Kenya

In Nairobi, recycling is an important part of the everyday economy. It is common for people to collect and make use of other people's rubbish.

Waste tips are scavenged for any recoverable or recyclable materials. For instance:

- old car tyres are cut up and used to make cheap sandals
- washing machine doors are used as kitchen bowls, and the drums as storage units
- glass bottles are collected and returned to stores for refilling
- food waste is collected and fed to animals or composted for use on vegetable plots
- tin cans and old oil drums are used to make charcoal stoves, lamps, buckets and metal tips for ploughs

Waste management is an excellent example of the need to 'think globally, act locally'.

Transport and its management

The spread of houses into suburbs and small towns and villages of rural areas, while jobs remain concentrated in the central parts of cities, has created surges of morning and evening commuters. These surges are at their most extreme in London but occur in most other large towns and cities across the UK. They take place along roads (private cars and commercial buses) and railway networks. Other traffic flows, for shopping, entertainment and other commercial services, add to the overall problems of mass transportation. No matter how much money is spent on transport infrastructure, traffic jams, railway overcrowding and parking problems seem to get worse.

This problem is not new. The first London Underground line was opened in 1863, and the first deep tube electric railway in 1890. These were built to overcome the urban transport problems in London at that time. Interestingly, the average speed along the Underground in 1890 was 24 km h^{-1}, the same as the average speed of central London tube trains in 1995. In 1963, the Buchanan Report entitled *Traffic in Towns* showed that the private car was clogging the central parts of cities. Indeed, this report concluded that the only effective way to control car usage was through 'good cheap public transport' (Photograph 4.13).

However, despite mounting problems, government policy in the UK has continued to favour private road transport. Government figures show continued expansion of roads, road traffic and progressively heavier goods vehicles. Alongside this there has been relatively slow growth in railway usage. The number of railway passengers has increased, particularly in the London region, but this has

Dance and Jump

Photograph 4.13
Public transport is
one solution to urban
traffic congestion

been accompanied by problems of poor rolling stock, inadequate track maintenance, escalating fares, accidents and poor travelling experiences. It is difficult to persuade people to abandon their cars.

As further road building is likely to release suppressed demand and quickly fill up the extra capacity, greater emphasis should be placed on upgrading the public transport system. Finding a solution to the problem of urban transport has exercised town planners and traffic consultants for many years.

How and why is urban traffic increasing?

Car ownership is increasing throughout the world. Globally it is anticipated that the total number of motor vehicles will be greater than 800 million by 2010. Most will be concentrated in developed countries, and in the urban areas within these. In the UK more than 30% of households own two or more cars. There are several reasons for this growth.

A large urban working population

A high proportion of people work in the urban areas of the country but live in rural or suburban areas. These people make regular journeys to and from their homes by road and rail. However, changes are taking place in this pattern. Many commuter journeys are now between one suburb and another, rather than from suburb to town centre. Most public transport systems were developed for travel from suburb to town centre, not across town. Suburb to suburb journeys therefore have to be made by private car, resulting in congestion of suburban roads. It is expensive to expand public transport networks to keep pace with suburbanisation and counter-urbanisation. The car continues to be more convenient.

Economic growth

Commuting is not the only reason for the growing numbers of vehicles on the roads. Economic growth in retailing and other consumer services has led to more service vehicles (including supermarket lorries and the notorious 'white van') on urban roads. Freight traffic, such as delivery vans, is likely to increase as e-commerce (internet shopping) becomes more important in retailing.

The growth in urban incomes

Earnings in urban areas are usually higher than in rural areas and these higher incomes allow more car ownership. Incomes have risen faster than the relative rise in car prices, leading to multiple car ownership in many families.

The growth in the number of journeys

As the number of cars increases, so does the number of journeys that people make in them. There is a corresponding fall in the use of public transport. Research in the USA has suggested that not only does the number of journeys increase with car ownership, but so does the distance travelled. Many of these extra journeys are for leisure purposes.

Urban transport solutions

There are four main approaches to dealing with these problems.

Road schemes and restricted access

London has had chronic road traffic problems for many years. In the 1970s and 1980s new radial routes around the city were thought to be the solution. The London orbital motorway, the M25, was built, but this increased the number of cars on the road. The M25 has been widened in places in response to demand. Plans for other new radial routes were abandoned in the 1990s, although work was completed on some.

The Congestion Charge was introduced in central London in 2003 and extended to parts of west London in 2007. Those choosing to drive through these zones of the city on a weekday are charged a toll. This model is likely to be followed by other cities in the future though it was rejected by the people of Manchester in 2008.

On a smaller scale, the creation of bus lanes with priority at junctions is an effective way of encouraging public transport use and decreasing car traffic (see case study, page 178).

Road traffic management schemes

Many provincial cities suffer from severe traffic congestion but do not have the option of a new ring road or new arterial routes. In towns such as Oxford, bypasses and inner ring roads already exist, in some cases formed by the amalgamation and upgrading of existing routes. Despite these, traffic problems continue.

Some of the strategies being introduced in these smaller towns and cities are as follows:

➤ strict on-street parking controls, and expensive car parks
➤ restrictions on access for cars, for example, pedestrianisation of large areas of the centre
➤ one-way systems and traffic calming measures
➤ encouraging use of public transport, for example, park and ride schemes

Streamlining of public transport

Around 30 years ago, Passenger Transport Authorities were set up to run and maintain efficient integrated public transport within their areas. In Merseyside the authority, under the name Merseytravel, is responsible for the Mersey tunnels, the Mersey ferries, Merseyrail and the Merseytravel bus services. It operates in a difficult geographical area, serving the Wirral peninsula as well as the county of Merseyside to the east of the Mersey estuary.

The key to the public transport system is Merseyrail. One third of the area's population lives within 1 km of a Merseyrail station and the system is intensively used for public access to the city centre. There are three main lines, the Wirral line that links Liverpool city centre with New Brighton, West Kirby and Hooton, the Northern line that serves Kirby, Ormskirk and Southport, and the City line to Wigan and Crewe. There are constant new initiatives, such as new stations (for example, at Whiston), updating of electrified lines and a centralised control system.

Commercial bus companies operate bus services, with some Authority provision for the disabled. Two ferry routes cross the Mersey, from Liverpool to Birkenhead and from Liverpool to Wallasey. However, they operate at a slight loss. Both Mersey tunnels are operated by Merseytravel. With just over 1 million vehicles a year passing through, the tolls provide a small profit.

New mass transit systems

Mass transit systems have been used to provide low-cost public transport from the suburbs to the city centre. Two recent examples include the Supertram in Sheffield and the Metrolink in Manchester (see case study). It has taken a number of years for British traffic managers to recognise the benefits of modern electrified tram systems. They did not have to look far to see these benefits. In Germany, France, the Netherlands and Switzerland light mass transit systems based on trams have eased traffic congestion and provided an effective public transport system for years.

Case study **The Manchester Metrolink**

The Manchester Metrolink opened in 1992 and there have already been some extensions to the network, for example to the Salford Quays and Eccles (Figure 4.15). The initial link ran from Bury in the north to Altrincham in the south, serving 18 stations on the conventional rail network as well as 6 street-level stations in the city centre. There are plans to extend the network to Oldham and Rochdale, Manchester

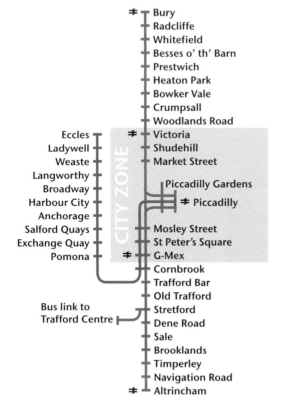

Bury
Radcliffe
Whitefield
Besses o' th' Barn
Prestwich
Heaton Park
Bowker Vale
Crumpsall
Woodlands Road
Eccles — Victoria
Ladywell — Shudehill
Weaste — Market Street
Langworthy
Broadway — Piccadilly Gardens
Harbour City — Piccadilly
Anchorage
Salford Quays — Mosley Street
Exchange Quay — St Peter's Square
Pomona — G-Mex
Cornbrook
Trafford Bar
Old Trafford
Bus link to — Stretford
Trafford Centre — Dene Road
Sale
Brooklands
Timperley
Navigation Road
Altrincham

CITY ZONE

Photograph 4.14 Manchester Metrolink tram at St Peter's Square

Airport, Ashton-under-Lyne, the Trafford Centre, and Didsbury and Stockport.

Interchange facilities are provided at Manchester's mainline railway stations, Piccadilly and Victoria. The Metrolink operates at intervals of 5 minutes at peak periods, and 12–15 minutes at less busy periods. There were inevitable problems of disruption during construction of the tracks, but the longer-term benefits are now becoming apparent. There is a fleet of 32 vehicles making 52,000 journeys every day — 19 million journeys every year. Research by Metrolink suggests that at least 3.5 million car journeys along the Metrolink corridor have been prevented each year. As its website states: 'By providing an efficient and pleasant alternative, Metrolink is persuading commuters to get out of their cars and onto the trams. And that's good news for us all!'

Figure 4.15 The Manchester Metrolink

Case study   The A638 Quality Bus Corridor (QBC), Doncaster

The QBC stretches along the A638 York Road (from Green Lane to the North Bridge) to the north of Doncaster and along the A638 Bawtry Road (from the Racecourse Roundabout to Parrott's Corner) to the south (Figure 4.16).

Features include:

- new dedicated bus lanes on the approach to the town centre, in addition to existing lanes of traffic
- upgraded bus stops along the route providing better waiting areas and information, including new shelters with lighting and seating to make waiting for the bus safer and more comfortable, textured paving to help people with visual impairments, raised kerbs to make it easier for people with mobility problems or pushchairs to get on and off the bus, electronic information about waiting times
- two new park and ride sites at the north and the south with 400 car-parking spaces at each. Each has a ticket office, covered waiting facilities with seating, toilets and baby-changing facilities, security staff and CCTV
- state-of-the-art buses with the latest low-emission engines

The A638 QBC has been designed to integrate with Doncaster's new public transport interchange at Frenchgate in the centre of the town, which is close to the railway station.

Photograph 4.15 State-of-the-art buses are used on the corridor

A638 QBC

Figure 4.16 A638 Doncaster's Quality Bus Corridor

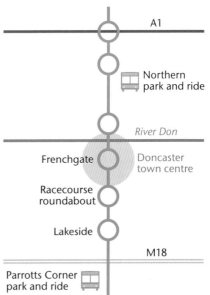

Development and globalisation

Chapter 5

Development

Defining development

The term **development** refers to an improvement in a number of different characteristics of a population. Development can suggest economic, demographic, social, political and even cultural changes:

➤ **Economic development** — an increase in a country's level of wealth. This could be accompanied by a decrease in the numbers employed in agriculture and an increase in those involved in manufacturing (at first) and services. There could also be greater access to, and use of, natural resources, with more energy used per head of population. The environment is exploited in an increasingly sustainable fashion.

Photograph 5.1 Children in Rwanda, classified as a least developed country

Jennifer Reynolds

➤ **Demographic development** — an increase in life expectancy and an overall fall in the death rate (including the infant mortality rate) combined with falling birth rates.

➤ **Social development** — can include a range of changes affecting the quality of life of the population. For example, improved levels of education and literacy, access to medical facilities (a decrease in the number of people per doctor within the country), improved levels of sanitation, better housing and increases in personal freedom.

➤ **Political development** — freedom means that people have a greater say in who forms the government and therefore the impact that it can have on their lives

➤ **Cultural development** — greater equality for women and better race relations in multicultural societies.

Measuring development

The most commonly used measurement of development is a country's **gross domestic product (GDP)** or **gross national product (GNP)**:

➤ **GDP** is the total value of all finished goods and services produced by a country in a year, usually expressed in amount per head of population.

➤ **GNP** is the total value of all finished goods and services produced by a country in a year, plus all net income earned by that country and its population from overseas sources. This is also expressed in amount per head of population. Both GDP and GNP are usually given in US dollars so that comparisons can be made.

Using such measurements an early classification of development divided the world into three groups:

➤ **First World** — also known as the **developed** world, including western Europe, North America, Japan, Australia, New Zealand

➤ **Second World** — covered the state-controlled communist countries such as the former USSR and the countries of eastern Europe

➤ **Third World** — also known as the **developing** world, containing all the other countries in Africa, Asia and Latin America

Key terms

Development gap The difference in affluence between the richer countries (those of the developed world) and the poorer countries of the developing world. This gap has increased with time.

Foreign direct investment (FDI) Investment by a transnational corporation in countries other than its parent.

Globalisation The increasing interconnection of the world's economic, cultural and political systems.

Newly industrialised countries (NICs) Countries in the developing world that have undergone rapid industrialisation since the beginning of the 1960s.

North–South divide The imagined line that separates the richer countries of the north from the poorer ones in the south. It was first proposed by the Brandt Report in 1980. The North consists of North America, Europe, Russia, Japan, Australia and New Zealand.

Sustainable development Development that meets the needs of the present without compromising the ability of future generations to meet their needs.

Transnational corporations (TNCs) A TNC is a company that has the power to coordinate and control economic operations in more than one country. The company does not have to own the operations outside its home country.

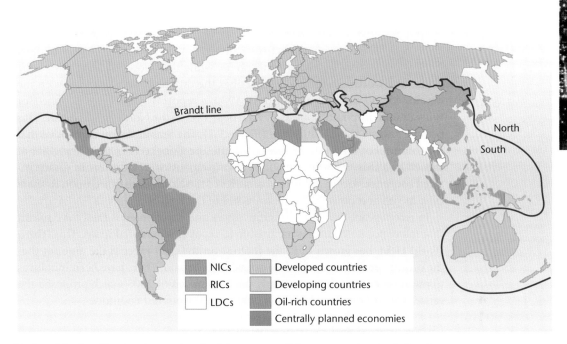

Figure 5.1 Global economic groupings

Today, this classification is too simple. It is now possible to recognise the following (see Figure 5.1):

➤ **developed countries** — the most highly developed countries, whose populations enjoy high living standards
➤ **developing countries** — countries at a lower stage of development
➤ **least developed countries (LDCs)** — countries with very low living standards, low life expectancy, high infant mortality, low levels of education, etc. This category includes a number of sub-Saharan African countries
➤ **newly industrialising countries (NICs)** — countries that have begun to develop through industrialisation in the last 40 years. Some of these, such as Singapore, could be classified as developed countries. It is also possible to recognise a group that has only just started on this process, known as **recently industrialising countries (RICs)**
➤ **centrally planned economies** — communist countries still exist, but only a few. North Korea is a good example
➤ **oil-rich countries** — these have a high GNP per head, although wealth may be concentrated in the hands of few people. Without oil, these countries would probably fall into the developing group. Saudi Arabia is a good example

As countries develop, they pass from one condition to another. The transition is gradual, with no abrupt points of change. The development process, with countries at various stages of development and developing in different ways, is referred to as the **development continuum**.

The development gap

The more developed countries have high levels of economic growth and GNP per capita, but low levels of population growth, infant mortality and numbers of people per doctor. Less developed countries have the reverse of this. There is therefore a **development gap** between these groups of countries. Most developed countries are in the northern hemisphere, while the poorer countries lie to the south. The **North–South divide** describes the difference in wealth between the developed and developing world. In 1980, a report by the German chancellor Willy Brandt proposed a line as a visual depiction of the North–South divide. This became known as the Brandt line (Figure 5.1). The Brandt Report demanded that the countries of the South be integrated into the global economic system. Brandt argued that this would bring about improvements in conditions in disadvantaged countries. Richer industrial countries of the North were called upon to share their means and power with the countries of the South.

In recent years, falling commodity prices and rising interest rates have meant that many poorer countries are unable to repay international loans. This 'Third World Debt' has grown until the interest on the debt exceeds the amount that the country produces, so the debt can never be repaid. There have been initiatives to resolve the situation, particularly the G8 summit of 2005 which proposed the cancellation of over $40 billion of debt from the poorest countries.

Other measures of development

Using GNP or GDP to measure development is flawed. There may be differences in wealth between regions of a country and between various groups (the country might have a high GDP but the wealth may be concentrated in the hands of a few people). These measures also fail to take into account the local cost of living and thus the purchasing power of people's incomes (wealth can be expressed as purchasing power parity or PPP instead of GDP/GNP). One widely used alternative measure of development is the UN **human development index (HDI)**. This measures:

➤ life expectancy at birth
➤ adult literacy, and enrolment in education at primary, secondary and tertiary levels
➤ real GDP per capita (based on the purchasing power of people's incomes, PPP)

The HDI has been criticised because some countries traditionally placed in the developing world have the same HDI as some countries in Europe. This occurs because countries can promote human development even though their income is low.

Table 6.9 in Chapter 6 (page 268) gives the HDI ratings for selected countries. The highest figure a country can achieve is 1.0. A figure below 0.5 is considered to represent low levels of development and in 2006 all 22 countries within that category were located in Africa.

Case study   Sub-Saharan Africa

Figure 5.2 shows the HDI for countries south of the Sahara. Many of these countries would occupy the lowest places on any list of development. Their biggest challenges are poverty, hunger, disease and high birth rates that leave them vulnerable to many types of disaster. The lack of roads, healthcare,

Photograph 5.2 Kibera slum in Kenya. Even this relatively well-developed sub-Saharan country has one of the biggest slums in the world

teaching provision and power sources all mean that countries are unable to provide basic needs for most of the population (Photograph 5.2). The widespread occurrence of HIV/AIDS and the frequent conflicts across the region have not helped. To move upward on the development ladder, these areas need foreign investment, either in the form of aid or direct investment by foreign companies. For example, investment in preventative rather than curative medicine would dramatically improve the health prospects of millions of people.

In 2006, the sub-Saharan countries with the highest HDI were Gabon and South Africa, ranked 119th and 121st, respectively. The lowest were Niger with an HDI of 0.311, Sierra Leone with 0.335 and Mali with 0.338.

Human development index
- Most developed
- (intermediate)
- Least developed

Figure 5.2 The human development index in sub-Saharan Africa

Globalisation

Globalisation is the increasing interconnection in the world's economic, cultural and political systems. One writer, Philippe Legrain, described globalisation as 'the way in which people's lives are becoming increasingly intertwined with those of distant people and places around the world, in economic, cultural and political terms'. **Transnational corporations (TNCs)** and nation-states are two of the major players in the global economy. Peter Dicken, an authority on the role of TNCs, has shown that globalising processes can be seen as a system of interconnected elements and scales (Figure 5.3). The growth of TNCs has been particularly rapid since the 1970s. In 1975 there were around 7,000 TNCs, today there are more than 60,000.

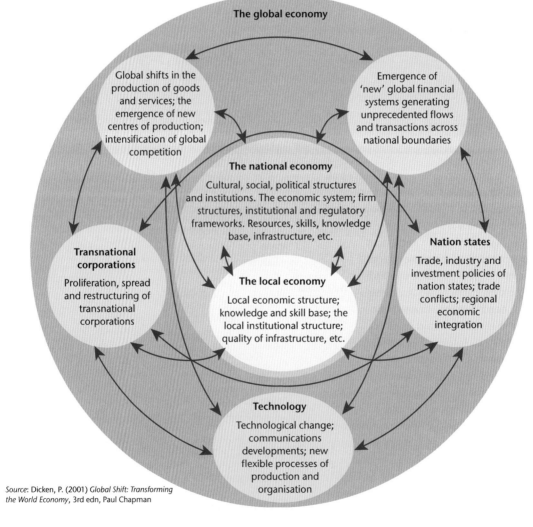

Source: Dicken, P. (2001) *Global Shift: Transforming the World Economy*, 3rd edn, Paul Chapman

Figure 5.3 Globalising processes as a system of interconnected elements and scales

There are three main forms of globalisation:

- **economic** — under both the General Agreement on Tariffs and Trade (GATT) and its successor, the World Trade Organization (WTO), world trade has expanded rapidly. TNCs have been the major force in increasing economic interdependence and several generations of newly industrialised countries (NICs) have emerged
- **cultural** — Western culture has diffused to all parts of the world through television, cinema, the internet, newspapers and magazines. This has been reflected in media, art, sport and leisure pursuits
- **political** — the influence of nation states has diminished in many areas as more and more countries organise themselves into trade blocs. The influence of Western democracies on developing countries (many of them ex-colonies) has also been strong

Globalisation can be seen in terms of:

- **urban** — a hierarchy of global cities has emerged to act as centres for the global economy
- **demographic** — the growth of international migration and the rise of multi-cultural societies
- **linguistic** — the emergence of English as the working language of the 'global village'
- **environmental** — the impact of activity in one country has a clear impact in others — for example the spread of pollutants and the impacts of global warming

History of globalisation

Some commentators believe that globalisation actually began in the late nineteenth century when:

- transport and communication networks expanded rapidly around the world
- world trade began to grow, with an increase in the level of interdependence between rich and poor nations
- capital flows began to expand as European companies started operations in other parts of the world

Events in the early twentieth century, such as the Great Depression, caused countries to fall back on their own resources, with the production process being mainly organised within national economies. Since the 1950s, however, a new global division of labour has emerged, reflecting:

- the fragmentation of production processes across national boundaries which has changed the geographical pattern of specialisation at a global scale
- international trade becoming increasingly complex
- the emergence of an increasing number of NICs such as Singapore and Taiwan
- new generations of NICs (second generation, e.g. Malaysia; third generation, e.g. India)
- the integration of the Soviet Union and the countries of eastern Europe into the capitalist system
- the opening up of the large economies of China and India to the outside world

Markets

In the late twentieth century, two major events shaped the processes of globalisation:

➤ the emergence of **free market** ideas which were promoted in the 1980s by the governments of Margaret Thatcher in the UK and Ronald Reagan in the USA. These radical ideas spread and were copied, to a varying degree, by other economies

➤ the **deregulation of world financial markets**. Prior to this, the activities of financial institutions such as banks, insurance companies and investment companies had been confined mainly within national boundaries. Financial companies were now able to scour the world looking for the best returns on their capital

Labour markets are not as advanced as financial markets in the process of globalisation. People move less easily around the world than money, because of restrictions on immigration, and the affinity that people feel to the country of their birth. However, in the late twentieth and early twenty-first centuries there has been an increasing movement across international borders of people seeking employment. Much of this has been from the developing countries (of Africa, south Asia and Latin America) to the richer areas of North America and Europe. In recent years, with the growth of the European Union, there has been a large cross-border flow of peoples from the relatively poorer eastern European member nations such as Poland and Estonia to the richer west, particularly the UK.

Trade and trade blocs

World trade has been the continuing basis of global interdependence. By the 1970s, an international economy had been established. The **General Agreement on Tariffs and Trade (GATT)** (established in 1947) sought to gradually lower the barriers to international trade, with free trade as its aim. Reaching agreements has not been easy, but average trade tariffs have shrunk to a tenth of their level when GATT first began operating. World trade has therefore been increasing at a much faster rate than GDP. In recent years, however, agreements have become increasingly difficult to reach.

Since the 1950s, countries have joined together to form trade blocs in order to stimulate trade between themselves and to obtain economic benefits from cooperation. There are various mechanisms for this, including free trade areas, customs unions, common markets and economic unions such as the European Union, of which the UK is a member.

The IMF and the World Bank

The International Monetary Fund (IMF) and the World Bank play major roles in running the world economy, although there is criticism of the way in which these two organisations operate.

The **IMF** was established to oversee the global financial system. It offers financial and technical assistance to its members, making it the international lender of last resort. One of its briefs is to renegotiate the terms of debt on behalf of nations in financial difficulties. To prevent the problem occurring again, the

IMF usually imposes conditions on its financial assistance. These conditions often include severe cuts in welfare and education spending by governments in developing countries and this has caused controversy.

The **World Bank** (International Bank for Reconstruction and Development) deals mainly with internal investment projects, usually in developing countries, with the stated aim of reducing poverty. Loans are set at the current market rate. However, one branch of the bank, known as the **International Development Association (IDA)**, provides interest-free loans (with long repayment periods) to countries with very low per capita incomes. Since the 1990s, the bank has claimed that it promotes sustainable development, with most funding going to small-scale projects. However, its critics argue that conditions attached to loans have not always had the effect of reducing poverty and dependency.

Case study   Barbie and Taiwan

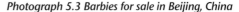

Barbie dolls (Photograph 5.3) were first produced in 1959 by the American toy company Mattel in Japan. In the late 1960s the company, wishing to lower its labour costs, moved its main factory to the island of Taiwan. This was widely seen as the 'trailblazer' for the outsourcing of production by TNCs that was to make eastern Asia the workshop of the world. At its height, the Taiwan factory produced over half the Barbie dolls made. However, within 20 years, rising incomes in Taiwan led Mattel to look again for a cheaper labour source. In 1987 Mattel opened its first factory in China where wages were much lower and gradually production was moved there. Today, Mattel still makes Barbie dolls in two Chinese factories but also has production centres in Malaysia and Indonesia (a lower wage economy).

Photograph 5.3 Barbies for sale in Beijing, China

The Taiwanese economy has benefited further from globalisation. The island is now home to many of the companies, whose names would not be recognised in the UK, responsible for making most of the world's laptops, personal organisers and MP3 players:

- **Asustek** makes iPods and Mac minis for Apple. It also makes the motherboards for one in three of the world's desktop computers.
- **Quanta** is the world's largest manufacturer of laptop computers. Quanta and other Taiwan firms make 75% of laptops for Dell, Sony, Compaq, Hewlett-Packard and other well-known brands.
- **TSMC (Taiwan Semiconductor Manufacturing Company)** is the world's largest manufacturer of outsourced computer chips with around 50% of the market.
- **UMC (United Microelectronics Corporation)** has another 25% of the computer chip market.
- **BenQ** is a major manufacturer of mobile phones, cameras and MP3 players. In 2005, it bought the mobile phone division of Siemens, one of Europe's largest manufacturing companies.

Taiwan is concerned that these high-tech industries will also move to mainland China (Asustek and BenQ already operate factories in China). Taiwan's rulers, however, seem confident that their reputation for reliability will allow them to remain in the ascendancy in these industries for the foreseeable future.

Global marketing

Global marketing has been defined as 'marketing on a worldwide scale, reconciling or taking commercial advantage of global operational differences, similarities and opportunities in order to meet global objectives'. When a company becomes a global marketeer, it views the world as one market and creates products that fit the various regional marketplaces. The ultimate goal is to sell the same thing, the same way, everywhere.

Coca-Cola is an example of a company with a single product — only minor elements are tweaked for different markets. The company uses the same formulas (one with sugar, the other with corn syrup) for all its markets. The bottle design is the same in every country but the size of bottles and cans conforms to each country's standard sizing.

Patterns of production, distribution and consumption

Globalisation brought about a new international division of labour. It is possible to recognise two main groups:
- the highly skilled, highly paid decision-making, research and managerial occupations. On a global scale, these are largely concentrated in developed countries

> the unskilled, poorly paid assembly occupations. These tend to be located in developing countries that have low labour costs

This simple division has undergone radical changes in the last 40 years. Many countries that were classified as developing countries have become NICs, and even within this group it is possible to recognise at least three generations, all at various stages of development.

Manufacturing

In 1954, around 95% of manufacturing was concentrated in the industrialised economies. Since then, decentralisation has occurred, largely as a result of **foreign direct investment (FDI)** by TNCs in those developing countries able to take on manufacturing tasks at a competitive price. This filtering down of manufacturing industry from developed countries to lower wage economies is known as **global shift**.

Another reason for this is that high technology is no longer associated with high productivity and high wages. The **transfer of technology** enables many countries in the developing world to increase their productivity without raising their wages to the same levels as developed countries. This could widen the development gap, as workers in the developing world are paid less to make the same products as those in developed countries. By the beginning of the twenty-first century, more than 50% of all manufacturing jobs were located in the developing world and over 60% of exports from those countries to the developed world were of manufactured goods.

Services

The provision of services has become increasingly detached from the production of goods. The financial sector, for example, has no direct relationship with manufacturing. Therefore, as manufacturing has become more dispersed worldwide, high level services have increasingly concentrated in places other than the old centres of manufacturing. The top of the service hierarchy is to be found in cities such as London, New York and Tokyo, which are the major centres of global industrial and financial control. Other prominent cities include Frankfurt, Chicago, Paris, Milan and Los Angeles.

In the 1990s a growing number of transnational service conglomerates emerged, seeking to extend their influence on a global scale, particularly in banking and other financial services, and advertising.

A recent trend has been the decentralisation of low level services from the developed to the developing world. Call-centre operations, for example, have moved from the UK to India where employment costs are generally 10–20% of those in the UK. This globalisation of services is following the pattern seen in manufacturing over several decades.

One of the consequences of global shift has been **deindustrialisation** in the richer countries. Global shift is not the only factor — outmoded production methods, products at the end of their life cycles and poor management have all contributed to the decline in manufacturing in those regions.

Patterns and processes

Newly industrialised countries

First phase

A key element in the process of globalisation has been the emergence of newly industrialised countries (NICs) — countries that have undergone rapid industrialisation since the early 1960s. When TNCs looked for areas where labour and other costs were lower, the countries of east Asia were targeted.

Japanese TNCs were among the first to seek new areas for their operations and it was logical that they should look to their less developed neighbours, particularly South Korea and Taiwan. These countries, along with Singapore and Hong Kong, became collectively known as the **Asian Tigers**. The advantages of these countries for the development of manufacturing industry were:

➤ a reasonably well developed level of infrastructure such as roads, railways and ports
➤ relatively well educated populations with existing skills
➤ cultural traditions that revere education and achievement
➤ good geographical location — Singapore, for example, is situated between the Indian and Pacific Oceans
➤ government support, for example offering low interest rates on bank loans
➤ less rigid laws and regulations on labour, taxation and pollution than in TNCs' parent countries, allowing more profitable operations

As the economies of NICs grew, large indigenous firms began to grow, helped by the economic climate and government aid. The *chaebols* (huge business conglomerates) of South Korea, helped by the government, were able to expand.

Second phase

As the economies of these NICs grew, wage levels and the cost of operating within those countries began to increase. As a result, Japanese, US and European TNCs looked for a second generation of countries that could support their operations. Such areas had recent improvements in both physical and human infrastructures but wage levels that were still low. At the same time, companies that had grown in the original NICs, such as the *chaebols* in South Korea, also began to move routine manufacturing tasks to their neighbours, such as Malaysia and Thailand.

Third phase

In recent years, both China and India have emerged as targets for FDI by TNCs. Since 1990, both countries have shown rapid and sustained economic growth. China's growth is the fastest experienced by any country, at one time averaging a real per capita growth of more than 10% per year.

Case study: China transforms its economy

In 1978, the Chinese leadership began moving from a centrally planned economy to a more market-orientated system. Led by Mao's successor, Deng Xiaoping, the Chinese sought to bring to an end the relative economic isolation of the country by encouraging foreign investment that would lead to huge increases in exports, as had been the case in other east Asian countries.

Initially, there was strict communist control of the way industries operated, but gradually this was relaxed. The decision-making powers of local officials and plant managers were increased, and the government permitted a wide variety of small-scale enterprises in services and light manufacturing. Agricultural output doubled in the 1980s as farmers were encouraged to make profits for themselves.

Special economic zones (SEZs) were established, where foreign companies were encouraged to set up manufacturing plants in return for preferable tax rates. The government designated 14 coastal cities as **open cities**, offering incentives for foreign

Table 5.1 China's exports and imports, 1952–2007 (US$ billion)

Year	Exports	Imports	Balance
1952	0.82	1.12	−0.30
1962	1.49	1.17	0.32
1970	2.26	2.33	−0.07
1973	7.26	7.49	−0.23
1980	18.12	20.02	−1.90
1985	27.35	42.25	−14.90
1990	62.09	53.35	8.74
1995	148.78	132.08	16.70
2000	249.20	225.09	24.11
2001	266.10	243.55	22.55
2002	325.60	295.17	30.43
2003	438.37	412.84	25.53
2004	593.40	561.40	32.00
2005	762.00	660.00	102.00
2006	969.00	791.00	178.00
2007	1,220.00	955.00	265.00

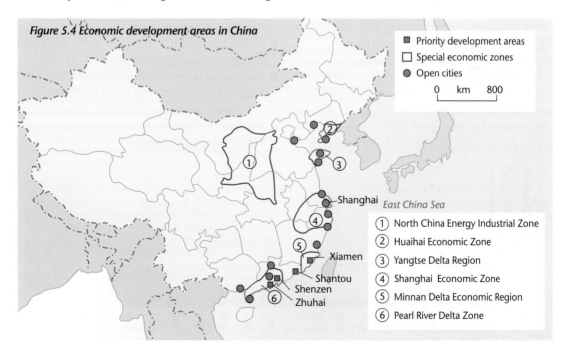

Figure 5.4 Economic development areas in China

- ■ Priority development areas
- ☐ Special economic zones
- ● Open cities

0 km 800

East China Sea

Shanghai

Xiamen
Shantou
Shenzen
Zhuhai

1 North China Energy Industrial Zone
2 Huaihai Economic Zone
3 Yangtse Delta Region
4 Shanghai Economic Zone
5 Minnan Delta Economic Region
6 Pearl River Delta Zone

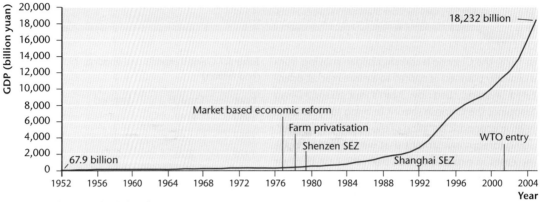

Figure 5.5 The growth of China's GDP, 1952–2005

companies to invest. The SEZs were initially concentrated on the coast facing Taiwan and the Pacific, particularly in the area around Hong Kong. Other industrial zones were established in the country including the Yangtze River delta near Shanghai and the Pearl River delta in Guangdong Province (Figure 5.4).

Large amounts of FDI led to economic growth. Since the early 1990s, China has averaged a real per capita growth of more than 8% a year, with over 10% in certain years (Figure 5.5). In the early part of the twenty-first century, China was receiving over $50 billion per year of inward investment (Figure 5.6). In 2006, the figure had climbed to $63 billion, which represents the highest figure for any developing country.

A significant step in the country's economic progress was China's entry into the WTO in December 2001 following several years of detailed negotiation. This has given China better access to global markets and, as a result, trade has boomed;

exports of $266 billion in 2001 had rocketed to $969 billion in 2006 (Table 5.1).

However, the rapid economic growth has not been without its problems. The major concerns are:

- a dramatic increase in the income gap between rich and poor despite high GDP growth (although it has been estimated that the number of Chinese living on less than $1 a day fell by 150 million between 1990 and 1999)
- the relative poverty of much of the interior of the country and the mountain areas which has led to massive rural–urban migration
- unemployment has grown in some areas and people are moving to find work
- the environment is deteriorating in many areas. Soil erosion has resulted in large losses of arable land and there is serious concern about air pollution
- the economy is driven by exports and investment rather than by consumption

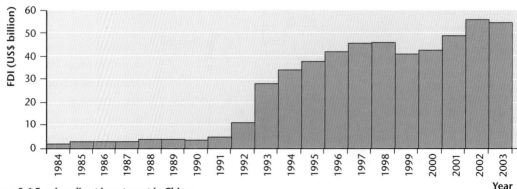

Figure 5.6 Foreign direct investment in China

Photograph 5.4 Women working in a textile factory in Tianmen

TopFoto

Case study India: a third generation NIC led by the service sector

Unlike the other emerging Asian economies, recent transformations in the Indian economy have been based more on the service sector than on the manufacturing growth which has occurred in countries such as Taiwan, South Korea and Malaysia.

Until recently there has been a fairly low level of foreign direct investment (FDI) in the Indian manufacturing sector (recent economic reforms are beginning to change this). It is the service sector which has been the main engine of economic growth. Services accounted for around 50% of GDP at the beginning of the twenty-first century (Figure 5.7)

India's great advantage lies in the number of highly qualified professionals in its workforce whose skills are in demand in many areas across the English-speaking world. This has resulted in a great deal of outsourcing of work from developed countries to Indian companies, particularly those operating in software and IT services. Other sectors

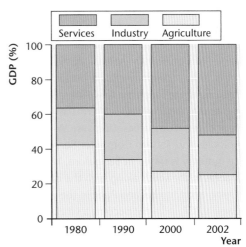

Figure 5.7 Division of India's GDP by sector

which have shown large growth include media, retailing, financial services, entertainment, advertising and tourism.

This growth, though, has mainly been of benefit to the English-speaking middle classes and certain areas of south India. The primary sector still dominates the country in terms of employment, with around 70% of the population still engaged in agriculture and other primary activities. Much of the farming is at subsistence level which accounts for the very high degree of rural poverty.

Outsourcing of work to India from developed countries began with software development, but rapidly progressed to call centres and a wide range of other business services (Figure 5.8). This led to the outsourcing of the administration and maintenance of overseas firms through ICT systems. India's advantage in this respect was based upon:

■ a large English-speaking workforce (estimated to be over 50 million)
■ much lower labour costs (one source estimated that for every 1,000 jobs relocated to India, a British company would save £10 million)
■ the fact that many developed countries had significant ICT skills shortages

The early growth of the sector was driven by foreign companies, mainly from the USA and the UK. Many skilled Indian workers migrated to such countries and gained valuable experience there. They used this experience to set up companies on their return to India. This allowed the number of home-grown ICT companies to significantly increase in the 1990s. In 1999, the Indian company Infosys became the first from the country to list on the New York stock market and in that year there were four IT firms listed among India's top ten companies (Infosys, Wipro, NIIT Technologies and Satyam Computer Services). This service industry is based in Bangalore, Hyderabad and Madras in the south along with the capital city, New Delhi, and Mumbai and Pune in the west.

As well as ICT, India has become a world leader in **'back office functions'**, properly known as IT-enabled services. These are operated by Indian firms for companies in countries like the UK and include:

■ call centres to deal with sales and customer enquiries for companies like British Airways,

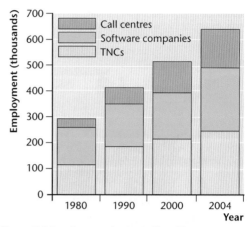

Figure 5.8 Employment in the Indian IT sector, 1980–2004

Lloyds TSB, Prudential, HSBC, Barclays, BT, British Gas and Norwich Union (Aviva)
■ dealing with accounts (American Express, Citigroup)
■ data entry and conversion, such as medical and legal transcription
■ knowledge services, which require specialists using databases to solve customer problems

The growth of India's service industry has not been without problems and critics:
■ Unions in the developed world are concerned about job losses and in some cases have pressurised firms to bring jobs back to the USA and UK.
■ Various organisations in the developed world have voiced concerns about standards of privacy and data protection in Indian IT companies.
■ Tata Consultancy Services (TCS), another large Indian IT company, operates in over 40 countries worldwide and employs over 100,000 people. In 2007 it reported that it was to outsource Indian jobs to Mexico because of a shortage of skilled operatives and the rising value of the rupee. Other companies, such as Wipro, Infosys and Satyam, have set up operations in China where an excess of well-trained software engineers has kept salaries low.

Growth in the twenty-first century

In the twenty-first century there is a new, evolving stage, in which new markets are emerging. This has given a boost to many of the 'older' economies. These emerging markets represent at least three-quarters of the world's population. They include India, China, Korea, Brazil, United Arab Emirates (UAE), Chile, Turkey, Saudi Arabia, Russia, Argentina and South Africa.

Many emerging economies are moving from centralised political and economic systems to more open market models as a result of:
➤ relaxations of controls on foreign exchange
➤ greater autonomy for financial institutions
➤ removal of trade barriers
➤ political reforms that in turn facilitate more change

The momentum for such changes has been the need to:
➤ raise living standards
➤ increase opportunities for the local population
➤ attract foreign investment

Although some of the emerging markets continue to receive foreign aid, the most successful have broken that dependency by raising their markets to international standards, thereby becoming more attractive to foreign investors.

Case study Dubai

Dubai lies on the Persian Gulf and is one of a number of states that make up the United Arab Emirates (UAE). Its geographical position (Figure 5.9) has always made it an important port of call for foreign traders, chiefly those from India, and until the 1930s it was well known for its pearl exports.

Its economy boomed with the discovery of oil in the 1960s. This led to an influx of foreign workers — it has been estimated that the population of Dubai City grew by more than 300% between 1968 and 1975. To widen the base of its economy, Dubai has invested in new developments, particularly those associated with new technologies, and it has encouraged the flow of foreign capital into the country. It has built the largest man-made harbour in the world, and using new building technologies it has constructed some of the world's tallest skyscrapers, such as the Emirates Tower. Most of its current revenues are from trade, real estate and financial services. Revenues from oil and natural gas now contribute less than 5% to Dubai's GDP.

Figure 5.9 Map showing the location of Dubai

Tourism

The construction of Burj Al Arab, the world's tallest freestanding hotel (Photograph 5.5), and the creation of new residential developments were used to market Dubai for tourism. This has prompted the building of gigantic shopping malls, theme parks, purpose-built resorts and sporting stadiums.

One of the newest developments is the Palm Islands, one of the largest land-reclamation projects in the world. Once completed, these islands will have hotels, apartment blocks, villas, marinas, water theme parks, restaurants, shopping malls and sports facilities.

Business

Dubai is increasingly a hub for service industries such as IT and finance, with the new Dubai International Financial Centre (DIFC) and Dubai Internet City (DIC), which is an information technology park used as a base by companies targeting emerging markets. Ownership and taxation benefits have led many internationally known companies to establish there, including Microsoft, IBM, Oracle Corporation, Sun Microsystems, Cisco, HP, Nokia, Sony Ericsson and Siemens. The country has also recently opened Dubiotech (the Dubai Biotechnology and Research Park), dedicated to life science industries including pharmaceuticals and biotechnology.

Photograph 5.5
Burj Al Arab hotel
at night

TopFoto

Countries at very low levels of economic development

Since 1968 the poorest countries in the world have been categorised as **least developed countries** (Figure 5.10). The United Nations described them as 'the poorest and most economically weak of the developing countries, with formidable economic, institutional and human resource problems, which are often compounded by geographical handicaps and natural and man-made disasters'. By the beginning of the twenty-first century, the UN recognised 50 countries in this category. In the UN review of 2007, Cape Verde was removed from that list (Table 5.2). Of the countries that remained 33 are in Africa, all south of the Sahara. Other

Afghanistan	Gambia	Rwanda
Angola	Guinea	Samoa
Bangladesh	Guinea-Bissau	São Tomé and Principe
Benin	Haiti	Senegal
Bhutan	Kiribati	Sierra Leone
Burkina Faso	Lao People's Democratic Republic	Solomon Islands
Burundi	Lesotho	Somalia
Cambodia	Liberia	Sudan
Cape Verde	Madagascar	Timor-Lesté
Central African Republic	Malawi	Togo
Chad	Maldives	Tuvalu
Comoros	Mali	Uganda
Democratic Republic of the Congo	Mauritania	United Republic of Tanzania
Djibouti	Mozambique	Vanuatu
Equatorial Guinea	Myanmar (Burma)	Yemen
Eritrea	Nepal	Zambia
Ethiopia	Niger	

LDCs are in southeast Asia, and a number of small island states in the Pacific such as Kiribati, Samoa, Solomon Islands, Tuvalu and Vanuatu (not shown on Figure 5.10).

Table 5.2 Least developed countries, 2006

LDCs are defined by the following features:

➤ low incomes, measured as less than $800 GDP per capita per year averaged over a 3-year period
➤ human resource weaknesses, based upon indicators of nutrition, health, education levels and literacy: specifically life expectancy at birth, per capita

Figure 5.10 The least developed countries

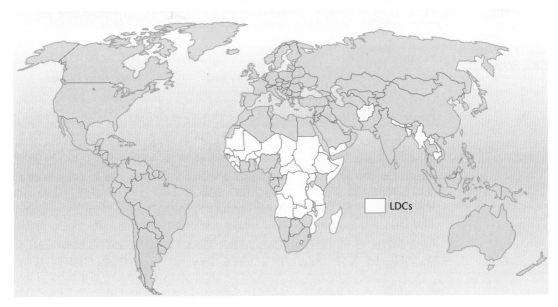

LDCs

calorie intake, combined primary and secondary school enrolment, and adult literacy rates
➤ economic vulnerability, shown by the low level of economic diversification, which is based on the share of manufacturing in the GDP, the share of the labour force in manufacturing industry, the annual per capita energy consumption and merchandise export concentration levels. Vulnerability can also be measured by the percentage of the population displaced by natural disasters

As well as extreme poverty, many LDCs also suffer from some of the following:
➤ ongoing and widespread conflict (including civil war and ethnic conflict, e.g. Darfur in Sudan, see pages 246–249)
➤ extensive political corruption
➤ a lack of political and social stability
➤ a form of government that is authoritarian in nature, such as a dictatorship

Quality of life

People live in poverty in all LDCs. A large proportion of the population has an income too small to meet their basic needs. The resources in the economy, even when equally distributed, are not enough to provide the needs of the population on a sustainable basis. The economic freedom of the majority of the population is therefore seriously constrained. In 2005 it was estimated that 277 million people within LDCs were living on less than $1 per day (Table 5.3).

In some cases the incidence of poverty has been falling, but a high population growth rate means that the actual number living in extreme poverty (on less than $1 per day) has increased over the long term (Figure 5.11). Table 5.3 also shows that there is a sharp contrast between African and Asian LDCs. Poverty is much higher in Africa — 374 million Africans have an income of less than $2 per day compared with 203 million Asians.

Table 5.3 Poverty in LDCs, 1990–2005

| | Population living on... | | | | | | | |
| | ...less than $1 a day | | | | ...less than $2 a day | | | |
	1990	1995	2000	2005	1990	1995	2000	2005
Percentage of total population								
All LDCs	40.4	40.8	38.9	36.1	81.6	80.4	78.8	75.7
African LDCs	49.7	49.3	46.9	43.9	83.9	83.1	82.2	79.9
Asian LDCs	26.9	28.3	26.9	24.0	78.3	76.4	73.6	69.2
Millions								
All LDCs	212.4	245.2	264.6	277.0	428.8	483.0	535.1	580.8
African LDCs	154.9	176.1	192.0	205.6	261.4	296.5	336.4	374.6
Asian LDCs	56.9	68.4	71.9	70.6	165.6	184.5	196.7	203.9
Island LDCs	0.6	0.7	0.8	0.8	1.8	2.0	2.1	2.3

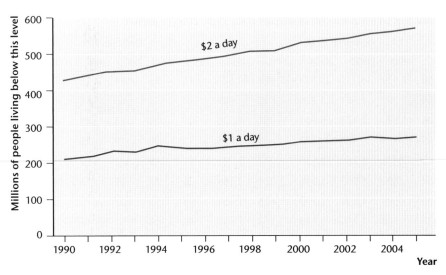

Figure 5.11 Growth of poverty in LDCs, 1990–2005

Despite some economic growth in certain LDCs, they are still very much dependent on external finance because this growth is failing to trickle down into improved wellbeing for the majority of their population. In 2006, net aid payments reached the record level of $28 billion, with bilateral and multilateral aid mostly funding social infrastructure and services. In 2006, the share of aid going to education, health, population programmes, water supply and sanitation was higher than in previous years, reflecting the focus on the Millennium Development Goals (see below) and the concern to improve the governance of such countries.

Debt

From the 1970s onwards, as a result of borrowing money from banks in the developed world, developing countries (particularly LDCs) found themselves in a debt crisis. Experts have attributed the problem to increasing oil prices in the 1970s, higher interest rates in the 1980s, falling export prices and problems of domestic economic management.

There was no hope of these debts being repaid (Table 5.4) and interest accumulating on them made the chances of repayment even more remote. This situation made it impossible to halt socioeconomic decline.

In 1996, the International Monetary Fund (IMF) and the World Bank, after lobbying by NGOs and other bodies, produced the **Heavily Indebted Poor Countries (HIPC)** programme (Figure 5.12). This provided debt relief and low-interest loans to reduce external debt repayments to sustainable levels, on condition that countries met a range of economic management and performance targets.

In 2005, the G8 countries, meeting at Gleneagles (Scotland), proposed to cancel the entire debt of the eligible HIPCs under a scheme known as the **Multilateral Debt Relief Initiative (MDRI)**. Countries would become eligible for debt relief if they met all of the following conditions:

Table 5.4 External debt and debt service payments of selected LDCs, 1985–2006 ($ million)

Country	External debt						Debt service					
	1985	1990	2000	2004	2005	2006	1985	1990	2000	2004	2005	2006
Bangladesh	6,658	12,439	15,717	20,129	18,928	20,521	195	495	684	646	769	624
Benin	854	1,292	1,591	1,916	1,855	824	41	33	60	54	60	81
Ethiopia	5,206	8,630	5,483	6,644	6,261	2,326	111	201	123	89	80	160
Gambia	245	369	483	672	668	725	1	30	19	25	25	28
Guinea	1,465	2,476	3,388	3,538	3,247	3,281	61	149	131	149	131	141
Haiti	757	890	953	1,044	1,034	1,189	21	15	29	72	45	48
Madagascar	2,520	3,689	4,691	3,790	3,466	1,453	94	155	102	75	66	67
Malawi	1,021	1,558	2,705	3,428	3,183	850	76	103	51	49	60	70
Maldives	83	78	206	353	368	459	9	7	19	32	33	33
Mali	1,456	2,468	2,980	3,320	3,025	1,436	34	43	68	79	70	79
Mauritania	1,454	2,113	2,378	2,333	2,316	1,630	76	118	66	45	54	69
Mozambique	2,871	4,650	7,257	4,869	4,637	3,265	57	64	84	62	66	53
Myanmar	3,098	4,695	5,928	7,239	6,645	6,828	185	57	75	105	92	70
Nepal	590	1,627	2,869	3,358	3,197	3,409	13	52	95	115	116	136
Senegal	2,559	3,744	3,607	3,940	3,883	1,984	103	225	185	297	168	198
Sierra Leone	711	1,197	1,226	1,728	1,682	1,428	15	16	19	24	20	27
Uganda	1,239	2,606	3,497	4,753	4,427	1,264	56	84	47	70	133	110
United Republic of Tanzania	9,105	6,454	6,931	7,805	7,796	4,240	140	136	150	86	75	101
Zambia	4,487	6,905	5,722	7,455	5,378	2,325	87	171	177	211	194	147

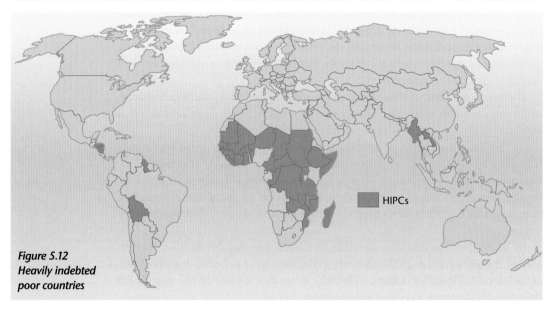

HIPCs

*Figure 5.12
Heavily indebted
poor countries*

> satisfactory economic performance under an IMF poverty reduction and growth facility programme
> satisfactory progress in implementing a poverty reduction strategy
> an adequate public expenditure management system that meets minimum standards for governance and transparency in the use of public resources

By October 2007, 16 LDCs were receiving debt relief under the HIPC initiative, all of which were in sub-Saharan Africa. These countries further benefited from MDRI, their total debts being reduced from $54.7 billion in 2005 to $25.7 billion in 2006.

Social problems

It is clear that LDCs have many problems apart from lack of income. In September 2000 world leaders adopted a **UN Millennium Declaration**, which targets a broader range of human development indicators. It commits countries to a new global partnership to reduce extreme poverty and sets a number of targets with a deadline of 2015. These goals are to:
> eradicate extreme hunger and poverty
> achieve universal primary education
> promote gender equality and empower women
> reduce child mortality
> improve maternal health
> combat HIV/AIDS, malaria and other diseases
> ensure environmental sustainability
> develop a global partnership for development

A number of specific targets have been set to meet these aims in LDCs. They are:
> halving, between 1990 and 2015, the proportion of people whose income is less than $1 per day
> halving, between 1990 and 2015, the proportion of people suffering from hunger
> ensuring that, by 2015, all children (both boys and girls) are able to complete a full course of primary schooling
> eliminating gender disparity in primary and secondary education as soon as possible, but certainly no later than 2015 at all levels of education
> reducing, by two-thirds, between 1990 and 2015, the under-5 mortality rate
> halving, by 2015, the proportion of people without access to safe drinking water
> halving the proportion of people without access to sanitation

 Case study **Malawi**

Malawi (Figure 5.13) is one of the poorest countries in the world. In the 2005 United Nations' human development index it was ranked 165th of 177 countries and its GDP per capita is one of the lowest in the world (around $170 per head, taking into account purchasing power). In recent years it has been seriously affected by drought. In 2005 it faced a serious food shortage with an estimated 4.85 million people (around 40% of the population) requiring emergency food support.

Malawi was originally known as Nyasaland, and was ruled by the British from 1891. In 1953 it joined with Northern and Southern Rhodesia (now Zambia and Zimbabwe) to form the Central African Federation. In 1963 this was dissolved and Nyasaland was granted full independence by Britain, becoming a republic in 1964. Originally a one-party state, under its president, Dr Hastings Banda, Malawi became a multi-party democracy in 1994.

It is one of sub-Saharan Africa's most densely populated countries, with 115 people km^{-2}. The population growth rate is high — 2.6% per year at the start of the twenty-first century (Figure 5.14), with 5.7 births per woman. The population increased from 9.93 million at the 1998 census to an estimated 13 million in 2007. The economy is dependent upon the export of agricultural products which are vulnerable to external trade factors and drought in the country. Malawi also has high import costs — all fuel except fuelwood has to be imported.

HIV/AIDS is one of the more serious problems faced by the country. More than 1 million of the population are believed to be HIV-positive which results in around 90,000 deaths every year. It is estimated that there are now more than 1 million orphans in the country, half of which are a direct result of deaths from AIDS. Life expectancy has fallen below 40 years.

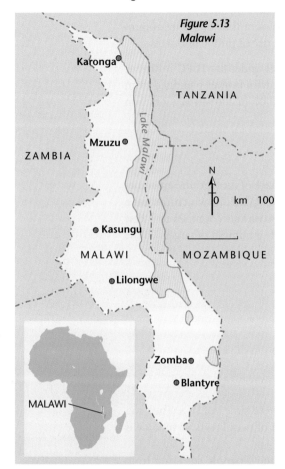

Figure 5.13 Malawi

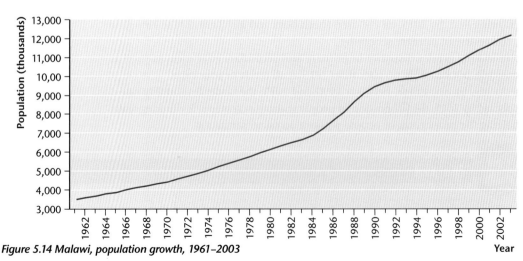

Figure 5.14 Malawi, population growth, 1961–2003

Photograph 5.6 Children in a Malawi school

Malawi was officially classified by the World Bank as a low-income country when it was estimated that the ratio of its debts to the value of its exports was over 300%. In 2000 it became eligible for the HIPC initiative but it failed to meet the conditions set by the IMF, particularly because of higher than expected government spending caused by famine and the need to import food. By repaying £440 million by 2006, however, the country became eligible for further debt relief under MDRI and more than £2 billion of its debts have been cancelled. This has released a large amount of capital that would have been spent on debt repayments and which can now be invested in public services.

Global social and economic groupings

The North–South divide

In the section on development (see page 181) we saw how a development gap has grown between the richer countries of the 'North' and the poorer ones in the 'South'. The line which divides these two groups is known as the North–South divide or the Brandt line because it was first set out in the Brandt Report of 1980 (see Figure 5.1, page 181).

Between 1950 and 1980, the North accounted for almost 80% of global GDP but contained only 20% of the world's population, whereas the South accounted for 80% of the population but generated only 20% of global income. Since then, globalisation has resulted in huge levels of growth and interdependence. To many economists this has made the concept of the North–South divide obsolete. Figure 5.1 shows how a number of global economic groupings have emerged, all part of the ongoing development process known as the development continuum.

One view is that instead of two groups (i.e. rich/poor), the world's economies fall into four groups:

➤ **Group 1** comprises the affluent countries, such as the USA, most of Europe and Japan. For the past 50 years they have dominated the global economy, but other countries are now emerging to contest their supremacy.

➤ **Group 2** contains these emerging economies, around 30 countries whose per capita GDP growth rates are 3.5% or greater. This group has a total population of over 3 billion or roughly 50% of the world's population. It includes China and India. The high levels of growth may mean that these countries replace much of the first group as the engines of the global economy.

➤ **Group 3** consists of more than 50 countries and contains over 1 billion people. Many have important natural resources, for example around 60% of proven oil reserves. To date they have not been able to translate the wealth obtained from their natural resources into sustained economic growth.

➤ **Group 4** comprises those countries that are lagging behind. These are the world's poorest economies and are home to another billion people. They continue to stagnate or decline economically, being isolated from the global economy and facing crucial development challenges. Most of these countries are in sub-Saharan Africa.

This development patchwork (some refer to it as a development continuum) has occurred because many countries of the South tried to achieve economic improvement relative to the rich countries of the North, and wealth-generating activities were redistributed from the richer zones to the poorer ones. States in the South have attempted to:

➤ increase their ability to pursue autonomous industrial policies
➤ change trade rules
➤ secure higher levels of development assistance
➤ encourage a transworld movement that makes the global economy more equitable

Social and economic groupings of nations

As countries sought to further their economic development, they looked for alliances that would stimulate trade between countries (**trade blocs**) and provide other economic benefits. There are different types of alliances:

➤ **Free trade areas** — countries agree to abolish tariffs and quotas on trade between themselves but maintain restrictions on goods coming from outside the area. Examples include the North American Free Trade Agreement (NAFTA; see case study, page 206) and the European Free Trade Association (EFTA).

➤ **Customs unions** — member countries operate a tariff on imports from outside the group. The South American Regional Trade Agreement, known as Mercosur, is such a union.

➤ **Common markets** — these are like customs unions but also allow the free movement of labour and capital. The European Union once existed in this form.

➤ **Economic unions** — members are required to do all the above, and to adopt common policies in such areas as agriculture, transport, pollution, industry, energy and regional development. The present form of the European Union is such an organisation.

The major trade blocs in the world are:

➤ **European Union (EU)** — see below
➤ **North American Free Trade Agreement (NAFTA)** — see below
➤ **Association of Southeast Asian Nations (ASEAN)** — consisting of Brunei, Cambodia, Indonesia, Laos, Malaysia, Myanmar (Burma), Philippines, Singapore, Thailand and Vietnam
➤ **European Free Trade Association (EFTA)** — once much larger (the UK, among others, was a member) but now containing only Iceland, Norway, Switzerland and Liechtenstein
➤ **Southern Africa Development Community (SADC)** — consists of Angola, Botswana, Congo, Lesotho, Madagascar, Malawi, Mozambique, Mauritius, Namibia, Seychelles, South Africa, Swaziland, Tanzania, Zambia and Zimbabwe
➤ **Mercosur (Mercado Comun del Sur)** — consists of several South American countries including Argentina, Brazil, Paraguay and Uruguay
➤ **Andean Community** — consists of Bolivia, Colombia, Ecuador and Peru
➤ **Caribbean Community (CARICOM)** — an organisation of Caribbean nations and dependencies

Consequences of international groupings

Positive consequences include the following:

➤ a greater chance of peace with international understanding (particularly true for Europe post-1945)
➤ increased trade as barriers are removed, which improves the economy, leading to better living standards
➤ a greater overall democratic function
➤ particular sectors of a national economy can be supported (e.g. agriculture within the EU member states — Common Agricultural Policy)
➤ remote regions within countries receive support from the larger organisation (e.g. the EU Regional Fund helps regions such as southern Italy and western Ireland, Photograph 5.7). Also support for declining industrial regions
➤ possibility of developing a common currency to prevent large currency fluctuations and simplify transactions
➤ people seeking work can move between countries more easily

*Photograph 5.7
Peripheral areas
of the EU, like
Connemara in
western Ireland,
have benefited from
EU funding*

Jane Buekett

➤ smaller nations have a bigger representation in world affairs

Negative consequences include:
➤ a loss of sovereignty — decisions are centralised by what some see as an unde-mocratic bureaucracy
➤ some loss of financial controls to a central authority such as a bank (e.g. European Central Bank, which oversees monetary policy in the euro zone)
➤ pressure to adopt central legislation (for example in Europe, the Social Chapter, Bosman ruling on soccer transfers, food rules)
➤ certain economic sectors are damaged by having to share resources (for example, the UK sharing its traditional fishing grounds with other EU nations such as Spain and France)
➤ elites within the system can hold a disproportionate amount of power through voting systems
➤ the drive towards federalism from some countries is opposed by others
➤ smaller regions within large countries demand a greater voice which has led to separatist movements (see the section on separatism in Chapter 6)

Case study North American Free Trade Agreement

The North American Free Trade Agreement was signed by the USA, Canada and Mexico in 1994 (Figure 5.15). The immediate objective was to gradually phase out tariffs between the member countries by 2010. The main driver for this agree-ment was the challenge presented by trade blocs from other parts of the world, particularly Europe. Mexico had got into debt in the 1970s and 1980s, and hoped that economic growth and higher employment would result from joining NAFTA.

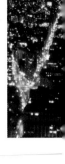

NAFTA's main aims are:

- gradual elimination of all trade barriers
- promotion of economic competition between members
- increased investment opportunities
- generally improved cooperation between the three member states

Supporters of NAFTA have pointed out that:

- trade between member countries tripled between 1993 and 2007 (£306 billion to $930 billion)
- manufacturing grew in the USA, with increased employment
- Mexico received increased foreign investment (as foreign companies established plants in the country in order to gain access to Mexico's NAFTA

trading partners' markets), higher wages for Mexican workers and increased sales from the agricultural sector

Opponents of NAFTA have pointed out that:

- some Canadian companies have closed because of competition from lower-cost US firms
- some US firms have moved to Mexico, and American jobs have been lost
- food surpluses from the USA and Canada could be dumped in Mexico affecting the peasant agricultural economy
- the growth of US-owned, labour-intensive, export-orientated companies (known as maquiladoras) on the Mexican border keeps wage rates down
- Mexico could be exploited because of its less stringent pollution laws

Figure 5.15 Area covered by NAFTA

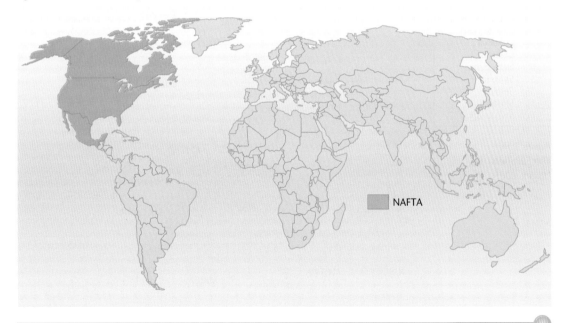

Growth of the European Union (EU)

In 1957, the signing of the Treaty of Rome created the European Economic Community (EEC). The original six members were added to over the years to give a membership of 15 at the end of the twentieth century. Since then another 12 nations have joined, bringing the total membership to 27 in 2008 (Figure 5.16). The organisation changed its name, first to the European Community (EC) and then to the European Union (EU). In its early days it was known as 'the Common Market' in the UK. Countries joined as follows:

➤ **1957** — the original six members were France, Italy, West Germany (now Germany, since reunification of East and West), Belgium, the Netherlands, Luxembourg
➤ **1973** — UK, Ireland, Denmark
➤ **1981** — Greece
➤ **1986** — Spain, Portugal
➤ **1995** — Austria, Sweden, Finland
➤ **2004** — Cyprus, Czech Republic, Estonia, Hungary, Latvia, Lithuania, Malta, Poland, Slovakia, Slovenia
➤ **2007** — Bulgaria, Romania

☐ EU countries

A	Albania
B	Belgium
BO	Bosnia
C	Croatia
CZ	Czech Republic
L	Luxembourg
M	Moldova
MA	Macedonia
N	Netherlands
S	Slovenia
SE	Serbia
SL	Slovakia
SW	Switzerland

Figure 5.16
The European
Union, 2009

The 1957 treaty was established to develop closer economic ties between the member nations. It was considered important to tie West Germany to an economic union that could promote prosperity and guarantee future peace on the continent. The aims of economic integration have been promoted through the years by:

➤ reducing tariffs and other barriers to trade between members
➤ establishing a common external tariff on imports from outside the union
➤ allowing free movement of labour, capital and other factors of production

➤ establishing common policies on agriculture, fishing, industry, energy and transport

Countries have developed greater interdependence and, as their economies have become more integrated, living standards have risen across Europe. Trade has encouraged competition and promoted a greater efficiency through economies of scale as each producer has had access to much larger markets. The Treaty of Maastricht (signed in February 1992) paved the way for monetary union in 2002. The members at that time (except the UK, Denmark and Sweden) adopted a common currency (the euro). Since then, Cyprus, Malta and Slovenia have been accepted into the euro zone and it is hoped that all nations that joined in 2004 and 2007 will eventually adopt the euro. Slovakia joined in 2009.

As more countries push for closer integration, the focus has been on the establishment of a constitution. Its main aims would be to:
➤ replace the existing, overlapping treaties that have grown up through the life of the EEC/EC/EU
➤ codify human rights legislation
➤ streamline the decision-making process within the EU

The original treaty setting out the constitution was signed by all members in 2004 but it could not come into force as it was rejected in referendums in France and the Netherlands. A new treaty, the Treaty of Lisbon, was signed in December 2007. The major features of this treaty were:
➤ the creation of a European president
➤ the creation of a common foreign policy to increase the EU's profile
➤ the number of commissioners reduced from 27 to 18
➤ national vetoes removed in about 50 policy areas
➤ voting weights between member states redistributed

The process has again been thrown into question by the rejection of the treaty in a referendum of the Irish electorate.

Aspects of globalisation

Transnational corporations

A transnational corporation (TNC) is a company that operates in at least two countries. Its organisation is hierarchical, with the headquarters and research and development (R&D) department often located in the home country (country of origin), while the centres of production tend to be overseas. As the organisation becomes more global, regional headquarters and, in some cases, regional R&D will develop in the manufacturing areas. The 20 largest companies in the world according to sales figures in 2007 are listed in Table 5.5 and other UK companies in the world's top 150 are given in Table 5.6.

*Table 5.5
World's largest
companies, 2007*

Company	Country	Sector	Sales ($ billion)
Wal-Mart	USA	Retailing	378.8
ExxonMobil	USA	Oil & Gas	358.6
Royal Dutch Shell	UK/the Netherlands	Oil & Gas	355.78
BP	UK	Oil & Gas	281.03
Chevron	USA	Oil & Gas	203.97
Toyota Motor	Japan	Vehicles	203.8
Total	France	Oil & Gas	199.74
ING Group	The Netherlands	Insurance	197.93
General Motors	USA	Vehicles	181.12
General Electric	USA	Industrials	172.74
Ford Motor	USA	Vehicles	172.46
ConocoPhillips	USA	Oil & Gas	171.50
Citigroup	USA	Banking	159.23
AXA Group	France	Insurance	151.70
Volkswagen	Germany	Vehicles	149.00
HSBC Holdings	UK	Banking	146.50
Daimler	Germany	Vehicles	145.11
Dexia	Belgium	Banking	140.78
Allianz	Germany	Insurance	139.12
Sinopec	China	Oil & Gas	133.79

*Table 5.6 Other UK
companies in the
world's top 150,
2007*

Company	Sector	Sales ($ billion)
Royal Bank of Scotland	Banking	108.45
HBOS	Banking	100.32
Tesco	Retailing	83.61
Aviva	Insurance	81.83
Barclays	Banking	79.70
Prudential	Insurance	70.34
Vodafone	Telecom services	61.23
Lloyds TSB	Banking	58.74
Unilever	Food/hygiene	54.82
GlaxoSmithKline	Pharmaceuticals	45.07

TNCs take many different forms and include a wide range of companies involved in the following primary, secondary (manufacturing) and tertiary (service) activities:

➤ **Resource extraction**, particularly in the mining sector, for materials such as oil and gas (five of the top ten companies in Table 5.5 are oil and gas extractors and refiners — ExxonMobil, Royal Dutch Shell, BP, Chevron and Total).

- ➤ **Manufacturing** (in three main sectors):
  - **high-tech industries** such as computers, scientific instruments, microelectronics and pharmaceuticals (Photograph 5.8)
  - **large-volume consumer goods** such as motor vehicles, tyres, televisions and other electrical goods (the vehicle manufacturers Toyota, General Motors, Ford, Volkswagen and Daimler all appear in Table 5.5)
  - **mass-produced consumer goods** such as cigarettes, drinks, breakfast cereals, cosmetics and branded goods.
- ➤ **Service operations** such as banking/insurance, advertising, freight transport, hotel chains and fast-food outlets (the ING Group, Citigroup, AXA, HSBC, Dexia and Allianz in Table 5.5 are all in the financial sector).

Photograph 5.8 Hi-tech companies such as Vodafone are among the big TNCs

The significance, growth and location of TNCs

TNCs control and coordinate economic activities in different countries and develop trade within and between units of the same corporation in different countries. Because of this, they can often control the terms of trade and can reduce the effect of quota restrictions on the movement of goods.

They are able to take advantage of spatial differences in factors of production at a global scale. They can exploit differences in the availability of capital, labour costs and land/building costs — for example, they can take advantage of cheaper labour costs in the least developed countries. In 2002, the household appliance manufacturer Dyson moved its production from a plant in Wiltshire to Malaysia to take advantage of cheaper labour. The company did retain several hundred jobs in Wiltshire, where research is carried out.

TNCs can also locate to take advantage of government policies such as lower taxes, subsidies and grants, and less strict legislation (if any) on employment and pollution. They can get round trade barriers by locating production within the markets where they want to sell. Japanese motor vehicle firms, for example, have been attracted to locations in the EU because of quota restrictions on the import of Japanese-made vehicles into Europe. By producing vehicles within Europe, they are considered to be European manufacturers and gain entry to the European markets.

Nissan, Honda and Toyota all have vehicle plants located in the UK. The first to locate here was Nissan at Washington (near Sunderland), followed by Toyota (at Burnaston, near Derby) and Honda. Honda's facility at Swindon (Photograph 5.9) consists of two car assembly plants and an engine plant. In 2008 it employed more than 4,000 workers (most of them on the production lines) producing over

Honda

*Photograph 5.9
An aerial view of the
Honda factory near
Swindon*

200,000 vehicles annually, mainly for the European market with some exports to the middle east, Africa and North America. As the recession hit in 2008/2009 Honda laid off workers and closed the plant for some periods. Such companies have geographical flexibility and can shift resources and production between locations at a global scale in order to maximise profit.

The large size and scale of operations of many TNCs enables them to achieve economies of scale, allowing them to reduce costs, finance new investment and compete in world markets. Large companies also have a wider choice when locating a new plant, although governments may try to influence decisions as part of regional policy or a desire to protect home markets. Governments are often keen to attract TNCs because inward investment creates jobs and boosts exports which assist the trade balance. TNCs have the power to trade off one country against another in order to achieve the best deal. Within a country, TNCs have the financial resources to research several potential sites and take advantage of the best communications, access to labour, low cost of land and building and government subsidies.

TNCs and globalisation

TNCs serve a **global market** and they can globalise their manufacturing operations in several ways:
➤ by producing just for the country in which the plant is situated
➤ by producing for a number of countries, e.g. the Honda car plant above
➤ by integrating production, so that each plant performs a separate part of a process. Linkage takes place across national boundaries in a chain sequence (vertical integration) or components are moved to a final assembly plant in one country (horizontal linkage)

Manufacturing industry

TNCs often locate in areas of industrial concentration, or their presence may encourage such concentrations. A major factor promoting this is **external economies of scale (agglomeration economies)**. These advantages arise from outside the company, unlike internal economies of scale that result from the large-scale operation of the production plant. External economies of scale can be categorised into:

➤ **Localisation economies,** which occur when firms linked by the purchase of materials and finished goods locate close together. This reduces transport costs between suppliers and customers, leading to faster delivery times (which in the case of TNCs could enable **just-in-time** operations) and allowing better communication and personal contact between firms (important in monitoring and maintaining quality).

➤ **Urbanisation economies**, where cost savings result from an urban location, enabling linkages to develop between manufacturing and services. In some cases it is cheaper for manufacturing plants to contract work to specialist companies. Savings also result from the economic and social infrastructure of the area that exists before the arrival of new companies.

Service industry

In recent years there has been a shift of investment towards service industries:

➤ Services now account for the largest share of the inward FDI in many countries. Figure 5.17 shows the shift from manufacturing investment to service sector investment that has taken place over the last 10 years in Europe.

➤ The continuous process of liberalisation and deregulation of key services has led to a large inflow of FDI into industries that were previously dominated by the state or domestic private-sector firms.

➤ A growing number of the world's largest TNCs are in the service sector. Even among the largest manufacturing TNCs, services account for a growing proportion of value added. Table 5.5 shows that of the world's 20 largest companies in 2007, six were service providers, including three banks (Citigroup, HSBC, Dexia) and three in insurance (ING Group, AXA, Allianz).

➤ The ICT revolution has opened up overseas investment in tradeable services. As information can now be sent across the world at little cost, services can be

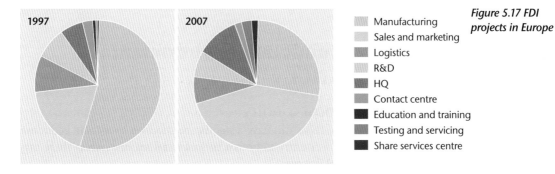

Figure 5.17 FDI projects in Europe

split into components, each of which can be located in countries that are able to provide them most efficiently and cost-effectively. IT-enabled services are increasingly globalising in the same way that manufacturing has been for several decades.

Case study — The accountants' network

Mirroring the transnationalisation of various industries that draw upon its services, the accountancy industry has also become global. Today, it is a large and highly regulated industry dominated by four large firms:

- Deloitte Touche Tohmatsu (HQ in New York)
- PricewaterhouseCoopers (HQ in New York)
- Ernst & Young (HQ in both New York and London)
- KPMG (HQ in Amsterdam)

These companies have grown through the formation of networks and partnerships with local accounting firms under a brand name and through mergers. Originally they were the 'Big Eight', but mergers between firms and the dissolution of Arthur Andersen in the 1980s and 1990s reduced the number of firms to four by the end of the twentieth century. The present 'Big Four' are much larger than all the other accounting firms. They each have thousands of partners, tens of thousand of employees, offices around the world and annual revenues of billions of dollars (Table 5.7). They provide both accounting and management consulting services, although the trend is increasingly towards the separation of these activities. The combined revenues of these four companies account for around 30% of the total global market for accountancy services.

Historically, accounting firms went abroad to service foreign clients. Today, these large firms have global operations and are among the most transnationalised business service enterprises, with a presence in most countries of the world. Because of regulatory controls in many parts of the world, these firms usually expand operations by acquiring new members and creating a network of firms that are legally separate, locally owned and managed.

The global expansion of the Big Four firms presents problems for local small and medium-sized accounting firms, which, for example, lack the capacity and capital to compete for the audits of large national and public companies.

Table 5.7 The 'Big Four' accounting firms

Name	Total revenue ($ billion)	Employees
Deloitte Touche Tohmatsu	27.4	165,000
PricewaterhouseCoopers	25.2	146,000
Ernst & Young	21.1	125,000
KPMG	19.8	123,000

Social, economic and environmental impacts of TNCs

Impacts on the host country

Inward investment by TNCs can have a significant effect on social and economic developments within a country, at both a national and regional scale. There may also be environmental impacts.

Positive impacts

Countries can gain a number of important advantages through the location of TNCs:

➤ **Employment** — for example in the UK in 2007, FDI generated more than 700 projects which created over 50,000 jobs. This is not huge compared with the size of the UK workforce, but these jobs were financed with foreign money (as opposed to government grants, although some TNCs qualify for subsidies) and they can have a big impact on local communities.

➤ **Multiplier effects** — at a local level, such investment can trigger more employment through the process of **cumulative causation**, bringing wealth into the local economy. The location of a TNC in a region has the potential to create jobs in:
  - companies that supply components to the plant
  - companies that distribute goods from the new plant
  - companies that supply services to the new plant, from servicing plant machinery to supplying the canteen

➤ The arrival of a TNC can inject capital into the local economy (in the form of wages). More disposable income in the area will create a demand for more housing, transport and services. All this promotes an upward spiral (virtuous circle) in economic terms.

➤ **New methods of working** — TNCs may introduce methods of working that are new to the country. These have included quality management systems which monitor the standard of output in supplier firms, and just-in-time (JIT) component supply. They **transfer technology** to the host country, creating a more skilled workforce. They may also create more opportunities for female employment in low-skilled manufacturing jobs, particularly in developing countries.

Negative impacts

Many of the negative impacts apply to developing countries, although the impact of FDI in more developed countries is not always positive:

➤ **Competition** — TNCs may be in direct competition with local firms, which may be less efficient and so lose business and, eventually, employees. In Russia, for example, the arrival of Western chocolate manufacturers had a very adverse effect on the home confectionary industry.

➤ **Environmental concerns**— TNCs may cause damage to the atmosphere, water and land. Many developing countries have less strict pollution laws than those in the developed world. Agricultural land may be lost, along with wildlife habitats.

➤ **Labour exploitation** — it has been alleged that some TNCs exploit cheap, flexible, non-unionised labour forces in developing countries. Many large, well-known TNCs, however, have established a basic standard of operation which involves setting up training facilities for workers, and providing promotion opportunities for host-country employees and minimum wage and age limits.

➤ **Urbanisation** — establishment of a TNC in a city of a developing country increases urbanisation as younger workers migrate to the city to work

Julio Etchart/Still Pictures

Photograph 5.10
Migrant peasants from the Andes in a shanty town in Lima, Peru

(Photograph 5.10). This can have serious effects in rural communities with the loss of people of working age resulting in an increasingly elderly population.

➤ **Removal of capital** — the capital generated by TNCs does not all stay in the host country.

➤ **Outside decision making** — decisions on whether or not plants stay open in other countries are made by the head office of the TNC. Decisions are not made in the interest of the host country but for the benefit of the TNC and its level of profitability.

Impacts on the country of origin

If TNCs transfer production overseas the economic impact on the country of origin can be negative. There is likely to be unemployment, both in that company and in component suppliers. The amount of disposable income within the region will decrease, leading to a downward spiral (vicious circle), which is the multiplier effect working in reverse. Traditional industrial regions that rely on one or two industries for their economic base can be hard hit.

The transfer of Dyson's vacuum cleaner production from Malmesbury (Wiltshire) to Malaysia cost 800 UK jobs. The company claimed that the move would cut around 30% from production costs. Other recent moves have included Kenwood's decision to move production of the Chef food mixer to China, Clarks shoes moving a lot of its production to Romania and Black & Decker moving production from its factory in Spennymoor (County Durham) to a plant in the Czech Republic.

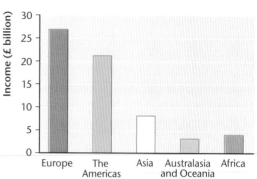

It is not only manufacturing employment that can be moved abroad. Companies including British Airways, Prudential, HSBC, Barclays and Norwich Union (Aviva) have call centres and back office functions in countries such as India. Such countries offer a much lower cost base as wage levels are only about 20% of those in the UK.

On the positive side, higher-salaried jobs often stay in the country of origin. Dyson, for example, retains several hundred jobs in the UK in administration and R&D. TNCs that move to locations with cheaper labour usually increase their profitability, which benefits the host country as profits are returned for distribution to shareholders. Government revenues from company taxation are also increased. Figure 5.18 shows the earnings from direct investment by UK companies in 2004, broken down into regions of the world. The total revenue earned by UK companies overseas in that year totalled £63.8 billion.

Figure 5.18 Net earnings from direct investment overseas by UK companies in 2004

Case study **Unilever: a manufacturing TNC**

Unilever owns many of the familiar consumer brands on our supermarket shelves. It operates in two main product areas:

- **food and beverages** — Unilever owns such well-known brands as Ben and Jerry's, Blue Band, Bovril, Colman's, Flora, Hellmann's, Knorr, Lipton, Marmite, PG Tips, Walls and Pot Noodle
- **home and personal care** — Unilever owns, among others, Cif, Comfort, Domestos, Dove, Lynx, Lux, Persil, Sunsilk, Surf and Vaseline

Unilever was created in 1930 by the merger of the UK soapmaker Lever Brothers and the Dutch margarine producer Margarine Unie. There was logic to the merger, as both companies used palm oil as a major ingredient in their products and there were economies of scale to be had through the larger organisation. They were also involved in the large-scale marketing of household products and both companies used similar distribution channels.

In 2008, the company had over 300 manufacturing sites in more than 100 countries across every continent. It employed more than 170,000 people and had an annual company revenue of over $50 billion in 2007 (see Table 5.6).

Research and development is important to a company involved in such markets and Unilever has several centres for this purpose. Two are located in the UK, and one each in the Netherlands, USA, India and China (Figure 5.19). The company has headquarters in both Rotterdam and London.

Like many other large manufacturing TNCs, Unilever has attracted a variety of criticisms from political activists and environmental groups. Issues have included testing products on animals,

mercury contamination, using child labour and deforestation. The allegations have been denied by the company. Where a problem has been identified, Unilever has often worked hard to resolve any issues. As recently as April 2008 the company was targeted by Greenpeace activists protesting about the removal of Indonesian rainforest to make way for palm oil production, which has seriously reduced the habitat of the orang-utan. Unilever maintains that it is leading research into the problem and will attempt to deal only with those suppliers who guarantee sustainable practices in palm oil production.

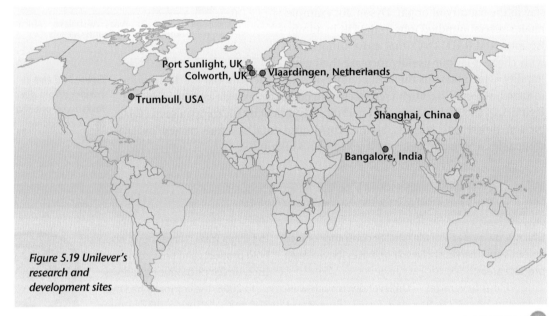

Figure 5.19 Unilever's research and development sites

Development issues

Trade vs aid

Since the 1940s, efforts to create development in the poorer countries of the world have centred around two approaches:

➤ the use of trade to promote economic growth
➤ the provision of aid by the developed countries of the North (and latterly the oil-rich states) to the poorer countries south of the Brandt line

Trade

Economic growth is essential to economic development of a country. Growth increases the amount of wealth being generated, allowing living standards to rise. In the early part of this period, economists believed that the way forward for the

South was a process of industrialisation that would help provide more goods for export (exporting manufactured goods creates more income than the basic raw materials which many countries were exporting). This increase in trade would allow more revenue to flow into such countries, promoting increased wealth and living standards. These ideas were based on the assumption that the countries of the South needed to go through the same process that the richer countries of the North had experienced since the middle of the nineteenth century.

This was partly dependent on three factors:

➤ adoption of Western-style capitalism, which also had political implications as it tends to foster democratic institutions that can be fairer

➤ economic growth 'trickling down', providing extra money and resources for new industry to be established, with more goods produced, more trade resulting and even more economic growth

➤ promotion of free trade, where markets were as open as possible. Key international organisations such as the IMF have been strong supporters of making trade as free from restriction as is possible. Such ideas became associated with the ideology known as **neoliberalism**, a set of free-market policies adopted by Thatcher and Reagan in the 1980s

In support of these ideas, many economists point to the growth of NICs such as Singapore, South Korea and Malaysia. These countries, undeveloped at the beginning of this period, experienced huge rates of economic growth and industrialisation as they opened up their markets. However, critics have pointed out that there were many factors that enabled this development, among them the fact that their governments often applied protectionist policies — quite the opposite to neoliberalism.

Some economists doubt that poorer countries with problems such as HIV/AIDS, war, and drought can ever become developed through trade and economic growth. They argue that:

➤ Less developed countries cannot be competitive in the global market because of the great difference in wealth between them and the developed countries. They cannot invest in industrial and technological development at the same level as richer countries.

➤ Many poorer countries depend upon agricultural exports, the price of which, until recently, has been falling. They cannot make much profit from this sector, particularly as richer countries often subsidise their own farmers through such schemes as the European Common Agricultural Policy and the terms of trade negotiated through WTO.

➤ The wealth generated by trade does not always 'trickle down' to the majority of the population. Benefits are often confined to the richer members of society and the gap between rich and poor has widened in these countries.

➤ The debt suffered by many poorer countries has put them in a difficult position. In order to receive financial help they have had to accept changes based on the neoliberal ideas of the IMF and World Bank, which often include cuts in spending on health and education .

Aid

There are three main systems through which aid can be supplied:

➤ **Bilateral aid** — aid given directly by the government of one country to another.
➤ **Multilateral aid** — aid given by governments to international organisations which use the money to assist programmes in poorer countries. Such organisations include the World Bank and UNESCO.
➤ **Non-governmental organisations** — these distribute aid in a variety of ways. Many of them are charities, such as Oxfam, which raise money for development projects, ensuring aid is directed at the people who need it most.

Aid does not have to be money. It can take the form of goods or technical assistance in the building up of infrastructure, agriculture and industry.

Aid can be distributed in several different ways:

➤ **Short-term aid** — given in response to a sudden problem within a country. This usually follows a disaster such as Hurricane Mitch in the Caribbean (1998), the Gujarat earthquake (India, 2001) or the Indian Ocean tsunami of 2004 (Photograph 5. 11).
➤ **Long-term development projects** — such investment can help agriculture, industry, energy supplies, infrastructure, education and medical facilities.
➤ **'Top-down' aid** — a responsible body (internally or externally) directs the operation 'from the top'. Building dams to provide irrigation water and hydro-electric power is a good example.
➤ **'Bottom-up' schemes** — also known as grassroots initiatives. Such projects are often funded by NGOs, working closely with local communities and using local ideas and knowledge to bring about change.

Aid is therefore diverse in both the way it is delivered and the objectives of any programme. Supporters of aid as a means to development believe its greatest

*Photograph 5.11
A US navy helicopter delivering supplies of water to Aceh, Indonesia, following the 2004 tsunami*

strength is that, while it can be directed to economic development, it can also be given for humanitarian purposes, social development or environmental improvement.

Critics of aid as a means toward development in the South point out that:

➤ Aid does not always reach those who most need it. Even if it does get through, it is not always used effectively. Corruption is a problem in many of the receiving countries.

➤ Some countries lack basic infrastructure and this makes it difficult to use aid effectively. For example, it is difficult to invest money in educational and medical programmes in parts of rural Africa that lack transport systems and power resources.

➤ **Aid dependency** can be created when aid becomes a substantial proportion of national income. Aid agencies hesitate to provide food and other help for extended periods following emergencies, for fear that this may create dependency.

➤ Aid often comes with strings attached — the recipient has to agree to conditions laid down by the donor. One example is **tied aid**, where the recipient has to agree to spend the money on goods and services in the donor country. Indebted countries that receive help under MDRI have to agree to a set of stringent conditions. The IMF has recently introduced Poverty Reduction Strategy Papers which have to be adopted to qualify for the IMF and World Bank's HIPC programme (see page 199).

Poverty Reduction Strategy Papers (PRSPs) are prepared by governments in low-income countries through a participatory process involving domestic stakeholders and external development partners, including the IMF and the World Bank. A PRSP describes the macroeconomic, structural and social policies and programs that a country will pursue over several years to promote broad-based growth and reduce poverty, as well as external financing needs and the associated sources of financing.

PRSPs aim to provide the crucial link between national public actions, donor support, and the development outcomes needed to meet the United Nations' Millennium Development Goals (MDGs), which are centered on halving poverty between 1990 and 2015. (IMF Factsheet)

Economic vs environmental sustainability

Sustainable development in its widest context has been defined as 'development that meets the needs of the present without compromising the ability of future generations to meet their own needs'. It is a process by which human potential (level of wellbeing) is improved and the environment (the resource base) is used and managed to supply people on a long-term basis. This implies social justice as well as long-term environmental sustainability. The global economy depends on the natural environment as a source of resources and as a sink for emissions. The capacity of natural systems to provide resources and to absorb increasing levels of pollution is the critical threshold controlling how far population can increase and the economy expand.

Sustainability was first expressed in the form of **environmental objectives**, to:
➤ maintain ecological processes and life-support systems
➤ preserve genetic diversity
➤ ensure the utilisation of species and ecosystems without destroying them

From this, the concept of **economic sustainability** followed. This examines the ability of economies to maintain themselves when resources decline or become too expensive, and when populations dependent on those resources are growing.

In 1992, the UN's Rio Earth Summit set out the sustainability principles described below.

Environmental principles

➤ People are at the heart of concerns for sustainable development.
➤ States have the right to exploit their own environment, but they should not damage the environment of other states.
➤ Environmental protection should be an integral part of the development process.
➤ People should be informed and states should make people aware.
➤ There should be environmental legislation and standards, but these must not affect other countries.
➤ Laws should be enacted regarding liability for pollution and compensation.
➤ The relocation and transfer of activities and substances that are harmful to health should be prevented.

Photograph 5.12 Burning off natural gas in the middle east. What economic changes are necessary to ensure sustainability?

Corel

> **Environmental impact assessment (EIA)** should be undertaken for all proposed economic activities.
> States should pass on information about natural disasters and notify neighbouring states of the foreseen and accidental consequences of any activities that might cross boundaries.
> The environmental and natural resources of people under oppression, domination and occupation should be protected.
> There should be a precautionary approach to the environment in all states, according to their capabilities.

Economic principles

> The right to development must be fulfilled so as to meet equitably developmental and environmental needs of present and future generations.
> All states should cooperate in eliminating poverty in order to decrease disparities in standards of living.
> The special needs of developing countries, particularly the least developed and environmentally most vulnerable, should be given priority.
> States should cooperate to restore the Earth's ecosystem. The developed states acknowledge the responsibility they bear for the demands their societies place on the global environment, and the technologies and financial resources they command.
> Unsustainable production and consumption patterns should be eliminated and appropriate demographic policies should be promoted.
> Scientific information and innovative technologies should be transferred to improve understanding.
> States should support an open economic system. Trade policies should not contain arbitrary or unjustifiable discrimination. Unilateral actions to address issues should give way to international consensus.
> National authorities should endeavour to promote the internationalism of environmental costs, taking into account that the polluter should pay.

Figure 5.20
The pillars of sustainability

The World Summit in New York (2005) declared that, to be effective, action on sustainability must involve cooperation across three sustainability 'pillars': environment, society and economy (Figure 5.20). Environmentalists emphasise the global environment as the ecological and material basis of human existence that is being progressively degraded. They believe that, by placing such strong emphasis on economic growth and investing little effort in protecting the environment, we are on a road to self-destruction. Many people see sustainability only in environmental terms — reducing human impact on the Earth's resources to a sustainable level — without considering the social and economic changes needed to achieve this.

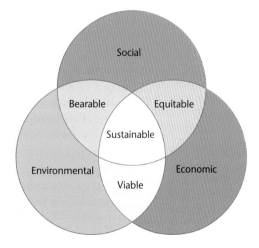

The Center for International Earth Science Information Network (CIESIN) of Columbia University (NY), in cooperation with Yale University and various European agencies, has set up an **environmental sustainability index (ESI)**. Twenty-one variables have been used to place countries on an index from 0 (bad) to 100 (good). The results for 2005 are shown on Figure 5.21.

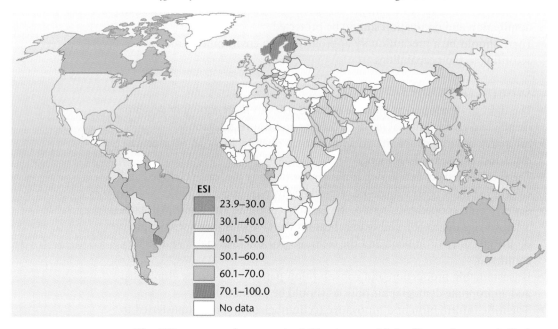

ESI
- 23.9–30.0
- 30.1–40.0
- 40.1–50.0
- 50.1–60.0
- 60.1–70.0
- 70.1–100.0
- No data

*Figure 5.21
Environmental
sustainability index,
2005*

The ESI suggests that sustainability has multiple dimensions and distinct challenges for developed versus developing countries. Developed countries must find ways to manage the environmental stresses of industrialisation and consumption of natural resources, particularly those which are non-renewable. Developing countries face the risk of depleting renewable resources such as water and forests as well as the challenges of funding investments in environmental protection and regulating the impacts of economic growth.

Economic conditions affect environmental outcomes, but a country's level of development is not the only driver of its performance and ESI score. Richer countries tend to score better on social issues, while poorer countries have lower environmental impact.

Figure 5.22 shows a comparison between Spain and Indonesia. Both have an ESI of 48.8. It shows that Spain must deal with burdened ecological systems and high levels of environmental stress but, like others in the developed world, it has a reasonably strong capacity to handle the harm which it faces. Indonesia in contrast has less environmental stress in several areas, but much less capacity to manage the challenges it must address, including severe water quality issues.

Figure 5.23 shows the relationship between ESI and GDP per capita. It shows that there is an obvious correlation between wealth and environmental sustainability, but the relationship is not always straightforward. As indicated by their position above the regression line, the Scandinavian countries have high GDP

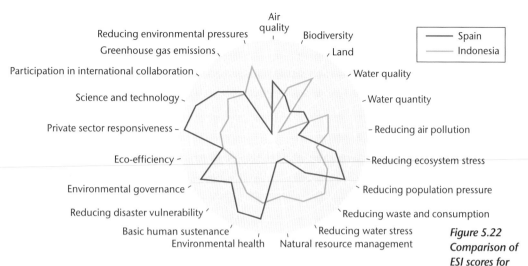

Air quality

Reducing environmental pressures

Greenhouse gas emissions

Biodiversity

Land

Participation in international collaboration

Water quality

Science and technology

Water quantity

Private sector responsiveness

Reducing air pollution

Eco-efficiency

Reducing ecosystem stress

Environmental governance

Reducing population pressure

Reducing disaster vulnerability

Reducing waste and consumption

Basic human sustenance

Reducing water stress

Environmental health

Natural resource management

Spain
Indonesia

Figure 5.22 Comparison of ESI scores for Spain and Indonesia

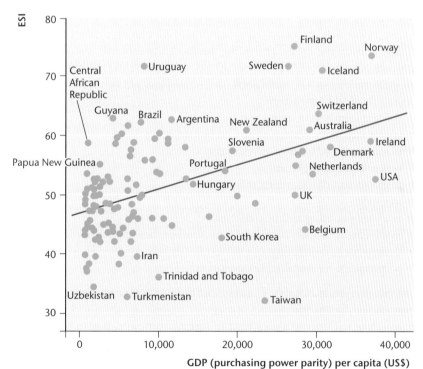

Figure 5.23 Comparing ESI and GDP/PPP

per capita but even higher ESI scores than their wealth might forecast. The USA, UK and Belgium, on the other hand, fall well below the regression line — given their level of wealth they do not perform well.

Sustainable tourism: myth or reality?

There is a fundamental relationship between the environment and tourism. The environment attracts the tourist in the first place, be it scenery or historical heritage. In theory, the relationship should be mutually beneficial: as tourists enjoy beautiful environments, so the revenue generated is used to maintain their quality. However, as tourist flows increase, tourism can cause major environmental problems. Unless successful management strategies are evolved, the cost of tourism can soon outweigh the benefits. This is especially true where there is overuse of relatively small areas of land or ocean that are vulnerable to damage. Pressures on coasts, mountains, National Parks, historic monuments and historic city centres are of particular concern.

There are many examples where the impact of tourism has been damaging. People have lost land to golf courses, which have then overused scarce water supplies to the detriment of local farmers. Coral reefs have been damaged deliberately and accidentally as water sports have spread into the reef areas, e.g. in the Lingayen Gulf (Philippines) where scuba divers and sports fishermen have contributed to the degradation of the coral reef system.

Tourism that does not destroy what it sets out to explore is known as **sustainable tourism**. The term comes from the 1987 UN Report on the Environment, which advocated development that meets present needs without compromising the future. Following the Rio Earth Summit, the World Travel & Tourism Council (WTTC) drew up an environmental checklist through a programme known as Green Globe. This named areas in which travel and tourism operations could take action:

➤ waste minimisation, reuse and recycling
➤ energy efficiency, conservation and management
➤ management of freshwater resources
➤ waste-water management
➤ management of hazardous substances
➤ transport
➤ land-use planning and management
➤ involvement of staff, customers and communities in environmental issues
➤ designs for sustainability
➤ partnerships for sustainable development

The pressure group, Tourism Concern, defines sustainable tourism as 'tourism and associated infrastructure that:

➤ operates within capacities for the regeneration and future productivity of natural resources
➤ recognises the contribution of local people and their cultures
➤ accepts that these people must have an equitable share in the economic benefits of tourism
➤ is guided by the wishes of the local people and communities in the destination area'

Sustainable tourism is therefore, in its purest sense, an industry committed to making a low impact on the natural environment and local culture, while helping to generate income and employment for local people. There are many ways in which individual tourists can work towards the aims of sustainable tourism including:

- being informed of the culture, politics and economy of the areas visited
- anticipating and respecting local cultures' expectations and assumptions
- contributing to intercultural understanding and tolerance
- supporting local cultures by favouring businesses that conserve cultural heritage and traditional values
- supporting local economies by purchasing local goods and participating with small, local businesses
- conserving resources by seeking out businesses that are environmentally conscious
- using the least possible amount of local resources, particularly non-renewables

Case study — Aldemar Hotels, Greece

Aldemar is a leading Greek hotel chain. It has worked with local communities on environmental issues for years. Its current environmental programme is called Mare Verde and aims to reduce the impact of the hotels on the environment.

What does the programme involve?

- The protection of water resources by using water sparingly and introducing biological cleaning systems.
- Automatic deactivation of the electricity supply to hotel rooms when guests go out.
- The use of environmentally friendly materials in the construction of hotels.
- Reducing use of packaging materials and recycling waste paper.

- Using solar energy.
- Sourcing fruit and vegetables from the company's own farm in Greece.
- Tree planting campaigns and involvement by staff in environmental activity.

Guests can contribute by:

- Not requesting clean sheets and towels each day.
- Turning off the supply of electricity to their rooms while they are out by removing the key card.
- Using Aldemar bags (made from a mixture of paper and fabric) instead of plastic bags.
- Turning off the taps while shaving or cleaning teeth and taking a quick shower rather than having a bath.
- Supporting local environmental groups.

Ecotourism

Ecotourism, or ecological tourism, is a form of sustainable tourism, conserving the environment for future generations. It has been described as 'an economic process by which rare and beautiful ecosystems and cultural attractions are marketed internationally to attract tourists'. The contradiction within that statement is that once the flow of tourists increases, the damage becomes harder to manage and it escalates. Environmental and sociocultural interests have to be balanced against purely economic aims. At its best, ecotourism is notable for the way it approaches the planning and management of tourism environments as it:

- aims to build responsible tourism by developing tourism with dignity and by managing capacity

➤ encourages conservation, through the education of both local people and tourists

➤ develops a focus on the environment by solving environmental problems and exporting ecotourism ideas around the world

Ecotourism's claim to sustainability is questioned. Many travel companies have been quick to pick up on the public enthusiasm for exotic environments. Expensive small-group tours to remote and faraway places, often based in luxury accommodation, may be marketed as ecologically sound. Environmentalists dismiss many of these tours as *egotourism*, claiming they are ordinary tourism dressed up as politically correct. Some ecotourism is genuinely sustainable, but much is not. Sustainable ecotourism has to meet two conditions:

➤ the number of visitors must be limited to a level that the environment can sustain

➤ it must be set up and run in cooperation and consultation with local people

Ecotourism is one of the fastest growing sectors of the tourism industry. It has been developed largely by small, dedicated tour companies but still constitutes less than 5% of the market. Ecotourism does not sit well with the large multinational companies that

Photograph 5.13 Posada Amazonas in the Peruvian rainforest is an ecolodge managed by the local community in partnership with Rainforest Expeditions

Mike Ritter

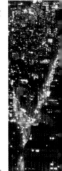

dominate the tourism market. Many companies, particularly hotel chains, are, however, seeking to become more environmentally aware through the management of waste, water and energy (see Aldemar Hotels case study). Others have carried out green audits of their business practices and reward green tourist initiatives. Cynics claim that these strategies are designed to generate a good public relations image.

Case study — Small-scale ecotourism in the Napo region, Ecuador

The Napo region is in the rainforest of eastern Ecuador (Figure 5.24). In 1990, after a group of tourists came to stay with a local family who were paid for their hospitality, the indigenous population of Quicha Indians had the idea of developing ecotourism.

In 1991, Action Aid (a British charity) carried out a research project which recorded how the rainforest in the Napo region was being destroyed by a combination of oil exploitation and rainforest tourism,

thus threatening the Quicha's traditional lifestyle. The ecotourism project was developed in an attempt to strengthen the community and to create a sustainable income for the indigenous people.

The Quicha people insist that all visitors must abide by certain rules and regulations:

■ Exchanges of clothing or other personal items with community members are not allowed; nor are community members allowed to accept gifts.

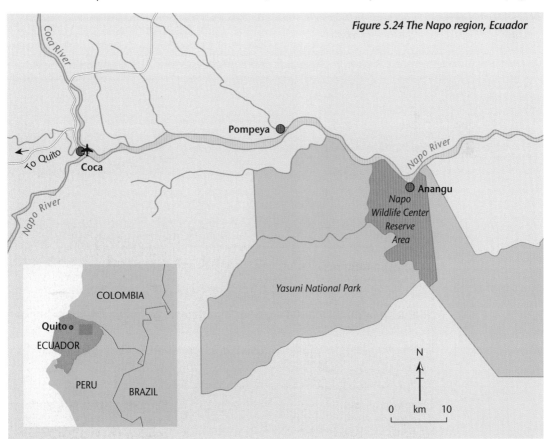

Figure 5.24 The Napo region, Ecuador

- Visitors must not enter people's houses without being invited and are asked not to make promises they may not be able to keep (e.g. sending back photos after the visit).
- All rubbish (e.g. empty bottles and cans) must be taken away by visitors.
- When walking in the rainforest tourists are asked:
  - not to touch any branches without looking carefully first — they may have thorns or carry dangerous insects or even snakes
  - not to pull on branches or vines — they may fall down
  - if they need to go to the toilet and facilities are not immediately available, go to the side of the rainforest track, never in, or near, a stream or lake
- Visitors must avoid displays of affection, even with close friends. In this community it is considered rude to hold hands or kiss in public.

- Plants, insects or other animals must not be collected without permission to do so.
- Visitors must never go off for a walk alone. It is easy to get lost in the rainforest.

Visitors come from the USA and Canada and are usually committed environmentalists. They travel into the area by canoe, and have a 2-hour hike through the forest to their destination. Stays last for up to 6 days and include walks through the 'jungle', and visits to community projects such as the Garden of Medicinal Plants and to see pottery making. Tourists, in groups of up to 12, stay in buildings built by the local people.

The Quicha use their expert knowledge of the forest as the basis of the guided tours. They have trained their children, via an ecological training programme in the village school, to recognise plants and their uses. Money from tourism has led to major improvements to services in the villages.

Contemporary conflicts and challenges

Chapter

6

The geographical basis of conflict

Causes of conflict

Identity

Identity is a sense of belonging to a group or geographical area where there is the same generic character, or a similarity of distinguishing character or personality. The identity may be determined by, or be apparent in, ethnicity, language and religion (Photograph 6.1). People can be very protective of their identity and seek to maintain it at all costs.

Photograph 6.1 Identity can be complex. A Belorussian Jewish poet, Herb Reles, who lives in a country that was part of the Soviet Union, and writes in Yiddish. He is shown with his Yiddish typewriter

Jane Buekett

Identity can be evident at a number of scales:

➤ **Nationalism** — loyalty and devotion to a nation. This can create a sense of national consciousness, exalting that nation above all others. The culture and interests of only that nation are promoted.

➤ **Regionalism** — consciousness of, and loyalty to, a nation or a distinct region with a population that shares similarities. It can sometimes lead to the development of a political or social system based on one or more such areas.

➤ **Localism** — an affection for a particular place. Localism rarely manifests itself in a political sense. However, it can be demonstrated in 'nimbyism' ('not in my back yard') which occurs when people are reluctant to have their local area affected by development for the national good.

Ethnicity

Ethnicity is the grouping of people according to their ethnic origins or characteristics. In narrow terms it describes the racial make-up of a population — whether people are caucasoid, mongoloid, negroid or polynesian. More recently the term has broadened in meaning to refer to groups of people classed according to one or more common racial, national, tribal, religious, linguistic or cultural origins or backgrounds.

Culture

In a geographical sense, culture is the customary beliefs, social norms and traits of a racial, religious or social group and the set of shared attitudes, values and practices that characterise that group. The origins of many groups are historical and may be lost in time. Hence, as with identity, culture is something of which groups of people are inherently proud, and which they seek to protect. Within the same nation, for example the UK, France or Italy, there are many variations in culture — this diversity enriches the country.

Territory

Territory is a geographic area belonging to, or under the jurisdiction of, a governmental authority. The territory may be an administrative subdivision of a country, or a geographic area dependent on an external government, but having some degree of autonomy (for example a country which is a colonial possession). Conflict can occur where there is dispute about who does or should have authority over an area. This can happen in areas where there are low levels of population (e.g. deserts, Photograph 6.2) or where borders depend on natural phenomena (e.g. rivers, estuaries and mountains).

Key terms

Challenge A task or issue that is perceived as being provocative, threatening, stimulating or an incitement to debate. The opportunity to examine and deal with the issues that arise from challenges often causes alternative views to be expressed, usually in a peaceful manner, though sometimes the views may be extreme or polarised.

Conflict A state of discord or disagreement caused by the actual or perceived opposition of needs, values and interests between people. In a geographical sense it is often the result of opposing views about the ways in which a resource might be developed or used. The result is stress or tension and negative feelings between the parties. A conflict can range from a disagreement or clash, to a fight, which may consist of harsh words or may involve the use of force, armed conflict or war. In political terms, 'conflict' refers to an ongoing state of hostility between two or more groups of people.

Corel

Ideology

Ideology is a systematic body of concepts regarding human life or culture. It can result in a set of integrated assertions, theories and aims that together constitute a sociopolitical programme. Some ideologies can be extreme and at odds with those elsewhere in the world and their supporters may seek to press their views on others by force. The Western views of democracy, and the alternative views of the Taliban in Afghanistan, could both be described as ideologies.

Photograph 6.2
Conflict over borders can occur in deserts

Patterns of conflict

There are four main scales of conflict in the world:
➤ **international** — where conflict involves the participation of more than one country
➤ **national** — where the conflict takes place within a country
➤ **regional** — where conflict takes place within an area of one country, or across the borders of one or more countries
➤ **local** — where the conflict is restricted to a small part of one region of a country

The expression of conflict

Non-violent

Conflict of this nature does not involve force or armed struggle. Statements of discontent are made by word, sign, marching or silent protest. Some forms of non-violent protest have been very successful. In Ukraine in 2004 thousands of people took to the streets of Kiev to demand political change (see case study on the Orange Revolution). On the other hand, non-violent protest by large numbers of monks in Burma in 2007 was less successful, as it was met by forced opposition from government-controlled forces.

Case study | **The Orange Revolution in Ukraine**

A series of protests and political events took place in Ukraine from late November 2004 to January 2005 (Photograph 6.3). This followed the run-off vote of the 2004 Ukrainian presidential election, which was compromised by massive corruption, voter intimidation and direct electoral fraud. Kiev, the Ukrainian capital, was the focal point of the movement, with thousands of protesters demonstrating daily. Nationwide, the democratic revolution was highlighted by a series of acts of civil disobedience, sit-ins and general strikes organised by the opposition movement.

The protests were prompted by reports from several domestic and foreign election monitors, as well as widespread public perception, that the results of the run-off vote of 21 November 2004 between leading candidates Viktor Yushchenko and Viktor Yanukovych had been rigged by the authorities in favour of the latter. The nationwide protests succeeded. The results of the original run-off were annulled and a re-vote was ordered by Ukraine's Supreme Court. Under intense scrutiny by domestic and international observers, the second vote was decreed 'fair and free'. Yushchenko was declared the official winner and, with his inauguration on 23 January 2005 in Kiev, the Orange Revolution peacefully reached its successful conclusion.

Photograph 6.3 Demonstrations in Kiev during the Orange Revolution

TopFoto

Political activity

Political activity relates to groups operating within a country who seek to acquire and exert political power through government. The groups, known as parties, develop a political programme that defines their ideology and sets out the agenda they would pursue should they win elective office or gain power through democratic means.

Political activity often involves **debate**: the formal discussion of a motion before a deliberative body according to the rules of parliamentary procedure. This occurs when new laws are debated in the House of Commons in Britain, for example. It takes the form of a regulated discussion of a proposition between those in favour and those against.

Terrorism

Terrorism is the systematic use of fear among the public as a way of trying to force the authorities into action for a political, or more frequently an ideological, end. During the latter part of the twentieth century and the first part of the twenty-first century, international terrorism has become increasingly widespread. Bombings, often by suicide bombers, have occurred in places across the world.

Insurrection

Insurrection is an act or instance of revolt against civil authority or an established government, usually involving rebellion against the rules of that government. People engaging in insurrection are called **insurgents**, and typically engage in regular or guerrilla combat against the armed forces of the established regime, or conduct sabotage and harassment in order to undermine the government's position.

War

War is a state of open and declared armed hostile conflict between states or nations. The armed forces of the states involved are the main protagonists of the conflict.

Conflict resolution

Conflict resolution is the means by which conflict at a variety of scales can be brought to an end. The expression of conflict — debate, political activity, war — can sometimes lead to its resolution. Different forms of conflict can be resolved by differing means, as the remainder of this chapter illustrates.

Conflict over the use of a local resource

There have been a number of conflicts in the UK over large building projects that have achieved public and national notoriety. These include the Newbury bypass

Photograph 6.4 A demonstration against the building of Terminal 5 at Heathrow

TopFoto

in Berkshire, the second runway at Manchester Airport, the new container terminal in the Southampton area, Terminal 5 at Heathrow (Photograph 6.4) and the building of the Olympic site in London for the 2012 games. There are also many examples locally across the UK where people have disagreed, for example about the construction of a new shopping complex, landfill site or housing estate.

Resolving the conflict

Such conflicts are resolved by market processes, planning processes or, in some cases, a combination of the two.

Market processes operate where the ability of the organisation undertaking the project to pay the going rate takes precedence over any local or national concerns. Often, objectors cannot afford to outbid the developer and the development goes ahead with the minimum of consultation. When it does occur, consultation often takes the form of an opportunity to voice objections or propose counter-arguments, but with no right of independent arbitration or appeal.

Planning processes (Figure 6.1) are an attempt to provide a means by which local authority planners:
➤ listen to the local community (more democratic)
➤ listen to the organisation responsible for a proposal
➤ have overall development control

*Figure 6.1 The
planning process*

Submit an application
(with fee)

No ← Is application valid? → Yes

Advise applicant of
invalid reasons

Register
application

Register: 3 days

Carry out public consultations

Planning officer assesses application

Optional
Yes

Amendments required?

Additional information
received

No

Decision: 8–13 weeks

Decision

Council officer decides
using delegated powers

Development control
committee of councillors

Decision notice issued

Appeal:
up to 3 months

Grant
permission

Refuse
permission

Resubmit: up to 1 year

Lodge an appeal

Resubmit application

A local authority's refusal to grant planning permission may lead to an appeal by
the developer, either to the local planning committee or to a higher body, for
example the Department for Environment, Food and Rural Affairs (DEFRA).
Planning processes are costly for local authorities, in both time and money
(Photograph 6.5). Planning committees may:

➤ require or negotiate modifications to be made to offset the opposition
➤ request additional provision of facilities (such as better road access) that the
developer or authority would have to provide if the development went ahead,
and that might placate local opposition

Photograph 6.5 Planning is an important part of the work of local authorities

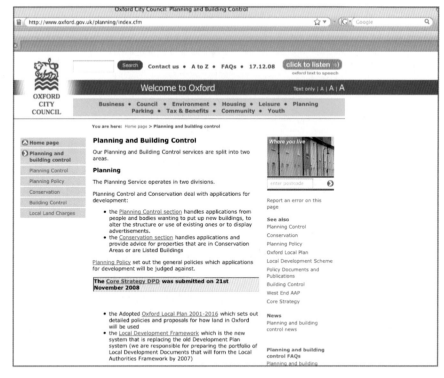

Planning committees need to weigh up:

➤ the gains from the proposal against its negative aspects
➤ the conflicts between differing groups within a local community
➤ the wider benefits of a scheme versus the local opposition

Case study

The Sandyforth open-cast mining site, Wigan

An example of a conflict over the use of a resource is that of the Sandyforth open-cast mining site in Wigan (Figure 6.2). When the Cobex mining company, which had been mining coal from the site, went into liquidation the area was abandoned, leaving a large hole in the ground (see Photograph 6.6). Wigan Metropolitan Borough Council spent a lot of money on making the area safe so that 'dirty' water would not pollute nearby water pipes or roads. In 2002 the council was approached by a company, H. J. Banks (www.hjbanks.com), that wished to use the site as a landfill to dispose of domestic waste.

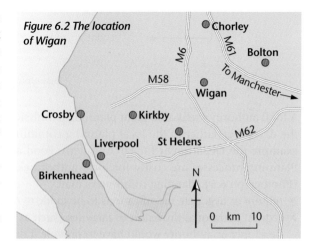

Figure 6.2 The location of Wigan

Phil Banks

Photograph 6.6 The abandoned opencast mine at Sandyforth

Objections to the landfill scheme

A campaign to prevent the scheme going ahead was launched, led by the group PALS (People Against Landfill Sites). A number of **objections** to the scheme were made by residents, including the following:

Unless the council can be 100% certain that the waste is totally inert and will not cause harm or danger to all life forms (human, animal or plant) then on environmental grounds alone this venture should not be allowed to proceed.

Without sampling and analysing the cargo of every single lorry before it arrives at the Sandyforth site there is no guarantee that it will not contain trace elements of heavy metals such as lead, cadmium or mercury or other toxic substances. Therefore, what policing measures will be put in place to protect against dangerous substances being hidden within so-called legal loads of waste?

Will the tipping area be fully lined with an impervious high impact liner so that in the event of toxic substances being tipped they will never enter the surface or underground watercourses?

Typically the site will be filled within 5 years, usually by which time the contractor has gone and it is left to the tax or ratepayer to fund any clean up costs.

What evidence does the council have to demonstrate that there will never be any ground movement or subsidence in the vicinity of the Sandyforth site? If ground movement is likely it is almost impossible to guarantee that any liner installed at the site will not become damaged, thus allowing uncontrolled leachates to discharge from the site.

Will leachates be collected in a holding tank and rendered harmless before they are discharged into the surrounding environment?

How will the council ensure that underground watercourses remote from the site are monitored to establish that they have not become polluted?

If light materials such as paper or polythene are tipped in windy conditions, they could become airborne and blow straight across the M6 thus posing a danger to traffic.

What controls will be put in place to prevent obnoxious smells entering the atmosphere? If they are uncontrolled, life could be extremely unpleasant for the residents of Ashton, Billinge, Bryn, Garswood, Highfield, Marus Bridge and Winstanley.

There does not appear to be any obvious route to the site that can cater for heavy traffic. Most have schools on them or the roads are unsuitable.

What will be done with this site when it has been filled with waste? Will the surface be capped and if so what methods will be used? How will pollution discharges be monitored once the site is no longer operational and who will pay for this?

The campaign against the proposal

Campaigning took a variety of forms. People objecting to the scheme were invited to send this letter to the council:

Dear Sir/Madam

We wish to formally object to the Sandyforth opencast mine, off Ashton Road, Windy Arbour, being used as a domestic waste tip. The reasons are as follows:

1 It will damage the environment by polluting the land, air and watercourses.
2 The M6 already pollutes the local environment.
3 Wigan MBC should be introducing recycling schemes to reduce waste.
4 The transport links to the site are unsuitable for heavy traffic.
5 It will cause noise pollution.
6 It will attract seagulls, flies, bluebottles, mice, cockroaches and other vermin to the surrounding area.

Yours faithfully,

Copies of the following article were distributed to residents:

Women living near landfills in the UK are more likely to have smaller babies or babies with congenital defects, according to the largest recorded study of the health effects of living near landfills. Although further research is needed to establish a causal link, the UK government is taking the study seriously, according to the country's deputy chief medical officer.

The study was conducted by a team of the Small Area Health Statistics Unit (SAHSU) at Imperial College, London. SAHSU researchers surveyed the 8.2 million live births that occurred within a 2-kilometre (km) radius of all 9,565 landfill sites that were operational in the UK between 1982 and 1997 and found that those babies had a 1% higher than expected risk of suffering from congenital abnormalities, such as neural tube and abdominal wall defects. That risk rose to 7% if the landfill contained hazardous waste. The researchers also found a 5% greater risk of low birth-weight babies for mothers living within 2 km of a landfill site.

'This is an important study, and the government is taking it seriously', said Pat Troop, deputy chief medical officer of the UK government. However, he says that the government is not changing its advice to pregnant women. And the government's expert committee on chemicals toxicity called the findings 'inconsistent', in part because there was no evidence that risk increased after landfill sites were opened.

The SAHSU researchers admit that factors such as smoking, drug use and infections during pregnancy may have influenced the data. Women living near landfills could also be exposed to other contaminants, because landfills are often located on land formerly used for industrial processes or close to current industrial activity. Nonetheless, Lars Yarup, SAHSU's assistant director, said a 1% risk cannot be dismissed: 'There may be a small set of locations with landfills that carry a substantial risk and some that have no risk. We have to try and identify these areas'. (Burke, M., 2001, 'Landfill link to birth defects strengthened', *Environmental Science & Technology*)

A website was set up for locals to express their opinions. Here are some responses:

Eddie from Wigan (Winstanley) says:

Forget it Wigan Council, its not happening! This area should be turned into a place of beauty, a nature reserve or something.

Ronnie from Bryn says:

Nobody wants a landfill site but who's offering any alternative ideas for waste disposal? It's got to go somewhere. If the council and the town's residents showed real commitment to recycling, we might not be in this situation.

Ged from Bryn says:

Look what happened when they used Billinge Hill Quarry for landfill. When the wind blew Upholland Road was covered in rubbish. We don't want the same for our district. Spend some money on it Wigan!

Pete from Abram says:

We already have over 20 conservation areas and numerous SSSIs. Sandyforth Pit would be prohibitively expensive to turn into a ecologically sound 'nature reserve or something', as has been suggested and it would take decades too. It is, however, geologically sound to be used to store waste which can then be covered over and landscaped to look just like the miles and miles of open countryside which surround it. Not one person saying we should not use Sandyforth has offered another location within the Borough for the Borough's waste.

Dave from Marus Bridge says:

A quarry is an ideal training ground for motocross and many disused quarries are used partly for this purpose. There is not a single facility for the sport that I love anywhere in the Wigan Borough and I would like to change that. Sandyforth Quarry would be ideal.

The outcome

The application was rejected by the planning committee of Wigan Metropolitan Borough Council. The company, H. J. Banks, went to appeal in February 2006. The appeal was rejected.

Vice chairman (PALS) from Garswood/North Ashton, said:

Congratulations to PALS on the victory over H. J. Banks. Once again David slew Goliath.

After the rejection of the appeal the site was filled in (Photograph 6.7).

Photograph 6.7 The Sandyforth site after the former opencast mine was filled in

Phil Banks

The geographical impact of international conflicts

You are required to study the 'social, economic and environmental issues associated with major international conflicts that have taken place within the last 30 years' using one or more case studies. The aim of this part of the specification is for you to study contemporary events as they are happening. The background to two on-going conflicts is described below: the Israeli/Palestinian conflict in the middle east and the war in Darfur. You should update this background with information from news media about events as they occur.

Figure 6.3 Map showing the location of Israel

The Israeli/Palestinian conflict in the middle east

Historical background

Before the First World War Palestine was a district ruled by the Turkish Ottoman empire. The Ottomans were defeated by Britain and its allies in the war. After the First World War Britain took control of Palestine, but there were many troubles between the Arabs who lived there and Jews who also wanted to live there. After the Second World War, Britain let the United Nations (UN) decide what to do with Palestine. The UN suggested separating Palestine into two countries, one Arab and one Jewish.

The Arab leaders did not agree to this plan, but the Jewish leaders accepted it and, in 1948, declared the state of Israel. The president of the USA gave his support to the new state.

Arab leaders were outraged by this. In 1948 war broke out between Arab nations in the region (including Egypt and Jordan) on one side and the new country, Israel, on the other. After months of intense fighting and extensive international diplomacy Israel and its Arab neighbours agreed to stop the war. However, relations between them have continued to be tense and more conflict has followed.

Who are the Israelis?

Israelis are people who live in Israel, which is at the eastern end of the Mediterranean Sea (Figure 6.3). Israel began as a homeland for Jewish people. Jews have historical and religious ties to the land dating back thousands of years. In the early part of the twentieth century, before it became

Israel, thousands of Jews moved to the area to start new lives and set up new communities. Many Jews were escaping persecution in Europe and Russia. At the end of the Second World War, after the Holocaust, a lot of Jews moved to Israel, including some from Arab countries. About one-fifth of the Israeli population are Arab. These people are the descendants of the Palestinians who remained in the country at its creation, despite the first Arab–Israeli war of 1948.

Who are the Palestinians?

The Palestinians are mostly Muslim Arabs, although some are Christians, who live in the middle east but are also scattered around the world. Palestinians do not have a country to call their own. Most of the land they come from, which they call Palestine, was given to Israel in 1948. The remainder of their land, known as the West Bank and Gaza Strip, was captured from Jordan and Egypt, respectively, by Israel in a war in 1967.

In the 1960s many Palestinians grew frustrated at not having their own state. They formed political groups, the largest of which is the Palestine Liberation Organisation (PLO). Militant Palestinian groups — some of whom were allied to the PLO — carried out violent attacks against Israelis. Eleven Israeli athletes were killed after they were taken hostage by one of these groups during the Olympic Games in Germany in 1972. Most died when a rescue attempt by the German police went wrong and ended in a gun battle. Other groups have hijacked aircraft and boats.

The start of the current conflict

In 1987 Palestinians living in the West Bank and the Gaza Strip, territories occupied by Israel, began demonstrating and fighting against Israeli soldiers and settlers in what was called the **Intifada**, or uprising. In the 1990s peace talks began and the Israelis withdrew from much of the West Bank and Gaza Strip. The PLO agreed to stop attacks against Israelis. But the uprising started again even more violently in 2001 when peace talks failed.

The Occupied Territories

The Occupied Territories are the two separate areas of land — the West Bank and the Gaza Strip — where many Palestinians live. After the 1948 war, Jordan took control of the West Bank and Egypt took control of the Gaza Strip. Both were captured by Israel during a war in 1967. Israel set up many Jewish settlements — some tiny, some as big as small towns — in both the West Bank and the Gaza Strip. These settlements are considered illegal under international law, although Israel does not agree with this.

In August and September 2005 Israel withdrew all of its settlers and troops from the Gaza Strip. It maintained control of the area's borders, coastline and airspace. Four settlements in the northern West Bank were also evacuated. The architect of the withdrawal plan was the Israeli prime minister, Ariel Sharon. However it was unpopular with many Israelis, especially the settlers, who resisted strongly at the time of withdrawal.

The impacts of the conflict

During the 1948 and 1967 wars hundreds of thousands of Palestinians left, or were forced out of, their homes and became refugees in neighbouring countries.

More than 4 million Palestinians are now refugees, many living in camps in countries such as Syria, Jordan and Lebanon. The two sides disagree on how to help the refugees.

Human rights groups believe the Israeli army sometimes treats the Palestinians too harshly in the Occupied Territories. For example, the Israelis have put up many check points on roads between villages. According to the army, this is to prevent potential suicide bombers from harming Israelis. But Palestinians say it makes it much harder to get to work or school, or visit friends and family. Some Palestinians compare the restrictions on their lives to being in prison.

Israel has built a massive barrier in the West Bank. It is mostly a strong fence, but some of it is a concrete wall. The Israeli government says the barrier will help prevent Palestinian suicide bombers travelling to Israeli cities. It also says that the barrier is only temporary and can be removed once a peace agreement is reached. Palestinians don't like the barrier. They say it is creating a new border and cutting into land they hope will form a future state of Palestine. They also say the barrier cuts through Palestinian villages, preventing farmers from getting to their land.

To try to create a better atmosphere for peace talks between the two communities, Israel has released many Palestinian prisoners.

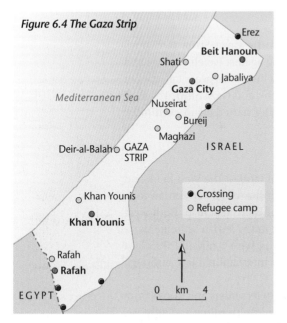

Figure 6.4 The Gaza Strip

The Gaza Strip

The Gaza Strip is one of the Occupied Territories to the southwest of Israel. It occupies 363 km^2 northeast of the Sinai Peninsula (Figure 6.4). The official population is more than 1 million people, but the actual population is much larger. Gaza City was a prosperous trading centre for much of its history. The area's main economic problem is now the extreme poverty of the large number of Palestinian Arab refugees living there.

In 1987, rioting among Gaza's Palestinians marked the beginning of the first Intifada. Continued unrest led in 1993 to an agreement between Israel and the PLO, granting limited self-rule to the Palestinian population of the Gaza Strip and West Bank. A breakdown in further negotiations in 2000 led to another outbreak of violence. In an attempt to stem the fighting, Israel withdrew all its soldiers and settlers from the Gaza Strip in 2005, and control of the territory was transferred to the Palestinians.

Gaza is not an easy place to live at the best of times. It is one of the most crowded areas of the world, where unemployment is high, people are poor and the economy is crippled by an international boycott and Israel withholding desperately needed Palestinian tax revenues. More than 50% of Gazans are 17 years of age or younger. Most feel they have no prospects at home but no way to get out. Foreign powers, Israel and Egypt, control all of Gaza's borders, opening and closing them at will. Gaza is also awash with illegal weapons. This is an ongoing, explosive mix of internal and external pressures.

The situation in 2007/08

In 2006 Palestinian elections were held under a peace process brokered by the international community. The elections were won by a radical group called Hamas, the Islamic Resistance Movement that calls for the establishment of an Islamic state and which does not recognise the state of Israel. The USA, Israel and European governments refused to acknowledge the result and imposed sanctions on the Palestinians.

A power battle has ensued, which reaches the highest levels of Palestinian politics. Fatah gunmen are loyal to the Palestinian president, Mahmoud Abbas;, Hamas gunmen to the Palestinian prime minister, Ismail Haniya. Despite repeatedly announced ceasefires between these factions street battles in Gaza are commonplace, preventing people going about their lives and crippling investment in the area (Photograph 6.8). Since October 2007 Hamas has been in control.

According to the UN Office for Humanitarian Affairs, more than 150 Palestinians died and more than 650 were wounded in internal violence in the first 8 months of 2008. This spells more misery for ordinary Gazans, many of whom stay in their homes for fear of being caught in the crossfire.

Things got so bad that an Egyptian security delegation stationed in Gaza publicly appealed to the warring factions for a lull, to allow people to shop for food and to go to the mosque for Friday prayers without dodging bullets.

*Photograph 6.8
Israeli soldiers on an operation in Gaza, 2008*

TopFoto

Israel is also conducting air strikes. Israel says these are pinpoint attacks on Hamas targets in Gaza in response to volleys of rockets regularly aimed at Israeli towns by the movement's military wing. Israel's military has made cockpit footage publicly available to show the high-tech precision of its air strikes. But in crowded Gaza, innocent bystanders often get hurt.

Israel has said it will continue to do 'whatever it takes' to stop the rocket fire from Gaza. In addition to the air strikes, it has stationed a number of armoured vehicles on and just over the Israeli–Gaza border — to act as a deterrent. The land on the border is blasted and empty, flattened by the Israelis to give soldiers stationed on the high concrete border wall a clear field of fire. However, neither Israeli incursions, nor air or artillery strikes, have stopped the rocket fire from Gaza, which to a greater or lesser extent, has been constant over the last 6 years. Armed Palestinian groups say that it will continue as long as Israel occupies land they view as Palestinian.

In January 2008, militants blasted a hole in the Egyptian border near the town of Rafah in defiance of the blockade of Gaza. Thousands of Palestinians streamed across the border into Egypt to stock up with much-needed food and fuel. The Egyptian side of the border became an open air market. Egyptian police could not control the numbers involved. However, under pressure from both the USA and Israel, the border was re-closed in February 2008.

During the summer of 2008 Israeli soldiers continued to raid refugee camps such as the Bureij refugee camp in Gaza seeking terrorists. It is inevitable that innocent people are killed in these raids. Israel now allows only the barest essentials into Gaza. There is little fuel, so the streets are full of carts pulled by horses and donkeys. The economy has collapsed — 87% of private businesses have gone bust. There are also increasing problems of water provision and sewage disposal. In some areas of the Strip water is only available for 8 hours a week. In Gaza City itself, over 50 million litres of raw sewage is being pumped directly into the sea every day. Not only is it causing problems for the immediate coastline, but the Mediterranean drift takes the sewage north into Israeli waters.

In late 2008/early 2009 Israel invaded Gaza with tanks, soldiers and air strikes to stop continued rocket attacks from Hamas. Over 1,000 Palestinians, many of them children, lost their lives in the devastation.

This ongoing conflict affects neighbouring countries including Lebanon and Syria. There have been many attempts to engineer peace and all of them have failed owing to the complexity of the situation and the difficulty of resolving some of the underlying issues.

Darfur, Sudan

Darfur is a semi-arid western province of Sudan — Africa's largest country (Figure 6.4). Darfur alone is the size of France. Though Sudan is an Arab-dominated country Darfur's population is mostly black African. For years there have been tensions between the mostly African farmers and the mostly Arab herders, who have competed for land. There was a long-running war in the south of Sudan that ended in 2005.

The arid and impoverished Darfur region of Sudan has been suffering civil war since 2003. This is how the BBC website described the crisis in May 2005:

> The world's worst humanitarian crisis has been unfolding in Sudan's western region of Darfur. More than 2 million people are estimated to have fled their homes and at least 180,000 are thought to have died during the crisis. Sudan's government and the pro-government Arab militias (the Janjaweed) are accused of war crimes against the region's black African population, although the United Nations has stopped short of terming it a genocide.

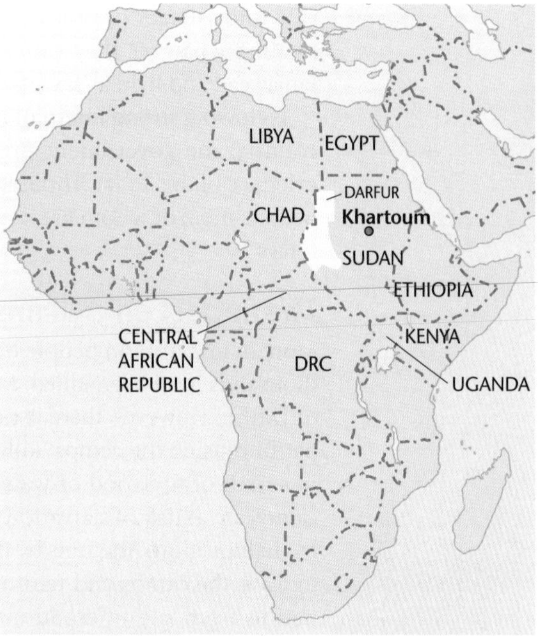

The start of the conflict

The conflict began in the Darfur region early in 2003. Rebel groups began attacking government targets, claiming that the region was being neglected by central government in Khartoum. These groups, the Sudan Liberation Army (SLA) and the Justice and Equality Movement (JEM), say that the government is oppressing black Africans in favour of Arabs.

Figure 6.5 Map showing the location of Darfur

The response of the Sudanese government

The government admits to mobilising 'self-defence militias' following the attacks by the black rebel groups. However, it denies links to the Janjaweed Arab militia groups accused of trying to 'cleanse' large swathes of territory of black Africans. Refugees from Darfur describe how, following air raids by government aircraft, the Janjaweed

Boris Heger/Das Fotoarchiv/Still Pictures

Photograph 6.9 A family displaced by fighting living in a shelter under a tree

ride into villages on horses and camels, slaughtering men, raping women and stealing whatever they can find. Many women report being abducted by the Janjaweed and held as sex slaves for more than a week before being released.

Following strong international pressure and the threat of sanctions against the country, the government promised to disarm the militias, but there is little evidence of this so far. Thousands of extra police have been deployed but the local people, most of whom are now refugees, have little faith in the Sudanese security forces.

The impact on civilians

More than 2 million people have left their homes in destroyed villages and many thousands have been killed. Most have taken refuge in camps in the main towns of Darfur. However, there is not enough food, water or medicine. The Janjaweed patrol outside the camps, killing men and raping women if they venture too far in search of firewood or water. Aid workers report that many thousands in the camps are at risk of starvation and disease, and 1 million children are threatened by malnutrition. Attempts by the Sudanese security forces to persuade the refugees to leave the camps and return home have led to violence and brought condemnation from the international community. Meanwhile, a drought and a big reduction in the number of active farmers means a poor harvest and heavy dependence on food aid.

As many as 200,000 people have sought refuge in neighbouring Chad. Many are also camped along a 600 km stretch of the border and remain vulnerable to attacks from Sudanese militia groups. The government of Chad is worried that the conflict could spill over the border, as its eastern areas have a similar ethnic mix to that in Darfur.

What is being done to help?

There are many aid agencies working in Darfur. However, they are unable to gain access to large parts of the region. They accuse the government of blocking access to some areas by demanding visas and imposing other bureaucratic obstacles.

The government and the two rebel groups signed a ceasefire in April 2004, but this has not held. The African Union (AU), a group of African countries, has organised peace talks and has made progress on some agreements, such as banning military flights and allowing in humanitarian aid. In 2006 a peace deal was signed between some of the various factions resulting in 7,000 African Union troops being deployed in Darfur as 'blue-helmeted' observers. The Sudanese government resisted any further increase in numbers of peacekeepers. The UN was criticised for doing too little, too late. Its Security Council agreed to impose travel bans and to freeze the assets of those who commit atrocities in the area.

The situation in 2007/08

Towards the end of 2007 it was agreed that a new combined UN-African Union peacekeeping force should be sent to Darfur, with the approval of the Sudanese government. It was to comprise 26,000 troops and 6,000 police under the

command of the former head of Nigeria's armed forces, General Agwai. Expectations were high, though successful outcomes were likely to be slow. One of the first problems was how to get troops into an area where there are few roads, no airport and little water. By August 2008 only 8,000 troops had been deployed.

A major problem was that only two of the rebel factions had signed the 2006 peace deal. There are estimated to be 13 rebel factions in Darfur, and there is now conflict between these. There are also concerns that the Sudanese government could create obstacles, as it has done in the past. Although enough troops have been promised — from Africa and elsewhere — wealthy Western nations have not guaranteed the necessary military hardware, such as helicopters. Such resources are tied up elsewhere in the world. By August 2008, no helicopters had arrived.

In the summer of 2008, the UN estimated that 5 years of conflict in Darfur had left 300,000 people dead and more than 2 million homeless. The aid agency Oxfam believed that about 1,000 people were being displaced every month in the region (Photograph 6.10). The Sudanese government, however, stated that the scale of the violence and suffering was exaggerated by the West for political reasons. It continued to deny that it had organised the Arab Janjaweed militias accused of widespread atrocities against Darfur's black African population.

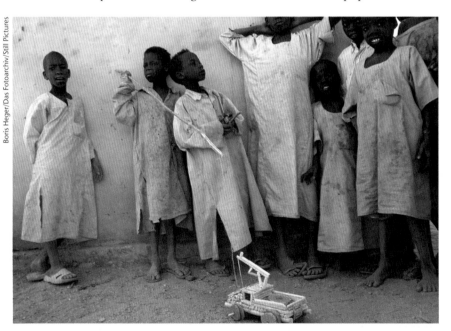

Photograph 6.10
Children in a refugee camp in Chad with a wooden toy they have made. It looks like the trucks they saw attacking their village before they fled

In July 2008, the political heat of the situation was increased when the prosecutor at the International Criminal Court in The Hague (the Netherlands) asked judges to issue an arrest warrant against Sudan's President Omar al-Bashir for alleged war crimes during the conflict in Darfur. The chief prosecutor stated that 'there are reasonable grounds to believe that Omar Hassan Ahmad al-Bashir bears criminal responsibility in relation to 10 counts of genocide, crimes against humanity and war crimes'.

Multicultural societies in the UK

Migration of ethnic groups leads to the creation of multicultural societies. In most countries there is at least one minority group and, while they may be able to live peacefully with the majority, it is more likely that there will be a certain amount of prejudice and discrimination leading to tensions and conflict. This is therefore an emotive and sensitive issue, particularly when cultural differences are interpreted as racial differences.

Current scientific research suggests that most modern humans are descended from three main racial types: caucasoid, mongoloid and negroid, but the distinctions between them are now so blurred that race has little scientific status. Skin colour remains a visible distinguishing feature but people also differ in their ethnic background, which is expressed in terms of language, religion and culture.

Multicultural societies are often the product of migration, but they may also be the stimulus for it, as persecuted groups leave a country to escape oppression. The level of integration of minorities varies between societies. In some societies there is a lack of integration, whereas in others there are more tolerant attitudes.

Ethnic segregation is the clustering together of people with similar ethnic or cultural characteristics into separate urban residential areas. There are numerous examples of this in the UK. The largest ethnic minority in the country is the Indian population, which forms 27% of the total ethnic minority population. The next largest is the Pakistani ethnic minority (17%), followed by the black Caribbean (15%). Smaller, but still significant, ethnic minorities of Bangladeshi, black African and Chinese people also live in the country. In addition to these 'ethnic' minorities,

Photograph 6.11
A Polish restaurant
in Oxford

there are significant numbers of migrants from other parts of the world, particularly Germany, the USA and most recently Poland (Photograph 6.11). Migration into the UK is so great that migrants are now classed as 'born abroad'.

In the 2001 census there were 57 million people in the UK. Of these, 4.3 million (7.5% of the population) were people born abroad. This had increased to 5 million in 2006. Between 1991 and 2001, half of the UK's population growth was due to immigration. There is no doubt that immigration will continue, though the areas of origin are likely to change.

Reasons for the development of multicultural societies

Multicultural societies are formed by migration. There have been a number of significant migrations into the UK over the last 200 years. The descendants of these immigrants, and the inter-marriage that has taken place since, have created the multicultural society that now exists.

The main migrations that have taken place into the UK are:

➤ **nineteenth century** — Jewish arrivals from Russia/Poland, escaping persecution
➤ **nineteenth century** — Irish people escaping from poverty in rural Ireland
➤ **1930s–40s** — Jews and Poles escaping fascism and the Second World War
➤ **1948–60s** — Caribbean workers invited to help rebuild postwar Britain, mainly in public services
➤ **1950s–60s** — Asians from India, Pakistan and Bangladesh escaping poverty and seeking work in public services and textile industries
➤ **1970s** — east African Asians (mainly from Uganda) escaping persecution and Vietnamese escaping war
➤ **1980–90s** — eastern European refugees escaping from war and political unrest in Romania and former Yugoslavia
➤ **2000s** — economic migration from eastern Europe caused by the enlargement of the European Union

Table 6.1 The top 10 countries of origin of people born abroad, 2001

The origins of people born abroad

The 1991 and 2001 censuses included questions that allowed detailed analysis of the origins of people born abroad and living in the UK. The top 10 countries of origin of people born abroad in 2001 (excluding the Republic of Ireland) are shown in Table 6.1.

Table 6.1 illustrates some interesting points:

➤ No single country of origin contributes 1% of the UK population (note that these figures do not include second or third generation migrants — people born in the UK to migrant parents or grandparents).
➤ The numbers of people from the Caribbean have fallen, albeit by a small number.

Country	Number 1991 (000s)	Number 2001 (000s)	As % of all people in the UK (2001)
India	409	466	0.82
Pakistan	234	321	0.56
Germany	215	262	0.46
Caribbean	267	255	0.45
USA	144	155	0.27
Bangladesh	105	154	0.27
South Africa	68	140	0.25
Kenya	112	129	0.23
Italy	91	107	0.19
Australia	73	106	0.19

Source: Institute for Public Policy Research

> There have been significant increases in people from unexpected areas such as South Africa and Australia.
> Surprisingly, the third and fifth largest countries of origin are Germany and the USA, respectively.

However, these figures do not show that since 2001 there have been significant and sudden increases in migrations from countries in eastern Europe, most notably Poland. Between April 2004 and December 2006, more than 370,000 Polish migrants came to the UK and registered for work. It is thought that an additional 100,000 self-employed workers, such as builders and plumbers also arrived, although no accurate figures are available. The Polish embassy estimated that the number of Polish workers in the country by this date was over half a million. However, most of them have stayed for less than a year and many have gone home regularly, making accurate estimates almost impossible.

Geographical distribution of cultural groups

Ethnic minorities are concentrated in the major urban areas of the country, particularly London (1.8 million migrants) and the southeast (0.6 million migrants), the west and east midlands, Manchester and West Yorkshire (Figure 6.6). Over 50% of ethnic minorities live in London and the southeast, which has only 30% of the white population, so the concentration here is highest. A significant proportion of ethnic minorities consists of people born in the UK, descended from migrants who came from the former Commonwealth countries in the 1950s, 1960s and 1970s.

Table 6.2 The UK population by ethnic group, 2001

Ethnic classification	Total population (000s)	%	% of ethnic population
White	54,154	92.1	Not applicable
Mixed	677	1.2	14.6
Indian	1,053	1.8	22.7
Pakistani	747	1.3	16.1
Bangladeshi	283	0.5	6.1
Other Asian	248	0.4	5.3
Black Caribbean	566	1.0	12.2
Black African	485	0.8	10.5
Black other	98	0.2	2.1
Chinese	247	0.4	5.3
Other	231	0.4	5.0
All ethnic population	4,635	7.9	100
All population	58,789	100	

Source: 2001 Census

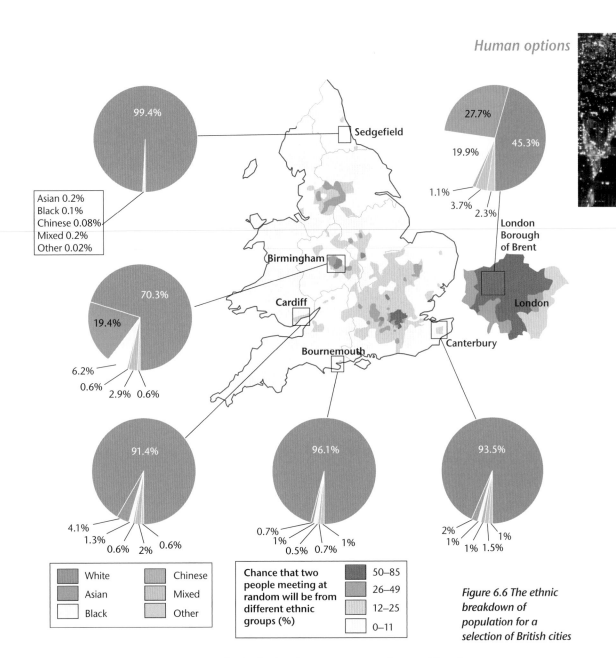

Asian 0.2%
Black 0.1%
Chinese 0.08%
Mixed 0.2%
Other 0.02%

Figure 6.6 The ethnic breakdown of population for a selection of British cities

The 1991 and 2001 censuses asked which ethnic group people considered themselves to belong to, as well as where they were born. In 2001, the term 'mixed' was used for the first time. Tables 6.2–6.4 show the census results.

Some variations in the geographical distribution of ethnic groups result from factors in the early days of immigration, such as employment in specific industries. For example, there are large concentrations of the Indian ethnic minority in the east and west midlands (e.g. Leicester, Wolverhampton and Sandwell) and Greater Manchester — areas where labour-intensive industries such as clothing and car manufacture were located. The Pakistani minority is concentrated in parts of Bradford, Leeds and Birmingham, and there are large Bangladeshi communities in Luton, Oldham and Birmingham.

Table 6.3 UK resident population by ethnic group, 2001

Region/country	White (%)	Mixed (%)	Indian (%)	Pakistani (%)	Bangladeshi (%)	Other Asian (%)	Caribbean (%)	African (%)	Other black (%)	Chinese (%)	Other (%)
UK	92.1	1.2	1.8	1.3	0.5	0.4	1.0	0.8	0.2	0.4	0.4
Northeast	97.6	0.5	0.4	0.6	0.2	0.1	0.04	0.1	0.02	0.2	0.2
Northwest	94.4	0.9	1.1	1.7	0.4	0.2	0.3	0.2	0.1	0.4	0.2
Yorks and Humber	93.4	0.9	1.0	2.9	0.2	0.2	0.4	0.2	0.1	0.2	0.2
East midlands	93.5	1.0	2.9	0.7	0.2	0.3	0.6	0.2	0.1	0.3	0.2
West midlands	88.7	1.4	3.4	2.9	0.6	0.4	1.6	0.2	0.2	0.3	0.3
East	95.1	1.1	1.0	0.7	0.3	0.2	0.5	0.3	0.1	0.4	0.3
London	71.2	3.2	6.0	2.0	2.2	1.9	4.8	5.3	0.8	1.1	1.6
Southeast	95.1	1.1	1.1	0.7	0.2	0.3	0.3	0.3	0.1	0.4	0.4
Southwest	97.7	0.8	0.3	0.1	0.1	0.1	0.2	0.1	0.05	0.3	0.2
England	90.9	1.3	2.1	1.4	0.6	0.5	1.1	1.0	0.2	0.5	0.4
Wales	97.9	0.6	0.3	0.3	0.2	0.1	0.1	0.1	0.03	0.2	0.2
Scotland	98.0	0.2	0.3	0.6	0.04	0.1	0.04	0.1	0.02	0.3	0.2
Northern Ireland	99.2	0.2	0.10	0.04	0.01	0.01	0.02	0.03	0.02	0.2	0.1

Source: 2001 census

Region	Total numbers 2001 (000s)	As % of all people in that region
East midlands	225	5.4
East of England	328	6.1
London	1,779	24.8
Northeast	67	2.7
Northwest	280	4.2
Scotland	168	3.3
Southeast	580	7.2
Southwest	218	4.4
Wales	77	2.7
West midlands	342	6.5
Yorks and Humber	235	4.7

Source: Institute for Public Policy Research

Table 6.4 Distribution of people born abroad, 2001

The 1991 and 2001 censuses revealed some geographical variations within urban areas between ethnic minorities. Bangladeshi and black Caribbean groups are concentrated in high-density inner-city areas characterised by low levels of owner occupancy and high levels of unemployment. In contrast, people of Chinese origin are distributed across a wide range of areas — from deprived inner-city areas to more affluent suburbs. Some research suggests that ethnic segregation is more geographically pronounced in northern areas than in London.

Table 6.5 shows that London has a high proportion and diversity of ethnic minorities. Sixty per cent of the UK's black Caribbean population and 52% of the Bangladeshi population lives here, but only 18% of the Pakistani population. The majority live in inner-city areas, and some areas are dominated by certain ethnic groups (for example, Bangladeshi people in Tower Hamlets), but there is wider diversity in other localities such as Brent and

Newham. There is a strong concentration of black Caribbean people south of the River Thames in Lambeth and Southwark. Even within these areas, there are some pronounced variations. For example, in the Northcote ward of Ealing, nearly 70% of the population is Indian, and over 90% of the population of that ward is non-white. The London Borough of Brent has the most diverse ethnic structure, with large concentrations of black Caribbean, black African and Indian people, as well as a large subsection of the white community which is Irish-born.

Table 6.5 also illustrates some of the difficulties regarding information on this topic. The data show people born abroad — it is unlikely that the high numbers of foreigners resident in Kensington and Chelsea are from areas such as India, Pakistan and the Caribbean. It is more likely that they are from other areas of the world, such as Germany and other European countries, Australia, the USA and the Gulf states.

Table 6.6 shows areas in the UK, excluding London, with high concentrations of people born abroad. It is a fair assumption that the migrants in these areas are predominantly from India, Pakistan and Bangladesh.

Area	Total numbers 2001	As % of all people in that area
Wembley	18,258	51.9
Hyde Park	32,128	48.4
Southall W	30,573	47.4
East Ham N	23,293	46.6
Kensington	28,757	45.8
Chelsea	26,429	43.1
Sudbury	21,109	42.9
Queensbury	15,641	40.9
Tottenham S	19,716	40.9
Tottenham N	24,801	40.5

Source: Institute for Public Policy Research

Table 6.5 Local areas with the highest proportion of people born abroad (all in London)

Area	Location	Total numbers 2001	As % of all people in that area
Belgrave	Leicester	19,126	40.1
Knighton	Leicester	19,744	36.2
Sparkbrook	Birmingham	22,301	35.2
Handsworth	Birmingham	18,339	34.3
Bradford (University district)	Bradford	18,579	32.0
Ladywood East	Birmingham	15,595	28.7
Ladywood West	Birmingham	14,036	28.4
Slough East	Slough	14,173	26.3
Luton Central	Luton	13,743	25.2
Oxford West	Oxford	9,310	24.8

Source: Institute for Public Policy Research

Table 6.6 Local areas with the highest proportion of people born abroad (outside London)

The Office for National Statistics (ONS) has devised a diversity index from census data to assess the ethnic diversity of particular areas. This is based on the probability that any two people chosen at random from a particular area would be from different ethnic groups. Using this index the most diverse areas are Brent (London) (85%), Slough (62%), Leicester (57%) and Luton (56%). Easington in County Durham is one of the least diverse (2%). This index has also been applied to religious composition, which showed that the most religiously diverse area of the country is Harrow (London) — 62%.

Issues related to multicultural societies

Housing

In the initial phases of immigration, multiple occupancy of rented accommodation in inner-city areas (terraced houses) was widespread. As migrants are often a source of cheap labour in low-paid construction, transport or health service jobs (in the UK in 2000, 27% of London Underground's staff, 26% of all workers in the health services and 14% of all workers in the catering industry were foreign born), they have tended to concentrate in the areas of poorest housing in major cities. Such concentrations are reinforced by later migrants who seek the support and security of living near friends and relatives within an ethnic community.

Ethnic minorities have also been less successful in securing mortgage loans. This has forced them to use less conventional and more expensive forms of financing which limit what they are able to afford. The prospect of an expensive mortgage on a sub-standard property in a deprived area has contributed to the low rate of owner occupancy among the ethnic minority population.

Ethnic minorities have also been discriminated against in access to local authority housing and tend to be disproportionately represented among council-house tenants. This has led in some urban areas to the development of internal networks of housing provision, where landlords belonging to an ethnic group provide housing for members of that group — a process known as the 'racialisation of residential space'.

More recently owner occupancy has increased and some more wealthy individuals have moved into suburban areas. In addition, many members of ethnic minorities run small businesses such as shops, and live in part of the same building. Despite this, geographical segregation is clear, as is inequality. On average, Asian households are the largest of all ethnic groups, contain the most

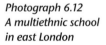

*Photograph 6.12
A multiethnic school
in east London*

dependent children, are the most overcrowded and have the highest rates of unemployment.

Education

Concentrations of minorities in inner-city areas have led to some schools being dominated by one ethnic group, which has affected education requirements. For example, special English lessons may be needed for children and their parents (mothers in particular) and bilingual reading schemes may be introduced. In some areas, religious provision for minority groups has resulted in separate schooling, known as 'faith schools', but this is rare. There is greater integration in communities such as Leicester and Bradford, where holiday patterns, school timetables and school meals are modified to reflect the ethnic mix of the areas. This helps to enhance mutual understanding of culture, particularly among the young.

Variation in the educational attainment of different ethnic minorities is still being examined. There is some evidence to suggest that children from black Caribbean backgrounds are underachieving compared not only with the white population but also with other ethnic groups. Conversely, the performance of children from Indian, Pakistani and Chinese backgrounds appears on average to be better than that of white children. Ofsted has stated that the white 'working-class' male is currently the lowest achiever in schools.

Healthcare

In the past there has been a lack of resistance to childhood diseases among the children of newly arrived immigrants, and fears about immunisation. Literature has been produced in ethnic minority languages to inform parents about the benefits of immunisation. However, as literacy and educational standards have improved, particularly among second and subsequent generation ethnic minorities, there have been fewer concerns.

Many ethnic minority groups continue to live in run-down inner-city areas and there remains a higher concentration of communicable and transmittable disease in such areas. However, this is more a reflection of the living standards in these areas than of the people who live in them.

Language

New migrants can find it difficult to obtain employment and to integrate if they do not speak English. Second-generation migrant children, educated in the UK, grow up speaking English and have different aspirations from their parents. They are more likely to integrate, and this can cause tension within the ethnic group if they adopt the culture of the host country.

Religion

Migrants from the Indian subcontinent, and other parts of Asia, are likely to follow a different religion from the host population. This may cause friction with employers and authorities when migrants wish to adhere to their own religious calendars and practices.

Country of birth	New immigrants (%)			Settled immigrants (%)		
	Employed	Low earners	High earners	Employed	Low earners	High earners
India	66.0	16.4	18.1	62.9	15.9	7.9
Pakistan	44.0	35.4	3.7	43.9	23.0	6.8
Germany	68.8	20.5	13.3	75.5	21.0	7.6
West Indies	n/a	n/a	n/a	n/a	14.8	0.1
USA	68.1	7.8	40.6	76.1	18.1	16.3
Bangladesh	42.8	63.3	2.2	40.0	39.0	4.3
South Africa	81.5	10.3	13.6	75.8	15.1	18.4
Kenya	60.9	19.6	5.9	77.1	12.8	11.1
Italy	73.4	13.3	13.3	72.1	22.6	4.5
Australia	90.6	6.8	27.0	81.9	12.0	14.4
UK				73.5	21.1	7.0

Source: Institute of Policy Research

Table 6.7 Immigrants' economic performance (from the top 10 countries of origin), 2004

Economic issues

In the UK, there has been legislation on anti-racism, employment rights and equal opportunities to combat discrimination, prejudice and racism. However, the cost of state benefits for migrants' housing, education and unemployment may still cause resentment and racial intolerance from members of the host population. The government policy of constructing centres to house asylum seekers in rural areas of the UK has caused concern and resentment among local residents.

Migration is often welcomed in periods of economic growth but resented during economic recessions, when migrants are accused of taking jobs. This has happened in Germany and France as well as in the UK. However, in 2002 it was calculated that the net tax contribution of migrants to the UK economy was £2.5 billion per year and that a 1% population increase through migration can lead to a 1.25–1.5% increase in GDP (UK Home Office statistics, May 2002).

There has been extensive research on the economic impact of immigration and in 2007 the Institute for Public Policy Research published further figures. It became clear that there was a wide disparity in economic performance between and within nationalities (see Table 6.7). For example, Bangladesh-born people tend not to earn high incomes, whereas those born in the USA and Australia do well. In Table 6.7, low earners are people earning less than £149.20 a week (half the UK median wage in 2004), high earners are people earning more than £750 a week. Figures for people born in the UK are given for comparison.

Migrants now account for one in eight of the UK's working-age population, which it is estimated boosts economic output by £6 billion (2007). Much of this labour is employed in unskilled and low-skilled work (Photograph 6.13). There is anecdotal evidence to suggest that UK-born people are unwilling to do such jobs in agriculture, hotels and catering . A government report published in 2007 (*The Economic and Fiscal Impact of Immigration*) concluded 'Migrants are filling jobs that natives will not do'. There is also evidence to suggest that employers prefer to employ immigrant workers because of their willingness to work for lower wages, to put in longer hours, and for their better work ethic compared with UK-born workers.

*Photograph 6.13
A middle eastern
taxi driver in
Manchester*

Contrary to popular belief, most immigrants are not employed in manual work. Banking and finance employ 13% of migrants, followed by the hotel and restaurant trade (12%). Construction accounts for just 7% while another 5% work in agriculture and fishing.

Other social issues

Despite the obvious economic gains there are still major concerns about the social impact of widespread immigration from other countries. The Home Office has stated that an increasing number of immigrants is putting pressure on public services (health, education, social services) and some chief constables are concerned about increased crime and disorder. One recent concern is that multi-cultural issues are beginning to emerge in areas of the country that have little or no previous experience of them, such as the northeast of England. However, in most urban areas, ethnic groups are well integrated and have a high profile in the local community, with representatives on local councils or as MPs.

There are times when multiculturalism is viewed negatively, however, for example when there are terrorist incidents on UK soil. The '7/7 bombings' in London in July 2005 and the terrorist attack at Glasgow airport in 2007 — both carried out by 'home-grown' Islamic fundamentalist terrorists — illustrate this.

Immigration controls

Many countries are tightening their rules on immigration and allocation of work permits. This makes it more difficult for both economic refugees and genuine asylum seekers to gain entry. There has been growing pressure for external controls to restrict immigration into Europe now that movement within the EU is easier.

Some people are concerned that Europe's traditional role as a place of sanctuary is being replaced by an attitude of hostility — it is becoming a 'fortress Europe', repelling migrants.

In January 2002, the UK government announced a scheme under which some workers would be allowed to enter the country, depending on their 'educational qualifications, work experience and past earnings'. Initially, such migrants were to be allowed to stay for only 1 year. In 2004, another ten nations joined the European Union. As the EU allows free movement of labour between its member countries, an increase in migration into the EU's more prosperous nations, such as the UK, was anticipated and this did occur, mainly from Poland. When Romania and Bulgaria joined the EU in 2007, the UK government announced restrictions on movement from these two countries. This was allowed under the accession treaty and was a clear change of policy.

All of the above is based on 'official' figures. There is no way of knowing how many migrants come into the UK illegally, where they come from or where they live.

Separatism within and across national boundaries

The nature of separatism

When the people of a region feel alienated from central government, they often seek to gain more political control. Such groups may have a different language, culture or religion from the rest of the state and are often geographically peripheral. They feel remote from centralised government and feel that they do not receive adequate support, particularly with economic development.

Reasons for separatism

Reasons for separatist pressure in a region include:
➤ an area which is economically depressed compared with a wealthier core
➤ a minority language or culture with a different history
➤ a minority religious grouping
➤ the perception that exploitation of local resources by national government produces little economic gain for the region
➤ peripheral location to the economic/political core
➤ collapse of the state, weakening the political power that held the regions together (e.g. the former USSR, Yugoslavia)
➤ the strengthening of supranational bodies such as the EU, which has led many nationalist groups to think they have a better chance of developing economically if they are independent

There are examples of separatist movements all over the world. Some have succeeded in their aims, while other struggles for independence are ongoing. In a few cases they have become bitter and violent. Some of the best known are:

Key terms

Autonomy The right to self-government.

Separatism The attempt by regional groups to gain more political control from central government over the area in which they live. Some groups want total independence.

➤ in Spain, the **Basque** area (northern Spain and southwest France) and **Catalonia** (northeast Spain), which now has the autonomy to decide many of its own affairs. The Catalan language, for example, has been taught in all schools in the region since 1983 and has become the official language in education

➤ the collapse of **Yugoslavia** and the formation of Croatia, Slovenia, Bosnia-Herzegovina and FYR Macedonia

➤ in Canada, the question of independence for French-speaking Quebec , and pressure from the Inuits in the north that led to the creation of a self-governing region known as **Nunavut** in 1999

➤ the break-up of the former **Soviet Union** (USSR) into its 15 constituent republics, including Russia, Moldova, Latvia, Ukraine, Georgia, Kazakhstan and Lithuania (Photograph 6.14)

Photograph 6.14 Vilnius, the capital of Lithuania, on the anniversary of independence from the former Soviet Union

➤ national groups *within* former Soviet republics seeking independence, for example **Chechnya** in the Russian republic. Rebels have been put down with extreme force by the Russian army

➤ **Czechoslovakia**, which separated into the Czech Republic and Slovakia in 1993

➤ **Belgium**, which consists of a Flemish-speaking north and a French-speaking south (Wallonia), is almost two countries

➤ in France, where concessions on self-government have been granted to **Corsica**, but there is also a movement for autonomy in **Brittany** (Breton nationalism)

➤ in **Italy**, where the Northern League has been agitating for autonomy for some of the northern provinces, particularly Piedmont and the Veneto (Venice-Verona region)

➤ **East Timor**, which sought independence after being annexed by Indonesia in 1976. After a long and bloody struggle between the separatists and militia gangs supported by the Indonesian Army, the UN took control in 1999, handing over to a new government in May 2002

➤ the bitter struggle against the Sinhalese majority in Sri Lanka by the **Tamils**, who want to set up their own state in the northern part of the island. The civil war began in 1983, and since then has claimed over 60,000 lives, including that of the Indian prime minister, Rajiv Ghandi

➤ the southern region of **Sudan**, where the population is mainly Christian and is fighting for independence against the majority Muslim population of the north

➤ **Western Sahara**, which has been fighting for independence since 1975 when armed forces occupied the country and incorporated it into Morocco following Spain's withdrawal

➤ **Scottish** nationalism. Before its union with England, Scotland was a separate kingdom and it still has its own national church (Presbyterian), separate education and legal systems and its own language (Gaelic) which is spoken in parts of the country. The Scottish National Party (SNP) feels that the exploitation of North Sea oil and gas has done little to develop the economy of Scotland. The drive for independence was partly satisfied by the establishment in 1999 of a parliament with limited tax-raising powers. In 2007, the SNP became the largest party in the Scottish Parliament

➤ **Welsh** nationalism. Wales has its own language and culture, and its nationalist party, Plaid Cymru, has gained increasing power. The drive for independence has been partly satisfied by the creation in 1999 of a Welsh Assembly (with some devolution of decision-making powers, but not tax raising)

Consequences of separatism

The consequences of separatist pressure may be peaceful or non-peaceful. Those desiring more autonomy have used a wide range of activities to create or press for it. In increasing order of extremism, they include:

➤ the establishment and maintenance of societies and norms with clear separate cultural identities within a country (e.g. the Bretons in France)

➤ the protection of a language through the media and education (e.g. Welsh, Catalan)

➤ the growth of separate political parties and devolved power (e.g. the Scottish and Welsh Nationalists)

➤ civil disobedience (e.g. the Friends of Owen Glendauer)

➤ terrorist violence (e.g. the Basques, Chechnya)

➤ civil war (e.g. East Timor, Tamil Tigers)

Reasons and consequences can be studied through a range of case studies. The example given here is the Kurds in the middle east.

Case study · The Kurds

The Kurds are said to be 'the largest ethnic group without a country of their own'. They live in an area which crosses the borders of Iraq, Iran, Syria, Turkey and parts of the former USSR — Armenia and Azerbaijan (Figure 6.5).

The Kurdish Human Rights Project estimates their number at about 40 million, including the **diaspora** (those who have moved to other parts of the world). They are unlike the Turks, Arabs or Persians, who form the majority populations in the countries where they live. They have a separate language, culture and history. The culture and identity of the Kurds are often not recognised by or have been oppressed by the regimes of the nations in which they currently live.

The Kurds are the only ethnic group in the world with indigenous representatives in four geopolitical blocs:

■ the Arab world (in Iraq and Syria)
■ NATO (in Turkey)
■ the south Asian-central Asian group (in Iran)
■ the former Soviet bloc (in Armenia and Azerbaijan)

Kurdistan

Kurdistan is made up of the mountainous areas of the central and northern Zagros, the eastern third of the Taurus and the Pontus, and the northern half of the Amanus ranges. The relationship between the Kurds and their mountains is strong — the Kurds' home ends where the mountains end. There are also two Kurdish enclaves: in central and north central Anatolia in Turkey and in the province of Khurasan in northeast Iran.

Language and religion

The Kurdish language is part of the northwestern subdivision of the Iranic branch of the Indo-European

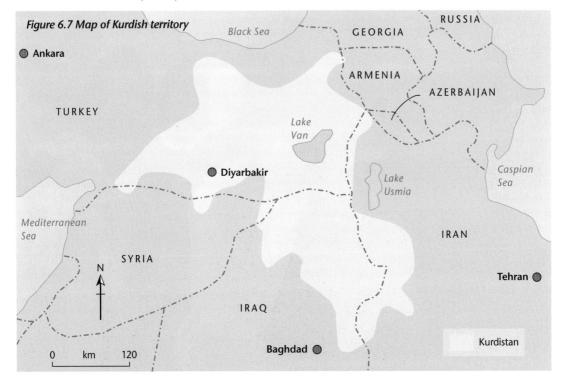

Figure 6.7 Map of Kurdish territory

Black Sea · RUSSIA · GEORGIA · Ankara · ARMENIA · AZERBAIJAN · TURKEY · Lake Van · Diyarbakir · Lake Usmia · Caspian Sea · Mediterranean Sea · IRAN · SYRIA · N · Tehran · IRAQ · 0 km 120 · Baghdad · Kurdistan

family of languages, which is like Persian and, by extension, related to the European languages.

Nearly three-fifths of the Kurds are Sunni Muslims; there are also Shiite and Sufi Muslims. There are also several indigenous Kurdish faiths of great age.

Brief history

There has never been a recognised Kurdistan nation in the way that there is a Turkish or Iraqi state. Small kingdoms and tribes were alternately united or at war over hundreds of years. The break-up of the Ottoman empire at the end of the First World War did nothing to help the creation of a state. The Treaty of Sèvres in 1921 allowed for an independent Kurdish state covering large portions of Ottoman Kurdistan, guaranteeing self-determination to the Kurds. However, the area was strategically important as the gateway between Europe, central Asia and the middle east, and Britain and France had colonial ambitions here. In addition, the area contained important resources, especially oil and natural gas. Consequently, France and Britain divided up

Ottoman Kurdistan between Turkey, Syria and Iraq in the Treaty of Lausanne (1923). The Kurds of Persia (later Iran) were kept where they were by Teheran. This division of Kurdistan and the defence of these boundaries by the newly created states kept Kurdish society fragmented.

Separatist movements

Despite their independent language, culture and traditions, the Kurds were expected to conform to the ways of the majority. They were expected to use the official language of the respective three states (Turkish, Arabic or Farsi) and to identify with those nationalities. The Kurds were treated differently in the three countries. For example, the Iraqi Kurds enjoyed an official autonomous status in a portion of that nation's Kurdistan. On 16 March 1988 Saddam Hussein ordered a poison gas attack on Halapja in Kurdistan and an estimated 5,000 Kurds were killed. The Kurdistan regional government — or 'Iraqi Kurdistan' — split from Ba'athist Iraq in an uprising in 1991 and later enjoyed the protection of the Allied

Photograph 6.15 Kurds at a refugee camp in Turkey

TopFoto

'no-fly zone'. The Kurds were granted a 'safe haven' after the first Gulf War.

Oppression by nationalist governments is not the only obstacle to Kurdish independence; the Kurds themselves are divided in their political objectives. Some political aims are based on ancient tribal structures, some are Islamic and some are left wing.

Most Kurdish groups want equal rights and autonomy, but not necessarily sovereignty. Even the relatively extreme political group in Turkey, the Kurdistan Workers Party (PKK), no longer claims independence, though it does want greater autonomy for Turkey's Kurds, particularly in the southeast of the country. On the other hand, militant Turkish Kurds stated in 2004 that they were ending their ceasefire: 'Tourists should not choose Turkey', the group said on a website. 'We appeal to people wanting to invest in Turkey not to come and invest in a conflict zone.'

In the autumn of 2007 there were renewed hostilities between the PKK and the Turkish army along the southern border with Iraq. There were casualties and the taking of prisoners, together with worrying signs that Turkey would invade northern Iraq in an attempt to close down the PKK camps in that area. During 2008 further bombing raids by the Turkish air force attempted to destroy Kurdish separatist bases in the Qandil mountains in northern Iraq. Turkey has accused Iraq of failing to stop the separatists from using the area as a safe haven.

The challenge of global poverty

In recent decades there has been increasing concern about the imbalance between population growth and the resource base of the world. In particular, there have been worries about inequalities in economic growth, development and welfare between countries. At the lowest end of the inequality scale lie those people living in poverty.

Indicators of poverty

Economic indicators

The simplest way to examine global inequality is to compare wealth, country by country. National wealth is usually measured by **gross national product per person** (GNP per capita) — the total value of the goods and services produced by the people of a country (including goods and services produced abroad), divided by its population. **Gross domestic product per person** (GDP per capita) is based on goods and services produced within the country. Both GNP and GDP are usually given in US dollars to make comparisons between countries easier.

Some geographers have used GNP per capita to divide the world into the more developed North with high GNP

> ### Key terms
>
> **Poverty** The latest estimates on poverty draw on over 500 household surveys from 100 developing countries, representing 93% of the population of the developing world. The **international poverty line** is based on a level of consumption representative of the poverty lines found in low-income countries. Since 2000, the international poverty line has been set at $1.08 a day, measured in terms of 1993 purchasing-power parity (PPP). Before this date, it was measured by the number of people living on less than $1 a day.

per capita and the less developed South with low GNP per capita. This division now tends to be seen as outdated and economic divisions have become much more complex as countries in the 'South' such as China and India industrialise.

Demographic and social indicators

In general, people in the richer North enjoy a better quality of life than those in the poorer South. However, a country's wealth does not paint the whole picture. To judge how developed a country really is, a number of other indicators are used. There is a wide range of such indicators, both demographic and social, including:

- birth rate
- death rate
- fertility rate
- infant mortality rate
- life expectancy
- access to drinking water
- children enrolled in primary school
- adult literacy
- number of people per doctor
- telephone ownership
- urban population

Each year, the Population Reference Bureau publishes details of many of these indicators in its Population Data Sheet. Details of some indicators for 20 selected countries (2007) are given in Table 6.8.

Composite quality of life indicators

In recent decades composite indices have been developed which measure a number of quality of life indicators. These are seen as a better measure of development than economic wealth.

The physical quality of life index

The physical quality of life index (PQLI) summarises infant mortality, life expectancy at 1 year and basic literacy on a 0–100 scale. The index enables researchers to rank countries, not by income but by changes in the quality of life in those countries. The developers of the index believed that the use by the World Bank of GNP as a basic indicator of human wellbeing was seriously flawed. The GNP ignores differences in prices and the distribution of income. It also fails to illuminate how efficiently income is spent. For instance in 1995, health expenditure per capita in the USA was the highest in the world but at least 22 countries had better infant and child mortality rates. The PQLI shows not how much has been spent but how effectively lives have improved.

One major finding in the initial use of this measure was the lack of congruence between GNP per capita and the PQLI. In 1995, the world average PQLI was 72. Industrialised countries in the developed world tended to rank high in the index, but other countries with high incomes, particularly the very richest middle eastern oil producers, had PQLIs in the low 30s. Some poor countries, for example Sri

Country	Population (millions)	Birth rate (per 1,000)	Death rate (per 1,000)	Infant mortality rate (per 1,000 live births)	Fertility rate (children per woman)	Life expectancy (years)
Afghanistan	31.9	47	21	166	6.8	42
India	1131	24	8	58	2.9	64
China	1318	12	7	27	1.6	72
Bangladesh	149	27	8	65	3.0	62
Chad	10.8	47	16	102	6.5	51
Mali	12.3	48	16	96	6.6	53
Niger	14.2	48	15	126	7.1	56
Rwanda	9.3	43	16	86	6.1	47
Egypt	73.4	27	6	33	3.1	71
Uganda	28.5	48	16	83	6.7	47
Malaysia	27.2	23	5	10	2.9	74
Thailand	65.7	14	7	20	1.7	71
Mexico	106.5	21	5	21	2.4	75
Brazil	189.3	21	6	27	2.3	72
Russia	141.7	10	15	10	1.3	65
Germany	82.3	8	10	3.8	1.3	79
France	61.7	13	9	3.7	2.0	81
Japan	127.7	9	9	2.8	1.3	82
USA	302.2	14	8	6.5	2.1	78
UK	61.0	12	10	4.9	1.8	79

Source: Population Reference Bureau 2007

Table 6.8 Demographic indicators, 2007

Lanka (PQLI of 82) and India (PQLI of 68), performed well, despite low monetary incomes.

In 1960, 53% of the world's population lived in countries with PQLI averages of less than 50. By 1995, only 11% lived in countries with averages of less than 50. This means that during that 35-year period, the number of people in the under-50 PQLI group fell from 1.7 billion to 584 million.

Between 1960 and 1995, the PQLI values of the economically poorest countries — those with incomes under US$450 per capita in constant 1980 dollars — rose from 31 to 64. This was a faster improvement than that which occurred in the higher income countries. Sub-Saharan Africa had the world's worst PQLI performances in 1960 and in 1995. Yet between 1960 and 1995, the average PQLI of sub-Saharan Africa rose from 21 to 50, quite inconsistent with the economic indicators.

The human development index

The human development index (HDI) was devised by the UN in 1990. It measures three variables:
➤ life expectancy

*Photograph 6.16
A school in Rwanda.
Educational
attainment is one of
the variables
measured by the
HDI*

Jennifer Reynolds

> educational attainment (adult literacy and combined primary, secondary and tertiary enrolment, Photograph 6.16)
> real GDP per capita (the GDP per capita of a country converted into US dollars on the basis of the purchasing-power parity of the currency of the country. It is assessed by calculating the number of units of a currency required to purchase the same representative basket of goods and services that US$1 would buy in the USA)

*Table 6.9 Selected
countries from the
Human
Development
Report, 2006*

Table 6.9 shows a selected sample from the *Human Development Report* (HDR) (2006) for 177 countries in the world. The final column, showing the difference

HDI rank	Country	Life expectancy 2004 (years)	Educational attainment index	Real GDP per capita 2004 (US$)	HDI	Real GDP per capita rank minus HDI rank
1	Norway	80	0.99	38,454	0.965	3
2	Iceland	81	0.98	33,051	0.960	3
3	Australia	81	0.99	30,331	0.957	11
4	Ireland	78	0.99	38,827	0.956	−1
64	Libya	74	0.86	7,570	0.798	7
65	Russia	65	0.95	9,902	0.797	−6
66	FYR Macedonia	74	0.87	6,610	0.796	16
67	Belarus	68	0.95	6,970	0.794	12
145	Uganda	48	0.67	1,478	0.502	7
146	Swaziland	31	0.72	5,638	0.500	−50
174	Burkino Faso	48	0.23	1,169	0.342	−17
175	Mali	48	0.24	996	0.338	−11
176	Sierra Leone	41	0.45	561	0.335	1
177	Niger	45	0.26	779	0.311	−7

between the key economic indicator of GDP per capita and the HDI rank, is important. A positive figure indicates that the HDI rank is higher than the GDP rank; a negative figure that it is lower.

Summary

In many ways, both PQLI and HDI measure poverty. In assessing the progress made in reducing global poverty, the HDR published by the UN notes that:
➤ in the past 50 years, poverty has fallen more than in the previous 500 years
➤ poverty has been reduced in some respects in almost all countries
➤ death rates of children in the less developed world have been cut by more than half since 1960
➤ malnutrition has declined by almost one-third since 1960
➤ since 1960, the proportion of children not in primary education has fallen from more than a half to less than a quarter

On the negative side, the HDR points out that there are still substantial problems, including:
➤ one-fifth of all people living in the less developed world still live in poverty, with nearly 1 billion living below the international poverty line
➤ nearly 1 billion people are illiterate; one child in five does not complete primary school. In sub-Saharan Africa a child has only a one in three chance of completing primary school. One in four school-aged children in south Asia is not being educated
➤ some 840 million people are hungry or face food insecurity
➤ more than 1.5 billion people lack access to safe drinking water
➤ women are disproportionately poor, with half a million women in the less developed world dying in childbirth each year. A woman in sub-Saharan Africa is 100 times more likely to die during pregnancy or in childbirth than is a woman in western Europe
➤ in much of the developing world, the HIV/AIDS pandemic continues to spread. More than 15 million children lost one or both parents to the disease in 2005 and the number of AIDS orphans is expected to double by 2010

The global distribution of poverty

Worldwide the number of people in developing countries living below the international poverty line fell to 980 million in 2004 — down from 1.25 billion in 1990. The proportion of people living in poverty fell to 19% over this period (Figure 6.8).

Levels of poverty in east, southeast and south Asia fell due to rapid economic development in these areas. In contrast, poverty rates in west Asia more than doubled between 1990 and 2004. In sub-Saharan Africa, the proportion of people living in poverty fell from 47% in 1990 to 41% in 2004. Most of this progress has been achieved since 2000. The per capita income of seven sub-Saharan countries grew by more than 3.5% a year between 2000 and 2004. Another 23 had growth rates of more than 2% a year, providing a degree of optimism.

Figure 6.8 Proportion of people living on less than $1 a day, 1990, 1999 and 2004 (%)

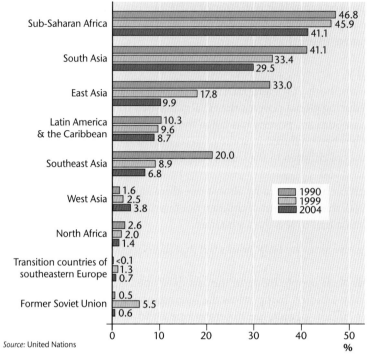

Source: United Nations

The poverty gap ratio, which reflects the depth of poverty as well as its incidence, has decreased in all regions except west Asia, where the rising poverty rate has caused the poverty gap to increase, and in the transition countries of southeast Europe. In contrast, the poor in east, southeast and south Asia have made important gains. In spite of some improvement, the poverty gap ratio in sub-Saharan Africa remains the highest in the world, indicating that the region's poor are the most economically disadvantaged in the world (Figure 6.9).

Figure 6.9 Poverty gap ratio, 1990 and 2004 (%)

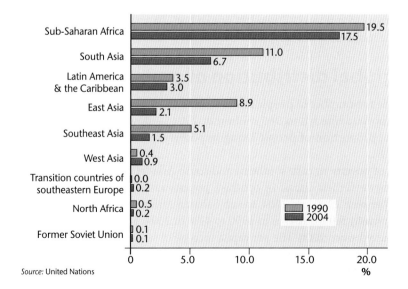

Source: United Nations

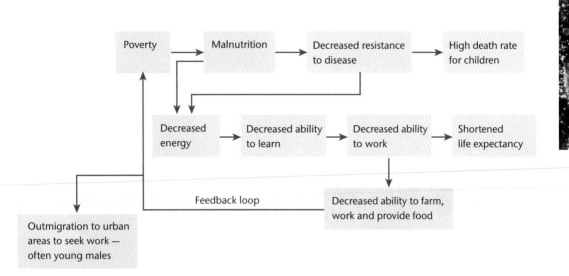

Figure 6.10 Effects of the cycle of poverty in subsistence farming economies

Much poverty in the less developed world occurs in rural areas. Figure 6.10 summarises the main effects of the cycle of poverty in subsistence farming economies, which stems from the inability of people to provide themselves with adequate food. There are long-term problems of malnourishment made worse by shorter-term disasters. Floods, drought, plagues of locusts and wars take place in many countries, particularly in Africa, at different times and in different years. These add to the endemic problems arising from low economic development.

Addressing poverty on a global scale: the UN Millennium Development Goals

The Millennium Development Goals (MDGs) were originally developed by the OECD and emerged from the eight chapters of the United Nations Millennium Declaration, signed in September 2000. The eight goals are aimed at the global *causes* of poverty. They are to:

1 **Eradicate extreme poverty and hunger.**
   – Reduce by half the proportion of people living on less than US$1 a day.
   – Reduce by half the proportion of people who suffer from hunger.
2 **Achieve universal primary education.**
   – Ensure that all boys and girls complete a full course of primary schooling.
   – Increased enrolment must be accompanied by efforts to ensure that all children remain in school and receive a high-quality education.
3 **Promote gender equality and empower women.**
   – Eliminate gender disparity in primary and secondary education preferably by 2005, and at all levels by 2015.
4 **Reduce child mortality.**
   – Reduce the mortality rate among children under 5 years by two-thirds.
5 **Improve maternal health.**
   – Reduce by three-quarters the maternal mortality ratio.

Photograph 6.17
A nurse in Kenya demonstrates how to use mosquito nets to prevent malaria

6 **Combat HIV/AIDS, malaria and other diseases.**
  – Halt and begin to reverse the spread of HIV/AIDS.
  – Halt and begin to reverse the incidence of malaria and other major diseases (Photograph 6.17).

7 **Ensure environmental sustainability.**
  – Integrate the principles of sustainable development into country policies and programmes; reverse loss of environmental resources.
  – Reduce by half the proportion of people without sustainable access to safe drinking water.
  – Achieve significant improvement in the lives of at least 100 million slum dwellers by 2020.

8 **Develop a global partnership for development.**
  – Develop further an open trading and financial system that is rule-based, predictable and non-discriminatory. Includes a commitment to good governance, development and poverty reduction — nationally and internationally.
  – Address the least developed countries' special needs. This includes tariff- and quota-free access for their exports, enhanced debt relief for heavily indebted poor countries, cancellation of official bilateral debt, and more generous official development assistance for countries committed to poverty reduction.

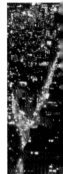

- Address the special needs of landlocked and small island developing states.
- Deal comprehensively with developing countries' debt problems through national and international measures to make debt sustainable in the long term.
- In cooperation with the developing countries, develop decent and productive work for youth.
- In cooperation with pharmaceutical companies, provide access to affordable essential drugs in developing countries.
- In cooperation with the private sector, make available the benefits of new technologies — especially information and communications technologies.

In 2007 the United Nations Secretary-General Ban Ki-moon launched the Millennium Development Goals Africa Steering Group with major development partners (African Union, European Union, African Development Bank, Islamic Development Bank, International Monetary Fund (IMF) and World Bank). The aims of the group were to target the goals in Africa, and to boost Africa's failing efforts to meet the goals on cutting poverty, hunger, maternal and infant mortality and other social ills by 2015.

'We are concerned that many African countries are off track, particularly for the countries in sub-Saharan regions. That is the only region in the world where not even a single country is on the track. We must help those countries so that they can join on the track', he added, noting that the group had agreed to strengthen its collaboration to expedite achievement of the MDGs.

The group resolved to address three challenges.

1 To identify effective mechanisms for implementing the MDGs for health, education, agriculture and food security, infrastructure and statistical systems.
2 To improve aid predictability. 'Our organisations will make our own aid more predictable', they said. 'We will also work with other donors to help establish country-by-country schedules for official development assistance to rise to meet existing commitments, so that African governments can plan effectively for the practical investments needed to achieve the MDGs.'
3 To strengthen joint efforts at country level. 'Starting in a sub-set of African countries, we will launch an intensive collaboration among our organisations to support governments in preparing and implementing strategies that are ambitious enough to achieve the MDGs', they declared.

There has been criticism by many, including the campaigner Sir Bob Geldof, that promised international support has not been forthcoming. The commitments of aid made in Monterrey in 2002 and at the Gleneagles summit in 2005 have not reached Africa. Critics have stressed that not only must the donors fulfil their promises but African countries also must have every opportunity to reach the targets. In this, they stress the importance of trade. They say that there cannot be sustainable development without strong support on trade. Trade brings prosperity and jobs and can give states the means to bring basic services to their people.

The UN Millennium Declaration established 2015 as the target date for most of the MDGs, with 1990 generally used as a baseline. World leaders came together in

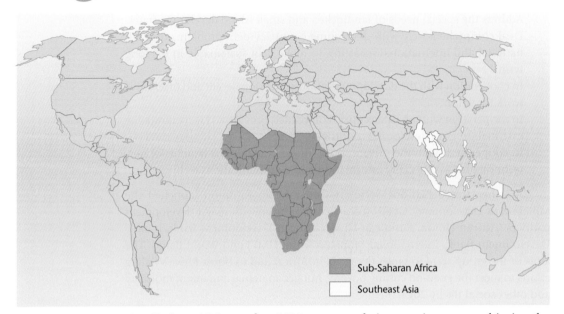

Sub-Saharan Africa

Southeast Asia

Figure 6.11
Map showing the regions discussed in Table 6.10

New York on 25 September 2008 to renew their commitment to achieving the Millennium Development Goals by 2015 and to set out concrete plans and practical steps for action. Table 6.10 shows progress as of June 2007 for two regions (Figure 6.11), based on data for selected indicators in each of the eight goals. Note the difference in progress between the African countries and those in southeast Asia.

Addressing poverty on a global scale: think global, act local

Considerable debate takes place between development experts about how best to raise living standards in the developing world, particularly in remote rural areas where environmental conditions are harsh and constraints are enormous.

Much government and World Bank aid has funded large capital projects (for example, mega-dams that are intended to be multi-purpose catalysts to regional development). In theory, the wealth that is generated by such **top-down** projects trickles down to the poorer peripheral areas. In fact, many of these projects make the lives of the rural poor worse, rather than better, and they have been severely criticised.

Bottom-up, small-scale projects are better at raising living standards in poor areas. This is because the development is initiated in consultation with local people and is more targeted to local needs. Bottom-up schemes:

➤ grant greater self-determination to rural areas by using communal decision making
➤ are often small scale and tailored to local needs
➤ use limited funding effectively to make a difference
➤ give priority to projects that serve basic needs — for example health and education

Goals and targets	Sub-Saharan Africa	Southeast Asia
Reduce extreme poverty by half	Very high poverty	Moderate poverty
Reduce hunger by half	Very high hunger	Moderate hunger
Universal primary schooling	Low enrolment	High enrolment
Equal girls' enrolment in primary school	Almost close to parity	Parity
Women's share of paid employment	Medium share	Medium share
Women's equal representation in national parliaments	Low representation	Low representation
Reduce mortality of under 5-year-olds by two-thirds	*Very high mortality*	Moderate mortality
Measles immunisation	Low coverage	Moderate coverage
Reduce maternal mortality by three-quarters	*Very high mortality*	High mortality
Halt and reverse spread of HIV/AIDS	*Very high prevalence*	Low prevalence
Halt and reverse spread of malaria	*High risk*	Moderate risk
Halt and reverse spread of tuber-culosis	*High mortality*	Moderate mortality
Reverse loss of forests	*Medium forest cover*	*High forest cover*
Halve proportion without improved drinking water	*Low coverage*	Moderate coverage
Halve proportion without sanitation	*Very low coverage*	Low coverage
Improve the lives of slum-dwellers	Very high proportion of slum-dwellers	Moderate proportion of slum-dwellers
Youth unemployment	High unemployment	*High unemployment*
Internet users	*Very low access*	Moderate access

Table 6.10 Millennium Development Goals: progress chart, 2007

Note: Italics indicate that there is no progress towards meeting the goals, a deterioration or a reversal.

➤ give land to the people by land reform
➤ use external physical resources only when local resources are inadequate
➤ improve rural–urban and internal village communications
➤ mobilise local indigenous human resources to create employment and increase labour-intensive activities
➤ emphasise the need to work with local environments and culture on development projects that are sustainable

The emphasis of such schemes is on using **appropriate or intermediate technology** (Photograph 6.18). The main features of appropriate technology are that it:
➤ is affordable for many villagers
➤ involves local people in design

Sean Sprague/Still Pictures

➤ is constructed locally by local people
➤ should be simple to build, small scale and appropriate to the needs of local communities
➤ provides local employment
➤ should be easy or cheap to repair and maintain
➤ should cause limited damage to the environment
➤ may use local materials
➤ develops local skills
➤ promotes self-sufficiency and self-reliance
➤ often relies on renewable sources of energy — for example solar power or mini-hydro schemes
➤ is low cost but is more efficient than traditional methods

Photograph 6.18 Building a house in El Salvador using a wooden frame, chicken wire and cement. It is cheap, quick to build and safe in earthquakes

Case study — Appropriate technology: PATH

Each year, about 57 million women worldwide give birth without the help of a trained health worker. These births often take place at home, where the risk of infection is high. Some 1,600 women per day die from complications (usually infection) associated with pregnancy or childbirth. Around 2,600 newborns also die from infection each day. The clean-delivery kit is a simple approach to reducing these deaths. It helps women and newborns avoid life-threatening infections.

Over the past decade, the non-governmental organisation PATH has helped develop such kits in Bangladesh, Egypt and Nepal. Most kits contain a small bar of soap for washing hands, a plastic sheet to serve as the delivery surface, clean string for tying the umbilical cord, a new razor blade for cutting the cord and pictorial instructions that illustrate the sequence of delivery events and hand-washing.

Research and field-testing during development ensured the cultural acceptability of the kits and allowed PATH to customise them for local conditions.

In Nepal, for example, it is traditional to cut the umbilical cord on a coin, for good luck. Out of respect for this custom, kits produced in Nepal contain a plastic rupee to serve as a clean cord-cutting surface.

Once the kits were in use in Nepal, PATH conducted interviews and role-plays to gauge the responses of women who had used them. Mothers and birth attendants generally appreciated the kits and found them affordable.

PATH recently quantified the positive impact of a delivery kit on the health of women and children in Tanzania. The study, conducted with funding from the US Agency for International Development, involved more than 3,200 participants. Results suggested that women who used the kit were substantially less likely to develop genital-tract infections and their infants were substantially less likely to develop cord infections.

With each delivery kit project, PATH's goal is to make sure the kits are available to the women who need them. It does this by building the capacity of

The delivery kit

local organisations and small businesses to produce and distribute or sell kits. In Egypt, PATH helped community health promoters develop a plan to use kits as an income-generating activity that would

contribute to their health programmes. In Nepal, it gave a local, woman-owned business a head start. The campaign that it funded promoted the kit via wall paintings, advertisements, street dramas and training for community-health volunteers. Within a year, sales increased from 28,800 to 46,800 kits per year, contributing to the long-term stability of the company. Maternal and Child Health Products Ltd continues to make kits available to Nepali women at prices they can afford.

Reproduced from the PATH website at www.path.org

'No development without security and no security without development'

This issue can be discussed with reference to recent events in Afghanistan (Figure 6.12).

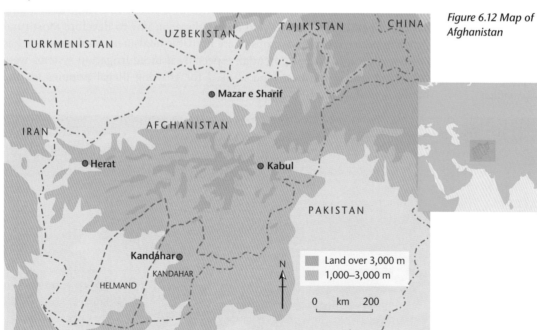

Figure 6.12 Map of Afghanistan

Demographic background

It is notoriously difficult to obtain statistics from Afghanistan. Censuses are rarely conducted and when they are, accuracy is questionable. The Population Reference Bureau estimated the population at 31,900,000 in 2007. What is certain is that Afghanistan's population is growing rapidly. It is typical of a stage 2 country in the demographic transition model and its economy is largely subsistence agriculture.

Birth rates remain high, while death rates, despite two decades of war, have decreased significantly. UN estimates suggest a population growth rate of 3.9% per annum between 2000 and 2005; it is now quoted at 2.6%. Forty-five per cent of the population are aged under 15 and only 2% are 65 or over. The infant mortality rate is one of the highest in the world at 166 per 1,000 live births. The fertility rate is 6.8 children per woman.

Afghanistan is relatively sparsely populated at 42 persons km^{-2}. Most people (78%) live in rural areas and 20% are nomadic, making data even more difficult to collect. Of the 22% urban dwellers, most are in the capital Kabul (2,536,000 people). The second city is Herat (349,000), followed by Kandahar and Mazar e Sharif (324,800 and 300,600, respectively, according to the Central Statistics Office, Afghanistan). Urban population growth rates are even higher than the national average at 6.9%, the result of high natural increase plus in-migration. The situation is complicated by people migrating in both directions between countryside and city to escape fighting.

War has been an almost constant feature of life in Afghanistan for 20 years. It is estimated that 3 million people have died in wars since the last official census in 1988, while up to 6 million have crossed borders seeking safety in Pakistan and Iran. Some have emigrated as far as the USA.

Afghanistan's demographic characteristics are unlikely to change until a long period of peace with external aid allows the economy to develop. Most rural people produce subsistence crops or are nomadic herdsmen, yet the country has considerable agricultural potential, especially if more irrigation systems were employed. Today the best land is used for growing illegal poppies for the production of heroin (Photograph 6.19).

Photograph 6.19 Poppy-growing in Afghanistan

TopFoto

The political and social systems in Afghanistan hold it back economically and demographically. When the Taliban took over in 1996, educational and career opportunities for girls and women ended. In 2000, 89% of the female population aged over 14 had no schooling at all, 6% had attended primary school and 4% secondary school. Only 1.3% had been to university. Under the Taliban, a woman's place was in the home. Girls' schools were closed and professional women (e.g. teachers, lecturers, doctors) were no longer allowed to work. Women had no access to medical attention, as male doctors were not allowed to treat them.

This is an extreme example of lack of opportunity, the worst in the world today. The situation has improved since the Taliban government was ousted in 2001, but the current political situation limits economic development. Without economic opportunity and a huge change in attitude to gender roles, the demographic situation in Afghanistan is unlikely to change.

Political background

Afghanistan is strategically placed between the middle east, central Asia and the Indian subcontinent. For centuries, foreign armies have fought over it and tried to conquer it. Many have been defeated by the rugged terrain — mountains cover four-fifths of the land — and fierce resistance from the different tribal groups. As well as the terrain, ethnic, religious and regional rivalries have made it hard for the authorities in Kabul to rule the country.

The overthrow of Afghanistan's King Zahir Shah in 1973 sparked a chain of events that led to decades of unrest. Reforms imposed by a Moscow-backed regime sparked rebellions and, in 1979, Soviet troops invaded Afghanistan. US-backed Islamic fighters known as mujahideen — among them Osama Bin Laden — fought the Soviets and the country became a Cold War battleground. In 1989, the USSR withdrew in defeat, leaving behind a devastated country and hundreds of thousands of dead Afghans.

After the Soviet forces left, a number of Afghan factions continued to fight for control of the country. In 1994, the hard-line Islamic Taliban emerged. By the late 1990s, they controlled most of Afghanistan with their strict version of Sharia law. The Taliban angered the international community by allowing Bin Laden, and other al-Qaeda members, to remain there. In 2001, after the 9/11 attacks on the USA, the Taliban refused to hand Bin Laden over, paving the way for a new war.

In October 2001, the USA and its allies launched a bombing campaign against the Taliban, marking the beginning of America's 'war on terror'. Within weeks, US-led troops and local fighters forced the Taliban from Kabul and drove them from power. But Taliban leader Mullah Omar and Osama Bin Laden evaded capture and are thought to have survived the offensive. Several thousand NATO (including British) troops remain in Afghanistan hunting Taliban supporters who have regrouped since 2003.

Years of fighting have left Afghanistan in ruins — it is one of the poorest countries in the world. International donors have pledged more than $10 billion, but the government says it needs more. In 2004 a constitution was signed and

Hamid Karzai won the country's first direct presidential elections. In 2005 national assembly elections were held.

Islamic militants, warlords and the booming drugs trade are among the greatest threats to stability. The authorities have limited power outside Kabul. Huge swathes of the country are controlled by warlords once funded by the USA to fight the Taliban. Many of these powerful regional militia chiefs have a history of drug trafficking and human rights abuses. The state of lawlessness is fuelled by the opium trade. Despite a ban on poppy crops, Afghanistan still produces about 90% of the world's opium, which accounts for about one-third of the country's economy.

Two alternative views regarding Afghanistan are given below.

No development without security

A survey published to coincide with the anniversary of 9/11 in 2008 suggests that an increasing number of people want British military involvement in Afghanistan to end. Others believe that this would be a serious mistake.

One aim of deploying armed forces there is to create a more stable environment in which a democratic and prosperous society can develop. Better security means that essential work, such as the building and repairing of vital roads, can begin. This would allow the transportation and export of goods produced in the country and an easier, more efficient distribution of aid to the areas where it is needed. The only products that can survive the uncertain journey at present are opium and hashish, generating around 60% of the country's economy. Afghanistan is the source of 95% of the 30 tonnes of heroin used in the UK each year and it is hard to know how much of the money made by those who traffic it is financing the Taliban.

The British government spends around £1.5 billion every year combating the impact of drug use in the UK. This ranges from drug awareness campaigns such as 'Talk to Frank' and school drug policies to the building of cold storage sheds in other countries to allow thorough border searches of refrigerated lorries. One such facility was opened in Kapitan Andreevo, Bulgaria in 2002 at a cost of £150,000. This is the only entry point for such vehicles on a main smuggling route for heroin via Turkey. The building had not even been officially opened when seizures of 239 kg of heroin were made there. In the long run it is in the public's interest to reduce the amount of heroin available and therefore the number of addicts. One way to do this is to provide the Afghan farmer currently growing opium poppies with alternative reasonably paid work such as road construction.

Large sums of money have already gone into Afghanistan and almost everything, from the wages of government officials to its IT systems, is paid for by other nations. The country does not generate enough money to operate as a modern democracy. Much of the aid has disappeared. Helmand province, where most British forces are based, was supposed to have received $55 million of 'alternative livelihood' development in 2005 (around $55 for every person in the area, approximately one-quarter of the annual income there) but there is no real evidence of this investment. However, even this amount of aid does not match the amount the opium producers would have earned. And apart from the income it generates, local people continue to grow opium for fear of the Taliban and the drug traffickers.

Had more investment been made in Afghanistan following the 2001 invasion the situation might have been different. As it is, a proper assessment of the needs of Afghanistan is required, followed by adequate investment (including the additional military assistance of countries such as France and Italy). The Afghan government must expose and prosecute officials engaged in trafficking and corruption. Increased military assistance is vital (especially the training of Afghan personnel) to prevent the shifting of opium growing to more remote and poorly policed areas. There was a decline of production in Helmand of 10% in 2005 but an increase of 1,370% in neighbouring Nimroz. Only a heavy security presence can prevent this.

No security without development

The failure of international aid to make a difference to Afghanistan is having serious security consequences. A recent Red Cross report showed that the worsening conflict in the south is spreading to the north and west, alongside an upsurge of suicide bombing in Kabul.

The amount of money promised per head for Afghanistan was far lower than in other recent post-conflict countries, and too little of it has gone into increasing the capacity of the Afghan government to run things for itself. In a 2007 report, the World Bank warned of the dangers of an 'aid juggernaut', a parallel world operating outside the government economy, with Afghans not even able to bid for major infrastructure contracts, such as roads. The quality of much of what has been delivered remains low. Schools that officially have been rebuilt are still teaching girls in tents in the mud.

There have been some successes. President Hamid Karzai often reminds audiences that 40,000 Afghan babies would not be alive today but for improvements in Afghan healthcare. Some aid for basic services is successfully going through the state. One in 10 Afghan teachers has their salaries paid by British taxpayers, but as far as the teachers are concerned, their pay packets are not 'foreign aid' — they come from the Afghan education department. Some small rural schemes — drainage, clinics, small power projects and schools — are being built through the National Solidarity Programme, an international aid fund managed and distributed by the Afghan government. On a larger scale, in the summer of 2008 a huge HEP turbine was transported through Taliban territory in an attempt to improve electricity supplies in the Helmand region.

The Americans, the biggest spenders in Afghanistan, are beginning to put more of their aid money through the government. However, the change is slow.

Most international officials and consultants in Afghanistan are on high salaries and short-term contracts. This means that much of the aid to Afghanistan goes straight back to donor countries in the form of their salaries.

The Afghan government is concerned that the international community will not allow Afghanistan to determine aid priorities for itself. Rather than helping to fund the coordination unit for the eradication of heroin requested by the Counter Narcotics Ministry, the British government is funding a project for aerial photography that will cost more than $10 million. The Ministry would have preferred to use the money to employ local people to survey the poppy-growing areas on the ground.

Other concerns have been raised over a fund designed to provide alternative livelihoods for poppy farmers. Of $70 million earmarked for this project, little more than $1 million has actually been spent. Afghan officials blame bureaucratic obstacles for this. The UK Foreign Office admitted that there have been 'teething problems' for a fund that is operating 'in a challenging environment'. Behind the criticism about spending lies a more serious concern that the counter-narcotics policy is not working. Poppy cultivation in Afghanistan is on the increase again, and rising fastest in areas under British control. A number of officials believe that the problem is now out of control, and that the international community has lost the war on drugs.

Assessment exercises 1
Section A

Plate tectonics and associated hazards

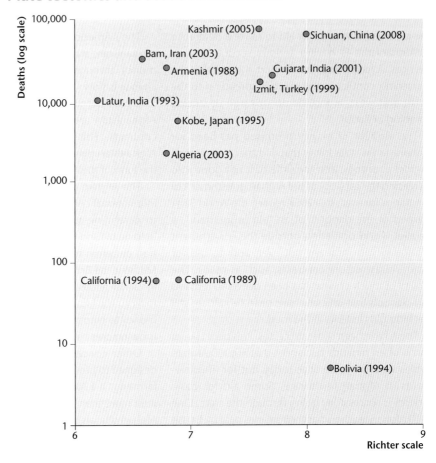

Figure A The size of recent earthquakes and the associated death toll

1 **a** Describe and comment on the information given in Figure A. (7 marks)
  b Explain the causes of earthquakes. (8 marks)
  c With reference to examples, discuss the effectiveness of hazard management schemes in areas where earthquakes have taken place. (10 marks)

Weather and climate and associated hazards

2 **a** Using Figure B, describe and comment on the responses to Hurricane Floyd in September 1999. (7 marks)
  b Explain the causes of tropical revolving storms. (8 marks)
  c With reference to *one* tropical region that you have studied, describe and explain the characteristic features of the climate of that region. (10 marks)

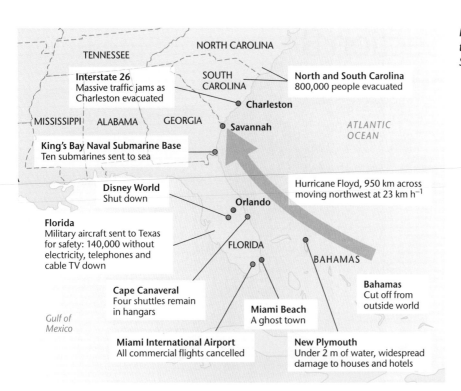

Figure B Responses to Hurricane Floyd, September 1999

Interstate 26
Massive traffic jams as Charleston evacuated

NORTH CAROLINA

SOUTH CAROLINA

North and South Carolina
800,000 people evacuated

TENNESSEE

● Charleston

MISSISSIPPI ALABAMA GEORGIA ● Savannah

ATLANTIC OCEAN

King's Bay Naval Submarine Base
Ten submarines sent to sea

Disney World
Shut down

● Orlando

Hurricane Floyd, 950 km across moving northwest at 23 km h^{-1}

Florida
Military aircraft sent to Texas for safety: 140,000 without electricity, telephones and cable TV down

FLORIDA

BAHAMAS

Gulf of Mexico

Cape Canaveral
Four shuttles remain in hangars

Bahamas
Cut off from outside world

Miami Beach
A ghost town

Miami International Airport
All commercial flights cancelled

New Plymouth
Under 2 m of water, widespread damage to houses and hotels

Photograph A Urban niches on a derelict site

Ecosystems: change and challenge

3 a Study Photograph A. Describe the various processes by which colonisation of this wasteland can take place. (7 marks)

b Explain how distinctive ecologies develop along routeways. (8 marks)

c With reference to one or more example(s), discuss the effectiveness of ecological conservation areas. (10 marks)

Section B

World cities

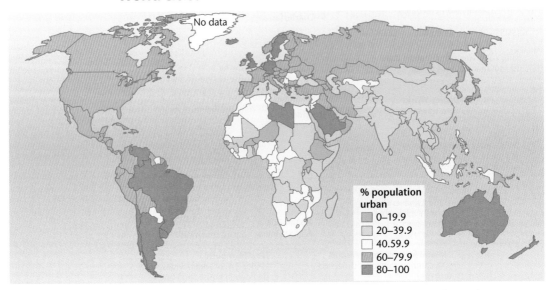

Figure C
Global pattern of
urbanisation, 2005

4 a Describe and comment on the pattern of urbanisation as shown in
  Figure C. (7 marks)
  b Explain the causes of counter-urbanisation. (8 marks)
  c Assess the effects of re-urbanisation on cities within countries at different
  levels of economic development. (10 marks)

Development and globalisation

*Table A The world's
top 10 companies,
2007*

Rank	Company	Country	Market value (US$ billion)	Sector
1	Exxon Mobil	USA	479	Oil and gas
2	General Electric	USA	396	General industrials
3	Microsoft	USA	287	Computer software
4	Toyota Motor	Japan	280	Automobiles
5	Royal Dutch Shell	UK	269	Oil and gas
6	Citigroup	USA	254	Banking
7	AT&T	USA	252	Telecommunications
8	Gazprom	Russia	251	Oil and gas
9	BP	UK	232	Oil and gas
10	Bank of America	USA	219	Banking

5 a Describe and comment on the information given in Table A. (7 marks)
  b Suggest reasons for the growth of transnational corporations (TNCs). (8 marks)
  c With reference to examples, discuss the social, economic and
  environmental impacts of TNCs on their host countries. (10 marks)

Contemporary conflicts and challenges

Table B UK resident population by ethnic group, 2001

Region/country	White (%)	Indian (%)	Pakistani (%)	Bangladeshi (%)	Caribbean (%)	African (%)	Chinese (%)	Other (%)
UK	92.1	1.8	1.3	0.5	1.0	0.8	0.4	2.1
Northeast	97.6	0.4	0.6	0.2	0.04	0.1	0.2	0.9
Northwest	94.4	1.1	1.7	0.4	0.3	0.2	0.4	1.5
Yorks and Humber	93.4	1.0	2.9	0.2	0.4	0.2	0.2	1.7
E. midlands	93.5	2.9	0.7	0.2	0.6	0.2	0.3	1.6
W. midlands	88.7	3.4	2.9	0.6	1.6	0.2	0.3	2.3
East	95.1	1.0	0.7	0.3	0.5	0.3	0.4	1.7
London	71.2	6.0	2.0	2.2	4.8	5.3	1.1	7.4
Southeast	95.1	1.1	0.7	0.2	0.3	0.3	0.4	1.9
Southwest	97.7	0.3	0.1	0.1	0.2	0.1	0.3	1.2
England	90.9	2.1	1.4	0.6	1.1	1.0	0.5	2.4
Wales	97.9	0.3	0.3	0.2	0.1	0.1	0.2	0.9
Scotland	98.0	0.3	0.6	0.04	0.04	0.1	0.3	0.6
N. Ireland	99.2	0.10	0.04	0.01	0.02	0.03	0.2	0.4

Source: 2001 census

6 a Describe and comment on the distribution of different ethnic groups in the UK as shown in Table B. (7 marks)
  b Suggest reasons for the development of multicultural societies. (8 marks)
  c With reference to examples, discuss the issues related to multicultural societies. (10 marks)

Section C Essay questions

Each question carries 40 marks.

Plate tectonics and associated hazards

7 'Volcanic and seismic events are major factors towards proving that plate tectonics theory is valid'. Discuss the extent to which you agree with the statement.

Weather and climate and associated hazards

8 'Urban areas have a significant impact on climatic characteristics.' Discuss this statement.

Ecosystems: change and challenge

9 'Development, biodiversity and sustainability are incompatible goals.' Discuss this statement in the context of the tropical biome you have studied.

World cities

10 Assess the impact of out-of-town centre retailing areas on the regions in which they occur.

Development and globalisation

11 'Global social and economic groupings have significant beneficial effects for their members.' Discuss the extent to which you agree with this statement.

Contemporary conflicts and challenges

12 With reference to one recent major international conflict, analyse and assess the geographical impacts of the conflict on the area(s) involved.

Assessment exercises 2
Section A

Plate tectonics and associated hazards

Photograph B The former capital of Montserrat, Plymouth, after the eruption of the Soufrière Hills volcano, August 1997

TopFoto

1 a Study Photograph B. Using Photograph B only, identify and comment on the impact that a volcanic eruption has had on the area shown. (7 marks)

b Describe and explain the characteristics of minor forms of extrusive
activity (geysers, hot springs and boiling mud). (8 marks)

c With reference to two recent volcanic events you have studied from
contrasting areas of the world, compare the ways in which their
impacts have been managed. (10 marks)

Weather and climate and associated hazards

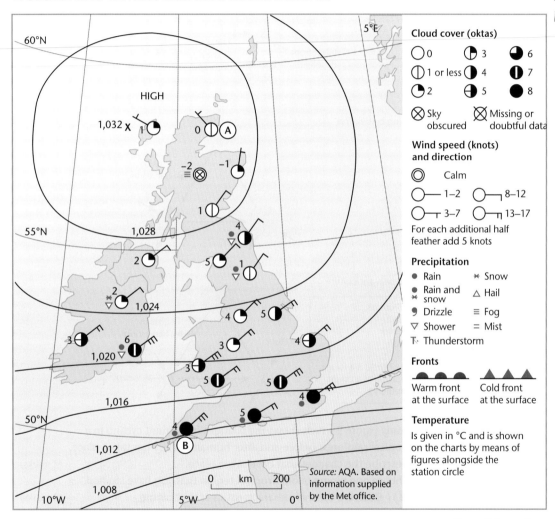

*Figure D Synoptic
chart for the British
Isles, 0900 GMT,
11 January 2001*

2 a Study Figure D which shows a synoptic chart for the British Isles at 0900 GMT
on 11 January 2001. Using map evidence only, describe and suggest reasons
for the differences between the weather conditions at Station A and those at
Station B. (7 marks)

b Identify the major air masses that affect the British Isles, and outline the
weather associated with each of them. (8 marks)

c With reference to one recent case study of a storm event, discuss the
responses to such events and their impacts. (10 marks)

Ecosystems: change and challenge

Figure E Nutrient cycling in a tropical rainforest

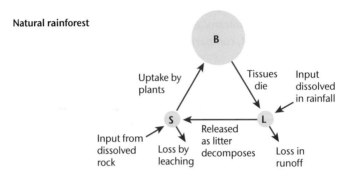

Natural rainforest

Shifting cultivation

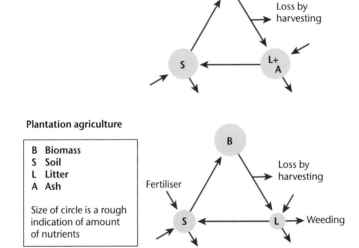

Plantation agriculture

B Biomass
S Soil
L Litter
A Ash

Size of circle is a rough indication of amount of nutrients

3 a Study Figure E which shows the changes in nutrient cycling in a tropical rainforest before and after human activity has taken place. Describe the changes that have taken place. (7 marks)

b Choose one biome of one tropical region that you have studied.
  (i) Describe the main characteristics of that biome. (8 marks)
  (ii) Discuss the ecological responses to the climate by both plants and animals. (10 marks)

Section B
World cities

4 a Study Photograph C. Describe and comment on the contrasts in the quality of living that can be seen in the urban area shown in the photograph. (7 marks)

*Photograph C
Housing in
São Paulo*

b With reference to examples, suggest reasons for urban decline.　(8 marks)

c With reference to one process of urban regeneration that you
have studied, discuss the effectiveness of that process in the
area(s) affected.　(10 marks)

Development and globalisation

*Table C Profile of a
country, 2006*

Characteristic		
Demography	Population: 39 million Urban population: 23%	Annual growth rate: 2.6%
Health	Life expectancy: 50 years Infant mortality: 78 per 1,000 live births Doctors per 1,000 people: 4 Access to safe water: 68% % of children under 5 that are underweight: 17	
Education	Adult literacy: 69%	School enrolment primary: 56% School enrolment secondary: 6%
Economy	GDP per capita: $674 Annual inflation: 6%	Annual economic growth: 2.7% External debt: $230 per capita
Main exports	Coffee, tea, cotton, sisal, diamonds	
Main imports	Oil, electrical goods, fertilisers	
Communications	Personal computers per 1,000 people: 35 Mobile phones per 1,000 people: 50 Landline telephones per 1,000 people: 6	

5 a Using Table C only suggest why this country can be classed as a country at a
very low level of economic development.　(7 marks)

b Explain what is meant by the term 'development continuum'.　(8 marks)

c Discuss the roles of both trade and aid in development issues.　(10 marks)

Contemporary conflicts and challenges

Figure F Population trends among Kurdish populations

(a) % of Kurds living in individual countries, 2005

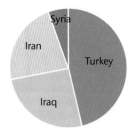

(b) Proportion of Kurds living in individual countries, 2005

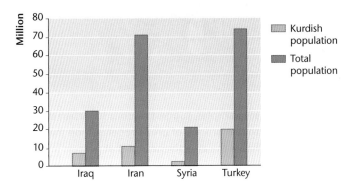

6 **a** Study Figure F. On the basis of this information only, analyse and comment on the degree to which separatist pressures are justified by the Kurdish people. (7 marks)

   b With reference to examples, explain the causes of separatism within and/or across political boundaries. (8 marks)

   c With reference to examples, discuss the consequences of separatist pressures. (10 marks)

Section C Essay questions

Each question carries 40 marks.

Plate tectonics and associated hazards

7 'The extent to which volcanic processes represent hazards depends on where and when they occur.' Discuss this statement.

Weather and climate and associated hazards

8 Critically evaluate the possible causes and possible effects of the phenomenon known as global warming.

Ecosystems: change and challenge

9 With reference to examples, critically evaluate the success of management schemes in fragile environments.

World cities

10 'Urban management issues are the same across the world.' To what extent to you agree with this view?

Development and globalisation

11 Discuss the reasons for, and consequences of, social and economic groupings of nations.

Contemporary conflicts and challenges

12 For a conflict over the use of a local resource, analyse the reasons for the conflict and assess the extent to which it has been/can be resolved.

Unit 4

4A: Geography fieldwork investigation

4B: Geographical issue evaluation

Geography fieldwork investigation

At A2, you are required to undertake investigative work in the field (Photograph 7.1). This allows you to develop skills associated with planning investigations, collection of primary and secondary data, and presentation, interpretation and evaluation of results. You are required to sit *either* Unit 4A — an examination consisting of structured and extended questions based on your own fieldwork investigation ($1\frac{1}{2}$ hours) — *or* Unit 4B — an examination consisting of structured and extended questions, including research-based skills questions, based on an advance information booklet, which is pre-released ($1\frac{1}{2}$ hours). Both papers carry 60 marks.

Amanda Barker

This chapter deals with the Unit 4A option. In this exam there are two sections: A and B. Section A (40 marks) assesses a personal fieldwork investigation that you have undertaken with the broad task of: 'the individual investigation of a geographical argument, assertion, hypothesis, issue or problem'.

The only restrictions on the type of topic studied are that it should be

*Photograph 7.1
Fieldwork*

geographical and include primary, and where relevant secondary, data collection. It should be based on a small area of study and be linked to the content of the specification. This is a very wide brief. It is also clear that this investigation/ fieldwork must be completed at a level above that done at AS.

Section B (20 marks) assesses fieldwork, investigative and research skills in a context that is unfamiliar to you. Questions require you to use data, skills and techniques to interpret, analyse and evaluate geographical information and apply understanding in unfamiliar contexts. Most of these skills are described in our *AQA AS Geography* textbook, and therefore will not be discussed again here. However, there are three additional A2 skills and these are described below.

Additional A2 skills

Weather maps

You need to be able to read weather maps, including synoptic charts. See chapter 2, p. 50 of this book for an example.

Comparative tests: chi-squared test

This technique is used to assess the degree to which there are differences between a set of collected (or observed) data and a theoretical (or expected) set of data, and the statistical significance of the differences.

The observed data are those that have been collected either in the field or from secondary sources. The expected data are those that would be expected according to the theoretical hypothesis being tested.

Normally, before the test is applied it is necessary to formulate a null hypothesis. In the example given here, the null hypothesis would be that there is no significant difference between the observed and expected data distribution. The alternative to this would be that there *is* a difference between the observed and expected data, and that there is some factor responsible for this.

The method of calculating chi-squared is shown below. The letters A–D in Table 7.1 refer to map areas A–D in Figure 7.1. In the column headed O are listed the numbers of points in each of the areas A–D on Figure 7.1 (the *observed* frequencies). The total number of points in this case is 40. Column E contains the list of *expected* frequencies in each of the areas A–D, assuming that the points are evenly spaced. In the column $O - E$, each of the expected frequencies is subtracted from the observed frequencies, and in the last column the result is squared. The relevant values are then inserted into the expression for chi-squared, and the result is 4.0.

Table 7.1

Map	Observed (O)	Expected (E)	(O – E)	(O – E)²
A	8	10	–2	4
B	14	10	4	16
C	6	10	–4	16
D	12	10	2	4
Sum	40	40	0	40

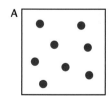 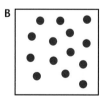 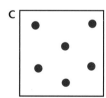 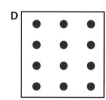

Figure 7.1

$$\chi^2 = \frac{\Sigma(O - E)^2}{E}$$

$$= \frac{40}{10}$$

$$= 4.0$$

Table 7.2 Critical values of chi-squared

Degrees of freedom	Significance level	
	0.05	0.01
1	3.84	6.64
2	5.99	9.21
3	7.82	11.34
4	9.49	13.28
5	11.07	15.09
6	12.59	16.81
7	14.07	18.48
8	15.51	20.09
9	16.92	21.67
10	18.31	23.21
11	19.68	24.72
12	21.03	26.22
13	22.36	27.69
14	23.68	29.14
15	25.00	30.58
16	26.30	32.00
17	27.59	33.41
18	28.87	34.80
19	30.14	36.19
20	31.41	37.57
21	32.67	38.93
22	33.92	40.29
23	35.17	41.64
24	36.42	42.98
25	37.65	44.31
26	38.88	45.64
27	40.11	46.96
28	41.34	48.28
29	42.56	49.59
30	43.77	50.89
40	55.76	63.69
50	67.51	76.15
60	79.08	88.38
70	90.53	100.43
80	101.88	112.33
90	113.15	124.12
100	124.34	135.81

Note: When there are *A* rows and *B* columns respectively, degrees of freedom = $(A - 1) \times (B - 1)$. If there is only one row, then there are $(B - 1)$ degrees of freedom.

The aim of a chi-squared test, therefore, is to find out whether the observed pattern agrees with or differs from the theoretical (expected) pattern. This can be measured by comparing the calculated result of the test with its level of significance.

To do this the number of degrees of freedom must be determined using the formula $(n - 1)$, where n is the number of observations, in this case the number of cells which contain observed data (4). So, $4 - 1 = 3$. Table 7.2 gives the distribution of chi-squared values for these degrees of freedom.

Then there are the levels of significance. There are two levels of significance: 95% and 99% (0.05 and 0.01 in Table 7.2). At 95% there is a 1 in 20 probability that the pattern being considered occurred by chance, and at 99% there is only a 1 in 100 probability that the pattern is chance. The levels of significance can be found in a book of statistical tables. They are also known as confidence levels.

If the calculated value is the same or greater than the values given in the table, then the null hypothesis can be rejected and the alternative hypothesis accepted.

In the case of our example, however, the value of chi-squared is very low (4.0), showing that there is little difference between the observed and the expected pattern. The null hypothesis cannot therefore be rejected.

Some further points on this technique

➤ The numbers of both observed and expected values must be large enough to ensure that the test is valid. Most experts state that there should be a minimum of five.

➤ The number produced by the calculation is itself meaningless. It is only of value for use in consulting statistical tables.

➤ As in Spearman rank test, only significance (or confidence) levels of 95% and 99% should be considered when rejecting the null hypothesis. Levels of confidence greater than these simply allow the null hypothesis to be rejected with even greater confidence.

➤ It is strongly recommended that you do not apply the test to more than one set of observed data because the mathematics become too complex.

Comparative tests: Mann–Whitney U test

To carry out the Mann–Whitney U test:
➤ set out the data in two columns
➤ rank each item of data in terms of its position within the sample as a whole; start with the lowest value first
➤ add the ranks for each column
➤ calculate the value of U by using the formula:

$$U = n_1 n_2 + \frac{n_1(n_1 + 1)}{2} - \Sigma r_1$$

where:
n_1 and n_2 are the two sample sizes
Σr_1 is the sum of the ranks for sample 1
➤ using a table of critical values, interpret the answer that you have calculated.

If the calculated value of U is less than or equal to the critical value at the chosen significance level, then the null hypothesis must be rejected. The null hypothesis is that there is no significant difference between the two data sets. Therefore, if the null hypothesis is rejected, there is a difference.

Worked example: Mann–Whitney U test

An investigation was carried out into the effect of the sea on a beach in the west of England at different times of year. Two samples of pebbles were taken, one in April and the other in October. The hypothesis is that the mean size of the beach material will be larger in October than in April. Therefore, the null hypothesis is that there will be no difference.

The size categories (phi categories) that were used in the survey are shown in Table 7.3.

Calculation of U

The mean particle sizes at six sites in October and April were calculated. After ranking, the data were recorded in a table (Table 7.4).

Table 7.3 Size categories of beach material

Phi (Φ)	Particle diameter (mm)	Size category (Wentworth grade)	
−6.0	64.0	Cobbles	
			60.0 mm
−5.5	44.8	Coarse gravel	
−5.0	32.0		
−4.5	22.4		
			20.0 mm
−4.0	16.0	Medium gravel	
−3.5	11.2		
−3.0	8.0		
			6.0 mm
−2.5	5.6	Fine gravel	
−2.0	4.0		
−1.5	2.8		
−1.0	2.0		
			2.0 mm
−0.5	1.4	Coarse sand	
0.0	1.0		
0.5	0.71		
			0.6 mm
1.0	0.50	Medium sand	
1.5	0.355		
2.0	0.25		
			0.2 mm
2.5	0.18	Fine sand	
3.0	0.125		
3.5	0.090		
4.0	0.063		
			0.06 mm

Table 7.4 Mean particle size and rank at six sites, October and April

Site number	Mean particle size (using phi scale) in October (x)	Rank (r_x)	Mean particle size (using phi scale) in April (y)	Rank (r_y)
1	−2.506	5	−1.567	1
2	−2.483	4	−2.286	3
3	−2.612	7	−2.562	6
4	−2.726	8	−3.368	11
5	−3.281	10	−1.772	2
6	−3.394	12	−2.727	9
		$\Sigma r_x = 46$		$\Sigma r_y = 32$

$$U_x = n_x n_y + \frac{n_x(n_x + 1)}{2} - \Sigma r_x$$

$$= 36 + \frac{42}{2} - 46$$

$$= 11$$

$$U_y = n_x n_y + \frac{n_y(n_y + 1)}{2} - \Sigma r_y$$

$$= 36 + \frac{42}{2} - 32$$

$$= 25$$

where:

n_x and n_y are sample sizes

Σr_x and Σr_y are the sum of the rank values of r_x and r_y respectively

Table 7.5 Critical values for the interpretation of the value of U

		Significance level	
Sample size		**0.05**	**0.01**
n_x	n_y		
6	6	7	3

Once the value of U_x is established as 11, it is necessary to interpret this value (Table 7.5).

The value obtained for U_x of 11 clearly exceeds the critical value of 3 or 7. This means that the null hypothesis must be accepted; the proposed hypothesis must be rejected.

Therefore, there is no significant difference in beach material size in April and October; the size in October is not larger than that in April.

Using comparative tests

It is important to note that both chi-squared and Mann–Whitney U test should only be used as a support for your own ideas on the geographical significance of your study. All results, and the statistical analysis of them, should be related to the original hypothesis and/or the established theory in that aspect of the subject.

Your results may support established theory or your hypothesis, or they may not. If they do not, there may be some reason or factor you can identify that is responsible. This could lead to further studies. Above all, your investigation should make geographical sense. This is far more important than demonstrating your ability to use mathematics or statistics.

Questions in Unit 4A

In this section the range of possible questions that may be asked in Unit 4A Section A is described, together with guidance on how to answer them.

As in Unit 2 at AS, all the questions are likely to begin with a 'stem', such as:

You have experience of geography fieldwork as part of your course...

or

With reference to a piece of fieldwork you have recently undertaken...

All parts of the questions will relate to this stem.

Sample question 1

a Explain why the location of your fieldwork was appropriate for the investigation. (12 marks)

Two elements are required for a response to this question: the location and its suitability for the investigation. The underpinning theory should be linked to the specification. The location is therefore expected to be suitable to investigate the aim and, by implication, the theory. So, in your answer make sure you link theory > location > investigation > theory.

Mark scheme

Level 1 The candidate is unable to set out the aim in full; much confusion may be apparent at the lower end of the band. Towards the upper end of the band, there may be background of relevance to the location, but not linked to the aim. Alternatively, the aim may be justified but there is limited reference to the location. There will be little reference to the candidate's own fieldwork investigation at the upper end, whilst this will be absent at the lower end of the mark band. (1–4 marks)

Level 2 There will be clear reference to both location and aim, but there is likely to be an imbalance. This will be very marked at the lower end, perhaps with implicit links, whereas at the upper end, the imbalance will be less and there will be reference to the appropriateness of the location. There will be some reference to the fieldwork undertaken, increasing up through the band. (5–8 marks)

Level 3 There will be detailed reference to both location and aim and this will be consistently integrated to demonstrate the appropriateness of the location for the investigation. There will be detailed and increasingly convincing reference to the fieldwork undertaken. (9–12 marks)

b (i) Assess the usefulness of one method used to collect data for the investigation. (6 marks)

The method selected must relate to the investigation. Only one method is required. Any appropriate method is acceptable.

Mark scheme

Level 1 There is likely to be a description of the method selected. This will be basic at the lower end, more structured at the upper end of the band. There will be no reference to the fieldwork undertaken at the lower end, with some, perhaps basic, reference at the upper end of the band. There will be little, if any, attempt to assess the usefulness of the method selected. (1–4 marks)

Level 2 There will be a clear assessment of the usefulness of the method selected. There will be increasing rigour demonstrated. There will be increasingly clear and convincing reference to the fieldwork undertaken. (5–6 marks)

(ii) Analyse the strengths and limitations of this method in meeting the aim of your investigation. (12 marks)

Any relevant method can be used, but it must be that selected in (i). Reference to strengths, limitations and a link to the aim of the specific investigation is expected.

Mark scheme

Level 1 There will be a basic awareness of strengths and limitations of the method selected. There is likely to be a strong focus on either strengths or limitations. There is likely to be a straightforward use of expression. Reference to any sampling used will be basic, if present. There will be basic reference to the aim of the investigation and the candidate's own fieldwork experience is unlikely to be mentioned.   (1–4 marks)

Level 2 There will be clear reference to both strengths and limitations, but there is likely to be an imbalance. This will be very marked at the lower end, perhaps with implicit links, whereas, at the upper end, the imbalance will be less and there will be clear reference to the aim of the investigation and the fieldwork experience undertaken, increasing up through the band. A clear reference to any sampling method used is expected.   (5–8 marks)

Level 3 There will be detailed reference to analyse both strengths and limitations and this will be consistently referenced to the aim of the investigation. A detailed commentary on the suitability of any sampling method used is expected. There will be detailed and increasingly convincing reference to the fieldwork undertaken.   (9–12 marks)

c Evaluate your investigation in the light of its aim and underpinning geographical theory.   (10 marks)

You should refer to the aim and underpinning theory as set out in (a). Evaluation of the investigation as a whole is expected, in the light of the fieldwork experience.

Mark scheme

Level 1 There will be basic awareness of the conclusions gained from the investigation. There is likely to be a strong focus on the conclusions, rather than any evaluation. There is likely to be a straightforward use of expression. There will be a basic or no reference to the aim of the investigation and the underpinning geographical theory in the light of the candidate's own fieldwork experience.   (1–4 marks)

Level 2 There will be clear reference to both the conclusions and evaluation of the investigation, but there is likely to be an imbalance. This will be more apparent at the lower end, perhaps with implicit links, whereas, at the upper end, the imbalance will be less and there will be clear reference to the aim of the investigation and the underpinning geographical theory. A clear reference to the fieldwork experience undertaken, increasing up through the band, is expected.   (5–8 marks)

Level 3 There will be detailed reference to the conclusions and there will be a meaningful evaluative theme. This will be consistently referenced to the aim of the investigation and the underpinning geographical theory. There will be detailed and increasingly convincing reference to the fieldwork undertaken.   (9–10 marks)

Sample question 2

a **Explain how your hypotheses/research questions evolved from the overall aim.** (5 marks)

The difference between an aim and hypotheses/research questions should be clear in your mind.

Note that at A2 it is better to have more than one hypothesis/research question.

Mark scheme

Level 1 Overall statement of aim given, together with a brief statement of hypothesis/research question. The links between the two are not well stated or made clear. (1–3 marks)

Level 2 Clear aim stated with statements of clear hypotheses/research questions and together with clear and logical link between them. (4–5 marks)

b **How did you assess the safety issues associated with your enquiry?** (5 marks)

This question assesses the degree to which risk assessment has taken place. The precise nature of the assessment will depend on the nature and location of the fieldwork undertaken. Risk assessment is an important element of fieldwork and should form part of your preparatory processes.

Mark scheme

Level 1 Simple statements of risk and of risk assessment. The answer could apply to any piece of fieldwork, there being no sense of appropriateness to the fieldwork being undertaken. (1–3 marks)

Level 2 Clear and precise statements of risk and of risk assessment. There is a clear sense of preparation prior to the fieldwork being undertaken, and being appropriate to the investigation undertaken. (4–5 marks)

c **Describe the use you made of modern technology in either data collection or presentation and assess its value.** (10 marks)

Clear evidence of the use of modern technology will be credited at a high level. There must be clear and detailed description of how the modern technology was used and not of the technology itself. Evidence of application of the technology to data collection or data presentation should be made clear. A strong answer will provide an indication of the benefits of using modern technology compared with not using it. An assessment of its value should include some evidence linked to the fieldwork undertaken rather than generic information.

Mark scheme

Level 1 Candidates offer limited description of the technology used which may be combined with limited assessment of value. Tends to be generic rather than linked to fieldwork across AS and A2 at bottom of level. (1–4 marks)

Level 2 Description of use of technology combined with assessment of value but partially related to fieldwork. Competent description but no assessment of value or vice versa. Answer may have poor structure with some inaccurate spelling and inaccurate use of geographical terminology. (5–8 marks)

Level 3 All aspects of indicative content covered in a fieldwork focused context. Well structured answers with accurate use of geographical terminology.

(9–10 marks)

d **Assess one method that you used to analyse your data. Explain why this method was suitable for your purposes.** (8 marks)

The method selected must relate to the investigation. Only one method is required. Any appropriate method is acceptable.

Mark scheme

Level 1 There is likely to be a description of the method selected. This will be basic at the lower end, more structured at the upper end of the band. There will be no reference to the fieldwork undertaken at the lower end, with some, perhaps basic, reference at the upper end of the band. There will be little, if any, attempt to assess the usefulness of the method selected.   (1–4 marks)

Level 2 There will be a clear assessment of the usefulness of the method selected. There will be increasing rigour demonstrated. There will be increasingly clear and convincing reference to the fieldwork undertaken.   (5–8 marks)

e **Explain how your investigation helped you to gain an understanding of the topic or the environment you were studying.** (12 marks)

You should make reference to the aim and hypotheses/research questions as set out in (a). Evaluation of the investigation as a whole is expected, in the light of the fieldwork experience.

Mark scheme

Level 1 There will be basic awareness of the conclusions gained from the investigation. There is likely to be a strong focus on the conclusions, rather than any evaluation. There is likely to be a straightforward use of expression. There will be a basic or no reference to the aim of the investigation and the underpinning geographical theory/environment in the light of the candidate's own fieldwork experience.   (1–4 marks)

Level 2 There will be clear reference to both the conclusions and evaluation of the investigation, but there is likely to be an imbalance. This will be more apparent at the lower end, perhaps with implicit links, whereas at the upper end, the imbalance will be less and there will be clear reference to the aim of the investigation and the underpinning geographical theory/environment. A clear reference to the fieldwork experience undertaken, increasing up through the band, is expected.   (5–8 marks)

Level 3 There will be detailed reference to the conclusions and there will be a meaningful evaluative theme. This will be consistently referenced to the aim of the investigation and the underpinning geographical theory/environment. There will be detailed and increasingly convincing reference to the fieldwork undertaken.   (9–12 marks)

Geographical issue evaluation

At A2, you are required to undertake investigative work in the field. This allows you to develop skills associated with planning investigations, collection of primary and secondary data, and presentation, interpretation and evaluation of results. You are required to sit *either* Unit 4A — an examination consisting of structured and extended questions based on your own fieldwork investigation ($1\frac{1}{2}$ hours) — *or* Unit 4B — an examination consisting of structured and extended questions, including research-based skills questions, based on an advance information booklet, which is pre-released ($1\frac{1}{2}$ hours). Both papers carry 60 marks.

This chapter deals with the Unit 4B option. Unit 4B is an issue evaluation exercise which requires you to use a range of geographical skills, knowledge and understanding. An advance information booklet (AIB) is released 2 months before the examination and you should study it carefully and in detail. You may also be told to investigate other sources of information such as maps, atlases and websites.

The process of issue evaluation

You must be able to:
➤ interpret a range of data and resources (provided in the AIB)
➤ use techniques to present and analyse these data
➤ consider how to collect additional information using methods such as fieldwork and internet research
➤ relate the data to the geographical knowledge and understanding you have developed at AS and A2
➤ carry out further research into the issue or the area referred to in the AIB, where necessary
➤ recognise and define an issue
➤ consider evidence from different points of view
➤ recognise shortcomings of the data and suggest sources through which those shortcomings could be remedied
➤ establish criteria for evaluation of the issue or for decision making
➤ evaluate a range of options concerning the management of an issue or of a decision
➤ identify and analyse potential areas of conflict
➤ consider ways of resolving or reducing conflict
➤ recommend a way to manage the issue or make a decision
➤ justify your recommendation

➤ suggest the possible impact of your suggested action
➤ review the process of issue evaluation

The examination

Unit 4B will be assessed in a $1\frac{1}{2}$ hour examination covering a selection of the skills set out above. The examination will test your knowledge and understanding of the subject matter in the AIB and its links with other aspects of geography. It will also assess your ability to have a critical approach to the techniques associated with data gathering, presentation and analysis. You should be aware of the findings of the investigation/task given to you and how it furthers your geographical understanding. You also need to understand the role of fieldwork inquiry in geographical study. You will be tested on your ability to apply your understanding of the enquiry process to unfamiliar contexts, using fieldwork stimulus material.

Succeeding in the examination

Doing well in this type of examination involves two main phases:
➤ preparation for the examination using the pre-released AIB
➤ performing well in the examination itself

It is important to note that the assessment is a single exercise. Although it may be divided into a number of separate questions, these are written in a clear order of progression. The initial questions help you to set the scene for the context within which the evaluation of the issue will have to take place.

The initial questions are intended to direct you towards certain issues or problems that should be considered when answering the later questions. Cross-references back to earlier points can be used to illustrate good intellectual and organisational skills. It is these skills that such exercises seek to assess.

Some questions will arise from the data given in the AIB, which can be answered from a fieldwork, or investigative, approach. You may be asked about aspects of data collection, presentation and analysis in the context of the information provided — you may even be asked to carry out a cartographic, diagrammatic or analytical technique using the data given. You should therefore have a thorough knowledge and understanding of the skills required at AS and A2.

Working with the AIB

Before the exam you are expected to make yourself familiar with the information in the AIB. You should undertake several hours of preparation — as a rough guide 10–12 hours in total. The following are guidelines for the kind of work that should be done:
➤ Read and re-read the booklet so that you are familiar with its content and layout.
➤ Look up the meaning of any unfamiliar words and phrases used in the booklet. There is nothing to prevent you asking your teacher for help with this.

> Use an atlas and other sources to become reasonably familiar with the geographical area in which the exercise is located.
> List the concepts, theories, processes, etc. that are referred to in the booklet, and make sure you are completely familiar with them by referring to course notes and textbooks.
> If necessary, carry out further research into the issue or the area referred to in the booklet.
> Consider some of the possible questions that might be asked, and think about how answers to such questions could be planned.

The internet

It is understandable that many candidates want to make use of the internet to support their background research into the geographical area and issue. However, bear in mind the following reservations:

> Information on some websites may be biased towards a particular outcome and may not be based on sound geographical evidence. In other words, the material may be unreliable.
> Information on the internet may be out-of-date, or indeed more up-to-date than the material that is provided in the AIB. It is dangerous to make use of such material because the decision you make has to be based on the information provided *within* the AIB, and nothing else. This is to ensure that all candidates can be assessed fairly on the same contextual material.
> Information on the internet may not be relevant to the question set. Examiners may well choose to use the context of a real-world issue for a slightly different purpose — one that makes a more effective assessment exercise. Again you are reminded that the material in the AIB is of most importance to you.

On the other hand, the AIB may refer you to specific websites. It is a good idea to investigate these sites. They have been 'flagged up' for a purpose and it is fair to assume that one or more questions will require the information contained in them.

Summarising the information

A number of techniques can be used to summarise the information presented in issue evaluation tasks:

> **Tabulation** — a visual display of summarised information highlighting the key issues. This technique tends towards brevity and simplicity, and is not a good method for evaluation, only for summary.
> **Ranking** — ordering options according to criteria, for example low priority to high priority, or most expensive to least expensive. Such a method is easier to apply to quantitative data than qualitative data.
> **Scaling** — subjective ranking of data/information on a personal basis to allow some comparison and analysis. This may be based on relative advantages or disadvantages, or on relative impacts such as positive or negative outcomes. This technique introduces an element of personal bias, but does involve a

degree of evaluation. The weighting of some factors may also feature here; for example, if the issue concerns flood control, then rainfall may have a greater influence than, say, vegetation type, and should be weighted accordingly.

➤ **Matrices** — a more complex form of diagram illustrating relationships between different aspects of the information. Matrices can be used to identify possible areas of conflict, or environmental impacts. Such matrices should *not* be used in the examination itself, unless specifically requested. All answers require continuous prose, and even matrices with explanations of codes or numerical scores do not fit this requirement.

Thinking about the question

It is not a good idea to second guess too confidently what the issue evaluation tasks will be. Sometimes the tasks are easier to predict and, where this is the case, the examiners will be aware that the task appears straightforward. They are then more likely to introduce a more unfamiliar context or sub-context into the final question.

The nature of the resources tells you exactly what topic the exercise will focus on. Clearly if all the data relate to flooding, you should spend time reading through your notes on this topic to make sure you understand all its concepts, for example hydrology and hydrographs. If the context appears to be the role of transnational corporations, then relevant general material should be read, and so on.

In many cases you will be given one or a number of opinions about an issue or problem in a particular area. It is useful to look at the issue or problem from the point of view of the 'owner' of the opinion. Is it based on professional research, fact or sheer emotion? Do the resources support the opinion in any way? Do the opinions conflict with each other?

While it is obviously not a good idea to prejudge the question, it is likely that you will have to compare the options in one way or another. This might, as explained above, involve weighing up advantages and disadvantages, socioeconomic benefits and negative impacts, or cost–benefit analysis. It is therefore a good idea to spend time looking at the alternative options and preparing a table of some sort to summarise the information.

The best answers usually demonstrate an intimate knowledge of the advance information. References to different items within it are brought together in interesting and relevant ways, which allow the candidates to show good insights. These answers are also often supported by useful information from within the booklet. Geographical theories and ideas are well integrated into the answers, and candidates demonstrate their knowledge and understanding of their previous studies. In simple terms, these candidates are well-prepared.

The worst answers show little familiarity with the advance information. They are often brief and unstructured. They may include large sections copied from the booklet, or with only small changes to the original wording. There are few developments of the ideas and concepts within the booklet, and little awareness is shown of the relevance of the candidate's previous studies within geography. In short, these candidates do not think geographically.

Answering the examination questions

You are not allowed to take your *annotated* pre-release material into the examination room. You may be provided with either a 'clean' set of material (for example a clean photocopy) or additional copies of the sheets that you need to use in the examination. You will also be given the task itself once you are in the exam.

You will be given a context within which you should answer the question. For example, you may be asked to imagine that you are a particular person or have a particular role. Alternatively, you might be given a set of guidelines that should form the basis for all or some of your answers. In some cases, you may even be told that you represent a certain body with a specific 'mission statement'. It is important that you empathise with this role, whatever it may be.

Remember:
➤ treat the whole paper as one exercise — all the questions are linked
➤ demonstrate familiarity with the data or information
➤ where there are maps and/or photographs, make sure you refer to them, and be accurate in your use of them (most maps and photographs will have grid squares on them — make sure you use these accurately)

The task itself will be varied, and divided into sub-tasks. There are many possible sub-tasks. For example, you may be asked to:
➤ summarise a given set of geographical information
➤ identify problems/issues/conflicts
➤ consider a variety of proposals
➤ evaluate each of these proposals
➤ place the proposals in a rank order according to the context of the whole exercise
➤ justify that rank order
➤ recommend the best way to manage the proposals in the light of possible problems/conflicts
➤ examine the difficulties that may arise in their implementation
➤ make a decision
➤ justify that decision

As in other forms of examination it is important that you answer the question(s) asked, and keep a close eye on the time. Appropriate use of the mark allocation will give an indication of the amount of time to be spent on each aspect of the exercise. By their nature the issue evaluation and/or decision-making elements and subsequent justification come at the end, so it is vital that you leave enough time to complete the task thoroughly.

The final question or section

When answering the final question or section, make sure you consider all or some of the following points:
➤ the short-term and long-term effects of each proposal

➤ the local, regional and national considerations
➤ the spatial (geographical) impacts of each proposal
➤ the social, economic and environmental impacts
➤ the costs and benefits of each proposal
➤ the effects of each proposal on different groups of people in the area

In addition, to access the highest mark ranges — Level 3 or 4 in most cases — you need to demonstrate the highest level of geographical skills, including:
➤ critical understanding of the issue(s) being considered, often showing an awareness of the complexity of the real-world situation
➤ maturity of understanding of the issue(s), which is identified through a coherent, well-reasoned and perceptive argument
➤ high levels of synopticity
➤ insight into the issue(s), possibly including elements of creativity and/or flair

Finally, you may be asked to justify your answer. The command word **justify** is one of the most demanding that candidates face. At its most simplistic, a response to this command must include a strong piece of writing in favour of the chosen option(s), and an explanation of why the other options were rejected.

However, issue evaluation is not straightforward. All the options in an issue-evaluation scenario have positive and negative aspects. The options that are likely to be rejected will have some good elements to them, and equally, the chosen option will not be perfect in all respects. The key to good issue evaluation is to balance up the pros and cons of each option and to opt for the most appropriate, based on the evidence available. A good answer to the command 'justify' should therefore provide the following:
➤ for each of the options that are rejected — an outline of their positive and negative points, but with an overall statement of why the negatives outweigh the positives
➤ for the chosen option — an outline of the negative and the positive points, but with an overall statement of why the positives outweigh the negatives

Try to avoid repetition, but make brief references back to the previous sections of the paper. Develop the points made earlier in the context of the final task and in the context of the role you have assumed. Be logical, use the evidence accumulated from the rest of the exercise, and always remember that it was conceived to be a complete task in its own right.

Guernsey issue evaluation exercise

Study carefully all of the information on the following pages (309 to 313). You should regard this information as an advance information booklet. Questions on these materials follow on page 313.

Background information on Guernsey

Figure 8.1
Map of Guernsey

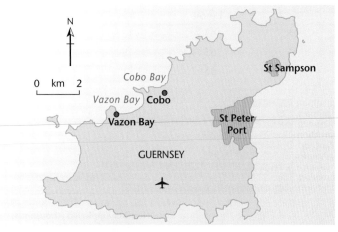

Figure 8.2
Population pyramid for Guernsey, 2001

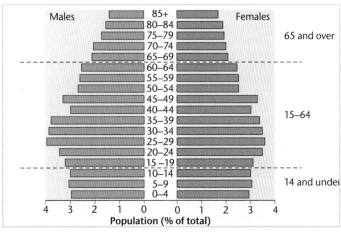

Figure 8.3
Guernsey population density, 2001, and population change by parish, 1991–2001

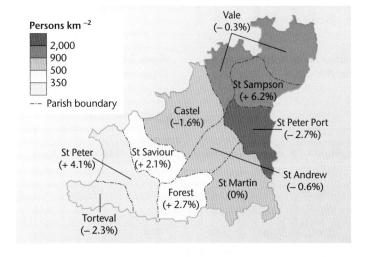

Year	Age group (% of population)			
	0–14	15–64	65+	Total
2001	18	63.2	18.8	60,542
2011 (est.)	15	66	19	62,021
2021 (est.)	14	65	21	63,808

*Table 8.1
Guernsey popula-
tion totals and
% in age groups,
2001–21
(estimated)*

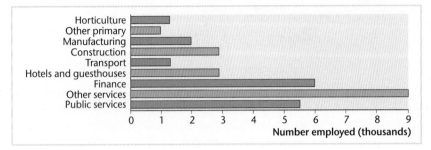

*Figure 8.4
Economically
active persons by
sector in Guernsey,
2001*

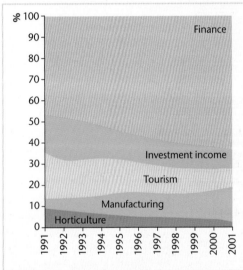

Figure 8.5 Contribution to Guernsey's exports
by industrial sector, 1991–2001

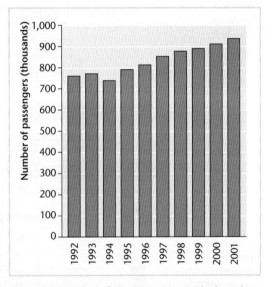

Figure 8.6 Number of air passengers (arrivals and
departures) to Guernsey airport, 1992–2001

	Type of visitor					
	Leisure	Business	Leisure (day trip)	Business (day trip)	Sailing	Total
1995	246	42	36	23	61	408
1998	316	52	31	16	66	481
2001	300	46	30	22	51	449
Average stay	7 days	2 days	1 day	1 day	3 days	

*Table 8.2
Number of visitors
to Guernsey,
1995–2001
(thousands)*

Proposal 1 To extend the runway at Guernsey Airport

A new terminal building has recently been built at the airport. This proposal is that the runway should also be extended. Here are some views on the proposed expansion:

> Unless the current runway is extended, the move to bigger aircraft will result in fewer airlines being able to operate here in future. The airlines that serve Guernsey will not be able to operate their larger aircraft. The island will become an insignificant backwater.
> *An aviation journalist*

> Our airline has invested heavily in short take off and landing aircraft to ensure we can and will continue to operate in Guernsey with the runway at its present length.
> *Channel Islands Airline manager*

> We had a cargo plane crash on approach in 2000 hitting a house to the east of the airport and narrowly missing a petrol station. Any extension to the runway with more people passing through on larger planes will increase the risks of living under the flight path. People to the west of the runway extension will see property prices crash and the quality of life decline. Some closer to the runway may even lose their homes.
> *Councillor for St Peter Port living in the vicinity of the airport*

> Why should we, living in the rural parish of St Peter, have to lose land of landscape value and suffer more noise to satisfy the bankers' and hoteliers' desire for more money? Hotels are never full and the bankers do not need larger planes.
> *Small farmer close to the airport*

James Harrison

Photograph 8.1
The new terminal building at Guernsey Airport

Proposal 2 To develop a waterfront area close to the centre of St Peter Port for a hotel and exclusive housing

This proposal is to demolish some of the existing buildings in the St Peter Port area and to build a new hotel development with exclusive residential property nearby. The following criteria must be satisfied:

- The development should be well designed, in keeping with the setting and should bring about significant improvements to the area.
- It should not occupy open space or block an important view.
- Adequate car parking should be provided.

Photograph 8.2 The sea front in St Peter Port

Here are some views on the proposed scheme:

A top quality hotel close to the financial district of St Peter Port is needed for business people and corporate entertaining. It could also provide quality accommodation in the summer months when business demand is lower.   *Overseas investment manager of a major offshore bank*

We don't need hotels; we need affordable housing, especially for the elderly Guernsey-born population. Financial services have created wealth for the island. The wealth should be distributed to make the island a good place to live for everyone and not just the bankers.   *Retired former glasshouse worker living in St Sampson*

House prices have doubled in the past 10 years and an average house costs £200,000. How on earth can a young person like me begin to afford one on this island where I was born?   *Recently qualified nurse*

The provision for future accommodation on the island should be made predominantly in the urban areas. A range of development possibilities, including the use of brownfield sites, should be investigated. Housing provision for those of modest means is also specified in a current policy.   *Planning department representative*

Proposal 3 To raise the sea wall along the western coast, starting with Vazon and Cobo Bays, to protect the coastal areas from rising sea levels

Vazon Bay is a popular place for tourists who want a beach holiday. It is important that the beach is maintained and that the land behind the existing sea wall is protected. Here are some views on the proposed scheme:

> We need to make sure that the sea defences are strong in order to protect the properties lying behind and below the beach ridge at Vazon. Our timeshare hotel and golf course are threatened by storms attacking the sea wall. Salt water has penetrated into the drained land on which the golf course is sited.
>
> *Manager of Vazon Bay sea front hotel*

> Without the sea wall raised at the head of the Cobo Bay a storm surge will overtop the defences and sea water will flow inland threatening our houses. It is all the fault of global warming. Planners seem more interested in new housing or airport extensions. *Cobo Residents' Association*

> Once we start raising the defences here, we have to do it all along the coast. It is better to let nature take its course. Those who live at or near high water mark have made their choice. You cannot stop natural processes! *A retired geomorphology professor living on the island*

> When winter storms rage, my cottage is already washed by spray. If the sea wall is not raised and strength-ened many coastal dwellers will have to move out. Defend what the island has, its existing cottages and homes. *Castel parish councillor*

Questions

1 Using only the information provided, summarise the main demographic and economic characteristics of the island of Guernsey. (15 marks)

2 Suggest possible conflicts that may arise in each case if each of the proposed schemes is approved separately. (15 marks)

3 Study Table 8.2. Using the information contained in Table 8.2, draw two proportional divided circles to illustrate the differences in the types of visitors to Guernsey in 1995 and in 2001. (10 marks)

4 Guernsey Planning and Finance Department has three strategic aims which guide the island's planning mechanisms:
- to improve the quality of life for all people on the island
- to manage the island in a cost effective and sustainable way
- to maintain and improve the quality of the environment

In the light of these strategic aims, conclude your report by ranking the three proposals in order for implementation, and justify your decisions. (20 marks)

Mark schemes

Question 1

Level 1   The answer simply re-states the information given in the data in written form. There is no interpretation of the data and no recognition of trends or of significance beyond the obvious. For example, the candidate may include figures of individual age groups from the population pyramid or numbers employed in particular industries. There is no evidence of cross-reference between two or more sets of data.   (1–6 marks)

Level 2   The answer demonstrates some recognition of trends from the information in the data. These trends may take the form of analysis over time or involve projections into the future; alternatively, they may group sets of data that demonstrate similar or related factors. The answer provides evidence that the candidate can see beyond the obvious, for example, recognising the possible consequences if trends do continue. The answer may also demonstrate some evidence of cross-referencing between two or more sets of data.

(7–12 marks)

Level 3   The answer must refer to both demographic and economic characteristics at the Level 2 standard to reach this level. Achieving Level 2 in both of these aspects would trigger the lowest mark within Level 3. (This is an example of a mechanical means by which Level 3 can be awarded in an examination answer.) The answer demonstrates wide-ranging synoptic ability. It refers to most if not all of the data provided and illustrates the degree to which the different elements within the data are interdependent — one impacts upon another, and not always in a straightforward manner. Short- and long-term implications of the trends in the information are stated clearly and effectively. The answer is written clearly and logically with a good command of the English language.   (13–15 marks)

Question 2

Level 1   The answer contains simplistic statements regarding possible conflicts that may arise for any of the proposed schemes. It is not clear from the answer that the candidate has recognised the location of the possible conflict — it could apply to any similar area. Participants in the conflict are identified in very general terms and are usually grouped as being either in favour of or against the schemes. Attitudes contributing to the conflict are also stated in very general terms with no clear sense of attribution — for example, sentences begin with the phrase 'Some people would think...'. Answers that examine only one proposed scheme cannot go beyond Level 1.   (1–6 marks)

Level 2   The answer contains detailed statements about the possible causes of the conflicts. There is an understanding of the factors leading to the possible conflicts, together with a recognition that there will be some variation of attitude within groups of participants. The answer is clearly linked to the named and located areas. Participants in the possible conflicts are clearly identified and their attitudes are clearly attributed. However, material copied

from the resources provided will not be credited at this level. The answer recognises that attitudes may vary over time, depending on the outcome of the decision-making process. (7–12 marks)

Level 3 The answer must contain Level 2 material on at least two of the proposed schemes to reach this level. The answer contains a thorough account of the possible causes of the conflicts, including background material on the area(s) and/or participants. There is some recognition of the variation in the basis of attitudes within each set of participants, depending on whether they would lose or benefit from the outcome of the conflict. There is also some consideration of the short- and long-term implications of the proposed schemes. There is evidence of critical understanding of geographical concepts and principles. The answer is written clearly and logically with a good command of the English language. (13–15 marks)

Question 3

As with many questions of this type, this cannot be levels marked. Marks are allocated for the process of drawing the diagrams, as follows:

Accurate construction of circles to scale: 4 marks (2 marks each)

1995: $r = \sqrt{A/\pi} = \sqrt{408/\pi} = 11.4$ mm

2001: $r = \sqrt{A/\pi} = \sqrt{449/\pi} = 11.9$ mm

If diagrams incorrect in size: credit 1 mark each for correct use of formula.

1 mark for circles drawn (whether or not to scale) — this allows subsequent credit for those who have NOT drawn the circles to scale.

1 mark for subdivision beginning at 12 o'clock

One mark for each circle for correct subdivision = 2 marks

1 mark for shading/identification of sectors

1 mark for titles

Total = 10 marks

Question 4

Level 1 A basic ranking is made, but any reasons given for this are little more than unsubstantiated assertions of pros and/or cons. The candidate does not make direct reference to the strategic aims given in the question and it is impossible to see any indirect recognition of their importance. (1–6 marks)

Level 2 A clear ranking is made, together with some appropriate justification supported by clear arguments. The justification tends to be constructed simplistically. For example, the reasons for the number one proposal outweigh the reasons for the other two, or only the negative aspects of the other two schemes are given. There is clear use of and reference to the strategic aims given in the question. However, there is no recognition that these may be contradictory or may also be ranked. (7–12 marks)

Level 3 The answer is detailed and developed. The ranking is justified thoroughly. The positives and negatives of each of the three proposals are examined in depth and compared with each other. There is clear use of and reference to the strategic aims throughout the answer. There is recognition that the decision-making process in such cases would be very complex. A variety of considerations is dealt with in detail. Issues are considered at different scales and from differing viewpoints. The answer is developing a high level of synopticity — the connections within and between the information given both at the outset, and for each of the three proposals, are developed. The answer is written clearly and logically with a good command of the English language. (13–18 marks)

Level 4 The candidate has completed the task thoroughly. The answer critically evaluates the task that has been given in relation to the context of the exercise. There is evidence of critical understanding of geographical concepts and principles. There is a clear acknowledgement that there is going to be disagreement when the outcome of the ranking process is announced/ published. There may be recognition that each of the different proposals would satisfy the three strategic aims but in different ways and that it is the relative ranking of these that could influence the decision-making process to a greater extent. The answer is carefully structured, shows real geographical insight, with a clear sense of place and an understanding of a variety of different needs. Synopticity is shown throughout the answer. (19–20 marks)

Candidate answer

A sample answer is given, followed by the examiner's comments.

Question 1

The demographic characteristics are shown by means of the population pyramid, the table and the population distribution map. The population pyramid indicates that there is a falling birth rate as the percentage of people at each age group gets less towards its base. There is a bulge in the middle section of the pyramid, in the 25–39 age groups. This could mean either that there was an increase in birth rate at that time or that there has been an in-migration of young adult males to the island of Guernsey. There is almost an equal proportion of over 65s to those under 15 on the island, with more females than males in the older age groups. This illustrates that women have a longer life expectancy than males.

The table shows that the proportion of people under the age of 15 is likely to fall, and the proportion of elderly people will rise. This could mean that more retired people will be coming to the island, which is also supported by the fact that the total population of the island is likely to increase by 2021. The island's population is going to get bigger and older.

The population distribution map illustrates that most people live in St Peter Port on the east of the island, with high densities in the northeast at St Sampson and Vale. Lowest densities are in the southwest of the island.

Over 30,000 people are economically active, in other words in employment, on the island of Guernsey. If you compare this with the data in the table, where approx-

imately 38,000 people are between the ages of 15 and 64, you can see this is a very high proportion of people who are in work. Unemployment is likely to be low. Over 20,000 of these people work in some sort of services — finance, public services and others. This is high at 66% of the workforce. Tourism is also important as shown by the fact that 3,000 people work in hotels and guest houses. The other sectors are low, with more people employed in construction than in manufacturing. Primary industries are low.

The information gives confusing data regarding tourism. The number of passengers to the airport shows signs of an increase and yet the number of people visiting the island shows a decrease between 1998 and 2001. However, it is clear that the contribution to exports that tourism has made is falling in proportion and is now only 10% overall. Although manufacturing employment is low the proportion of the island's wealth that comes from manufacturing is increasing. By far the biggest proportion of the island's wealth comes from financial affairs — over 70% if you combine finance and investment income. This is a massive proportion.

Examiner comments

The candidate has constructed an answer by carefully examining each of the resources in turn. Although this is an acceptable approach, its drawback is that some interrelationships can be missed. However, this candidate does manage to identify most of the characteristic trends in the data.

In the first paragraph the candidate identifies some of the major demographic trends and even seeks to explain them in general terms (for example, women having longer life expectancies). However, the candidate does not appreciate the scale of the estimated reduction in the number of under 15 year olds — a reduction of nearly a quarter in 20 years. Low Level 2 would be awarded for this paragraph. The second paragraph shows a good degree of insight and moves the response well into Level 2, but the third paragraph is poor. It makes only simplistic comments and the information relating to population change is not referred to at all: St Peter Port is declining in population, with a growth in the nearby parish of St Sampson; three of the four parishes in the southwest of the island are increasing their populations.

The paragraphs on economic characteristics are also of a Level 2 standard. The candidate has attempted to make detailed use of the data with varying degrees of success. There are 32,500 people who are economically active, and it is true that unemployment would be extremely low on the island. The comment about the importance of services would have been even more accurate if the candidate had recognised that hotels, guest houses and transport are also service industries — making the proportion employed in the service sector nearly 80%. Perhaps it would have been better to make the direct link to export contributions here, where again 80% of export earnings come from some form of service activity — finance, investments and tourism. No comment is made regarding horticulture — this is surprising given the Channel Islands' reputation for producing flowers and early vegetables.

Some interrelationships between the resources are established — for example, the comment regarding manufacturing — and both the demographic and economic

characteristics are referred to at Level 2 standard. Consequently, a low Level 3 can be awarded overall and this answer would score 13 marks.

Candidate answer

Question 2

The proposed extension to the airport runway will cause conflict between those who want it to go ahead and those who do not. The idea of runway extension has caused conflict in a variety of locations in the UK — the most recent high-profile case was at Manchester airport. Here the argument was between industrialists who wanted to increase the amount of aircraft traffic through Manchester in order to encourage more investment in the area, together with the owners of the airport itself who obviously would make more money, and the environmentalists who wanted to save farmland, woodland areas and rare habitats. Guernsey earns a lot of its export income from service industries and tourism. An efficient airport is essential for both of these — flying tourists in and out, and flying business executives in and out.

Airlines with bigger aircraft will want a full-length runway, otherwise they will not be able to use the airport, or may have to use smaller planes. The aviation journalist suggests therefore that the airline companies would want the expansion. He also suggests that it is in the interests of the island economically to have a longer runway — he says, if not, 'the island will become an insignificant backwater'.

However, both of these views are challenged by two of the other quotes. The airline manager states that an extension is not necessary due to investment in STOL aircraft. The councillor who lives near the airport, but represents St Peter Port 4 km away, who one may have thought would have supported the proposed extension, is against it on safety grounds. Perhaps he lives to the west of the airport and is worried that the value of his house may fall. If this is the case, he is not really representing the views of his constituents. The small farmers in the area are most likely to be against the expansion — they will lose land and still have to live under the noisy flight path. However, they are also most likely to gain compensation, so their views are likely to vary over time. They could even appear to be against the proposal, while actually being in favour of it.

The proposed development of the waterfront area in St Peter Port is likely to upset a lot of local people. They will be concerned that the appearance of the area will be greatly changed. You can see in the photograph that many of the properties are quite old — some of these will be demolished to make way for this new development. The people who own these properties and live there will be angry if the development goes ahead. However, the people who own the properties but do not live there will be delighted as they will make money out of the sale. The views offered also highlight some other opinions. Some people will say that this is not the kind of housing that is needed — housing should be provided for public service workers like nurses and teachers, and the elderly who will increase in number in the years to come. But then again, those supporting the development point to the fact

that as Guernsey depends a huge amount on financial dealings then it is right that there is somewhere for these people to stay and to be entertained.

The proposed development at Vazon Bay is very different from the other two. Most people would seem to be in favour of it — indeed it is difficult to contemplate much opposition, apart from those who want the other schemes to go ahead first. All sorts of people would be in favour: the people who have houses on the coastline, like the councillor; the people whose businesses depend on tourists coming to the beach, such as the hotel and golf course owner; even the tourists because then they are guaranteed a nice place to have a holiday. I don't really envisage much of a conflict here — the only dissenting voice comes from a geography professor who says that you can't stop nature, and that if you raise the sea wall here, there will be a knock-on effect somewhere else along the coast. This is true, as many places in the UK, such as on the Yorkshire coast, have seen the consequences of work on one part of a coastline affecting other parts in a negative way. But, I don't think many people would listen to that view.

Examiner comments

This is a good answer. The candidate has studied the background information and has weighed up the pros and cons of each of the proposed schemes. In answering this type of question, it is very tempting to lift material directly from the quotes provided and to reuse these to illustrate the possible causes of conflict. In this answer, the candidate has only done this once, and then has used quotation marks and has used the quote to highlight a key point made in the same sentence. Use of material in this way is perfectly acceptable — but it is not appropriate to construct an answer using the same words and statements found in the stimulus material. Candidates should demonstrate that they understand the material fully.

The section dealing with the runway extension demonstrates a good understanding of the issue, and the complexity of the arguments that may be put forward. It recognises that some of the participants may not have stereotypical views, namely the airline manager and the local councillor. It also suggests that other participants (for example, farmers) may have varying views as the issue progresses. The candidate refers to other similar conflicts — at Manchester Airport. This is a valid exercise, as it is highly relevant in this case. It also demonstrates a degree of synoptic ability. As the answer is clearly related to the area identified and is detailed it is well within Level 2.

Similarly, the examination of the possible conflict in St Peter Port is handled well. There is a clear sense of place, good use is made of the given quotations, and there is evidence of good geographical insight. The candidate relates the issue to the data provided for Question 1 — the importance of the financial sector for the island of Guernsey. There is also a recognition that views on the proposed development will depend on whether individuals will lose directly or gain directly. As is the case in many such conflicts, the views of the participants are not always clear cut. One concern is that the candidate has chosen, deliberately or by accident, to ignore the final quotation. However, this section also reaches a Level 2 range of credit in its own right. According to the mark scheme, this would mean that a cumulative low Level 3 could now be awarded.

The final paragraph is also good. The candidate actually challenges the basis of the question here, by stating that conflict is unlikely. This is evidence of critical understanding and/or critical thinking — a high-level skill. The answer therefore moves up higher into the Level 3 range of credit. As elsewhere, the participants in any possible disagreements are identified and their views are summarised. The reference to the Yorkshire coast is again evidence of synoptic knowledge and understanding. The final sentence also introduces an element of insight, demonstrating that the candidate is well in control of this task. Overall this is an excellent answer which would be awarded a high Level 3 and would gain all 15 available marks.

Candidate answer

Question 3

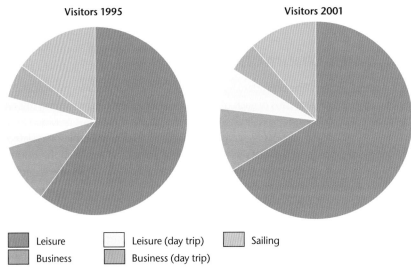

Note: These diagrams illustrate the correct techniques but have been enlarged

Figure 8.7

Candidate answer

Question 4

This particular task is not an easy one, but I will give my ranking as: first, the extension of the runway; second, the development of the waterfront area; and third, the raising of the sea wall.

There are a variety of ways in which this task can be examined. I have looked at the three strategic aims and in my opinion the best way to satisfy them is the rank order I have given them. I have also based my ranking on which schemes would harm least, but help most. I will now justify my ranking by taking each scheme in turn, in preference order.

I think the proposed extension to the airport will harm the least. The only people who will be affected by it are those directly in the flight path of the airport, and they will already be in that flight path, so what major effect will there be? They are selfishly thinking that the value of their houses will lower, but they would have known that when they first moved into that area. The airport has been there for many years. The farmers will not object really — they have the potential to make a lot of money out of the sale of the land. The population density of the airport area is low — so not many people will be directly affected. Against these objections are the possible benefits. There will be more tourists coming to the island, and as tourism is showing signs of declining it needs some form of stimulus. Business people will come in greater numbers on the bigger planes, increasing the potential for more business. We must also remember that Guernsey is an island. If the people want to go on holiday themselves, or visit relations in the UK or France, then they have to fly. A bigger airport will make that all the more easy, and may even lower costs if a budget airline gets involved. On consideration of the three strategic aims, the quality of life for more people will be improved, there will be little damage to the environment (a few extra metres of runway will not be noticed) and cost benefits are likely to outweigh any economic losses. This has to be the best scheme.

The second scheme I would implement is the development of the waterfront. Again this is connected to the economic growth of the island. Business, finance and tourism are vital to the island's economy. People who are involved in these need to be supported, and all the other important financial centres of the world like London and Frankfurt have high-quality hotels. The photograph of St Peter Port shows that there are no modern exclusive hotels there — it needs some modernising. The criteria for the development say that it must be well-designed, and in keeping with the area. It is a brownfield site — it is not building on new land. The planning department has acknowledged that there should be housing provision for those of modest means, but this does not mean that prestige developments should not go ahead. The reason I ranked it in second place is that it does not really satisfy the first of the strategic aims — it will not improve the quality of life for all people on the island, only a few — those who get jobs there.

In last place, I have identified the raising of the sea wall in Vazon and Cobo Bays. As a geography student I have learnt from my studies that trying to prevent nature from doing what it does is not easy. There are consequences of any such scheme, some of which can be predicted, but others cannot. It would be a very expensive scheme to implement, but the costs of it would not suddenly end. There will be on-going costs, in the bays themselves but also elsewhere on the coastline. This is not being cost effective, and certainly is not being sustainable. But who would the scheme benefit? The only beneficiaries are the owners of property and land in that area — the council-tax payers of the island would be paying to protect a small minority of people living in those bays, who again should have known that living in a coastal area will mean that you get flooded every now and again. The representative of the Cobo Residents' Association states 'Planners seem more interested in new housing or airport extensions', but that is exactly what they should be doing. I think this scheme satisfies the strategic aims the least, indeed it could be argued that it does not meet any of them.

In summary, extend the airport runway first, build the hotel second, and personally, I would not even consider the raising of the sea wall.

Examiner comments

The candidate has been very clear in the ranking process at the start of the answer. This is exactly what is required by the question and is to be encouraged. Some candidates assemble their argument first, and then give the final placings at the end of their answer. Although this approach is acceptable, it should be noted that it does not assist examiners in their task. It should also be noted that there is no definitive answer to this question — any ranking would be correct — it is the quality of the justification that is important.

Taken as a whole, the answer clearly accesses the Level 3 range of credit. It is detailed and thorough. Good use is made of the stimulus material, both at the start of the exercise (in Question 1) and in the evaluation of each of the proposals. This demonstrates a degree of synoptic ability. The ranking process is justified thoroughly. There is even some evidence of empathy with the people who will have to brief the various councils involved in the decision-making process. There are a number of statements that identify those who will benefit from each of the schemes in turn and those who will lose, and there is some limited comparison between the proposals.

The candidate recognises that the decision-making process is not straightforward and will depend on the standpoint of the people making the decision. Indeed, the answer to Question 2 has already highlighted a possible conflict of interest for one councillor on the island.

There is evidence of synoptic insight — the references to world financial centres and to previous work on coasts illustrate this. There are also frequent references to the strategic aims, which are the key to this question, and to the context of the exercise. Note that the student is working within the Planning and Finance Department of the island — its aims must be paramount.

The answer is well written and logical. All the criteria for Level 3 are satisfied so 17/18 marks would be awarded.

Improving the answer

Examine the mark scheme that appears with the question and work out for yourself how the answer to Question 4 could have accessed Level 4. To help you in this process, think about the following two points:

➤ Are the three strategic aims of equal importance and relevance for each of the three proposals? Should the candidate have given some consideration to this, and if so, how?

➤ Has the context of the exercise been fully appreciated by the candidate? Has the task been critically evaluated? Read again some of the views expressed by the candidate — how well are these likely to be received by the people involved as well as those in the decision-making process?

Bay of Naples issue evaluation exercise

Study carefully all of the information on the following pages (323 to 331). You should regard this information as an advance information booklet. Questions on these materials follow on page 331.

The Bay of Naples

Naples: the city

Background

Naples (Italian: *Napoli*) is a historic city in southern Italy that dates back more than 2,500 years. It is the capital of the Campania region and of the province of Naples (Figure 8.8). The city is noted for its rich history, art, culture and gastronomy. Naples is located midway between two volcanic areas: Mt Vesuvius and the Phlegraean Volcanic District, situated on the coast in the Bay of Naples.

Founded by the Ancient Greeks, it was important in 'Greater Greece' and then as part of the Roman Republic in the central province of the empire. Naples was the capital city of a kingdom which bore its name from 1282 until 1816. Then, in union with Sicily, it was the capital of the 'Two Sicilys' until the Italian unification.

In the area surrounding Naples, the islands of Procida, Capri and Ischia are reached by hydrofoils and ferries. Sorrento and the Amalfi coast are to the south of Naples. The Roman ruins of Pompeii, Herculaneum and Stabiae, which were destroyed in the eruption of Vesuvius in AD 79, are also found here.

Figure 8.8 Location map of Naples

Modern-day Naples

Today, the historic centre of the city is listed by UNESCO as a World Heritage site. The metropolitan area of Naples is the second most populated in Italy, with around 3.8 million people. Of these, 1 million people live in the central area of the city. The inhabitants are known as Neapolitans. The demographic profile for the Neapolitan province is relatively young: 19% are under age 14, while only 13% are over 65, compared with the national average of 14% and 19%, respectively.

Unlike many northern Italian cities there are few immigrants in Naples; 98.5% of the people are Italian. In 2006 there were approximately 19,000 foreigners in the city; the majority are eastern European, particularly from Ukraine and Poland. There are few non-Europeans, although there are some small Sri Lankan and east Asian immigrant communities. Statistics show that the majority of immigrants are female; this is because male workers tend to head to the more industrial north of Italy.

The geography of the Naples area

Naples enjoys a typical Mediterranean climate with mild, wet winters and warm to hot, dry summers (Figure 8.9). In Roman times its mild climate and geograph-ical richness made the Bay of Naples a favourite holiday location for emperors.

The regional economy in Italy is measured at a provincial level. The province of Naples ranks 94th out of a total of 103 provinces in terms of economic wealth. However, government statistics do not include wealth generated by the black market or untaxed wages.

It is not uncommon for Neapolitan workers to move north in search of jobs because unemployment in the area is around 28%. In recent times there has been a move away from a traditional agriculture-based economy to one based on service industries.

A breakdown of employment by sector in the province of Naples is given in Table 8.3.

Naples is well connected by major motorways, or autostrada. The A1 runs from Naples north to Milan and is known as *autostrada del sole* (motorway of the sun). It is the longest motorway on the peninsula. The A3 runs south to Reggio Calabria and the A16 crosses east to Canosa. The latter is called the *autostrada dei due mari* (motorway of the two seas) because it connects the Tyrrhenian Sea with the Adriatic Sea.

Public transport services in the city include trams, buses, funiculars and trolleybuses. There is also the Metro, an underground rapid transit railway system serving several stations. The mainline train station is Napoli Centrale, which is located in Piazza Garibaldi. Naples has lots of narrow streets, so compact hatchback cars are the usual form of private transport and scooters are especially common.

Figure 8.9 Climate graph for Naples

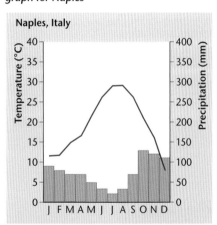

Table 8.3 Employment in Naples by sector

Sector	%
Public services	30.7
Manufacturing	18
Commerce	14
Construction	9.5
Transportation	8.2
Financial services	7.4
Agriculture	5.1
Hotel trade	3.7
Other activities	3.4

David Ball/Alamy

Photograph 8.3
Naples with Vesuvius
in the background

Several public ferry services operate out of the port of Naples. Most ferries serve places within the Neapolitan province such as Capri, Ischia and Sorrento, or the Salernitan province, such as Salerno, Positano and Amalfi. Naples International Airport lies within the suburb of San Pietro a Patierno. It is the most important airport in southern Italy, serving millions of people each year with around 140 flights daily.

One issue of major concern in the area is litter. As *The Lonely Planet Guide to Italy* states 'Litter-conscious visitors to the peninsula will be astounded by the widespread habit of Italians who dump rubbish when and where they like'. This is particularly evident throughout the Bay of Naples area.

Mt Vesuvius

Mt Vesuvius (Italian: *Monte Vesuvio*) lies on the coast of the Bay of Naples, about 9 km east of Naples close to the shore. It is a stratovolcano and the only volcano on the European mainland to have erupted within the last hundred years, although it is not currently erupting. The two other volcanoes in Italy (Etna and Stromboli) are located on islands.

Vesuvius is best known for its eruption in AD 79 that destroyed the Roman cities of Pompeii and Herculaneum. It has erupted many times since. Although it is not thought likely to erupt in the immediate future, it is today regarded as one of the most dangerous volcanoes in the world because of its tendency to produce sudden violent explosive eruptions and because 3 million people now live close to it. It is the most densely populated volcanic region in the world.

The most recent eruption took place in March 1944. A number of villages and orchards were partially destroyed and 26 people were killed, although it is thought that most of them died from heart attacks. Residents put pots on their heads to protect against rocks falling through the air. However, the rumblings soon stilled and the volcano has been quiet since.

What happens when Vesuvius erupts again?

The authority's emergency plan assumes that the worst case will be an eruption of similar size and type to one that occurred in AD 1631. In this scenario the slopes of the mountain, to about 7 km from the vent, may be exposed to pyroclastic flows while much of the surrounding area could suffer tephra falls. Because of prevailing winds, towns to the south and east of the volcano are most at risk, and it is assumed that tephra accumulation exceeding 100 kg m^{-2} (the level at which people are at risk from collapsing roofs) may be experienced as far as Avellino to the east or Salerno to the southeast. Towards Naples, to the northwest, the tephra fall hazard is assumed not to extend beyond the slopes of the volcano.

The plan assumes that there will be between 2 weeks and 20 days notice of an eruption. It foresees the emergency evacuation of 600,000 people, almost entirely from the *zona rossa* ('red zone'), i.e. the area at greatest risk from pyroclastic flows. The evacuation, by trains, ferries, cars and buses, is planned to take about 7 days. The evacuees will be sent to other parts of the country rather than to safe areas in the local Campania region, and may have to stay away for several months.

However, the dilemma facing those implementing the plan is when to start this evacuation. If it is left too late many people could be killed, but if it is started too early the eruption may turn out to have been a false alarm. In 1984, 40,000 people were evacuated from the Campi Flegrei area, another volcanic complex near Naples, but no eruption occurred.

Ongoing efforts are being made to reduce the population living in the red zone, by demolishing illegally constructed buildings, establishing a National Park around the upper flanks of the volcano to prevent the erection of further buildings and by offering financial incentives for people to move away (up to €30,000 per family). The underlying goal over the next 20 or 30 years is to reduce the time needed to evacuate the area to 2 or 3 days.

The volcano is monitored by the Osservatorio Vesuvio in Naples using extensive networks of seismic and gravimetric stations, a combination of a GPS-based and satellite-based radar to measure ground movement, and by local surveys and chemical analyses of gases emitted from fumaroles. This is to track magma rising underneath the volcano. So far, no magma has been detected within 10 km of the surface, indicating that any possible eruption is only in its very early stages.

Tourism to Pompeii

The Roman town is one of the best known sites in the world — and also one of the most threatened. Visitor numbers have increased from 863,000 in 1981 to

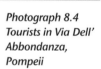

around 2 million a year today. Many of the houses open for viewing in the 1950s are now closed and in 2000 Pompeii was included on the world monuments' watch list of 100 most endangered sites. There are now proposals to restrict the number of tourists to the site.

Photograph 8.4
Tourists in Via Dell'
Abbondanza,
Pompeii

Further materials

Vesuvius

Item 1   Italians trying to prevent a modern Pompeii

Residents of San Sebastiano al Vesuvio in Italy believe that they will have plenty of time to leave when Vesuvius next erupts. In the 1944 eruption the lava flowed at only 5 km h^{-1}. Scientists say it is only a matter of time before it does erupt. 'It won't be tomorrow, it won't be next month, and maybe it won't be next year. But it is overdue', says Giovanni Macedonio, director of Osservatorio Vesuvio, the institute responsible for monitoring the volcano.

Since 1944 Naples has undergone urban sprawl and nearly 600,000 people now live in 18 villages in the shadow of the volcano. This population density, combined with Vesuvius' volatile nature, makes the volcano the most dangerous in the world. Rather than slow lava flows it emits devastating pyroclastic flows. The authorities have introduced plans to try and pre-empt another Pompeii-like disaster.

Officials estimate that at least 100,000 people have built illegal homes, hotels, restaurants and other buildings in the National Park of Vesuvius without permits or on land they don't even own. In 2003 the national government backed an appeal to legalise these constructions. Local planners say this shows how controversial are their efforts to crack down on population growth and demolish illegal buildings. It also illustrates the divisions between Italy's national government and the regional government in Naples. National Park staff removing illegal buildings have received death threats and have needed police protection.

The most ambitious aspect of the Vesuvius emergency plan is the permanent relocation of much of the local population. The director of urban planning estimates that it would take 2 weeks to evacuate the 580,000 people now living in the highest risk zones. The goal is to reduce the population by 150,000 within 15 years. Young people and retired people are being encouraged to relocate.

However, predicting a volcanic eruption is not an exact science. Vulcanologists can predict eruptions but it is difficult to get the timing right, and predicted eruptions don't always happen. If the authorities evacuated 580,000 people and no eruption occurred, residents would be unlikely to take any future threat seriously.

October 2003

Item 2 · Expert view

Professor Michael Sheridan (US National Academy of Sciences) believes that the next eruption of Vesuvius could be much more deadly than the Italian authorities are planning for. This is comparable with the US experience of Hurricane Katrina, when the authorities did not prepare adequately for a well-understood weather disaster.

The current planning in Naples doesn't take into account the maximum probable event. There is a high probability of a worst-case scenario because there have been eight large eruptions in the history of Vesuvius with intervals of 2,000–3,000 years, and it has been nearly 2,000 years since the last one.

Evacuating 3 million people from a major urban centre such as Naples is an enormous task. There are lessons to be learned from the aftermath of Hurricane Katrina. With an evacuation of such magnitude distribution of water, food and housing for the survivors and the nature of the escape routes must be carefully considered.

Waste disposal

Item 3 · Rubbish and the Mafia

A refuse crisis in Naples has presented the local Mafia with a lucrative business opportunity. In 2004 the waste situation reached crisis point when piles of rotting rubbish in the streets caused an environmental and public health emergency. Residents took the law into their own hands and set fire to mounds of refuse.

The city produces thousands of tonnes of rubbish every week and the landfill sites are full. Local opposition to incinerators means that none have been built and most Neapolitans do not recycle any of their waste.

However, rubbish is a goldmine for the local Mafia or Camorra, which control around half of the waste disposal industry. According to a parliamentary commission, the business generates around £4 billion a year for them. The Camorra dispose of household and industrial waste at competitive rates,

Photograph 8.5 Piles of rubbish in the streets of Naples

but have allegedly dumped it in rivers, fields and caves all over the Campania region. It is even claimed that industrial waste has been disguised by mixing it with tarmac and asphalt, and made into bricks used to build houses.

In some areas land and water have been contaminated by toxic waste. This has had a devastating effect on farmers affected by the pollution, who cannot sell their produce, and has led to further unemployment in the region and migration north to find work.

The authorities are trying to tighten up regulations. Part of the police force has been dedicated to tackling environmental crime. Fly-tipping — once a mere misdemeanor— is now a criminal offence with a 6 year prison sentence. However, no major convictions have yet been made.

July 2004

Item 4

Stinking Naples

Questions are being raised across Europe about the continent's reliance on landfill.

The European Commission has undertaken legal action, with the probability of large fines, against 14 member states for failing to enforce landfill regulations. Waste disposal crises have led to strikes and riots in Greece and Bulgaria. Britain has been warned that landfill capacity will be exceeded by 2016.

The southern Campania region of Italy — home to the beautiful Amalfi coast but also the slums of Naples — has faced a number of rubbish crises in recent years. Landfill sites fill up, and local

Photograph 8.6 Police clash with demonstrators in riots about the rubbish crisis

communities block government efforts to build new ones or create temporary storage sites. In 2004, a rubbish crisis prompted weeks of protests.

Naples' rubbish crisis may worsen with the planned closure of the only remaining landfill in the area at Villaricca, north of the city. Rubbish collectors have gone on strike because they have nowhere to take waste and angry residents have burnt refuse in the streets. The government has approved new landfill sites but they have been opposed by local people who do not want a rubbish dump in their 'back yard'.

May 2007

Item 5 — Naples battles with rubbish mountain

Naples – a city of nearly 4 million people – has run out of landfills. Traditionally old quarries were used as rubbish dumps but these are now full. At the same time the authorities have failed to implement EU legislation on recycling of waste.

Naples was once a popular winter tourist destination because of its mild climate and beautiful setting. However, in February 2008, its hotels were practically empty. Tour operators are worried about the appalling image of the city projected internationally by the rubbish crisis.

Vast areas of land are filled with mountains of unsorted compressed rubbish, in which toxic waste is often mixed with ordinary household refuse and the remains of old cars. More than 250,000 tonnes of waste lie uncollected along the streets in many outlying areas of the city. Municipal workers stopped collecting rubbish in December 2007. Although the city centre has now been cleaned up and the army has helped remove most of its waste, the emergency continues. There has been an increase in out-of-control fires as people try to burn the accumulated rubbish.

The newly appointed 'rubbish tsar' of Naples, Giovanni Di Gennaro, acknowledges that he has made limited progress. The former chief of Italy's national police, Di Gennaro has been given until 7 May 2008 to get waste disposal moving again. However, he knows that Naples is still creating rubbish faster than it can dispose of it.

He has met with the Cardinal Archbishop of Naples to elicit the help of the Catholic Church. One-tenth of the city's 281 parish priests are giving lessons to their parishioners on how to sort their rubbish into the different coloured containers for plastic, paper, glass and compost that are new to Naples but common in other parts of Europe.

A group of concerned citizens — doctors, ecologists, physicists, judges, geologists and journalists — monitor the waste crisis by holding regular weekly meetings. Luigi Berghantino, a member of the group, is satisfied with some of the decisions taken by Commissioner Di Gennaro. 'He has stopped the reopening of old landfills', Luigi says. 'He has created some new temporary storage facilities for waste, and he has understood that it is cheaper and more efficient to cart away Naples' waste by ship rather than by freight train to Germany as at present.'

Ferdinando Laghi, another member of the group, is a hospital doctor specialising in environmental medicine. He believes that waste disposal has been out of control for at least 15 years, with illegal dumps being created and rubbish left by the side of the road. He does not believe that incineration is a solution because it does not dispose of the waste or remove the health hazards. It simply creates toxic dust and ash. He says that big business all over Italy has paid the Mafia, at low cost, to dispose of their industrial waste by dumping it in the Naples area — one of the most fertile and agriculturally profitable parts of Italy.

February 2008

Questions

1 Using all the resources provided explain why the Bay of Naples area, including Naples, is a popular destination for tourists. (10 marks)

2 Analyse the main issues for the local authorities that may arise when Vesuvius erupts again. (15 marks)

3 Your A-level geography group has been asked to conduct a research enquiry into the issue of waste management in the Naples area. Design an appropriate enquiry to meet the objectives of the task by identifying:
- an appropriate hypothesis
- appropriate primary and secondary data sources
- appropriate methods of data collection, presentation and analysis (15 marks)

4 The task of local governments is to supervise the spending of the funds made available to them, and to prioritise the ways in which those funds are allocated. The authorities of the Bay of Naples area have a number of issues to manage:
- the provision of effective public services, including transport and waste management
- the provision of evacuation procedures following a major volcanic eruption
- supporting a thriving tourist industry

How would you prioritise the funding for these three issues? Justify your choice. (20 marks)

Mark scheme

Question 1

Level 1 Several causes of tourism in the area are stated. However, the answer is basic with no cause/reason explained clearly and thoroughly. At this level much of the answer relies on data lifted from the resources. (1–4 marks)

Level 2 The answer takes at least two of the causes/reasons for high levels of tourism and explains in detail why they are important factors, and with clear understanding. Clear links are made between information from the resources and the candidate's own knowledge and understanding. (5–8 marks)

Level 3 The answer is thorough and detailed, and a wide range of reasons/causes is analysed in detail and with thorough understanding. The answer is clearly synoptic, showing good all-round understanding of the topic. (9–10 marks)

Question 2

Level 1 The answer contains simplistic statements regarding possible issues that may arise. It is not clear from the answer that the candidate has recognised/understood the restraints regarding the location of the area — it could apply to any similar area. At this level much of the answer relies on data lifted from the resources. (1–6 marks)

Level 2 The answer contains detailed statements about the possible issues. There is a clear understanding of the factors leading to the possible issues, together with recognition that there will be some difficulties associated with them. The answer is clearly linked to named and located areas. There is some recognition that the attitudes of the local people will vary — the authorities may have to have a range of alternatives in terms of strategies. There is recognition of conflict within the management of the issues. There are elements of synopticity — the interrelationships between a range of factors. (7–12 marks)

Level 3 The answer contains a thorough and detailed account of the possible issues, including background/contextual material on the area and/or participants. There is some recognition of the variation in the basis of attitudes within each set of participants affected. There is also some consideration of the short- and long-term implications of the issues. There is evidence of critical understanding of geographical concepts, principles and issues. The answer is fully synoptic. (13–15 marks)

Question 3

Level 1 Simple statements of enquiry, with no real sense that the enquiry is feasible. Candidates at the upper end of this level have established an appropriate hypothesis but have not sufficiently developed methods to test the research question. (1–6 marks)

Level 2 Candidates display skill in identifying an appropriate hypothesis. They show sound knowledge and understanding of the data to be collected and a range of techniques that are appropriate for presenting and analysing evidence. (7–12 marks)

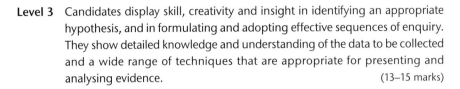

Level 3 Candidates display skill, creativity and insight in identifying an appropriate hypothesis, and in formulating and adopting effective sequences of enquiry. They show detailed knowledge and understanding of the data to be collected and a wide range of techniques that are appropriate for presenting and analysing evidence. (13–15 marks)

Question 4

Level 1 A basic ranking is made, but any reasons given for this are little more than unsubstantiated assertions of pros and/or cons. The answer does not make direct reference to the strategic aim given in the preamble and it is impossible to see any indirect recognition of its importance. (1–6 marks)

Level 2 A clear ranking is made, together with some appropriate justification supported by clear arguments. The justification tends to be constructed simplistically. For example, the reasons for supporting the first issue outweigh the reasons for the other two, or only the negative aspects of the other two issues are given. There is clear use of and reference to the strategic aim given in the preamble. (7–12 marks)

Level 3 The answer is detailed and developed. The ranking is justified thoroughly. The positives and negatives for supporting (or not) each of the three issues are examined in depth and compared with each other. There is clear use of and reference to the strategic aim throughout the answer. There is recognition that the decision-making process in such cases would be very complex. A variety of considerations is dealt with in detail. Each of the issues is considered at different scales and from differing viewpoints. The answer is developing a high level of synopticity — the connections within and between the information given both at the outset, and for each of the three issues, are developed. (13–18 marks)

Level 4 The candidate has completed the task thoroughly. The answer critically evaluates the task that has been given in relation to the context of the exercise. There is evidence of critical understanding of geographical concepts and principles. There is a clear acknowledgement that there is going to be disagreement when the outcome of the ranking process is announced/published. There may be recognition that each of the different proposals for support would satisfy the strategic aim but in different ways and that it is the relative ranking of these that could influence the decision-making process to a greater extent. The answer is carefully structured, shows real geographical insight, a clear sense of place and an understanding of a variety of different needs. Synopticity is shown throughout the answer. (19–20 marks)

Index

Page numbers in **bold** refer to definitions of key terms

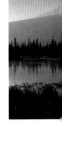

housing
    ethnic minorities 149, 256–57
    gentrification 146–48
    improvements 136, 137–38, 146–48
    inequalities 135, 148–50
    inner city 146–48, 152, 153, 157, 158–59
    LDCs 135–39
    rural 141–46
    substandard 135–37
    suburban 140–41, 143–45
Hull 168–69
Hulme City Challenge Partnership 157
human development index (HDI) 182–83,
    267–69
Hurricane Katrina 63–65
hurricanes and cyclones 60–66, 128
hydroseres 96
hypotheses 301

I

ice cores 77
ICT companies 194
identity, sense of 231–32
ideology 233
immigration 250–52, 258–60
India
    Calcutta 139
    Gujarat earthquake 30–31
    service industries 193–94
    slums 139
Indian Ocean tsunami 28–29
industrialisation *see* newly industrialised
    countries
industrial location, TNCs 211–12, 213
inequality (*see also* poverty) 135, 148–50
inner city (*see also* central business district)
    decline 148–53
    regeneration 153–59
insolation (solar radiation) 37, 43, 67, 68
insurrection 235
intermediate technology 275–77
international conflicts 242–49
international economic groupings 204–09
International Monetary Fund (IMF) 186–87, 221
international poverty line 265

internet, research using 305
inter-tropical convergence zone (ITCZ) 40,
    55–56, 57, 58, 102, 108
introduced species 117–18
isobars 39, 46, 50
Israeli/Palestinian conflict 242–46
issue evaluation 303–33
Italy *see* Etna, Mt; Naples; Sicily

J

jet streams 39, 42
Jewish/Arab conflict 242–46

K

Kenya 173
Kingston-upon-Hull 168–69
Kurdish separatism 263–65
Kyoto Protocol 86–87, 122

L

labour, new international division 185,
    188–89
labour markets 186
landfill 172, 238–41, 329–30
land use
    CBD 164–65
    suburbanised villages 143–45
languages 257
lapse rates 39, 44
latitude 39, 43
latosols 103–04
lava 14
lava flows 19
lava plateaux 14, 17
leaching (eluviation) 101, 104
least developed countries (LDCs) 181, 196–203
    urbanisation 134–39
Limits to Growth 121–22
lithoseres 96
lithosphere 4
localism 232
London
    conservation areas 120–21
    ethnic segregation 254–55
    gentrification 147–48

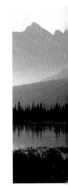